MYTH AND REALITY

IN

IRISH LITERATURE

Edited by

Joseph Ronsley

Canadian Cataloguing in Publication Data

Main entry under title:

Myth and reality in Irish literature

ISBN 0-88920-039-4 bd.   ISBN 0-88920-038-6 pa.

1. English literature—Irish authors—History and
criticism—Addresses, essays, lectures. 2. Irish
literature—History and criticism—Addresses, essays, lectures. I. Ronsley, Joseph, 1931-

PR8742.M98   820'.9'9415   C77-001382-1

Wilfrid Laurier University Press
Waterloo, Ontario, Canada
N2L 3C5

Cover design: R. D. MacDonald

Dedicated
to the memory of
His Excellency,
Joseph Shields,
Irish Ambassador to Canada

CONTENTS

PREFACE

Unity is one of the criteria by which an anthology of essays is often judged, but a glance over the essay titles of this book quickly makes apparent the fact that the dominant characteristic of the collection is not unity, but diversity. The book's title, it is true, serves to relate the disparate subjects to a single theme, and I think the recurrent preoccupation with myth, direct or implied, both in Irish literature itself and throughout these essays, demonstrates that the relationship is both real and useful. On the other hand, the scope suggested by "Myth and Reality" is so broad as to be able to include almost any subject concerning Irish literature, or perhaps any literature. Poetry takes over the function of myth in society as myth itself breaks down, David Greene tells us, and "exists because it is an expression of the myth." It is the ambiguity, between exclusiveness and inclusiveness, that characterizes the entire field of literary study, that gives an individual poem autonomy or that brings diverse works of literature into a common bond through myth, or that brings together two or more writers in each of several essays, or makes the student of Yeats interested in the early Christian Ireland over whose advent Oisin had so despaired. Any student of Yeats or Joyce, moreover, or of Synge, O'Casey, Beckett, or another, learns very quickly that while that author's great poems, novels, or plays had initially generated his interest—and generated it most often by transcending provincialism—it is impossible to escape an involvement with other Irish writers, and with Ireland itself—history, politics and art as well as myth. The mutual illumination between Ireland and individual Irish writers becomes more poignant the longer one is engaged. The binding effect of "Myth and Reality" aside, then, the real unity of this collection comes not in a concern with a single subject, or narrowly related subjects, but in the likelihood that the reader who has an interest in any one subject will naturally have one in several others as well, and that the interests themselves will overlap and combine.

Not only does this book contain variety of content, however, but also variety of form and style, although this variation offers a diversity which hardly needs explanation or apology. The scholarly-critical stance of Professors Clark, Rajan, and Theall, for instance, combines with the personal notes struck by Denis Johnston and Kate O'Brien—artists themselves in whom we have as much interest as we do in their subjects—and with a panel discussion that joins both. All this variety will, I hope, cohere into a mosaic image that represents one vista (there obviously could be no attempt at real comprehensiveness) of the Irish literary scene, and will provide vitality and reading pleasure of a kind at least related to that which Yeats found in the variety of Chaucer.

About half the pieces in this collection were originally delivered orally to the Sixth Annual Conference of the Canadian Association for Irish Studies, held March 21-25, 1973, at McGill University in Montreal. The inclusion of additional essays, of course, indicates that the book is not intended to be a record of the proceedings of that conference. Furthermore, an adequate record would be difficult to assemble because of the integral part played at the conference by dramatic presentations, films, concerts, an art exhibit, and, not to be overlooked, a vibrantly Irish congeniality. Finally, the essays which were originally delivered as lectures have in many cases been revised by the authors since the conference. With some exceptions—as in the panel discussion and Denis Johnston's banquet lecture—little of the conference remains in evidence in the essays.

Nevertheless, the conference did generate this book, and on behalf of its steering committee—Professors Brian John, Norman MacKenzie, Desmond Maxwell, Robert O'Driscoll, Balachandra Rajan, Ann Saddlemyer, and myself—I want to thank the following for financial assistance: Aer Lingus, The Canada Council, Corby's Distillers, Ireland Department of Foreign Affairs, Irish Mist Company, Irish Tourist Board, John Jameson Distillers, Knights of Columbus Council No. 284, McGill Debating Union, McGill English Department, McGill Graduate Faculty, St. Patrick's Society of Montreal, St. Paul's College of Winnipeg, Seagram's Distillers, and the United Irish Societies of Montreal. My personal thanks, too, for help of various kinds, are extended to Professor Donald Theall, Mr. Frank Phillips, Mr. Dan O'Brien, Judge Clarence Quinlan, Fr. Matthew Dubee and St. Patrick's Church, Mr. Theo Waddington, Mr. John Carey, Mr. Jeremy Craig, the CAIS Steering Committee, and a group of very dedicated students; and finally, to participants at the conference whose contributions could not be included in book form: A. Norman Jeffares, Lorna Reynolds, William Murphy, Helen H. Vendler, Michael Sidnell, David Clark, Balachandra Rajan, Gràinne Yeats, Jean Erdman and the "Open Eye" players, Peter Arnott, Tressa O'Driscoll, James McGoldrick, and The Chieftains.

The Book has been published with the help of a grant from the Humanities Research Council of Canada, using funds provided by the Canada Council. For this assistance I am most grateful.

Joanne, Jill, and John Ronsley gave me considerable help in preparation of the manuscript, as did Reta Lienhardt of Wilfrid Laurier University Press.

Montreal   J. R.

NOTES ON THE CONTRIBUTORS

RONALD AYLING
>   Professor of English at the University of Alberta. Literary executor to the Sean O'Casey estate. Editor of a posthumous selection of O'Casey's writings entitled *Blasts and Benedictions*, and an anthology, *Sean O'Casey: Modern Judgments*. Co-editor, *Sean O'Casey: A Bibliography*.

LEONARD E. BOYLE, O.P.
>   Professor of Paleography at the Pontifical Institute of Mediaeval Study, Toronto, member of the Comité international de paléographie. Author, *A Survey of the Vatican Archives and its Mediaeval Holdings*; editor, *Calendar of Papal Letters Relative to England and Ireland*; contributor to the *New Catholic Encyclopedia*.

DAVID R. CLARK
>   Professor of English and former Chairman of the Department, University of Massachusetts, Amherst. Author, *W. B. Yeats and the Theatre of Desolate Reality*, *Dry Tree* (poems), *Reading Poetry*, editor, *Irish Renaissance*, *A Tower of Polished Black Stones*, *Druid Craft*.

SEAMUS DEANE
>   Senior Lecturer of English at University College, Dublin, and poet. Author, *Gradual Wars* (poems, winner of AE Memorial Award for Literature, 1973), *Rumours* (poems); editor, *Atlantis*, 1969-75.

DENIS DONOGHUE
>   Professor of English at University College, Dublin. Author, *The Third Voice, Connoisseurs of Chaos, William Butler Yeats, Jonathan Swift: A Critical Introduction, Thieves of Fire, The Sovereign Ghost*; editor, *W. B. Yeats: Memoirs, The Integrity of Yeats, An Honoured*

Guest, Swift Revisited, Johathan Swift, The Honoured Universe: Soundings in Modern Literature.

DAVID GREENE
Professor of Celtic Studies at the Dublin Institute for Advanced Studies, former President of the Royal Irish Academy. Contributor to the Royal Irish Academy's *Dictionary of the Irish Language*; author, *Fingal Ronain and Other Stories*; editor, *A Golden Treasury of Irish Poetry, AD 600-1200.*

C. L. INNES
Currently teaching at the University of Kent, Canterbury. Has recently completed a comparative study of Irish and Black Nationalist writing.

DENIS JOHNSTON
Playwright, former Director of the Dublin Gate Theatre, BBC war correspondent, writer and producer for BBC Radio and Radio Telefis Eireann, Programme Director BBC Television, drama critic, Professor of Drama and Theatre; previous to all these, a Dublin barrister. Author of plays: *The Old Lady Says 'No!', The Scythe and the Sunset, A Fourth for Bridge, The Moon in the Yellow River, The Dreaming Dust, Strange Occurence on Ireland's Eye, Blind Man's Buff, a Bride for the Unicorn, Storm Song, The Golden Cuckoo*; other works: *Nine Rivers from Jordan, The Brazen Horn, In Search of Swift, John Millington Synge.*

THOMAS KILROY
Playwright and novelist. Author, *The Death and Resurrection of Mr. Roche, The O'Neil, The Big Chapel.*

THOMAS KINSELLA
Poet, Professor of English at Temple University, Philadelphia. Author, *Poems, Another September, Downstream, Nightwalker and Other Poems, Wormwood, Notes from the Land of the Dead, New Poems: 1968-1972, Selected Poems 1958-68*; translator of the *Tàin Bò Cuailnge.*

NORMAN H. MACKENZIE
Professor of English at Queen's University, Kingston, Ontario. Author, *The Outlook for English in Central Africa, Hopkins* (Writers and Critics Series); co-editor, *The Poems of Gerard Manley Hopkins*, 4th ed.; editor, *Poems by Gerard Manley Hopkins* (Folio Society).

JAY MACPHERSON
Poet, Professor of English, Victoria College, University of To-

ronto. Author, *Four Ages of Man, Nineteen Poems, O Earth Return, The Boatman and Other Poems, Welcoming Disaster.*

DOMINIC MANGANIELLO
Graduate student, Oxford University.

J. C. C. MAYS
Senior Lecturer of English, University College, Dublin. Engaged in preparation of a Samuel Beckett bibliography and in editing Coleridge's poems.

KEVIN B. NOWLAN
Professor of History and Chairman of the Department, University College, Dublin. Author, *The Politics of Repeal*; editor, *Ireland in the War Years and After, Travel and Transport in Ireland.*

KATE O'BRIEN (1897-1974)
Novelist and playwright. Author of novels: *Without My Cloak, The Ante Room, Mary Lavelle, Pray for the "Wanderer," The Land of Spices, The Last of Summer, That Lady, The Flower of May, As Music and Splendour*; plays: *Distinguished Villa, The Bridge, The Schoolroom Window*; other works: *Farewell Spain* (travel), *Presentation Parlour* (autobiography), *English Diaries and Journals, My Ireland.*

VERONICA O'REILLY, C.S.J.
Has taught at the University of Toronto and University College, Dublin.

SHOTARO OSHIMA
Professor Emeritus at Waseda University, Tokyo, President of the Yeats Society of Japan. Author, *W. B. Yeats and Japan, W. B. Yeats: A Study, William Blake and Celtic Literature, W. B. Yeats: A Critical Biography, Studies in English Prose and Verse, Among Shapes and Shadows* (poems), *Poetic Imagination in English Literature, The Development of the Celtic Temperament, Studies in Modern Irish Literature, Yeats: The Man and the Poet, Poems*; translator into Japanese of *The Collected Poems of W. B. Yeats.*

ANDREW PARKIN
Associate Professor of English, University of British Columbia. Editor, *Stage One: A Canadian Scenebook, The Canadian Journal of Irish Studies.*

BALACHANDRA RAJAN
Professor of English at the University of Western Ontario, Fellow of the Royal Society of Canada. Author, *Lofty Rhyme: A Study of*

Milton's Major Poetry, "Paradise Lost" and the Seventeenth Century Reader, W. B. Yeats: A Critical Introduction, The Dark Dancer (novel), *The Overwhelming Question*; editor, *T. S. Eliot: A Study of His Work by Several Hands, "Paradise Lost": A Tercentenary Tribute.*

ALEC REID

Scholar and drama critic for the *Irish Times*. Author, *All I Can Manage—More Than I Could: An Approach to the Plays of Samuel Beckett*; editor, *Time Was Away: The World of Louis MacNeice.*

JOSEPH RONSLEY

Associate Professor of English at McGill University, former Chairman of the Canadian Association for Irish Studies. Author, *Yeats's Autobiography: Life as Symbolic Pattern.*

ANN SADDLEMYER

Professor of English and former Director of the Graduate Centre for Study of Drama, University of Toronto; former Chairman, the International Association for the Study of Anglo-Irish Literature. Former Berg Professor, New York University, Fellow of the Royal Society of Canada. Author, *In Defence of Lady Gregory, Playwright, J. M. Synge and Modern Comedy*; editor, *The World of W. B. Yeats, The Plays of J. M. Synge, The Collected Plays of Lady Gregory, Letters to Molly: John M. Synge's Letters to Maire O'Neill, J. M. Synge to Lady Gregory and W. B. Yeats, Theatre Business, Management of Men: The Letters of the First Abbey Theatre Directors*; contributor, the *Oxford Companion to the Theatre.*

HENRY SUMMERFIELD

Associate Professor, University of Victoria, British Columbia. Author, *That Myriad-Minded Man: A Biography of George William Russell, "AE" 1867-1935.*

DONALD F. THEALL

Professor of English and former Chairman of the Department, McGill University, former Chairman of the Joint Departments of English, University of Toronto. Director of the Graduate Programme in Communications, McGill University and consultant, director, or member of several education, film, communications, and multi-media projects, including production of the film, *Let's Speak English*. First Canadian cultural exchange professor to the People's Republic of China. Author, *Let's Speak English, The Medium is the Rear View Mirror*; editor, *Studies in Canadian Communications.*

ANCIENT MYTH AND POETRY:
A PANEL DISCUSSION

**David Greene, Thomas Kinsella
Jay Macpherson, Kevin Nowlan
Ann Saddlemyer, moderator**

Ann Saddlemyer: About thirty years ago, Joseph Campbell, that
noted unraveller of many skeins, wrote the following:

> Throughout the inhabited world, in all times and under every circum-
> stance, the myths of men have flourished, and they have been the living
> inspiration of whatever else may have appeared out of the activities of the
> human body and mind. It would not be too much to say that myth is the
> secret opening through which the inexhaustible energies of the cosmos
> pour into human cultural manifestations. Religions, philosophies, arts,
> the social forms of primitive and historic man, prime discoveries in
> science and technology, the very dreams that blister sleep, boil up from
> the basic magic ring of myth.

This evening we are asked to consider the special relationship between
myth and poetry, and although the adjective "ancient" has been slipped
into the title, I suspect it has been done so in the nature of a catalyst
rather than a restriction. I would be very surprised and indeed disappointed if more recent applications did not boil up from that basic
major ring of myth.

I have asked our four outstanding panelists, each of whom is
intimately concerned in a different way with myth and its relation to
poetry, to speak for ten minutes or so first. We will then move to a less
formal interchange. I will ask the panelists, then, to speak in this order:
Professor Greene, Professor Macpherson, Professor Kinsella, Professor Nowlan.

David Greene: Thank you, Madam Moderator. Believe it or not,
myth does not exist to produce poetry, nor to produce professors of
poetry, nor professors of criticism of poetry. Myth is indeed—I wish I

could rehearse to you now the whole of Joseph Campbell's description of myth—but myth is simply the cement that binds society together. All societies have myths, of course, but, in what Frank O'Connor liked to call primary societies, the existence of these myths produces what we now, standing at a long distance from such primary societies, call poetry, because our societies are now so interpenetrated that we do not have that clearness of vision and singleness of view which is to be found in a primary society. We now have to chop up the myth into all sorts of different elements. One might take, for example, the first five books of the *Old Testament*, the *Pentateuch*, as one of the finest examples known to everybody—except no doubt to some of the younger members of the audience. (In my day it was fairly reliable to talk about the *Pentateuch*, but now it is an arcane subject for some people.) But in the *Pentateuch* one can find the dealings of God with the Jewish people outlined in a remarkable number of different forms, as we would have to describe them now. We can talk about them as history or law, or theology or myth, of course, or poetry—you might even think of elements of drama, and so on. But of course to the early Hebrews, any distinction like that was absolutely ridiculous, and unthinkable; it was all part of the same thing. It was all part of the national feeling—of the tribal feeling if you like, of the national inheritance. Poetry, in other words, does not exist at the early point any more than law exists because both poetry and law are what are already ordained by a tribe and its beliefs, and it is we that have invented words like "poetry" and "myth" and the rest to break them down. A similar situation obtained in ancient Ire-. land.

In ancient Ireland the equivalent of the *Pentateuch* of the Hebrews was the *Senchus*: that which was old, that which was inherited—not "antiquated" in the way we use that word now, when any house more than fifty years old must be razed to the ground to make way for something more important and useful. What was old was good, what was old was part of the tribal memory, and to be revered as such, and the old Irish *Senchus*, which, as we know, existed before the Christian missionaries arrived in Ireland, was incorporated into the Irish tradition. This *Senchus*, like the Hebrew *Pentateuch*, was not readily divisible into poetry, or history, or religion, or anything like that; it was all part of one seamless garment, and this attitude continued for a very long time. It continued in the consciousness of men long after the objective circumstances had changed irrecoverably. For example, take the Irish poet Eochaidh Ó'Heodhusa, who flourished I believe somewhere between the years 1550-1660, and who was an inheritor of an immemorial tradition of—of what? Of poetry? That is what we would say nowadays—and he did call himself in Irish by the name of *file*, and for the last fifteen hundred years the word *file* has been interchangeable with the word *poeta*, so from that point of view you can say that Eochaidh was a poet, and no doubt he knew the Latin word too and would have used it to describe himself. But *file* means a seer—that is the etymological sense—and the *file* in the *Senchus* was a person who, having undergone certain magical rites, was enabled to see the future. That is a very different thing from a poet in our sense of the word. A *file* was a practical sort of man whom you could actually consult about things that are going to happen. He was a useful member of society, unlike the poet of modern society. He could do a day's work for you. Eochaidh was a poet, therefore, only in a sense which is to be distinguished from that in which I think the word "poetry" is used in the title of this discussion. He was the inheritor, as I say, of an immemorial tradition. He in fact was practising what was nothing more than a journeyman trade—journeyman trade in the literal sense of the word because the bardic poet of his days was a man whose sole duty was to manufacture praise poems for princes, and who used to travel from place to place selling his poems to princes unless he was successful enough to be hired on a permanent basis by one of them. This kind of man, incidentally, was not dignified in early Ireland by the title of *file*. He was designated as *bard*, which has of course given us the English word "bard," but the old Irish *bard* was one of the lowest grades because his duty was simply to make praise poems, which was not recognized as nearly as good as being able to predict the future, naturally enough.

Now Eochaidh, despite the fact that he was practising what was the lowest form of the trade, still dignified himself by the name of *file*—that is, the seer, the foreseer of the future. Not only that, but he arrogated to himself all the powers of the *file*: the *file* was a shaman, he was a magician, he was a priest. I don't know really what the differences between shaman and magician and priest are, but I use the three words to appeal to your own personal tastes. This is the sort of person that the *file* was in the *Senchus*, and as you remember, Eochaidh's Elizabethan contemporaries—both Shakespeare and Spenser—knew that Irish poets were able to rhyme rats to death and indeed they were quite ready to satirize their contemporaries with full confidence that the satire could cause physical harm, if not death. Eochaidh was an inheritor of that extraordinary tradition, in spite of the fact that his work had shrunk to an almost journalistic sort of trade. Nevertheless, when he practised it he was still calling on the depths of the past. To every chief that he praised he would say that that man had been wedded to Ireland—wedded to Ireland always, because even if the man owned only a few acres of ground, you still thought of Ireland, the country, which is part of the *Senchus*—this unfortunate country which they tell us has never been politically united and nevertheless has been a cultural unity, a spiritual unity and a religious unity since the very earliest days of history and before the dawn of history itself. So the king he praised had to be wedded to Ireland, and if he had been wedded properly, of course, there were fish in the rivers, the trees were breaking their boughs under the weight of fruit, and so on, and so on. Here we have the whole of the myth of the past, going back probably to Indo-European ancestors, all embodied in a journeyman piece of work. And yet this very Eochaidh was working for a society which was broken down, of course, by the approaching English power, and was to collapse altogether, in his own lifetime probably. And he had already begun to show signs of breaking out of the thing. Even before Hugh McGuire had become chief of his name Eochaidh had written personal poems to him in which he demonstrated his special friendship for the man; that is to say, he spoke to him not in the correct traditional terms in which it is right to speak to a reigning prince, as a man wedded to his kingdom, but he spoke to him in personal terms, as a friend. This, of course, was a terrible break with the tradition. We can see now that as society decays, personal poetry advances.

The myth is to some extent decaying and the personal poet appears. The few examples of that sort of thing in the sixteenth century in Irish do not constitute enough on which to build a real picture. With the battle of Kinsale, which probably happened in Eochaidh's lifetime though we do not know when he died, the whole thing fell to pieces. But after that we can see what you may call the decay of myth; after that you can find the situation in which a poet will pick up some pieces of the myth of the past, what was a coherent and unifying force, and use them for poetical purposes. That is to say the myth is now transformed into the symbol.

Some poets even have invented whole mythologies of their own. The outstanding example, I suppose, in English, is William Blake who invented a highly organized and complicated mythology all of his own, which I think very few readers of Blake have mastered. And, of course, in modern times Irish poets have dipped into the myths of the past and used them to adorn their poems, sometimes with great success. I remember that in *Seven Types of Ambiguity* the line "For Fergus rules the brazen cars" is quoted and analyzed. It is a very good example of the use of words which may be thought to refer to the past for poetical purposes. Whatever chariots there were in ancient Ireland were certainly not brazen, and every student of Irish literature knows that Fergus had nothing particular to do with chariots. He hadn't a title like "Lord of the Chariots" or anything like that, but Yeats has found the word "Fergus" which is a fine word. Whether Yeats really knew that it meant "manly vigor" and that Fergus was undoubtedly some sort of representative of the virile principle, that I do not know. But brazen cars and manly principles and warriors are all damned good, and Fergus ruling the brazen cars certainly gives me the right sort of gooseflesh if somebody pronounces it in a suitably hieratic way. This, I understand, is what poetry is about. But it is not what myth is about because myth requires of the reader, if he is to relate to Fergus and brazen cars, that he should know what part in his life Fergus and brazen cars have and how it impinges on him and on every member of his society.

That I conceive to be the difference between myth and poetry. Myth is what is social, what is common, what pertains to the whole tribe, to the whole community. Poetry, as far as I can see, once myth breaks down, becomes a matter of private communication—not of course entirely private since nobody presumably speaks entirely to himself— but is addressed to a coterie on a hit-and-miss basis without much worry as to whether the poem will find the mark. The poem is good by itself. In the society where myth flourishes the poem does not exist as a poem. It exists because it is an expression of the myth. It is only later critical judgment which decides that some expressions of the myth will be called poetry. This is what I would think is the difference between ancient myth and poetry, and if by any chance I have perhaps made my categories a little too divergent, and if perhaps I have simplified unduly, it is merely with the thought of the eager speakers who are waiting to correct my obvious blunder.

Jay Macpherson: I have no possible Irish connection at all. I think what I am going to say has, however, a quite direct connection with what Professor Greene has just said. In essence, I think I am in agreement with him about the situation, but the emotional colouring with which I view it might be a little different from his. However, we shall see how that works out.

Although my main interest in life is the relation between literature and myth, I think this is the first time I have been asked to attempt a definition. So I am going to do that only very warily, broadly and hastily, and spend most of my time developing an example. I am going to take, in fact, half my time to read the example, which is a cut-down version of the original. In my view myth can be a practicable term, for classroom purposes, for any element in literature that has the effect of enlarging a work's scope beyond the merely descriptive. Ancient myth is one particular range of such elements. My illustration is a poem that I thought visitors here might like, called "Winter in Montreal," written late in the war by a British writer, Patrick Anderson. Actually, he ranks as a Canadian writer because of the amount of his production here. He spent some years in Montreal as a school teacher, and in fact he worked particularly hard at defining aspects of the Canadian imaginative scene. What he attempted I think nobody else has quite tried to do again, and I think he was surprisingly successful, considering that he had no observable Canadian tradition for the kind of thing he wanted to do.

Winter in Montreal

. . . .

One day I woke and took the milk like a flower
protruding its frozen neck on the outdoor steps
and a pole from my battered skis that were stacked
      in the hall
and began to jab furiously at a wonderful crystal
chandelier that had grown down from the roof in the night,
a theatrical piece of ice,

and the next day it had grown again to glisten
exactly as before, and a fungoid mirror
had sealed the garbage can to the balcony floor.
O when shall we be free of the winter palace?
Armorial in air my breath was plantagenet
and my heels were spurred.

And, climbing the Mountain, I saw in a bird's eye view
the city below with its way of a photograph,
its iron wood brick but never quite real tones—
I had not thought such silver in statistics
could play such a trick in the mist. Around me the skiers
rushed silently. The snow like chloroform
masked my face. And I turned to one
of the skiers whose nervous curve neatly missed me
and saw his heart spread out in a fluttering tartan
for the delicate pleasures which he was suffering,
and I said: Can you tell me? Is this Canadian,
to ski—I mean, to dare so silently
with nothing in front and blue behind like a railway?
I waited for his answer but it was
wafted away in the sanitarium snow
where the skiers flushed like the hectic tubercular
schussed down the fever of their feathery pillow.

And afterwards on the rinks boys mashed their sticks
in the vivid colours of their awkward age
with D'Archy-M'Gee and Loyola over their breasts
knots on their knees bunches of lumps on their shoulders
and on their loins a strap and a codpiece—
in the extreme rabble of their being suspended
within the tarnished mirror of their game and their
      youth I glided

. . . .

In this swan neck of the woods, these crystal sticks,
a hick town, icicle thick, such frozen bumpkins,
knockabout boys, knobbly with sex, flick their black
puck in the net. But I moralise
on the riotous quiet that makes the colony:
those who live in the capitalists' crystal
surge like a revolutionary future about me.

The double windows closed upon January
I hear the decrepit movement of this time
crepitate with ice and creep with shadow,

precipitate dust and frost in my room.
I hear the skinny wind in the chimney slightly
moaning all night. I wonder what will come—
what comes with a limping stride is February

and on my pane a prism burns in the fern
the frost has made, a wind begins to gnaw
at an ivory tower as if it had found a bone,
and in the suspension of the hour that is
not really so immobile at all, I hear
Ortona, Anzio and the bombing of Rome!

In the routine of snow and the dreaming season
I hear the avalanche fall from the villa roof
like the plush of a crash in sleep's debility
or Berlin dying, the gloved and female gash
of a great wound gliding into a soldier's body—
a crumpled thunder and faintness so far away
that the listener does not stir nor the skier wake
nor I, nor I. Drowsing upon this poem
which puns and purrs in the gap the armies make.

Anderson is not any sort of a textbook mythological poet, but he manages to draw a large suggestiveness around his subject by allusion to areas outside it. A first stanza, which I omitted, calls up its scene of old-fashioned echoing midnight streets in the language of the movie westerns. Montreal Mountain with "sanitarium snow" becomes an ambiguously magic mountain infected from another strain of contemporary mythology. Again, the question "Is this Canadian?" is one of those passwords like "explain to me that chalice and that bleeding lance." The boys on the "tarnished mirror" of the ice rink play out their interschool rivalries in the names of different brands of Canadian Irish Catholic heroism—D'Arcy McGee and Loyola—and the winter itself takes on a mythic presence, almost palpably near the end, as a monster about to leap, and more pervasively throughout, as a magical, dream-like, charmed suspension of existence reflected in the narrator's charmed immunity as he referees the boys' hockey game, and again in the climate of unreality that he feels in watching the war in Europe from this continent. The sense that the charmed suspension cannot last, that for better or worse something must come to break it, generates, incidentally, those Marxist Audenesque phrases about the capitalists' crystal, drawing in yet another distinct mythology.

The stanza I would like to focus down on is the one I read first, with the frozen milk, the outdoor stairway to an upstairs apartment, the overhanging chandelier-like icicle, the garbage pail frozen in a "fungoid mirror" to the balcony floor. And one line in particular: "O when shall we be free of the winter palace?" The imagery of the stanza is baroque. It recalls to me, for example—me as isolated reader just as he is isolated poet making poetic rather than perhaps technically correct historical or mythological illusions—it recalls to me my favourite movie, Cocteau's *La Belle et la bête*, or one not too unlike it, *Last Year at Marienbad*, with its statuary, its crystal drops, its haunted mirrors and its cast of Orpheus, Eurydice, Hades. Like the capitalists' crystal, it suggests simultaneously beauty, wealth, guilt, imprisonment. Like, again, the mirror world of the cold heart that entraps the child hero of Hans Anderson's story, "The Snow Queen," which is related in turn to the glass coffin that holds Snow White in her trance. Overlaid with no matter what layers of baroque decoration, or adumbrated by whatever imagery of romantic captive maidens gliding through its corridors or ferried on its black underground streams, the original winter palace belongs to Pluto, the god or riches as well as of death, and its original captive is the spring maiden, Persephone, "the youth of the heart and the dew of the morning." And as spring maidens in captivity become transformed inevitably into wintry queens of the dead, full of heiratic gestures, Anderson armours in glittering wit this poem that is about, finally, a tranced inability to respond with full feeling to events that are all too real. Not only, say, the capitalists, but also the speaker and the poem are in a sense trapped, held in stasis.

It is that kind of many-leveled enlarging and ramifying effect that I think some element of mythological language gives to, in fact, most modern poems. Or, looking in this context at the classical myth rather than at the poem, one sees not just its stability, its durability, but also its metamorphic power, the protean flexibility and, if one can say it, venerean openness that has belonged to the life of such elements since they were fully released from religion into art.

Thomas Kinsella: I am not sure that any kind of coherence is going to emerge from our various contributions. It seems that we have all reacted differently to the allotted topic.

What I would like to do is to talk briefly about the poetic process as I understand it, and the part that myth—however understood—may possibly play in it. What I say will have to be a little sketchy: it is a matter of running rapidly over complicated ground without stopping to go into any detail.

There are a number of stages in the process. It begins with the ingestion of experience and continues as the imagination (or whatever the agency may be) sieves that experience for its significance. The significant experience, so ingested, spends a period in the depths of the mind, forming relationships with other material similarly collected and stored. And then it lies ready, in a kind of ever-saturating solution, to be "crystallized out" at the moment of inspiration. At this point, a significant cluster—a structure of imaginatively processed reality —responds to some particular impulse (and the word "particular" is important) and there is suddenly the possibility of a poem.

I believe that myth plays a part at that point in the process when significant material is being digested, and imaginative relationships are forming.

Unless a poet is totally eccentric, he is likely to undergo in his own experience (if it is important enough) the basic experiences that are enshrined in myth. Responding as an individual, to a specific event, he does so in a way that is characteristic of our fundamental human origins and the course of our evolution. Relating certain references together in pursuit of a private order, or of some important obsession—handling material that has been taken in under unique, specific circumstances—he causes the primary mythical process to take place again, for the nth time. And so a kind of foundation is provided, both for communication and for understanding—the poet's understanding of reality, of what his own life, his ordeal, is about.

I could give a great deal of illustration if we had the time, but I will confine it to one instance (not strictly confined to the terms of myth) that struck me recently. In Donne's "Ecstasie," in the "diagram" of the thinking, as the "mixed souls . . . mix again," and make one, this fused soul is made up of interchanged atoms, produced by a kind of breaking down of the loving persons, and the intermingling of their fragments; a new person is constructed out of the results, with a stronger element of permanence. It seems eccentric, but I believe it is merely an extraordinarily precise statement of a not uncommon perception. What struck me, lately, is that much the same diagram occurs in William Empson's "Chinese Ballad"—a translation of a ballad set in modern China during the war with Japan. Not a setting that seems to have much in common with Renaissance England. The guerilla fighter and his beloved are parting. Her idea is that he should make models of them both out of river mud. The models, once made, are to be smashed and their particles mixed together. Then two final models will be made out of these married atoms. The theme of the original ballad was apparently borrowed from an earlier classical poem, or poems, and transposed into popular form.

What I am trying to suggest is that the human mind tends to respond in a certain way when faced with any important reality. And I believe that this is partly what poetry is about, and this is why it remains a useful and necessary human function, however marginal, or remote, or arcane, it may seem. (I would be prepared to argue that it—or art in general—is the most useful and necessary of human functions, but that would be for another night.)

To get closer to the subject of myth, if I can: these clusters and constellations of digested experience—"involutes," as DeQuincey called them—may be static or dynamic. Insofar as they were dynamic they are what I understand by myth: clusters of related *events*, rather than of relationships. In his attempt to come to terms with something that is vital to him, an individual poet will find himself undergoing for the nth time (as I have suggested) the primary mythical experience of death and rebirth, imaginatively understood; or of the night sea-journey; or of Persephone's time in Hell; of encounters with the Snake; of the breaking open of the egg, the hatching of things. All of these can be aids in the muscular, imaginative struggle for understanding. If they help toward understanding they also help toward communication, because they are *not* eccentric—they are shared. Even though the good reader may not understand everything in the specific references he will, in completing the act of communication, undergo in his turn a primary mythical experience.

It has been speculated that this is possibly where the notion of being "moved" by poetry comes in. Something in one's own depths is stirred by something in another's, something that carried the particulars of the poetry. The point about myth, as Professor Greene has said, is that it is, in a sense, a generalization of human experience. The point about poetry is that it is a particularization.

Kevin Nowlan: I would like, as a historian, to take up the definition of Professor Greene, that myth is the "cement that binds society together," and perhaps make it my own. One of the important developments in the 19th century is the way in which men involved in political nationalism began to seek in many lands a justification for their claims of individuality for their own people, for their own group, for their own tribe. A fascinating thing about the history of Ireland in the 19th century, and one which brings it very firmly into the main pattern of European history—European nationalism, that is—was the very conscious attempt to link Ireland of the 19th century, with all its misery, all its problems, to a very romantic age, a very heroic age. Here Ireland is not unique—you will find, for example, in Czech literature, and in the literature of the Baltic peoples of this period, a conscious effort to rediscover the past.

I think Ireland of the 19th century, and especially the Young Irelanders along with lesser political poets like Samuel Ferguson, saw in the myths as they conceived them of Celtic Ireland a sort of vitamin pill to justify 19th-century nationalism. And I think one of the fascinating problems for the political historian, as well as for the cultural historian, is first of all to trace the genesis of this fascination with the "cement which binds society together," and secondly, to see to what extent in the course of the 19th century there emerged a new myth which, using the material from the historic or prehistoric past, purported to create a new nation. Now I think one can see, for example, in the writings of the Young Irelanders, in the kind of poetry found in *The Nation*, indeed even in the sometimes doggerel, sometimes very attractive writings of Thomas Moore or of Thomas Davis, a deliberate use of themes to glorify the notion that although we may now be in the mire, we were once great, we were taller than Roman spears. Moreover, in addition to these themes, we find in the works of Samuel Ferguson—in "The Tain-Quest" or "The Death of Dermid"—the use, in the rather Walter Scott style of balladry or of *The Nation*, of Gaelic words and terms, of heroic words. All this sort of thing was presumably intended to create a sense of maturity, a sense of confidence that the history of the past could justify a distinctive nationality in the present. This is not purely Irish; it is part of a wider European progression, and there is a big area of Irish cultural history which needs to be more fully investigated—the way in which these ideas came to Ireland, the way in which they were matured and developed in the 1830s, '40s and '50s. The word "romantic" trembles on one's lips, but since it is so abused a term I am not going to use it.

Now I think an important development of the myth in the context of Ireland was, of course, its use in poetry, because one of the fascinating things about many aspects of 19th century nationalism was the way in which the medium of poetry, of verse at least, was used to propagate a concept of society, a concept of history, a concept of a collective memory. Again, myth is a very convenient form of shorthand for collective memory. In some ways within the Irish context, the 1830s and '40s—the age of the Young Irelanders, of *The Nation* newspaper, of Ferguson, of Mangan—embraced a sort of first amateurish experiment in looking to the kind of learned past which David Greene has very brilliantly interpreted. But the curious thing about Ireland —perhaps not curious if we look at it hard enough—is that there was a second go, it seems to me, at looking at the Celtic past. Of course you had sort of intermediate developments, for example, the Ossianic Society, the writings of a man like Standish O'Grady, the Society for the Preservation of the Irish Language, and so on. But in the 1890s you had a tremendous upsurge of feeling that all that was particularly Irish was disappearing. In the 1820s and '30s the priests were not particularly worried about the survival of the Irish language, or about the moral merits of crossrow dancing. Indeed, their views of crossrow dancing would suggest that it was not particularly moral. But by the end of the 19th century we suddenly find that things Gaelic, things Celtic, become pure and important, so if you wear Irish tweeds and dance a crossrow, you are doing something morally superior. You have, I think, from the 1890s onwards, a new form of myth that will return to the Gaelic past, and this is where the curious mixture of folklore and a more formalized myth—a return to all these things —elevates you morally.

What form the elevation was to take was to cause rather bitter disputes. Whether you could regard, for example, Diarmuid, the writings of Yeats or AE or Lady Gregory, as morally elevating was of course an open question for the contributors to *The Leader* and to the *Gaelic League Journal*. But nonetheless there was a feeling that myth, folklore, a past, was a moral purgative. And I think here again you will find Irish nationalism in the 19th century having a very strong link —and again it should be investigated more fully—with certain aspects of Continental nationalism. Take the Czechs, the way in which the Czech language from being the language of country people and servants was to be the language of a middle class and of a new industrial society in Bohemia in the 19th century. But this phenomenon took place not merely in a purely Marxist material context, but also in a moral context—that if you spoke Czech you somehow were morally better than if you spoke German. We can see, too, the so-called athletic movement among the Czechs, and its parallel with the Gaelic Athletic Association, that more virile form of nationalism in Ireland in the 1880s and '90s. In other words, the whole of man could fit into the myth, and I think one of the fascinating aspects of Irish history in the 19th century was the extent to which politicians became entangled with poetry, mainly due to the Young Irelanders (and I am using poetry not in a literary assessment of the value of what is written, but of the structure in which it was written, namely in verse). Poetry and myth, combined, do two things: first, they create a powerful moral conviction that we are an ancient people with a glorious past, and by implication a glorious future, and second, that given these two conditions our present misery is a product of outside forces. That gives one tremendous moral contentment to go on with revolution. However, myth and poetry have left modern Ireland with the unresolved problem of those who cannot identify themselves with Cuchulain of Muirthemne, or indeed with many of the other legends, real or otherwise, of Ireland. And so, in a sense, we are given a moral power and also presented in the middle of the 20th century with a moral dilemma. And I think this is our all-embracing message, despite the attempts to give Irish nationalism a universal pagan quality at certain points—which of course failed, given the Pierce 1916 interpretation of the past. While the legend was very important and a very powerful factor in a middle-class interpretation of Ireland's history and its making (leaving aside the land and rather more material factors) it has also left us with this predicament: how can you fit into the legend, into the myth, and into the poetry, people who don't want to fit into that myth, into that legend, and into that poetry?

Ann Saddlemyer: Ladies and Gentlemen, someone suggested that we might end up with four parallel views and that I would be in the unfortunate position of trying to find the connections between them. I don't think that is exactly what has happened. But before asking the panelists if they would like to question each other, I would like to have my opportunity. I have one question which I'll address to Professor Nowlan, but by implication I would like some of the other panelists to answer it also.

You are suggesting, Professor Nowlan, that from an interpretation of myth as truth and reality, we have moved—or certainly in Ireland there was a move—to myth as falsehood. Is this so?

Kevin Nowlan: No, I wouldn't quite put it that way. Myth, and I again go back to David Greene's rather fine definition, and hope again to have it right—"the cement which binds society together. . . ." Now to my mind it is totally irrelevant whether a myth is true or false, deceitful or otherwise. If a society accepts it as the cement which binds it together, that is the form of the ritual. Its truth, its moral value, is indifferent. It is merely the feeling, which is something set up. One worships; one must have something presumably to worship, and the myth is as good as anything else.

Ann Saddlemyer: Would any of the other panelists care to respond?

Thomas Kinsella: I am just wondering how you could assess, if the notion isn't ridiculous, the value of a society if that society is successfully held together by a series of misunderstandings, falsehoods, and so on.

Kevin Nowlan: Well, I think that is a totally different question. I am not discussing the worth of the myth, but most societies have some myth. When I came in here through the doors tonight I saw two figures, I think the Governor General on one side, and on the other side one which looked like a Chancellor of the university. Now this is presumably a form of statement of association—that it is noble to wear the robes and the Order of the Garter. It gives you a sense of community, of fulfillment, of involvement, of suggestion of power, of monarchy, and so on. But that is to my mind a myth. It could be a man with a hammer and sickle looking at the railway station—as you know, *To the Finland Station*—but it doesn't matter. Most societies have these clichés in which they live, and which, to my mind, bring myth down to prose. The myth is the cliché in which society lives. It has to have something.

Thomas Kinsella: How about that distinction between myth and symbol? You are able to get along well with a notion of nobility vaguely attached to robes of one kind or another, and other values attached to other trappings, while it seems to me the basic myth of a great deal of American society is of the young boy who grows up and makes a great deal of money regardless of what he does to anybody else in the process. That seems to me to be a fairly real myth in a society of this kind. The others are just ways of evading thought, or maintaining a kind of general attitude. I realize that I appear to be arguing for some kind of moral evaluation of the society, but I really am not. What I am trying to get back to is the way in which the robes would be created by this situation. At the moment it is a convention which makes them seem noble. At some point—there must have been a point—true nobility emerged in the form of that particular robe.

Kevin Nowlan: Well, we all seek nobility.

David Greene: I doubt very much whether we can really compare the artifacts of modern times in the shape of myths with what I began by talking about—the myths of primary societies. For example, Tom Kinsella is asking, can the cement which holds society together really be just a tissue of falsehoods? Well, let us take the most successful use of myth—because, after all, the word "myth" of course is a Greek word—and undoubtedly the most remarkable use of myth was by the Greeks. It doesn't matter if you are not really taken in by the Greek thing. We think that these myths are fairly ridiculous, fairly silly, fairly improbable. That is of no importance. They held Greek society together and they're there. One could accept that a myth might give offense, and one could apply this to all sorts of myths. Classical Greece is safely dead, however, so we can use our critical faculties to the full in this area without giving any offense. Nevertheless, Greek myth produced some of the noblest language and the noblest thinking the world has seen, and this arose only from the coherence of that small society. Whether in a modern society the artificial myth can ever really work we don't know. Undoubtedly myths have been evoked—some of them, as Kevin Nowlan has pointed out, just as artificial as our own—to invent societies like those, for example, of the Czechs or the Hungarians, just as the Hungarian and Czech languages were largely refurbished during the 18th century and provided with an artistic and technical vocabulary which they never had before. But all those words are now a part of Czech and Hungarian, so these myths have been woven in. Like anything else, I feel, whether in religion or in politics, the only crime is to fail. If the myth doesn't take, it begins to look pretty shoddy and pretty terrible. But I began with the myths of primary societies which, because they have come down to us from the distant past, were, by definition, successful.

Jay Macpherson: Could I suggest, perhaps, that the myths of the modern world that seem to us shoddy or thin, or, above all, not disinterested, which usually can be located in either politics or advertising (they're usually closely connected to one or other of those areas) draw what force they have from their power to recall what I think we would all recognize without being able narrowly to define, the authentic myths, the ones that have some imaginative force behind them, those that are in an imaginative, disinterested dimension—the return to innocence, the purification of society, the transformation of the self which advertising and politicians both promise us. They draw on these dreams. These are authentic desires which can be expressed either on the imaginative level or in the debased, corrupted form in which they are so very much more familiar to us through the media that make up so much of the texture of our everyday life. Is that a possible distinction?

Thomas Kinsella: I would just like to say that I only really get interested in myth when it returns us to its fundamental roots in some kind of significant reality, that is to say, to the origin of these robes of nobility, or reminds us that a fiction which is ridiculous on the face of it may also go back to the morality play, so to speak, that the psyche may have put on. Ridiculous that play may seem on stage but in fact it would be re-enacting a series of relationships and processes which are fundamental to our appreciation of reality on reality's own terms. But while it may be ridiculous, for instance, for Oedipus to have to push his own eyes out, nevertheless, the impulse to do that springs from something which has to do not with the pushing out of eyes on the stage, but the purgation of some kind of guilt. However, he may have been born with it or tricked into it, or whatever. It is this kind of psychic root of the myth that is interesting, and seems to me still to function at precisely the same fundamental level in the creation of poetry, even in the modern world.

Michael Sidnell [from the audience]:   Passionate feelings have been generated recently in discussions of "Bloody Sunday" [30 January 1972, when thirteen Roman Catholics were killed by British troops in the act of subduing an illegal protest in Londonderry]. Perhaps we are dealing here with a myth newborn and vigorous; and the panelists have been looking at myth from very different perspectives, Professor Nowlan's, I believe, distinctly ironical. My question arises from this variety of responses and the search for an overall pattern. It is addressed chiefly to Professor Macpherson: Is there, can we say, a characteristic morphology through which myths pass in the imagination? Are there typical transitions from, say, primitive or naive usages to, say, the symbolic or ironic, associated with myths and their recurrence?

Jay Macpherson: I think that a mythology that is no longer capable of change and absorbing new layers of possibility is a dead one that can only be studied from books. I feel in no position to say whether there is a distinct morphology through which, shall we say, our classical body of mythology must all inevitably travel in modern treatment. It seems to me that myths in their origins are of so vastly many different kinds, taking so many different kinds of material, ranging from the very primitive to the pretty invention, the attractive story, the sort of light fancy, that different groups of myths attract different writers, different users, different reworkers, and probably follow a great many different possible kinds of history. It seems to me that the life of myth is in its metamorphic capacity, but I would be very surprised if you could lay down two, three, four directions or regular stages and say that these are the ones through which any myth, even any myth from a given body of myths, must travel; because where they stay alive, I think they stay alive to the imagination, to people who work with the imagination, and that a vast number of imaginative uses become possible. It is a new question to me. It shouldn't be, but it is.

Ann Saddlemyer: Well, Ladies and Gentlemen, if we were appearing on the television screen, one of the instruments, as Professor Macpherson has reminded us, that have done so much to encourage a kind of mythologizing, I would be saved from any need to sum up; because at this moment passing before your eyes would be a series of credits while music drowned us out as we continued our discussion around the table. Since we do not have that machine, I must simply confess my inability to sum up. And further, to provide our own credits, that is, thanks from all of us to the panelists for a most interesting and stimulating discussion, and thanks to the audience for being so patient and interested.

SAINTS, SCHOLARS AND OTHERS, 500-800 A.D.

Leonard E. Boyle

Irish people, particularly those living abroad or those of Irish extraction, are accustomed to think fondly of medieval or early Ireland as a nation of "Saints and Scholars." This is not an unfounded assumption, but it is not always acceptable to those who are not in any way Irish. As a matter of fact, it seems to encounter a peculiarly dogged if not outraged resistance in those very areas of Europe which at one time or another were evangelized or, perhaps, reevangelized by Irish missionaries in the early Middle Ages, say between 500 and 800. And if in 876 Heiric of Auxerre was able to report straightforwardly and with justice that Ireland, "facing the dangers of the sea, came to our shores with her flock of learned men,"[1] his eulogy has not always found a ready echo in every circle of modern continental scholarship.

The Belgian Benedictine, Dom Cappuyns, when writing an excellent study in 1933 of Heiric's contemporary, the polymath and pungent controversialist, John Scotus Eriugena, found it difficult to understand how such an erudite man should have come out of such a backward and unlikely place as Ireland to grace (and on occasion to upset) the intellectual life of northern France, Belgium and the Rhineland.[2] More recently, an Italian Carmelite, Fr. Coccia, has cast serious doubts in a lengthy article on the scholarly calibre, if not on the competence, of most of the literary products of Irish monks, whether in Ireland or elsewhere, in these same years, 500-800.[3] And if to the

---

[1] "Preface," *Vita S. Germani*, ed. L. Traube, *Monumenta Germaniae Historica, Poetae Latini*, III (Berlin, 1896), p. 429.

[2] M. Cappuyns, *Jean Scot Erigène: Sa vie, son ouevre, sa pensée* (Louvain, 1933).

[3] E. Coccia, "La Cultura irlandese pre-Carolingia, Miracolo o Mito?" *Studi Medievali*, 3rd series, 8 (1967), 257-420.

naturalized Irish Austrian, Ludwig Bieler, Ireland was "The Harbinger of the Middle Ages" in, among other things, manuscript production, decoration and illumination,[4] M. Masai of Belgium and others in France and England are just as firmly convinced that much of the manuscript illumination with which Irish centers have been credited in the past could not possibly have been done in Ireland but is largely a product of northern English or Northumbrian monastic culture.[5]

One view that is not as well-known as it should be is that of the great U.S. palaeographer, E. A. Lowe. Since he was unable to differentiate with any great certainty between a manuscript which was supposed to have been written in England before 700 and one claiming to be an Irish product of the same period, Lowe devised a simple set of rules by which to form a judgment. With the departure of the Irish monks from Northumbria in 664, he argued, Irish influence waned, and the English genius for sobriety and orderliness began to assert itself. From then on, Lowe asserts, it is possible to distinguish an Irish product from an English one: the Irish type is freer, more incalculable, less bound by rules and regulations, than the English type modelled upon it; the Irish scribe often behaves as if the written line were something elastic, and he seems to be a prey to whim and fancy where the English scribe is circumspect and disciplined. As a result of these observations, Lowe arrived at the following general conclusion:

- if a manuscript looks haphazard and messy
- if the number of lines varies wildly from page to page
- if the ruling is missing or, if present, disregarded
- if the parchment is very rough to the touch or very greasy
- if odd or irregular scraps of parchment are used

THEN, "this otherwise undetermined manuscript is likely to be the work of an Irish not an English scribe."[6]

If I were an Englishman I should not feel too happy about the implication here that the English of the 7th and 8th centuries were as unimaginative and tidy-minded as Napoleon's "Nation of shopkeepers" and were, in fact, quite inferior in spirit to the creative, free-flowing, jaunty insouciance of their Irish contemporaries. As an Irishman, however, I have no intention of embracing an English cause, no more than I have any intention of dilating upon the surely obvious fact that E. A. Lowe has simply applied to the past some commonly accepted versions of "typical" Irish and English "national characteristics."

---

[4] L. Bieler, *Ireland, Harbinger of the Middle Ages* (Oxford, 1963).

[5] F. Masai, *Essai sur les origines de la miniature dite irlandaise* (Brussels, 1947).

[6] E. A. Lowe, *Codices Latini Antiquiores* II (Oxford, 1934; second ed. ibid., 1972), p. xii.

No. If I cite the opinions of E. A. Lowe and other scholars, this is simply to suggest how difficult it can often be for a foreigner, however learned, to give the Irish of the middle ages a tolerant hearing and to see beyond their undoubted vagaries to their equally undoubted seriousness. Scholars such as these, however, should be treated with great understanding if not with courtesy, for the period in which they have to work and to evaluate the supposed Irish scholarship is not too well documented and, where documented, presents so seemingly extravagant a picture that an innocent foreigner is all too quickly persuaded that the picture cannot possibly have a foundation in reality.

* * * * *

What, then, were the Irish really like in those days of the "Saints and Scholars," the manuscripts and the teeming piety? No ready answer to the question is possible—at least not at this time. But a few ragged, untidy, messy, "typically-Irish" pointers may be given which, if they do not scratch the surface of the subject may at least lay bare a few promising patches.

The period of the "Saints and Scholars" is, as I have said, from about 500-800, and my characters are saints as well as scholars and, to boot, a few saintly sinners. It is a period of thronging monastic and intellectual life, of plentiful commerce with Britain, Spain, France and Italy, and of the final (or so it seemed) victory of Christian over pagan ways.[7] Grammars of Latin were compiled then; collections of ecclesiastical legislation were put together; books of penance and the practice of penance were written which influenced the whole of Europe and the whole history of penance; annals were kept, and the intricacies of the computus explored.[8] The scholars even developed their own highflown, "hesperic," Latin, juggling with words in a manner as dazzling and inventive as that of Joyce.[9] According to Bernhard Bischoff, who has discovered some forty Irish works of exegesis, the Irish production of exegetical and grammatical works in the 7th and 8th centuries was greater in quantity than that of Spain, England and Italy combined.[10]

---

[7] In general see N. Chadwick, *The Age of the Saints in the Early Celtic Church* (Oxford, 1961); and K. Hughes, *The Church in Early Irish Society* (London, 1966).

[8] Most of these categories are discussed in detail in a work that is still unsurpassed, though now in need of some revision: J. F. Kenney, *Sources for the Early History of Ireland, I: Ecclesiastical* (New York, 1929).

[9] See L. Bieler, "The Island of Scholars," *Revue du Moyen Âge Latin*, 3 (1952), 212-31 at p. 220, although Bieler is inclined to place the *Hesperica Famina* in Britain rather than in Ireland.

[10] B. Bischoff, "Wendepunkte in der Geschichte der lateinischen Exegese im Frühmittelalter," *Sacris Erudiri*, 6 (1954), 189-281; "Il monachesimo irlandese nei suoi rapporti col continente," *Settimane di Studi del Centro Italiano di Studi sull'Alto Medioevo*, IV (Spoleto, 1967), 121-38.

At home, there were monasteries like Bangor, Clonmacnoise and Glendalough, all of which won international renown for their scholarship. Abroad, there were those Irish saints and scholars who embraced their peculiar form of "martyrdom" by deliberately (and almost "by nature," as Walafrid Strabo put it[11]) going into exile "for the love of Christ": Colmcille of Iona, Columbanus of Bangor, Luxeuil and Bobbio, Aidan of Lindisfarne, Fursa of Peronne, Gall of St. Gall in Switzerland, Fergal of Salzburg, Kilian of Würzburg. These and others made their way, often in frail boats, to the Orkneys, the Faroes, Iceland, Britain, France, Germany, Switzerland, Austria,and Italy.[12] It was due to their wanderings and curiosity that, for example, wheat was first introduced into Ireland and (or so it is said) the first bees began to hum in the country—the wheat coming in the shoe of St. Finian the Lame, the bees in the bell of St. Modomnoc: as the martyrology of Oengus puts it about the year 800: "In a little boat, from the East, over the pure-coloured sea, Modomnoc brought—oh wondrous thing—the gifted race of Ireland's bees."[13]

It was an age of scholars and miracles—and of some miraculous scholarship. If we omit such distinguished and well-known products as the *Cathach of Columba* (c. 600), the *Book of Durrow* (c. 650) and the *Book of Kells* (c. 800), this is because we must linger over one of the more spectacular feats of scholarship. Sometime in the 7th century a holy abbot Ailbe, who was a great friend of three saintly nuns called Tallulah, Tallitha and Squiatha, gladly answered a request of Squiatha to send her a scribe who would write out a copy of the Four Gospels for her monastery. Unfortunately, the scribe had time to complete only two of the Gospels before he died. Ailbe only discovered this some months later when he visited the monastery, but when he did discover it he was so annoyed that he went to the scribe's grave and ordered him out to complete the Gospels. The resurrected scribe did as he was told, completed the Gospels, and died in a great odour of sanctity some years afterwards.[14]

Ailbe's scribe was clearly not only an obedient but also a very competent scribe—unlike the personal scribe of St. Comgall, whose writing was so bad that Comgall decided to bless his hand in the hope that his handwriting would improve.[15] In general, scribes were a law unto themselves, and the margins of manuscripts are full of personal

---

[11] Walahfridus Strabo, *Vita S. Galli*, II. 46, ed. B. Krusch, *Monumenta Germaniae Historica, Scriptorum Rerum Merovingicarum*, IV (Hanover-Leipzig, 1902), p. 336.

[12] See in general L. Gougaud, *Christianity in Celtic Lands* (London, 1932).

[13] *The Martyrology of Oengus*, ed. W. Stokes (London, 1905), pp. 60, 113 (13 Feb.).

[14] *Vitae Sanctorum Hiberniae ex codice olim Salmanticensi nunc Bruxellensi*, ed. W. W. Heist (Brussels, 1965), p. 127.

[15] *Vitae Sanctorum Hiberniae*, ed. C. Plummer (Oxford, 1910), II, 13.

asides about food and drink and aches and pains.[16] Few scribes were as content and undemanding as the scribe of c. 800 who wrote so feelingly of the joy of writing a manuscript in the woods on a Summer's day:

> A hedge of trees overlooks me,
> A blackbird's lay sings to me . . .
> Above my lined book
> the birds' chanting comes to me.
> A clear-voiced cuckoo sings to me
> (what a nice way he does it)
> in a grey cloak from a forest of bushes.
> The Lord is indeed good to me:
> Well do I write beneath a forest of woodland.[17]

It was the period, too, when Women's Liberation was in its first fine flush in the country, and when Adamnán of Iona was persuaded by his mother to organize about 697 a public outcry at the age-old custom of sending women as well as men into battle. As a *Vita* of Adamnán has it, "It came to pass that Adamnán was travelling in Mag Breg with his mother on his back, and they saw two battalions smiting each other. It happened that Ronnát (Adamnán's mother) saw a woman, with an iron sickle in her hand, dragging another woman out of the opposite battalion, and her sickle was stuck in the other woman's breast. Then Ronnát, Adamnán's mother, said to her son: 'Thou shalt not carry me out of this place until women are freed forever from things of yon kind.' "[18] How successfully Adamnán lived up to the promise he gave his mother on that day is clear from the eulogy of him that Oengus the Culdee, the great poet from the monastery of Mael-ruain at Tallaght, composed a hundred years later in his Martyrology:

> To Adamnán of Iona,
> Whose followers are radiant,
> Noble Jesus granted
> The lasting liberation
> Of the women of Ireland.[19]

It was a period, too, when an outlaw who operated around Tara became a penitent under St. Kevin of Glendalough and a saint in the later Martyrologies under the rather improbable name of Glúnsalach, "the dirty-kneed one."[20] And speaking of Kevin of Glendalough,

---

[16] C. Plummer, "On the Colophons and Marginalia of Irish Scribes," *Proceedings of the British Academy*, 12 (1926), 11-44.

[17] Edited and translated from St. Gall, MS. 904, by W. Stokes and J. Strachan, *Thesaurus Palaeohibernicus*, II (Cambridge, 1903), p. 290. The version quoted here is that in G. Murphy, *Early Irish Lyrics* (Oxford, 1956), p. 5.

[18] *The Martyrology of Oengus*, ed. W. Stokes, pp. 210-11 (notes from the *Book of Leinster*).

[19] Ibid., p. 296 (23 Sept.).

[20] *Martyrology of Tallaght*, ed. H. J. Lawlor (London, 1931), p. 47; L. E. Boyle,

where else but in Ireland could a saint like Kevin himself, who lived to be 120 years old, have attempted to test his chastity by sleeping nude between two naked maidens (on a stone bed, I hasten to add)?[21] Or where else would one find an ancient saint whose great claim to immortality and a place in the Martyrologies seems to have been the fact that young maidens who visited his grave were made to twitch and giggle uncontrollably? And where else (to the great confusion of foreign scholars) would a saint like St. Cummine be found to subject the chastity of lovers to an "Ordeal by cohabitation"—putting them to bed together with an acolyte between them to observe and record their reactions?[22]

If some holy men of the period were as non-conformist as they were foolhardy, there were others who were as conceited as they were crustaceous. One such was Fintan Munnu. A Westmeath man, and a son of a druid, Fintan studied at Kilmore with Colmcille shortly before 563. After a spell at Colmcille's foundation at Iona in Scotland, he founded a monastery of his own at Taghmon, near Wexford Harbour, about 620. Between then and his death some sixteen or seventeen years later, this doughty old man spent his time fighting the introduction of the Roman reckoning of Easter into the South of Ireland.[23]

His great moment came in 630, when the leader of the Roman party, the scripture scholar St. Laisrén, convoked a synod at Whitefield, Co. Kildare, to debate the Easter question once and for all and to establish beyond doubt the reasonableness of the Roman reckoning. For it was old Fintan who dominated, if not cowed, the assembly. First of all, he arrived a day late, by which time the gathering was in a state of frustration at the delay. Then Fintan proceeded to show how contemptuous he was of the whole idea of an assembly of this sort and of open debate. For instead of debating the Easter question, as the Roman party had expected him to do, Fintan unexpectedly challenged Laisrén and the Roman party to a veritable trial by ordeal. One after the other, three choices were offered the Roman party by Fintan:

1. Each side would throw its own Easter reckoning into a fire to see which one would burn and which one would not.
2. A monk from each party would be locked into a house which would then be set on fire. The party whose representative would come out

---

"Glunsalach," *Bibliotheca Sanctorum*, VII (Rome, 1966), col. 62.

[21] *Vitae Sanctorum Hiberniae*, ed. C. Plummer (Oxford, 1910), I, 234-57.

[22] For the story of St. Cummine and the lovers Cuirithir and Liadan, see D. Greene and F. O'Connor, *A Golden Treasury of Irish Poetry, A.D. 600-1200* (London, 1967), pp. 72-77.

[23] *Vitae Sanctorum Hiberniae*, ed. W. W. Heist (Brussels, 1965), pp. 198-209; P. Grosjean, "Recherches sur les débuts de la controverse pascale chez les Celts," *Analecta Bollandiana*, 64 (1946), 200-44; L. E. Boyle, "Munnu di Tech Munnu," *Bibliotheca Sanctorum*, IX (1967), cols. 674-77.

of the holocaust unharmed would be the winner.

3. If neither of these trials appealed to the Roman party, Fintan generously suggested a third form of trial. Fintan and Laisrén would go to the grave of a monk who had died recently, call him back from the dead, and then ask him what reckoning of Easter was being followed in Heaven that year.

Now Laisrén was a distinguished and determined man himself, but he seems to have had a wholesome awe of old Fintan. For on behalf of the Roman party he resolutely refused to have anything to do with these methods of proof, saying that Fintan would surely win in each case, "since if Fintan were to ask God to make the local hills and plains change places, then undoubtedly God would oblige." Fintan, of course, now claimed that no further proof was required for the validity of the Irish reckoning of Easter, so he told the crowd to go home and have some sense.[24]

No less intriguing is the figure of Maelruain of Tallaght some one hundred and more years later. Personally, I have always been attracted to him, having lived for some years as a student in a Dominican house on the outskirts of Dublin which stands on the site of the monastery founded by Maelruain at Tallaght on 10 August 774.[25]

This Maelruain was the principal agent of attempts to breathe new life into the monasteries during a period of grave decline and secularization in the 8th century. And he seems to have been the spearhead of a religious movement called the "Culdees" ("Servants of God") which was centered on what were known as "The two eyes of Ireland": Tallaght, under Maelruain, six miles south of Dublin; Finglas, under Dublitir ("Blackletter"), some three miles north of the city.

Tallaght was the literary center of the Culdee movement. Its best-known product, perhaps, is the Stowe Missal, now in the Royal Irish Academy, Dublin. Written between 792 and 815, it was an attempt to give Tallaght and the whole Culdee movement an authoritative ritual.[26] Not less well-known are the two great Martyrologies, that of Tallaght about 800, and that of Oengus the Culdee, written in 805. To both of these we owe much of our knowledge, however fragmentary or allusive, of the saints and scholars of the preceding three centuries.[27]

The most interesting product of Tallaght, however, is a volume

[24] *Vitae Sanctorum Hiberniae*, ed. Heist, p. 207.

[25] E. J. Gwynn and W. J. Purton, "The Monastery of Tallaght," *Proceedings of the Royal Irish Academy*, 29 C (1911), 115-79; L. E. Boyle, "Maelruain," *Bibliotheca Sanctorum* VIII (Rome, 1967), cols. 484-89.

[26] Kenney, *Sources*, p. 699; Lowe, *Codies Latini Antiquiores*, II, no. 268.

[27] *The Martyrology of Tallaght*, ed. H. J. Lawlor (London, 1931); *The Martyrology of Oengus the Culdee*, ed. W. Stokes (London, 1905).

known as "The Teaching of Maelruain" (*Teagasc Maelruain*) which was compiled by a disciple of Maelruain some forty years after his death. If its author seems to have been determined to prove that Maelruain's Tallaght was a more ascetic place than Blackletter's Finglas some ten miles away on the other side of the Liffey, its chief value to historians is the lively picture it gives of Maelruain himself.

Maelruain's humanity is evident in the regulation that the divine office should be recited with each side of the choir alternately sitting and standing, "so as not to get too tired or to fall asleep." And although Maelruain had a high regard for manual work of the toughest kind, he nevertheless argued that "works of piety were more powerful than any others, for the kingdom of Heaven is guaranteed to those who study and to those who direct study."

Yet there is much in Maelruain of the unbending asceticism that was at the core of the Culdee movement. Cold water was the order of the day, whether to cool passions by standing in it for hours on end with arms outstretched, or as the regular beverage of monks and monasteries. Beer or drink of any intoxicating kind was uncompromisingly outlawed, as Blackletter of Finglas was to find out when he came to Maelruain urging him to allow his monks at Tallaght to drink ale on the three chief festivals of the year. For, as the *Teagasc* informs us, Maelruain replied, "So long as these monks are under my control and keep my commands, they shall drink no drop that causes them to forget God in this place." And when Blackletter went on to argue that his monks drank ale "and they shall be in the kingdom of God with thine," Maelruain retorted, "I am not so sure about that as you are. But this I know: every monk of mine that listens to me and keeps my rule shall have no need of judgment to be passed on him, nor of the fire of Domesday to cleanse him, because he shall be clean already. Not so your monks, Blackletter: they, ale-drinkers that they are, shall have somewhat that the fire of Domesday must cleanse."

If drinking was out, so also was any form of recreation. There was, for example, a luckless anchorite called Cornán ("little horn-player") who once sent a message to Maelruain saying that he would be pleased to play him a few skirls on his bagpipes. Maelruain's answer fell somewhat short of graciousness: "Tell Cornán that these ears of mine shall not be delighted with earthly music until they shall have been refreshed with the music of Heaven."[28]

To many, Maelruain may seem harsh and unfeeling, but to Oengus the Culdee, Maelruain's best-known disciple and the author of a great Martyrology, Maelruain was "the sun that shone in the South of the plain of Meath," the one "at whose pure tomb the wound of every

---

[28] See. E. J. Gwynn, "The Teaching of Máel-Ruain," *Hermathena* (second Supplemental Volume, Dublin, 1927), pp. 1-63.

heart is healed," the one whom he himself prayed would "take him to Christ."[29]

Oengus the Culdee was just as eulogistic about the great men and women of the preceding three centuries whom he commemorates in verse in his *Félire* or Martyrology.[30] And in his magnificent introduction to the *Félire* he rejoices in the state of Ireland about 800, after the heroic labours of men such as Maelruain, and in the final triumph of Christianity over the old pagan, secular order:

> The great settlement of Tara has died,
>   with the loss of its princes.
> Great Armagh lives on,
>   with its choirs of scholars.
> A great cutting off there has been:
>   The pride of Laegaoire has been stifled;
>   Patrick's splendid, revered name is spreading. . . .
> The fort of Emain Macha has melted away,
>   all but its stones,
> Thronged Glendalough is the sanctuary
>   of the Western Church. . . .
> Paganism has been destroyed,
>   though it was splendid and far-flung.
> The kingdom of God the Father
>   has filled heaven and earth and sea. . . .
> The great hills of evil
>   have been cut down with spear points,
>   while the glens have been made into hills.[31]

When Oengus penned these introductory verses some ten years after the death of Maelruain, he was in fact penning the obituary of all that he prized. Four or five years afterwards the first Viking raids began to wipe out most of the work of the saints and scholars of the previous three hundred years and to bring the reforms of Maelruain, Blackletter and the Culdees to nought. The invaders came in search of booty and found it in the churches and monasteries. As the *Cogadh Gaedhel re Gallaibh* has it, "Writings and books in every church and sanctuary were burned and thrown into the water."[32] It was the end, but for a handful of exceptions, of "the host of books" ("*sloged leber nErenn*") and "the multitudes of them" through which Oengus had searched when compiling his "martyrologies of the men of Ireland" ("*Felire fer nGoidel*").[33]

The new Ireland that was formed in the ninth century from the

---

[29] *The Martyrology of Oengus*, ed. W. Stokes, p. 26 (preface).

[30] On Oengus see L. E. Boyle in *Bibliotheca Sanctorum*, 9 (1967), cols. 1128-30.

[31] *The Martyrology of Oengus*, ed. W. Stokes, pp. 23-27 (preface).

[32] *Cogadh Gaedhel re Gallaibh*, ed. J. H. Todd (London, 1867), p. 140.

[33] *Martyrology of Oengus*, ed. W. Stokes, p. 270 (epilogue).

ruins of the old was a quite different one from the scholarly, saintly and marvellously eccentric Ireland of pre-800. From now on, Irish scholarship and wit and flair are to be found more in centers outside Ireland than in the homeland. Now, unlike the 6th, 7th and 8th centuries, the typical Irish exile is the Latin scholar and intellectual rather than the ascetic or missionary: Clemens Scotus at Aachen as head of the great imperial school; Dicuil at the same school as grammarian, geographer and astronomer; Sedulius Scotus at Liège, Metz and Cologne, where he proved to be an outstanding Ciceronian as well as an accomplished maker of gay drinking songs; John Scotus Eriugena in monasteries in the north of France, translating from the Greek and writing lengthily and profoundly of philosophical and theological subjects.[34]

These scholars-in-exile often felt lonely, cut-off, adrift, lamenting the quality of beer in Germany or looking back with nostalgia from the watery beverages of Italy to the manly drinks of their own land. But they continued to be as independent and as individualistic as their predecessors had been at home and abroad: as savage as Sedulius Scotus in his remarks on Rome:

> Who to Rome goes,
> Much labour, little profit, knows.
> And as for God:
> On earth though long you've sought him,
> You'll miss him at Rome—
> Unless you've brought him.[35]

Or as gentle as the Irish monk, deep in Austria, who scribbled a few famous verses on a scholar and his white cat, Pangur:

> Myself and White Pangur
> are each at his own trade:
> He has his mind on hunting,
> my mind is on my study.
> Better than any fame
> I prefer peace and a book,
> pursuing knowledge.
> White Pangur does not envy me,
> He loves his own childish sport.
>
> A tale without boredom
> When we are at home alone:
> For we each have (O endless fun)
> Something on which to exercise our skill.
> Sometimes, after desperate battles,

---

[34] In general see P. Wolff, *The Awakening of Europe, The Pelican History of European Thought*, I (Harmondsworth, 1968), pp. 64-104.

[35] Verses in Irish in Codex Boernerianus (Dresden) of Greek text of St. Paul, etc.—a codex probably written by Sedulius. For the text of the quatrain see *Thesaurus Palaeohibernicus*, II, p. 296; the translation used here is that of R. Flower, *The Irish Tradition* (Oxford, 1947), p. 39.

a mouse is caught in his net,
While into my net, too, there falls
   some hard and difficult legal point.

Pangur points his clear bright eye
   against a wall,
I point my own inquiring, if feeble, one
   against a wall of knowledge.

However long we are like that,
   neither disturbs the other.
Each of us enjoys his job—
   And enjoys it all alone.
The job he does every day
   is the one for which he is fit.
I, too, am competent at my own task:
Bringing light where there is darkness.[36]

   While the monk in Austria was immortalizing a literary cat, people
in Ireland were rebuilding with no great success on the ruins of the
Viking raids. Mercilessly efficient the Vikings in the first fifty years or
so of the 9th century, had laid waste all around them. If the Irish kings
and chieftains eventually learned enough of the new methods of warfare to contain and defeat the Vikings, they also learned far too much.
For they turned these methods on one another, and a series of deadly
wars soon wrecked what remained of the old Gaelic social order.
Monasteries were foremost among the victims of the Scandinavian
plunderers—and, unfortunately, of their Irish imitators. The heady,
vigorous world of Ailbe and Adamnán, Fintan and Laisrén, Blackletter and Maelruain, disappeared forever. There remained only the
memory of these men, a memory that heightened as the years passed
by and their comparatively blissful times receded into an unre-
coverable past. There remained, too, a yearning for the peace and
integrity and simplicity of those days of "The Saints and Scholars" that
is beautifully reflected in the 10th-century poem with which I shall
conclude:

O Son of the Living God, old Eternal King,
I desire a hidden hut in the wilderness
   that it may be my home:
A warm blue stream beside it and a clear pool
   for the washing away of sin
   through the grace of the Holy Ghost.
A lovely wood about it on every side
   to nurse birds with all sorts of voices
   and to hide them within its shelter.

---

[36] Printed and translated from MS. sec. xxv. d. 86 of monastery of St. Paul, Unter-
drauberg, Austria, in *Thesaurus Palaeohibernicus*, II, pp. 293-94. The version here is
adapted from Greene and O'Connor, *A Golden Treasury of Irish Poetry*, pp. 81-83. Another
translation, and some very useful notes, will be found in Murphy, *Early Irish Lyrics*, pp.
2-3 and 172.

A place looking south for heat
  and a stream through its land
  and good fertile soil for all plants.
A number of virtuous youths, too—
  I shall tell their number—
  Humble and obedient to beseech the king:
Four threes, three fours, suitable for all good service:
  two sixes in the church, one north, one south,
  six pairs besides myself
  praying forever to the king who moves the sun.
A beautiful draped church—a house for God from Heaven—
  and bright lights above the clean white Gospels.
One household to visit for care of the body,
  without lust or weakness or thought of evil.

The husbandry I would do and choose without concealment
  is fragrant fresh leeks and hens and speckled salmon and bees
and enough of clothing and food, from the King of fair fame.
And to be sitting for a while in peace
And praying God in every place.[37]

---

[37] For this 10th century poem see Murphy, *Early Irish Lyrics*, pp. 28-31 and 184-85.
The version here is that of Greene and O'Connor, *A Golden Treasury*, p. 150.

AUGUSTA GREGORY, IRISH NATIONALIST: "AFTER ALL, WHAT IS WANTED BUT A HAG AND A VOICE?"

Ann Saddlemyer

In 1928, looking back at a varied and active career, the sixty-six year old Augusta Gregory culminated a long list of public roles with the revealing comment: "And then 'a rebel' with the Nationalists all through—more than they knew or my nearest realised."[1] Unlike her two colleagues in the early Abbey Theatre, Lady Gregory was single-mindedly a rebel nationalist. When Yeats regretted the creation of a "People's Theatre" as "a discouragement and a defeat,"[2] she calmly asserted the duty of a national theatre to prepare for Home Rule.[3] While Synge celebrated the artist as vagabond and looked on Irish life with the romantic vision of self-imposed exile,[4] Lady Gregory planned folk-history plays aimed at educating the country towns. She routed Florence Farr, if not Maud Gonne, by offering Yeats collaboration in finding a theatre in Ireland. When that theatre's patron Miss Horniman begged him to put politics behind him, Lady Gregory sternly reminded him of his responsibilities to his nation. Her diary proudly

---

[1] Quoted in Editor's Foreward to *Lady Gregory's Journals 1916-1930*, ed. Lennox Robinson (New York, 1947), p. 8.

[2] *Explorations*, selected by Mrs. W. B. Yeats (London, 1962), pp. 249-50.

[3] *Our Irish Theatre*, 3rd ed. (Gerrards Cross, 1972), p. 29.

[4] Synge always considered himself the vagabond, the outsider; see Ann Saddlemyer, "Art, Nature, and 'The Prepared Personality,'" in *Sunshine and the Moon's Delight*, ed. Suheil Bushrui (Gerrards Cross, 1972), pp. 107-20.

bristles with acknowledgements of her ambition to restore to Ireland its native dignity: "O'Casey said, 'All the thought in Ireland for years past has come through the Abbey. You have no idea what an education it has been to the country.' " "The Union is holding a concert . . . and Jim Larkin would like to show the work of an Abbey playright to many who have never been inside the Abbey Theatre."[5]

Of the avowedly nationalistic plays presented by the Abbey Theatre company, Lady Gregory had a hand in most. As early as 1899 she and Yeats worked with Douglas Hyde to create plays in Irish for members of the newly established Gaelic League to perform; *Casadh an tSugan (The Twisting of the Rope)* was performed by the Irish Literary Theatre in October 1901, the first Irish play to be produced in any theatre. More significant perhaps, for her own future career, was her collaboration with Yeats in 1902 when she turned his "dream" of *Kathleen ni Houlihan* into country speech.[6] Years later Yeats claimed that he was not conscious at the time of the play as propaganda[7] (although under political necessity he was always prepared to take advantage of its popularity with the nationalists), but Lady Gregory had no doubts.[8] Certainly the patriotic sentiment of her own play, *The Rising of the Moon*, is undeniably a direct answer to the Old Woman's invitation in *Kathleen*.

Written in 1904 though not produced until 1907, *The Rising of the Moon* has a simple plot: an escaped Fenian is on the run; an upright Sergeant of the Royal Irish Constabulary encounters him at night on Galway quay; the Fenian in the guise of a ballad singer appeals to the sergeant's nationalist sympathies and is allowed to escape. "Well, good-night, comrade, and thank you. You did me a good turn tonight, and I'm obliged to you. Maybe I'll be able to do as much for you when the small rise up, and the big fall down . . . when we all change places at the Rising of the Moon." He disappears to a waiting boat and safety while the Sergeant, turning towards the reward notice, reads aloud, "A hundred pounds reward! A hundred pounds! I wonder now, am I as

---

[5] *Journals*, pp. 73 and 323.

[6] *Journals*, p. 264, quotes Yeats's admission in 1926, "I have never made one [play] in sympathy with my audience except *Kathleen ni Houlihan*, and that was you and a dream."

[7] See *Yeats and Patrick McCartan, A Fenian Friendship*, ed. John Unterecker (Dublin, 1965), p. 430. Though in a letter written to Lady Gregory in December 1904, he remarks, "*Kathleen* seemed more rebellious than I ever heard it." *Our Irish Theatre*, p. 36.

[8] Stephen Gwynn, in *Irish Literature and Drama* (Edinburgh and London, 1936), pp. 158-59, recalls the first performance in St. Teresa's Hall, Clarendon Street, on April 2, 1902: "I went home asking myself if such plays should be produced unless one was prepared for people to go out to shoot and be shot." Yeats finally asked himself this question in 1938 in "The Man and the Echo."

great a fool as I think I am?"[9]

Nourished on Fenian ballads sung by her old nurse Mary Sheridan, as a child the Loughrea bookseller's best customer for Fenian pamphlets,[10] she does not deserve Gogarty's malicious claim that Yeats wrote the play, nor could he have.[11] In her notes to the actors she takes great pains to point out that the Sergeant's actions were "not a change of mind," but the release and temporary ascendancy of "a deeper instinct, his Irish heart and memory of youth that had been moved unconsciously to himself."[12] Was it that same "deeper instinct" that led her to tear from a newspaper a lament on the death of Parnell; to study Irish in the early years of her marriage (a wish from childhood);[13] to begin collecting Irish ballads, improbably, among her husband's grandfather's Unionist papers;[14] to colour many of the comments in her edition of the state papers of that same Gregory with recognizably Home Rule sentiments?[15] Her first publication for the literary movement was again an edition, this time a collection of essays by Ireland's "image-makers"[16]—AE, D. P. Moran of the *Leader*, George Moore, Douglas Hyde, Standish O'Grady of *All-Ireland Review*, and W. B. Yeats—her private term for all the strong people whose dream is love of country. Her ambition as a playwright was equally patriotic: her first

---

[9] All quotations from Lady Gregory's plays are taken from the Coole edition, *Collected Plays*, vols. I-IV, ed. Ann Saddlemyer (Gerrards Cross, 1970).

[10] See her introduction to *The Kiltartan Poetry Book* (New York and London, 1919), pp. 7-9.

[11] Oliver St. John Gogarty, *As I Was Going Down Sackville Street* (London, 1968), pp. 291-92, and *It Isn't This Time of Year at All* (London, 1954), p. 216. Cf. Elizabeth Coxhead, *Lady Gregory*, 2nd ed. (London, 1966), pp. 7 and 103-04.

[12] Lady Gregory to George Roberts, 24 February 1904; the original letter is in Houghton Library, Harvard University. Even so, a few nationalists in the audience indignantly claimed that it was an unpatriotic act to represent a policeman as capable of any virtue at all. "How could the Dublin mob fight the police if it looked upon them as capable of any patriotic act?" Quoted by Yeats in his speech to the British Association on September 4, 1908.

[13] Introduction to *The Kiltartan Poetry Book*, pp. 7-9.

[14] *Seventy Years: Being the Autobiography of Lady Gregory*, ed. Colin Smythe (Gerrards Cross, 1974), p. 213.

[15] *Our Irish Theatre*, p. 41. Her reply was honest: "I defy any one to study Irish History without getting a dislike and distrust of England." In a letter to Bernard Shaw, October 5, 1912, she quotes Parnell, "an Irishman may betray us but an Englishman always does so, and it is what we have found," in "The Lady Gregory Letters to G. B. Shaw," ed. Daniel J. Murphy, *Modern Drama*, X, 4 (February, 1968), 341.

[16] Augusta Gregory, ed. *Ideals in Ireland* (London, 1901). In her editor's note, p. 11, she explains, "My object in collecting them is to show to those who look beyond politics and horses, in what direction thought is moving in Ireland."

attempt, *Colman and Guaire* (never to my knowledge produced), was "a little play in rhyme which might perhaps be learned and acted by Kiltartan school-children."[17] That ambition flourished with the establishment of the Irish National Theatre: "I had had from the beginning a vision of historical plays being sent by us through all the counties of Ireland. For to have a real success and to come into the life of the country, one must touch a real and eternal emotion, and history comes only next to religion in our country. . . . I still hope to see a little season given up every year to plays on history and a sequence at the Abbey, and I think schools and colleges may ask to have them sent and played in the halls, as a part of the day's lesson."[18] Doubtless to the discomfiture of Yeats, she revelled in their "folk-theatre" and its "return to the people."[19]

Her many translations from the Irish, collections of folklore, as well as her six "folk-history plays," all contain the simplicity of patriotic sentiment and appeal to the folk-imagination she valued in her countrymen. But even her comedies recognize the division of heart and mind, the tilting "between the two loyalties,"[20] which generations of an alien, often uncomprehending "over-government" exacted. The theme is rung throughout her work from the creation of Jo Muldoon, the slow-thinking policeman of *Spreading the News*, through all the heroes of the folk-tragedies—Grania, Dervorgilla, and especially Patrick Sarsfield of *The White Cockade*—to little vignettes such as *The Wrens*, where two singing, quarrelling vagabonds reflect the opportunism and inner turmoil which led to the 1799 Act of Union. The political allegory continues in one of her last published plays, *On the Racecourse* (itself an unsentimentalized re-writing of her first produced play), and is not difficult to trace in her adaptation of Don Quixote, *Sancho's Master*, where even the title is suggestive. Two further satires exist among her papers; one, *The Worked out Ward* (perhaps by her, perhaps by AE?), is a Sinn Fein parody of her comedy *The Workhouse Ward*, starring two inhabitants of a political ward, John Dillonel and Stephen Gwynnery, who refuse to go home with their countrywoman Mrs. Houlihan. The other is more interesting in that it was written in collaboration with Yeats, although clumsy and of no literary merit: entitled *Heads or Harps*, it bitterly attacks political turncoats and Trinity College unionism, and like Synge's essay on "National Drama," was better left unpublicized.[21]

---

[17] Augusta Gregory, *My First Play* (London, 1930), p. 1.

[18] *Our Irish Theatre*, pp. 57-58.

[19] *Our Irish Theatre*, pp. 50-51.

[20] See especially her notes to *The Canavans* in *Collected Plays*, vol. II.

[21] *Heads or Harps* was published finally in *Collected Plays*, vol. IV, pp. 343-50.

But the most significant patriot-dreamer in her canon is Charles Stewart Parnell. The first open reference to Parnell occurs in her three-act tragicomedy, *The Image*; written the year of Synge's death while still affected by the shock waves of *The Playboy* riots, she added a programme note, "Secretum meum Mihi." Set against the deluding dreams of a hero who never was, the wrangling between Brian Hosty of Connaught and Darby Costello of Munster represents in miniature the great split which occurred over twenty years earlier in Irish politics. *The Deliverer* followed a year later, ostensibly about Moses, really about Parnell, a strange, intense, bitter tragicomedy reflecting most clearly her own attitude toward her countrymen: "They were said to give him learning and it is bad learning they gave him. That young man to have read history he would not have come to our help." It is perhaps her most personal cry of disappointment and sorrow over the downfall of one more great leader and image-maker. A dozen years later the bitterness breaks out again in her Irish passion play, *The Story Brought by Brigit*, made all the more painful by the suffering of the civil war: "We wanted him and we got him, and what we did with him was to kill him." The lament of the keen in her most lyrical tragedy, *The Gaol Gate*, became even more applicable as the years passed: "It was not a little thing for him to die and he protecting his neighbour."

Like Yeats, Lady Gregory enjoyed a good fight in the theatre, particularly when it was aimed at the "over-government." She had fought against fellow nationalists for the *Playboy*'s right to be heard although she herself did not care for the play, and later on the Abbey's first American tour battled heroically for it in court, in the newspapers, and on the stage. But how much more this respectable widow of a colonial Governor enjoyed defying Dublin Castle! When her good friend Bernard Shaw's *The Shewing up of Blanco Posnet* was denied a hearing by the Lord Chamberlain's Office in England, she arranged to produce it in Dublin, confiding to her diary: "That should be a help to us and I don't know anything that would show up British hypocrisy so clearly."[22] Openly defying the Lord Lieutenant (a personal friend of long standing), she wrote exultingly to Shaw: "It is great fun the respectable Lord Aberdeen being responsible, especially as he can't come to see it, as vice-royalty doesn't like the colour of our carpets. We have never put down red ones, I always suggest their wearing red slippers."[23] (Red carpet was finally put down in 1926 when the theatre became subsidized; yet still she recognized the sensitivity of their posi-

---

Synge's "National Drama (a Farce)" was published in J. M. Synge, *Plays: Book Two*, ed. A. Saddlemyer (London, 1968), pp. 220-26.

[22] *Seventy Years*, p. 447. In her arguments with the Castle officials, she quoted Parnell, "Who shall set bounds to the march of a Nation?" *Our Irish Theatre*, p. 93.

[23] August 9, 1909, *Modern Drama* (February, 1968), p. 337.

tion, making a point of acting as "a barrier or a bridge" between the Governor General's party and some Fianna Fail friends she had invited to the theatre.)[24] The Castle was defied many times as more overtly political plays were produced at the Abbey: Thomas MacDonagh's *When the Dawn is Come* in 1908; Padraic Pearse's *The King* in 1913 (because the play was in Irish, few would recognize the significance of the closing speech: "Do not keen this child, for he hath purchased freedom for his people. Let shouts of exultation be raised and let a canticle be sung in price of God"). In 1914 Edward McNulty's *The Lord Mayor*, blatant anti-British propaganda, was produced, and in 1921, *The Revolutionist*, four months after its author Terence MacSwiney, Lord Mayor of Cork, died in prison while on a hunger strike. She commented in her diary, "I feel so happy that we have been able to keep the Abbey going if only for this one week, with the production of a national play of fine quality by one who has literally given his life to save the lives of others."[25] But her hopes for the end of such gestures were in vain, and two years later, this time defying her friend and fellow director, Senator Yeats, she and Lennox Robinson wrote an open letter to the people of Ireland pleading a halt to yet another hunger strike. "I feel more than ever a Republican without malice," she decided, and offered to move to a hotel, leaving her guest room at Yeats's house in Merrion Square.[26] After some deliberation Yeats felt that perhaps she had been right to send the letter; privately he wrote to Olivia Shakespear, "As she grows older she grows very strong and obstinate."[27]

As well as her strength, Yeats admired her courage and that accompanying sense of responsibility to herself and to others:

> Augusta Gregory seated at her great ormolu table,
> Her eightieth winter approaching: "Yesterday he threatened my life.
> I told him that nightly from six to seven I sat at this table,
> The blinds drawn up."
>
> ("Beautiful Lofty Things")

From her journals and articles we can gain a fairly clear image of her as landlord and Republican and of the unique mingling of duties. An unpublished article written in 1919 reveals much, including an inclination towards American Republicanism which might have horrified even her husband:

> I have long tried to do my work apart from politics, my formula has been "not working for Home Rule but preparing for it." And whatever may be done or left undone by Governments, I hope to continue to the

---

[24] *Journals*, pp. 95 and 337.

[25] *Journals*, pp. 63-64.

[26] *Journals*, p. 192.

[27] *The Letters of W. B. Yeats*, ed. Allan Wade (New York, 1955), p. 706.

end my endeavour to do for Ireland whatever task I may be best fitted for, in the constant care of our theatre, or as in these four years past in the effort to bring back Hugh Lane's pictures to Ireland according to his intention and desire.

As to the form of government I would prefer to see brought into being I have perhaps but little right to speak, for there remain to me at the most but a few years in which I may enjoy or endure it. Yet my persuasion, my confession to myself, though not as yet to others, has come to be that among us the essential forms of the philosopher's ideal state "temperance, courage, liberality, magnificence, and their kindred" would best thrive and grow in a commonwealth. That word, as its sister word "Republic" has a high and noble tradition that stirs the imagination, as "Dominion" in its dictionary sense of "a territory, region, district, considered as a subject" could never do in Ireland. For if, as it may be, imagination in the British Dominions sees its pole star over Westminster or Windsor, it is in part because of a tradition brought by men and women born and bred in the kingdom of England; whereas those of our kingdom who come to us or to whom we go over the ocean belong to no kingdom but to the great Republic that has been their refuge and become their home. Mr. Roosevelt, once talking to me of Ireland's difficulties said "We are too far off or she might be taken into our Union as a State — We can do those things." And though that may not be, it is certain that America would give the little republic that delighted, ungrudging welcome that is even the best help being a benediction having no savour of patronage.

I believe it is thus only in complete freedom, under complete sense of responsibility that our regeneration can come, and thus only that the root of bitterness, hurtful alike to us and England these 700 years can be dragged out.

Reasonable men from those lips we hear, as we should not have heard a while ago the word "Dominion" yet call out against "Republic" is a wasted cry, a thing out of reason. Yet changes come on the wind — and many prophets say that the impossible today may be the accomplished work of tomorrow. And I remember a poet [Yeats, in an earlier draft] saying to me a good while ago: "A prophet is an unreasonable person sent by Providence when it is going to do an unreasonable thing."[28]

As resident of Coole Park, she was loved and respected throughout the countryside, even during the height of the Civil War when her brother Frank was burned out of the family home at nearby Roxborough. Her granddaughter Anne recalls an incident from this time when two men in hiding insisted on walking Robert's two little daughters from the Nut Wood safely into the house garden, warning them not to return to the woods for at least three days: "Tell her Ladyship

[28] The original manuscript, dated July 24, 1919, and signed "A. Gregory," and an earlier draft dated July 6, are in the Gregory papers of the Berg Collection of the New York Public Library. All quotations from the Gregory papers in the Berg Collection are printed by permission of the Trustees of the New York Public Library: Henry W. and Albert A. Berg Collection, The New York Public Library, Astor, Lenox and Tilden Foundation. This appears to be the document she is referring to in her *Journals*, p. 189, August 27, 1923 ("Polling Day"). See also *Journals*, p. 61.

that we wouldn't hurt a hair of anyone in her Ladyship's family."[29]
Several weeks before this incident a car had been ambushed, and all the
passengers killed except one—Lady Gregory's daughter-in-law, Margaret.

Cryptic references in her journals to some articles published in
England explain in part the respect for and safety of Coole. "I had been
brought a message after the ambush," she wrote in August 1921,
"saying 'as long as there was a Gregory in Coole they need fear
nothing.' MacI. was grateful for what I 'had thought fit to do for him
the time the house was burned,' and besides that 'it was from Dublin
they had got word of my help' (I suppose the *Nation* articles)."[30] A
search through the files of *The Nation* disclosed six articles in the form
of a week's diary of local events. To prevent reprisals by the Black-
and-Tans, they are unsigned, the author described only as "a distinguished writer and landlord" from "a quiet part of Ireland, not
dominated by the Extremists." But the details are horrifying in their
honesty and by matching references with certain published portions of
her journals, one can quite definitely assign them to Lady Gregory.
Initials are given instead of names and places, but again they are
readily identifiable. Much of it is recorded conversation, some eyewit-
ness accounts, others hearsay, all substantiated by detail and recorded
in a dispassionate tone, and all but the hated Black-and-Tans given
their due:

> Old Patrick F working for me says: "There did two car loads of the
> Black-and-Tans come into G[ort] yesterday evening. They were a holy
> fright—shooting and firing. They broke into houses and searched them,
> and they searched the people in the street, women and girls that were
> coming out from the chapel and that came running down our street in
> dread of their life. Then they went into S's to drink, and got drunk
> there—it is terrible to let them do it. Look at I's, they burned all the
> bedding in the house and every bit of money he had, and nine acres of
> wheat and oats. They would have burned the hay, but they didn't see it.

> As we came from church the exits from the town had been bar-
> ricaded—carts drawn across and soldiers in a group. They let us pass
> without question. All the men coming from Mass were taken into a house
> and searched. In church we had "God Save the King"—it has been sung
> ever since military were sent to G[ort]—in the war time. One lesson, and
> all but one of the Psalms, were cut from the service at their asking, as they
> said the long service would keep them late for dinner, but that remains.

> The Connacht Tribune has an advertisement of "German toys in great
> variety of lowest prices," to be had from an agent in Belfast. Later in
> the day J. tells me, "It is true about the Loughnanes [two sons of a
> neighbouring widow murdered by the Black-and-Tans]. I met two boys

---

[29] Anne Gregory, *Me and Nu: Childhood at Coole* (Gerrards Cross, 1970), pp. 18-19.

[30] *Journals*, p. 157.

from Shanaglish. They had gone to the place where they were found and saw the bodies and they knew them, though they could not say what way they met their death. The flesh was as if torn off the bones. God help the poor mother."

A farmer coming on business says: "B[urke]'s house that was burned down and rebuilt by the neighbours has been raided again in the night by the Black-and-Tans. I hear they threatened to burn it again, but that the old police have said that if this is done by the Castle police the whole of them will resign."[31]

Yet despite her obvious Republican leanings and her keen admiration for the image-makers of her nation, Lady Gregory was not herself politically inclined. With great misgivings she stood for Senate at Yeats's instigation, but was relieved when defeated.[32] Of Yeats's At Homes in Merrion Square, she writes, "He is very kind, and would ask politicians and officers to meet me but thinks I don't care to meet them, and that is true enough. It is the creators that I like best to meet." The same entry in her diary includes the revealing words, "O'Casey, sheltering by me, interested me most."[33] Even before the Troubles and the Civil War, she had clearly aligned her sympathies with "the workers, the creators," rather than with the active politicians. She wrote to Shaw after the 1916 rising, "I couldn't feel much enthusiasm for Casement, but I wish something could be done for John MacNeill, a scholar to the backbone and most generous in his help to learners. There are such masses of MSS to be translated, while he is making sacks in gaol. He is our business because of what he has done for the intellectual life of Ireland."[34]

Yeats mourned, admired, and wondered at the terrible beauty of 1916. Lady Gregory lamented the loss of teachers and leaders who might have provided a blueprint for that Republic she so looked forward to. An essay exists among her papers, signed, dated 16 May [1916] and entitled, "What Was Their Utopia?" It reads in part:

> For many days the road that leads north, to Galway, was barricaded and held by armed men; the railroad that leads to Dublin had been torn up. The telegraph poles had been cut and the wires flung over walls. For

---

[31] There are six articles altogether: "A Week in Ireland," *The Nation*, 16 October 1920, pp. 63-64; "Another Week in Ireland," 23 October 1920, pp. 123-24; "Murder by the Throat," 13 November 1920, pp. 215-16; "A Third Week in Ireland," 4 December 1920, p. 333; "A Fourth Week in Ireland," 18 December 1920, pp. 413-14; "A Fifth Week in Ireland," 1 January 1921, pp. 472-73. See her *Journals*, pp. 133-46.

[32] *Journals*, p. 335.

[33] *Journals*, p. 260.

[34] 12 August 1916, *Modern Drama*, February, 1968, p. 343. In *Seventy Years*, p. 542, she says of the Rising, "One begins to distinguish between the leaders who had some ideals and the village tyrants."

news we were dependent on rumour, vague, alarming, for the most part false. When newspapers came again they told that the rising had been put down, and the chief among the leaders shot.

Since then the papers have been full of rumours as had been our roads; rumours of plans "for the better governance of Ireland." Perhaps these are known in London today, for the Prime Minister was to speak yesterday. But that news has not reached us yet; we only know he has been asking counsel, opinion, from men on one or the other side. That is a wise thing to do; and is it not a great pity it is too late to hear from their own lips what was the plan of government made for Ireland by those leaders who are dead? One would so gladly hear it; for these men who proclaimed their promise to all the citizens of Ireland of "religious and civil liberty, equal rights and equal opportunities"; who promised "to pursue the happiness and prosperity of the whole nation equally," must certainly have shaped some scheme in detail by which to work out these general principles. One desires to know by what means, by what reasoning they had meant to bring Ulster and Connacht into friendship; how so to enforce law as to bring the serenity of order into a long disordered land, how so to use their "Science and Poetry and thought" as to

> make the lot
> Of the dwellers in a cot
> Such they curse their neighbour not.

For as Shelley says "In men who suffer for political crimes there is a large mixture of enterprise and fortitude and disinterestedness, and the elements, though misguided and disarranged by which the strength and happiness of a nation might have been cemented." And these men, Irish and living in Ireland, living in this vision, this idea, must certainly have given to it an intensity of thought to which politicians can hardly attain. One covets to know the ground plan of their Republic, their Jerusalem, their Utopia; of how they would have attained Milton's aim that must be the aim of every free Commonwealth, to "make the people fittest to choose, and the chosen fittest to govern"; and all the more if we admit for them Whitman's proud claim for their "visions the visions of poets, the most solid announcement to any." We covet to know once again in this generation what was the poets Utopia. For these men were certainly poets. . . .

Now that Germany, thank God, can never gain a foothold here, I would humbly pray that John MacNeill be asked, as representing those leaders who are gone, to give full testimony as to the plan, the project, in which they had put their faith. It may be it would give some common meeting ground for all, as well the patient as the passionate, who wish our country well. And there would be compelling force behind it; for is it not the custom in Ireland as in tragedy for the victory to remain with the dead?[35]

At the same time she wrote to Yeats, "My mind is filled with sorrow at the Dublin Tragedy, the death of Pearse and MacDonagh who ought to have been on our side, the side of intellectual freedom, and I

---

[35] Original manuscript in the Gregory papers, Berg Collection, New York Public Library. See also *Seventy Years*, pp. 532-49.

keep considering whether we could not have brought them into the intellectual movement. . . . It seems as if those leaders were what is wanted in Ireland and will be even more wanted in the future, a fearsome and imaginative opposition to the conventional and opportunist Parliamentarians who have never helped our work even by intelligent opposition."[36]

The intellectual life of Ireland—this is perhaps the secret of that uneasy tension that hovers over Lady Gregory and her writings, and is reflected in Yeats's admiration of "all that pride and that humility." Her entire life was built on paradox—O'Casey once complimented her on struggling against her birth and class.[37] Certainly some of the conflicts in Ireland were represented in her own life. As a worker for Ireland she was a leader, as a creator she was a teacher, as a patriot she was a landlord. In the midst of her description of the Black-and-Tan terrorism, she can comment on the additional chilling horror of the retaliatory murder of officers in Dublin, "perhaps from its being in one's own class."[38] The Abbey Theatre was to be for the nation and for all, but the taste would be decreed by the few: "we went on giving what we thought good until it became popular."[39] The sagas must be translated, and she spent many years learning Irish, poring over old manuscripts, to make that material available. But her dedication to the people of her own district, Kiltartan, makes it clear that expurgation was also a responsibility: "I left out what I thought you would not care about for one reason or another."[40] The very emphasis on dignity in literature begs the question of realism; the early Irish Literary Theatre manifesto had stated, "We will show that Ireland is not the home of buffoonery and easy sentiment as it has been represented, but the home of an ancient idealism."[41] The famous autograph tree of Coole was approached only at her invitation and some visitors, penknife at the ready, were never asked. Poor plays were performed to keep the Abbey Theatre open, but O'Casey's experimental The Silver Tassie was rejected because it did not come up to the standard and style expected of the author, one of their discovered "geniuses." The pit was beloved more than the stalls, but chastized more frequently. It cannot be denied that the arrogance which characterized some of Yeats's most famous ut-

---

[36] Seventy Years, pp. 544-45.

[37] Journals, p. 105.

[38] "A Third Week in Ireland," The Nation, 4 December 1920, p. 333.

[39] Our Irish Theatre, pp. 63 and 68.

[40] Dedication, Cuchulain of Muirthemne, 1902 (5th ed., Gerrards Cross, 1970).

[41] Our Irish Theatre, p. 20. She prefaces the quotation from the statement of the Irish Literary Theatre with the admission, "it now seems a little pompous."

terances (and inspired some of his greatest poetry) belonged to Lady Gregory also.

But that very arrogance fed her nationalism as surely as did her love of country. "In questions like this one must go to one's own roots," she had written to Yeats over the Easter Rising.[42] Was it an urge to see herself as an image of the spirit of Ireland, as well as the urgency of the moment, that led her to step into the role of Yeats's Kathleen ni-Houlihan some three years later? An actress was delayed returning to the theatre; the bills were out; the audience had been promised. "After all," she argued defensively to her diary, "what is wanted but a hag and a voice?" And then, with the ruthless honesty and self-appraisal she demanded of all Ireland's would-be image-makers, added, "yet if all goes well I shall be glad to have done it."[43]

---

[42] *Seventy Years*, p. 545. See also p. 394. "The passionate love of Ireland is the foundation to work."

[43] *Journals*, pp. 56-58.

AE AS A LITERARY CRITIC

Henry Summerfield

*(Thanks are due to Messrs. Colin Smythe Ltd., for allowing me to reproduce some sentences from my biography of AE—*That Myriad-minded Man *(Colin Smythe; Rowman and Littlefield)—and from my introduction to the selection of articles from the* Irish Statesman *to be included in the firm's forthcoming edition of AE's* Collected Works. *That selection and the companion volume of pieces chosen from the* Irish Homestead *will include most of the articles cited in this essay.)*

AE (George William Russell) is famous for his participation in the Irish Renaissance as journalist, artist, poet, mystic, patriot, theatre organizer, and propagandist for Sir Horace Plunkett's agricultural cooperative movement. One of his greatest pleasures lay in seeking out new poets whom he supported with loans and gifts, assistance in getting their work published, and, not least, advice on the craft of writing. Despite his weakness for wearing out favourite words and phrases in his own verse, he was a rigorous critic of slipshod idiom in the productions of these young writers, and his influence helped to raise poetic standards in the Anglo-Irish literature of the twentieth century. While this aspect of AE's critical activity is quite widely known, it is less often recognized that in the *Irish Statesman*, which he edited from 1923 to 1930, he attempted to educate the general public on literary subjects. His voluminous contributions to his own paper include a rich body of critical writing marked by a supple, vigorous and individual style and to a large extent based on a consciously held theory of literature. Collectively this work embodies a synoptic view of the English, American, and modern Anglo-Irish literatures.

AE has suffered comparative neglect in recent years because his impact on his contemporaries depended largely on his unique personality, the expression of which is badly muffled in the prose and verse he himself published in volume form. From an early stage in his life, he adopted the practice of concocting a self-consciously literary prose, which he usually eschewed in his journalism where the printer's demands happily allowed little time for revision. The dated character of AE's formal prose is well explained in an unpublished letter in which he tells how he rewrote both *The Candle of Vision* and *The Interpreters* about a dozen times aiming, though rarely with complete success, at a style made musical by assonance and alliteration.[1] His lifelong friend, Yeats, reviewing *Song and Its Fountains*, contrasted its effete language with the forceful modern prose through which AE had influenced public affairs, and complained that he "writes as though he were living in the 'nineties, seems convinced that spiritual truth requires a dead language."[2] Yeats pointed to "Fiona Macleod" (William Sharp) as one of the authors whose mannerisms had infected AE's style.

In the mid-1890s, when AE's first identifiable book reviews appeared in the *Irish Theosophist* (1892-1897), he already had two prose styles. One, self-consciously poetic, he used for inspirational stories and essays:

> Parvati turned homeward, still half in trance: as he threaded the dim alleys he noticed not the flaming eyes that regarded him from the gloom; the serpents rustling amid the undergrowths; the lizards, fire-flies, insects, the innumerable lives of which the Indian forest was rumourous; they also were but shadows.[3]

The other, unaffected, straightforward and competent, he employed for exposition:

> Ireland was known long ago as the Sacred Island. The Gods lived there; for the Tuatha De Dannans who settled in Eire after conquering the gigantic races of Firbolgs and Fomorians (Atlanteans) were called Gods, differing in this respect from the Gods of ancient Greece and India, that they were *men who had made themselves Gods* by magical or Druidical power.[4]

AE developed this second style in the course of editing the *Irish Homestead* from 1905 to 1923, and as he campaigned on behalf of the agricultural co-operative movement, which the paper existed to support, he became a master not only of exposition but of satirical irony and invective. Bringing his new skill to bear on literary subjects, he learnt to conduct a critical argument with clarity, to convey a lively notion of the content and tone of a book, and to denounce lightheartedly the pretensions of a worthless publication. He displayed a particular talent for conveying concisely the individual flavour of a book or a character.

---

[1] To Miss Piercy, 25 February 1929 (Lilly Library, University of Indiana).

[2] W. B. Yeats, "My Friend's Book," *Essays and Introductions* (London, 1961), pp. 412-18.

[3] "The Meditation of Parvati," *Irish Theosophist*, 15 November 1893, pp. 151-53.

[4] "The Legends of Ancient Eire," *Irish Theosophist*, 15 March 1895, pp. 101-03.

Thus he described Carlyle as "a huge creature, for all his screaming and rant, with enough genius in him to furnish forth a score of artists, though he himself had too passionate, tattered and hasty a mind to be one of the great artists in literature."[5] In another article, a long sentence evoking with the aid of an extended metaphor the mercurial mind of John Butler Yeats is quickly followed by a selection of short sentences from his essays, a selection which illustrates AE's gift for lighting on enticing quotations from the books he reviewed:

> He marches gaily down the street of his mind ostensibly with one topic as companion, but he meets and nods at all kinds of intellectual acquaintances on the way, gives a sly dig at an enemy, or trips him up with a cleverly inserted epigram. And he contrives yet with all this side play, in which his Irish nationality is very apparent, to say a good deal that is interesting and stimulating on the topic he is ostensibly discussing. How delightful are his sentences. "When a belief rests on nothing you cannot knock away its foundations." "In Ireland we are still mediaeval and think that how to live is more important than how to get a living." "The woman does not believe in pleasures. She believes in happiness."[6]

AE could write detailed criticism with precision, as when he warned J. L. Donaghy that he would have to overcome his weaknesses to release his poetic talent:

> Let me take the poem which he calls *The Tigers*. He says he saw "a tiger (clearer to my sight than houses at early morning)," and then goes on to show how clearly he saw by reference to its claws, feet, muscles, etc. Now when it is obvious he sees clearly what is the point of saying he saw the tiger clearer than houses at early morning? What exact degree of precision of sight is suggested by this image or how does it bear on the seeing of claws, feet, etc.? It is quite unnecessary, it does not elucidate, and it is therefore mere verbiage.

Referring to the poet's phrase "lightning to cleave and kill," he commented firmly: "The first thing Lyle Donaghy has got to kill is his own wordiness."[7] At its finest, AE's prose attained a noble eloquence. Praising MacKenna's translation of Plotinus, he introduced his reader in three short sentences to the austere world of intellect and beauty in which the philosopher moved, and then his own phrases took wing as he reproduced the very phenomenon he described:

> There is not a word here which grates upon us. All is pure and cold and ecstatic as the vision the seer beholds. We are never let down to earth. The long sentences keep their upward flight like great, slow-moving

---

[5] Review of *The Glamour of Dublin*, by D. L. Kay, *Irish Homestead*, 14 December 1918, p. 819.

[6] Review of *Essays, Irish and American*, by J. B. Yeats, *Irish Homestead*, 13 July 1918, p. 467.

[7] Review of *At Dawn Above Aherlow*, by John Lyle Donaghy, *Irish Statesman*, 11 December 1926, p. 330.

birds which can soar upwards to the sun through the icy coldness of the
lofty air and yet live and be full of exultation.[8]

The composite image of birds, sun and sky makes concrete the qualities
abstractly described as "pure and cold and ecstatic," and only the
repetition in "upward . . . upwards" betrays the haste with which AE
was compelled to write.

Even before AE was appointed editor in 1905, the *Irish Homestead*,
though primarily an agricultural paper, carried some features on the
arts, and by 1911 he had formed the habit of contributing a review of a
book or periodical to his own editorial columns every few weeks. The
frequency of these reviews increased steadily during succeeding years
so that by the time the *Irish Homestead* was superseded by the *Irish
Statesman* in 1923, he was an experienced critic. He took this comparatively new role with great seriousness, regarding the critic as the pro-
moter and guardian of high standards in the literary life and especially
the poetry of his nation. Accordingly he felt duty-bound to blame as
well as to praise, for while he believed that the composition even of
indifferent poetry was spiritually good for the writer, he considered
publication another matter. Thus, confronted with the work of a
nineteenth-century poet whom he judged to be competent but unin-
spired, he admitted that "no doubt the writing of it kept open some link
between body and soul, and it is something to do that through a long
life."[9] Faced on the other hand with a contemporary book of what
seemed to him worthless verse, he did not allow his extraordinary
natural kindliness to prevent him from saying, "There are thousands
of people who do, we think, advantage their souls by trying to write
poetry, but they are restrained by modesty or the candid criticism of
their friends from making public their efforts."[10]

The spontaneity and naturalness of AE's literary articles came
from the intense instinctive delight he took in literature as in art. He
readily admitted: "I am not one of those supercilious persons who will
read nothing but the finest literature and who decline in art anything
but the masterpiece. I confess I get some pleasure from almost every
book I read or almost every picture show."[11] In criticism, however, he
sought some fundamental principles beyond the personal taste of the
writer, and he once complained:

We have little criticism of literature because we have no criterion other

---

[8] "The Genius for Translation," *Irish Statesman*, 6 December 1924, pp. 399-400.

[9] Review of *Collected Poems* by James Rhoades, *Irish Statesman*, 11 April 1925, pp.
152-53.

[10] Review of *Don Quixote and Other Sonnets*, by Grace Tollemache, *Irish Statesman*, 26
April 1924, p. 216.

[11] "Picture Exhibitions," *Irish Statesman*, 19 May 1928, p. 212.

> than personal opinion. It is possible to imagine criterions of the quality of thought based on Platonism, or as with Trotsky on a social order, or any of the great religions of the world. But unless there is some philosophy of the soul, of nature, of society, all criticism must be to a large degree personal opinion. . . .[12]

In 1913 a controversy he conducted in the editorial "notes of the Week" and the correspondence columns of the *Irish Homestead* led AE to formulate one of his major critical principles. The debate began when he wrote in the issue of 15 February of his revulsion at the election to high political office of men of straw who thought like second-rate businessmen and seemed more concerned about money than about people; he went on to speculate, like Sir Philip Sidney, that men had often become noble by emulating the heroes celebrated by the poets, and he suggested that modern authors were to blame since they presented no models of exalted character. In the next number of the weekly, James Stephens, writing under his pseudonym James Esse, defended the poets with his usual ebullience of style, insisting that the author was not the inspirer of men but merely their historian. AE commented that "Realism as a theory of literature is the most ignoble of all theories," and in the issue of 1 March he drew a distinction between the lesser work addressed to the individual reader and the greater work addressed to the nation. While acknowledging the "great gift of lovely song" his contemporaries, "singing a solitary song for the solitary listener in the byways," had bestowed on Ireland, he maintained:

> . . . when the work of a writer or artist is considered not with reference to the personal pleasure it gives individuals, but to the needs of a nation, it involves the setting up of a higher standard, and all writers must feel then that they have erred and strayed from the highway like lost sheep. We can talk with men as men, but the writer who would talk to a nation must use a lordly speech as one who talks to a god. The nation is a giant being . . . and can only be awakened by such cries as rang from the prophets of Israel or the majestic oratory of a Pericles.

Some weeks later, a contributor to the *Irish Review* challenged these beliefs on the grounds that the writer was merely engaged in self-expression, and in his reply, printed in the *Homestead* for 17 May, AE summed up his position. Asserting that "To write is self-expression, to print and publish is propaganda," he cited Wordsworth, Shelley and Whitman—"the greatest of the moderns"—in support of his claim that "the great poets did not take this view of their own genius. They identified themselves with their race. They sang because they believed their song would influence those who heard it." The craft of words, he argued, was on the same plane as the craft of the jeweller, and it was only recently that writers had presumed to demand for their verbal

---

[12] Review of *Lectures on Dead Authors*, by E. H. Lacon Watson, *Irish Statesman*, 7 January 1928, pp. 422-23.

skill the praise traditionally accorded to "the greatness of soul expressed through the craft," and he instanced the way in which "In the
baldest schoolboy crib translation of the Prometheus of Eschyllus [*sic*],
devoid of all literary merit, the lordly spirit shines through and we are
full of reverence." At an earlier stage in the controversy he had answered the argument that the writer must wait for inspiration with his
favourite dictum that inspiration comes as a response to aspiration, and
he now urged that the contemporary writer, who had in most cases
restricted himself to "a surface scratching of the human soil . . . should
first of all see whether he has something in himself worth expressing,
and if he has not it is his duty by fervent brooding to create a spirit and
an ideal worth giving to the world."

As a Theosophist, AE believed that the path to reality lay inwards,
and he never tired of insisting—Joyce made him do so in *Ulysses*—that
the criterion of greatness in a work of art is the depth of life from which
it springs. In the ancient Indian doctrine of four levels of consciousness—walking, dreaming, deep sleep, and the transcendental Turiya
or Fourth which he called spirit waking—he found a scale on which this
could be measured, a scale that he frequently employed during his
Statesman period. Thus he held that the best work of Spenser, Keats,
Coleridge, the younger Tennyson, and William Morris all originated in
the dream consciousness, as did that of most living poets among his
compatriots except Oliver St. John Gogarty, who was "singular among
modern Irish poets in being a poet of the waking consciousness."[13] Believing that most poets entered the dream consciousness while retaining
the waking mind's willpower and reason and so controlling the dream
images, AE demanded a poetry in which inspiration was combined
with reason, and he felt that the achievement of De Quincey's prose
was limited by the fact that "the entry into the dream consciousness has
been attained at the expense of the rational which the best poetry never
relinquishes."[14] De Quincey had tried to make prose, normally the
instrument of the waking consciousness, do the work of poetry. The
distinctive music of poetry was an echo of the musical nature which
man's being takes on as it rises in mystical experience towards the
Logos. "If you feel and think profoundly," he asserted, "you feel and
think musically, and it is not artifice but nature which prompts the
measured beat, echo or assonance."[15] In the act of composition, according to his belief, "an intense mood in the poet harmonises all sounds
and attracts to consciousness identities and assonances with the preva-
lent feeling."[16] Nevertheless AE was sufficiently interested in the

---

[13] Review of *An Offering of Swans*, by Oliver St. John Gogarty, *Irish Statesman*, 15
December 1923, pp. 436, 438.

[14] "Poetical Prose," *Irish Statesman*, 17 December 1927, pp. 350-51.

[15] Ibid. Cf. also AE, *Song and Its Fountains* (London, 1932), pp. 79-81.

[16] Review of *Poems*, by Sir Samuel Ferguson, *Irish Homestead*, 9 February 1918, p. 88.

mechanism of auditory effects to propound a theory, with which Yeats agreed,[17] that the poet's sounds, like the artists's pigments, produced their effects by contrast as well as harmony. In a letter published in the *Times Literary Supplement* of 19 May 1921, he suggested that, for example, the "o" and "i" sounds set one another off in Nashe's line, "Dust hath closed Helen's eye," and that a science of sound might help a great poet to amend a weak passage.

Prose, then, was usually rooted in the waking consciousness and poetry in the dream consciousness. No inspiration could proceed from the deep sleep state, but AE believed that the very greatest works of art were created only when the artist came in contact with the transcendental level Turiya, in which the psyche is aware of the unity of itself and of all things with Deity:

> I feel somehow that with Shakespeare and some others consciousness has transcended the dream state, and has come to a magical awakening beyond, perhaps corresponding to that stage which in India is called spirit waking, a state differentiated from bodily waking or dream, and I think in this state, higher than dream, the supreme works of art are created.[18]

AE's literary criteria are reflected in his views of entire literatures. In youth he seems to have been prejudiced against English (as opposed to Anglo-Irish) literature, for in 1895 he wrote scornfully to "John Eglinton" (William Magee): "I see the great tree of English literature arising out of roast beef and watered with much rum and beer. That is my feeling about most of it."[19] He could then see little even in Shakespeare, though he ardently admired some Romantic and Victorian poets. In maturity, his prejudice diminished and his critical articles show him making in effect his own analysis of the pattern of English literature from the sixteenth to the twentieth centuries.

Reviewing Norman Ault's masterly anthology *Elizabethan Lyrics* in the *Irish Statesman* of 26 December 1925, AE revelled in a poetry which embodied the vitality of a young people for whom everything was possible and who were too excited by the external world to achieve the spirituality which made intermittent appearances in the work of their successors. "They love," he wrote; "they kiss; they disdain love; they rage; they mourn; they run through all passional life and experience with a gusto never to be felt again in English poetry." Their technique was equal to their vitality, and "the more self-conscious artists of a later age might look in despair on the miracles of style born in a sudden affinity between soul and lips." After the Gaelic scholar Osborn Bergin

---

[17] Letter to W. B. Yeats, 10 March 1921, text in National Library of Ireland, MSS.9967-99, compiled by Alan Denson.

[18] "The Essays of W. B. Yeats," *Irish Statesman*, 7 June 1924, pp. 397-98.

[19] "Unpublished Letters from AE to John Eglinton," *Malahat Review*, April 1970, pp. 84-107.

lent him Sir Walter Raleigh's book on the greatest Elizabethan, AE came to find in Shakespeare a delightful sense of play—"a very fat laugh" and "sheer impish enjoyment"[20]—as well as an unequalled genius for characterization and flashes of a profundity comparable to that of the Greek tragedians. About the giant of the next century he had mixed feelings. While he responded to the resonant verse of *Paradise Lost*, recognizing that the sentence, not the line, was its unit,[21] and while he appreciated the overpowering image of Hell, he judged that Milton was a moralist of Tolstoy-like fanaticism rather than a spiritual man so that "when he ascended to Heaven his vision was rather of the intellect than the imagination."[22] In his book *The Interpreters*, he ascribed the unreal, somewhat ignoble quality of the Miltonic Heaven to the fact that unlike Irish poets Milton was not handling a mythology which had arisen from the spiritual experiences of his own race.

AE had only a little to say of Milton's contemporaries and near-contemporaries the Metaphysicals. He found some beauty in Donne,[23] while the gentle but strong-willed George Herbert was one of his favourite poets,[24] and in the work of Henry Vaughan he hailed the first appearance in English literature of a truly spiritual vision. Vaughan, however, he thought of as more pious than mystical, suspecting that a stronger personality, perhaps his brother Thomas, the Hermetist, had made him into an "interpreter who has heard or read the mystics, has intuitionally accepted them but never had pressed his own way far into the spiritual universe."[25] Faced with the poems of Bishop Henry King, AE, like T. S. Eliot, was enchanted by "the Exequy," but classified this author as otherwise "the cultivated man of letters, writing verse more as a pleasant occupation than because he has been obsessed by his daemon to sing."[26] He emphasized also the limitations of Andrew Marvell, but admitted that he combined the ability to distill an exquisite magic in occasional lines with "a kind of wisdom which would delight conservative minds"[27]—wisdom which spilled over from his prose into

---

[20] "What is Art?" *Irish Statesman*, 28 February 1925, pp. 787-89.

[21] Letter to James Pryse, 16 October 1923 (Berg Collection, New York Public Library).

[22] "The Anatomy of a Poet," *Irish Statesman*, 23 May 1925, pp. 338, 340.

[23] Ibid.

[24] C. C. Rea, *Some Less-known Chapters in the Life of AE* (Dublin: privately printed, 1939), p. 7.

[25] Review of *Poems*, by Henry Vaughan, *Irish Statesman*, 20 February 1926, p. 746. See also "The Youth of a Nation," *Irish Statesman*, 26 December 1925, pp. 494-95.

[26] Review of *Poems*, by Henry King, *Irish Statesman*, 4 July 1925, p. 532.

[27] Review of *Andrew Marvell*, by V. Sackville West, *Irish Statesman*, 5 October 1929, p. 98.

his "Horatian Ode upon Cromwell's Return from Ireland." In these assessments there is little awareness of the qualities of the metaphysical poets considered as a school.

One would have expected AE to have dismissed the Augustan period as an age of barren rationalism, but in fact, while lamenting the absence of close observation of nature and exclaiming "A wild Irishman is not the person to be just to this poetry,"[28] he was moderately appreciative. Praising Dryden, the father of English neoclassical poetry, as "one of the great energies in English literature," he noted that after his passing the Elizabethan vitality disappeared and "the Popes, Grays[29] and Priors made literature formal and dipped its wings."[30] Congreve as a fellow Anglo-Irishman was no doubt a special case, but AE displays an infectious enthusiasm over his "effervescent" wit, "the bubbles of which yet rise up out of the deeps rather than the surface of human nature," and he insists: "None of the moderns have depicted a witty woman better than Congreve, not Wilde or Shaw, and none of these has written so well as Congreve at his best."[31] Acknowledging the artistry of Pope as unmatched in its field and his "powers of offence and defence" as remotely rivalled only by Byron's, he speculated, in agreement with a thesis of Edith Sitwell, that "such unnatural intensities of hatred or contempt are possible only to natures which have dreamed of almost impossible sweetness of the affections."[32] He recognized the period attraction in the fainter charms of Gay, but found his work "all a great deal too easy" and concluded "Watteau was the true poet of that artificial world."[33] In the *Homestead*, AE would show in passing references his admiration for the trenchancy of Swift's prose, and he had some appreciation for the prose satire in the rational Augustan spirit which was still being written as late as the Romantic Revival. He alluded with pleasure to Jane Austen's light satiric touch[34] and to the intellect and "the slender vein of poetry" of Thomas Love Peacock, and praised in the latter "a certain aristocracy of mind, fostered by classical learning," which was sufficient to save "his humour from becoming commonplace."[35]

---

[28] Review of *The Oxford Book of Eighteenth Century Verse, Irish Statesman*, 18 December 1926, pp. 364, 366.

[29] Perhaps a misprint for "Gays."

[30] Review of *The Character of John Dryden*, by Alan Lubbock, *Irish Statesman*, 25 July 1925, p. 628.

[31] Review of *Comedies*, by Congreve, *Irish Statesman*, 26 September 1925, p. 89.

[32] Review of *Alexander Pope*, by Sitwell, *Irish Statesman*, 5 April 1930, p. 98.

[33] Review of *Poetical Works*, by John Gay, *Irish Statesman*, 8 January 1927, p. 436.

[34] "The Tale of Genji," *Irish Statesman*, 25 July 1925, pp. 622-23. Cf. review of *Pride and Prejudice: A Play*, by E. and J. C. Squire, *Irish Statesman*, 7 September 1929, p. 18.

[35] Review of *The Misfortunes of Elphin and Crotchet Castle*, by Peacock, *Irish Statesman*, 19 July 1924, p. 598.

The area of English literature in which AE felt most at home was certainly the poetry of the Romantic Revival, in which he saw the fitful visionary hints of Vaughan fulfilled. Its harbingers Collins, Gray, and Goldsmith returned to some extent to nature,[36] and in Blake, Wordsworth, Coleridge, and Shelley he encountered poets who had penetrated into his own world where physical nature was but a part of a greater entity.

AE's enthusiasm for Blake as artist and lyric poet went back to his twenty-first year, though he did not seriously explore the prophetic works apart from the early *Book of Thel*, until more than thirty years later, when, apparently infected by James Stephens' enthusiasm, he embarked on a more serious reading of them, which is reflected in some of his *Statesman* articles. At a much earlier date, however, he showed a lively appreciation of *The Marriage of Heaven and Hell*, making an illuminating comment, for example, in his *Homestead* editorial of 24 December 1910:

> It was part of Blake's philosophy that every man had in him a prophet, a voice which talked to the soul and told it what to do and what was coming to pass. He called the prophet in himself familiarly by the august name of "Isaiah," and he said the prophet "Isaiah" dined with him because this inner voice was never done talking to him, even during meal times.

Too early to benefit by recent research which has shown that Blake's obscurity was caused more by too much learning than by too little, AE accused him of becoming enmeshed in his own reason-created system, and claimed: "If he had read of Plato or Plotinus he might have found that others had adventured before him who reported of what they discovered in a speech which became universally intelligible, and his own message might have become more lucid." AE considered that Blake resorted to constructing an intellectual system in an attempt to make sense out of what he saw in the Mid-world—the realm of the dream consciousness—and valued most, apart from a psychological insight unmatched in English literature, those moments of vision when he rose above the dream consciousness and was inspired to compose such passages as the conclusion of *Jerusalem*: "Not any poet, not Dante, imagined a Paradise which lingers longer in our imagination than that brotherhood of all living things with which Blake ended his greatest song."[37]

AE was conventional in his view of Wordsworth, frequently quoting with approval from his early verse but seeing both a spiritual and a

---

[36] Review of *The Oxford Book of Eighteenth Century Verse, Irish Statesman,* 18 December 1926, pp. 364, 366.

[37] "The Prophetic Books of William Blake," *Irish Statesman*, 12 March 1927, pp. 14-16. See also review of *William Blake in this World*, by Harold Bruce, *Irish Statesman*, 10 October 1925, pp. 150-51.

literary decline in his later work. He loved especially the line, "Thy friends are exultations, agonies," from "To Toussaint l'Ouverture"; it "was written," he said, "by one who saw that for which all the long labours of the soul were undertaken."[38] Sensing a division between the rational, moralizing surface of Wordsworth's mind and a subconscious spirituality, he suggested that the latter might have touched off the flights into the Mid-world (the world to which Faery belongs) of the weak-willed Coleridge, arousing him from his customary "abnormal indulgence in sentimental dreaming"[39] to create "The Ancient Mariner," "Kubla Khan," "Christabel," and, years later, "A sunny shaft did I behold." AE's admiration for Shelley was less severely qualified, for he sympathized with one who "inwardly was living, if somewhat uncertainly, in the Golden Age, and had not learned to harmonise its ethics with the ethics of the Iron Age,"[40] but he acknowledged that the poet sometimes lost himself in "a vague cloudland where there is neither a clear view of the earth nor a clear view of the heaven."[41] In early youth he had preferred Shelley to Keats, finding the latter too rich and sensuous, but he came to see him as "the greatest artist in words in English poetry after Shakespeare."[42] Though there is no sign that he was aware of the philosophy behind Keats's work, he paid him the high compliment of attempting a Keatsian ode in his own poem "Natural Magic." He felt, however, that Keats, like Shelley, wrote from only a part of himself, whereas Byron, in his greatest work, *Don Juan*, wrote "with the whole being, and . . . exploited every phase of his rich vitality, from the cynical to the heroic,"[43] and he rejoiced that in Greece at the end of his life the hero in Byron was victorious over the demon.

The rich and varied literature of the Victorians aroused in AE certain misgivings. From childhood he relished the lyric poetry of Tennyson, and he especially loved "Ulysses" with its celebration of the human will, that power neither good nor evil in itself but essential for progress in the spiritual life. Rossetti, another poet of the Mid-world, had for AE a sinister aspect, for he wished to draw the beauty of that realm into the world of nature and drag Paradise down to earth, and to accomplish this he "was in painting and poetry seeking always to express psychic intensities, going in imagination beyond natural inten-

---

[38] "A Platonic Criticism," *Irish Statesman*, 22 June 1929, pp. 311-12.

[39] "Samuel Taylor Coleridge," *Irish Statesman*, 22 May 1926, pp. 297-98.

[40] Review of *Shelley's Lost Letters to Harriet*, by Leslie Hotson, *Irish Statesman*, 22 March 1930, p. 56.

[41] Review of *The Mount of Transfiguration*, by Darrell Figgis, *Irish Homestead*, 18 December 1915, p. 829.

[42] "Keats and His Circle," *Irish Statesman*, 14 March 1925, pp. 15-16.

[43] "Byron," *Irish Statesman*, 15 March 1930, pp. 31-32.

sities in an endeavour to sustain the passional life at its summits."[44] AE's reservations about Browning were literary rather than moral, for he admired his psychological subtlety while being troubled about his wordiness and his marked decline, ominous for the future of literature, from a Shelley-like prophet to a skillful versifier of conversation.[45] In the key article "A Gold Standard for Literature,"[46] he looked back longingly to the time before cheap printing had made publication easy when profound truths were often condensed into aphorisms readily committed to memory. Primarily he referred to the sayings of ancient Chinese and Indian philosophers, but he pointed to an English equivalent in *The Marriage of Heaven and Hell* of William Blake, who labouriously engraved his own text on metal plates. Turning to Browning, he asked despondently, "Has the [sic] *Ring and the Book* anything of the quality of *Two in the Campagna?* ... Can we imagine Browning, if he had, like Blake, to engrave, print, and decorate his own poetry, producing the *Ring and the Book?*" Extending his argument to prose fiction, he complained of long modern novels

> where the writer tells us how the room was furnished, what clothes everybody wore, what their personal appearance was like, how they spent their school days, their adolescence, and all their love affairs wringing out the last drop of emotion. We ought hardly to endure such minutiae about titans like Napoleon, but to have mountains of words piled about imaginary, commonplace characters revolts me.

This protest about excessive realism should be associated with AE's preference in fiction for romance like that of Dumas *père*, George MacDonald, and the Kipling of *Kim* and *The Jungle Book*, with his disgust at the failure of modern writers to provide characters of heroic stature, and with the thesis of his important essay "Is Literature in a Blind Alley?"[47] In this article he maintained that a work of literature which existed mainly for the portrayal of character could not be a work of the first rank. Contrasting Shakespeare with the Greek dramatists, he noted now as we watch *Oedipus Rex* "we suddenly become aware of an invisible presence, Nemesis, a deity, who puts down the mighty from their seats and exalts insignificance." Most of the greatest works of literature, such as the Greek tragedies, *The Divine Comedy*, and ancient Indian epic, showed man as existing "in an aether of deity" and revealed him to himself in his relation to the eternal and divine. Shakespeare, however, departed from tradition in concentrating on the portrayal of character for character's sake, and while he himself displayed

---

[44] "Dante Gabriel Rossetti," *Irish Statesman*, 5 January 1929, pp. 356-57.

[45] Review of *Poems, 1909-1925*, by T. S. Eliot, *Irish Statesman*, 9 January 1926, pp. 564, 566.

[46] *Irish Statesman*, 2 March 1929, pp. 516-17.

[47] *Irish Statesman*, 9 February 1924, pp. 685-86.

an intuition of man's cosmic place in brief passages like "We are such stuff / As dreams are made on," he exerted a regrettable influence on the British and Continental novelists of the eighteenth and nineteenth centuries, who, except for Balzac, were without such intuitions. Among the British novelists affected, AE named Fielding, Scott, Dickens, Thackeray, George Eliot, and—rather strangely—Hardy, and he concluded by expressing the hope that future writers might lead literature out of the blind alley into which it had strayed. In this argument AE, writing before the recovery by recent scholars of the Elizabethan world-picture, is unfair to Shakespeare, who can now be seen as representing mankind poised between Heaven and Hell. On the other hand, the contention that literature which has no aim transcending the portrayal of character can at best be of the second rank is readily defensible, and AE could have cited the fact that the modern novel evolved in the eighteenth century—he began his list with Fielding—the very age when Shakespeare took his undisputed place as the greatest English writer. Moreover the Elizabethan world-picture had by then already been forgotten, and the dramatist was seen as, in Dr. Johnson's words, "the poet that holds up to his readers a faithful mirror of manners and of life."

Since AE grew to manhood in late Victorian Ireland, it is not surprising that he found some difficulty in responding to the modern movement in literature. The decline in faith and the decay of a unified world-view had left Western man suspended in limbo with no stay for his ego, leading ultimately to the doctrine of the Absurd. Confronted with the poetry of T. S. Eliot, AE considered that he had unmistakable talent, that sometimes (as in *The Hollow Men*) he wrote "with beauty and distinction," but that most often he "has sunk into a pit where he talks to himself, not to the universal spirit in himself, but the personal ego looks at its own peculiarities in a mirror and the pit is often impenetrable in its intellectual murkiness."[48] He noted Eliot's "vague" derivation from Browning, who had also deserted the universal in man for the particular, but did not live long enough to welcome, as he surely would have done, Eliot's quest for timelessness and deity in *Four Quartets*. He did, however, give his warm approval to that side of T. S. Eliot which responded to the unified world-view in *The Divine Comedy*, claiming that his essay on Dante showed him to be a true critic, one who has an "appreciation of what is rare in beauty or noble in mind," and who, partly by his gift for quotation, "in a slight essay . . . gives us an impression of the vastness, the depths and heights of the whole poem" and "sends us back to Dante by suggesting his infinitude."[49] Not sur-

---

[48] Review of *Poems, 1909-1925*, by T. S. Eliot, *Irish Statesman, 9 January 1926, pp. 564, 566.*

[49] Review of *Dante*, by T. S. Eliot, *Irish Statesman*, 5 October 1929, p. 98.

prisingly, the "opacity," or lack of visionary windows, which troubled
AE in the poetry of T. S. Eliot, also troubled him in that of lesser
innovators, but he softened towards Ezra Pound when Eliot's skillful
selection from the verse of his mentor almost persuaded him "that the
man of talent, if he be serious enough about his art may approach the
work of genius." He praised the "marriage of beauty and wit" in
Pound's poetry, and, caring deeply about quality of sound, perceived
that "Free verse has never with Pound meant easy verse."[50] In spite of
such appreciation, however, AE probably remained more at ease with
fairly traditional poetry such as the lyrics of Ralph Hodgson, the best
verse of Kipling, who had "a lordly air at times, a line which has vision,
or magic, or wisdom in it,"[51] and *The Flaming Terrapin* by Roy Campbell,
which made him exclaim: "No poet I have read for many years excites
me to more speculation about his future. . . ."[52] Even the charming
experimental verses of Robert Bridges, which are still undeservedly
neglected, left him sighing for that writer's earlier songs.[53] He considered, indeed, that technique was an obsession with modernist poets,
but that they had not on the whole much that was worthwhile to say.[54]

When AE met with technical innovation in Anglo-Irish rather
than English or American works, he was inclined to respond with a
more open mind and a quicker sympathy, for the productions of his
fellow countrymen appealed to his most intimate feelings. His critical
writing on modern Anglo-Irish literature is so extensive that only a
brief survey is possible here. He customarily emphasized the debt
which the authors of the Irish Renaissance owed to Gaelic literature
and its translators, and in the poetry of Sir Samuel Ferguson he hailed a
pioneer example of the Gaelic spirit and even technique embodied in
English verse.[55] But while Gaelic literature was replete with spirituality
it was deficient in intellect, and AE rejoiced that the influx of Dane,
Norman and Saxon had enriched the Gaelic mentality making it into
something more complex yet allowing the old Irish element to remain
"the Mendelian dominant."[56] This element had re-emerged in the

---

[50] Review of *Selected Poems*, by Ezra Pound, *Irish Statesman*, 8 December 1928, pp.
279-80.

[51] Review of *Sea Songs and Ballads*, by C. Fox Smith, *Irish Statesman*, 3 November
1923, pp. 242, 244.

[52] Review of *The Flaming Terrapin*, *Irish Statesman*, 10 May 1924, pp. 276, 278.

[53] Review of *New Verse*, by Robert Bridges, *Irish Statesman*, 16 January 1926, p. 600.

[54] Review of *A Survey of Modernist Poetry*, by Robert Graves and Laura Riding, *Irish
Statesman*, 24 December 1927, p. 376.

[55] Review of *Poems*, by Ferguson, *Irish Homestead*, 9 February 1918, p. 88.

[56] "Anglo-Irish Literature," *Irish Statesman*, 22 January 1927, pp. 477-78.

early poetry of Yeats, which dazzled AE in his youth, and in the versions of Irish legend and history produced by Standish James O'Grady, sometimes in what now seems a grotesque prose imitation of the idiom of classical and Miltonic epic. So impressed was AE by the nobility of the characters that O'Grady pictured, especially in his *History of Ireland: The Heroic Period*, that he exempted this author from his general charge that modern Irish writers failed to offer society worthy models of national leaders. The entire first phase of the Renaissance seemed to him, in retrospect, to have been dominated by a distinctly Gaelic spirit of idealism and romance. In Yeats's poetry he had found "for the first time the revelation of the Spirit as the weaver of beauty,"[57] and James Stephens' fictions and Synge's dramas abounded in romantic fantasy. (AE's contention that the Abbey Theatre should not have staged *The Playboy of the Western World* realistically[58] is supported by the contrast between the plot of the comedy and the story on which Synge based it as given in his book *The Aran Islands*.) Even George Moore in his masterpiece *Hail and Farewell!* relied on "malicious phantasy," for, explained AE, he "has invented a group—invented with genius, it is true—but nonetheless invented people who never existed in Ireland and has called them by well-known Irish names."[59] Yet even in some of these authors AE noticed that imagination was coming closer to home, and in 1912 he wrote: "With writers like Synge and Stephens the Celtic imagination is leaving its Tirnanoges, its Ildathachs, its Many Coloured Lands and impersonal moods, and is coming down to earth intent on vigorous life and individual humanity."[60] As early as 1907, when Padraic Colum published *Wild Earth*, AE had seen signs of a new literary mood and had greeted him as "the first Irish poet who has chosen to write of the common life," a man "in love with the normal."[61] The trend towards realism, however, was of slow growth, and it only came to full fruition in the work of James Joyce, Sean O'Casey, Liam O'Flaherty, and Frank O'Connor. AE accounted for the literary see-saw in terms of a law of action and reaction,[62] and in private letters[63] he tried to explain it by an eccentric application of the Indian doctrine that each ascent into a heaven

---

[57] AE, *Imaginations and Reveries* (Dublin and London, 1915), p. 27.

[58] Alan Denson, ed., *Letters from AE* (London, New York, Toronto, 1961), p. 67.

[59] Review of *Twenty-five Years*, by Katharine Tynan, *Irish Homestead*, 25 April 1914, p. 326.

[60] *Imaginations and Reveries*, p. 43.

[61] Review of *Wild Earth*, by Colum, *Irish Homestead*, 14 December 1907, p. 972.

[62] "Heredity in Literature," *Irish Statesman*, 4 June 1927, pp. 304, 306.

[63] E.g. to Sean O'Faolain, 25 January 1927, text in National Library of Ireland, MSS.9967-69. Cf. "Notes and Comments," *Irish Statesman*, 3 April 1926, p. 89.

necessitates a corresponding descent into a hell, and hoping, despite his respect for much of the realistic literature, that there would soon be a new ascent, he speculated that this would probably lead to an intellectual rather than a second imaginative phase.

In spite of his reservations, AE had a lively appreciation of the major achievement of the later part of the Irish Renaissance. The most outstanding practitioner of the new realism was James Joyce, whose amazing talent for prose AE had noticed almost as soon as he had met him in 1902.[64] Initially taken aback by the brilliance, the scale, and the novelty of *Ulysses*, AE admired the intellect behind it but found its atmosphere unlikeable, and he fell into the habit of referring to it as an *Inferno* without a *Purgatorio* or *Paradiso*, but in a more appreciative mood he endorsed another critic's view that Joyce was "dredging the great deeps of personality" with the comment that "the great deeps in us all must be dredged so before our natures can truly be purified and porous to the sea of light,"[65] and two years later he claimed that America, for all her brilliant authors, had "no sky-touching genius, no one even who burrows so deeply as our James Joyce."[66] The first extracts published from *Work in Progress* (later *Finnegans Wake*) made AE suspect that Joyce had taken a wrong turning, but when *Anna Livia Plurabelle* appeared he greeted it with a delight almost as great as he used to display on discovering a new poet:

> ... this book is the really extraordinary part of the work which is in progress. ... As a technical feat, this strange slithery slipping, dreamy nightmarish prose is more astonishing than anything Joyce has yet written, and whatever else he may be, he is a virtuoso in the use of words.[67]

A few months later, in his review of *Shem and Shaun*, he refused to deliver a final verdict but insisted: "It was no bungler who wrote this, however misdirected his energies. ..."[68]

A parallel achievement to Joyce's *Ulysses* and *Finnegans Wake* was the later poetry of Yeats. Despite his passionate attachment to the early lyrics, AE could not help seeing that the work of his middle age made Yeats into a poet of much greater stature. Warming to the more modern style of the new verse, he was quick to commend to over luxurious poets like the young Austin Clarke "that beauty made out of

---

[64] *Letters from AE*, p. 43.

[65] Review of *Reminiscences of a Student's Life*, by Jane Ellen Harrison, *Irish Statesman*, 21 November 1925, p. 346.

[66] "A Study of American Culture," *Irish Statesman*, 19 February 1927, pp. 573-74, 576.

[67] Review of *Anna Livia Plurabelle, Irish Statesman*, 29 December 1928, p. 339.

[68] Review of *Tales Told of Shem and Shaun, Irish Statesman*, 6 July 1929, p. 354.

bare words to which Mr. Yeats came at last."[69] AE regretted what he thought of as a failure of will after the promise of Clarke's first book,[70] but applauded the emergence of his later and more original manner in *Pilgrimage*, where "a certain decorative treatment of images and ideas" made "the poetry the equivalent in words of some lovely antique tapestry glimmering with rich subdued colour. . . ."[71] When AE heard that Yeats was basing a book about his fundamental beliefs on Mrs. Yeats's automatic writing, he was, being highly sceptical about spiritualism, somewhat amused, and when *A Vision* was published, he politely expressed a fear that it implied that the soul went through a series of predetermined phases and had no power over its own destiny. It was only when Yeats returned reinvigorated to the work of the imagination and created a poetry "fresh and strange and beautiful" that AE was satisfied that the enormous intellectual labour behind *A Vision* had not been a sterile bypath:

> It is one of the rarest things in literature to find a poet of whom it might be said that his wine was like that in the feast in the Scriptures, where the best was kept until the last. Here in this later poetry is the justification of the poet's intellectual adventures.[72]

Standing quite apart from Yeats and Joyce, Bernard Shaw became one of the major Irish writers of the earlier twentieth century without participating in the Renaissance, but although he was an expatriate and a rationalist, AE showed his usual sympathy with literary compatriots when assessing his work. Shaw's wit and intellect, he believed, had revitalized the English and American theatres, and his arrogance was a mere pose to hide an inner humility, but however much the world needed his questioning of the accepted social order—and he was "a much saner critic of politics and society than Tolstoy"[73]—he suffered from the limitations of the man who relies on logic. "Shaw," he warned his readers in 1912, "has made a pure culture of his own cleverness and inoculated himself with it, and his mind is utterly incapable of taking in anything which has half-tones or quarter-tones and which cannot be translated into terms of pure reason."[74] When *Back to Methusaleh* appeared in 1921, AE detected signs that Shaw, unlike Wells and Bennett whose concentration on externals was a true reflection of their

---

[69] Review of *The Sword of the West*, by Clarke, *Irish Homestead*, 7 January 1922, pp. 4, 6.

[70] Letter to W. B. Yeats [late April 1932], text in National Library of Ireland, MSS. 9967-69.

[71] Review of *Pilgrimage and Other Poems, Irish Statesman*, 2 February 1929, pp. 437-38.

[72] "The Winding Stair," *Irish Statesman*, 1 February 1930, pp. 436-37.

[73] "Notes and Comments," *Irish Statesman*, 27 October 1928, p. 143.

[74] "Notes of the Week," *Irish Homestead*, 1 June 1912, p. 442.

shallowness, was "tormented by suppressed spirituality,"[75] and a few years later he extended his diagnosis by describing him as "a romantic, a true descendant of the writers of the old Irish Sagas," who had "decided when he was young that he would hide the leprachaun in himself under civilised clothing" and so "dressed his fairies and imps and leprachauns in hats and coats and boots."[76]

AE's friendly approach to the not very Irish Shaw was matched by his attitude to a writer who was neither Irish nor English. In youth AE had been interested in the work of "Fiona Macleod" as a symptom of a Celtic revival in Scotland parallel to that in Ireland, and by the 1920s he felt that there was indeed an Anglo-Scottish renaissance and that one of its major authors was "Hugh MacDiarmid" (C. M. Grieve).[77] When he first encountered the verse of MacDiarmid, the outstanding Scottish poet of the twentieth century, he admired its poignant emotion and subtle thought, but wondered whether the attempt to revive Lallans were not more heroic than practical.[78] Soon, however, he was dazzled by MacDiarmid's masterpiece, *A Drunk Man Looks at the Thistle*,[79] and by 1931, when he came to write his Introductory Essay to *First Hymn to Lenin and Other Poems*, he knew that Lallans literature had a distinguished past, and he not only praised the Scotsman for his philosophical depth—"I find hardly any character in contemporary poetry so intellectually exciting"—but envied his access to a vernacular which, unlike the Anglo-Irish peasant speech employed by Synge and Lady Gregory, could express the subtlest thought and emotion.

Having become acquainted with the Scots literary tradition and being a dedicated apologist for the concept of a distinctive Anglo-Irish literature, AE speculated on the reasons why the dominions had not yet produced authors of international rank,[80] and he was fascinated by the one colony that had already broken away to become a separate nation with its own literary identity. His interest in American literature went back to early youth, and throughout his life he regarded the New England Transcendentalists, and most of all Emerson and Whitman, as the spiritual center of American culture. In discussing Whitman, AE often pointed to his unique success in imbuing passages of his free

---

[75] Letter to W. B. Yeats [September 1921?], text in National Library of Ireland, MSS. 9967-69.

[76] Review of *Tales from Bernard Shaw*, by Gwladys Evan Morris, *Irish Statesman*, 14 September 1929, pp. 38-39.

[77] Review of *New Poems*, by Thomas Sharp, *Irish Statesman*, 21 November 1925, pp. 344-45.

[78] Review of *Sangschaw*, by MacDiarmid, *Irish Statesman*, 3 October 1925, p. 120.

[79] Review of *The Lucky Bag*, by MacDiarmid, *Irish Statesman*, 4 June 1927, p. 313.

[80] Review of *Modern Australian Literature*, by Nettie Palmer, *Irish Statesman*, 27 September 1924, pp. 86-87.

verse with a rich quality of sound, but in an article of August 1923, referring to his achievement in speaking with an authentically American voice, he emphasized a less technical point asserting that "Rude as his chants were, something almost like cosmic consciousness seemed to thrill in them," and he expressed disappointment that Whitman's successors had not yet appeared, perhaps because Americans were a busy, outward-looking people drawn away from inner spiritual depths to surfaces. Nevertheless he saw signs of promise in a few recent poems which seemed to have been "born in a different nature and with a spiritual atmosphere not European."[81] In a number of articles written during the next seven years, AE repeated his analysis, pointed to architecture as so far the great art of the unintrospective Americans, and expressed his confidence that the heirs of Emerson, Whitman, Thoreau, Melville, and Hawthorne—men seemingly "born with the spirit aged within them"[82]—would eventually appear. Meanwhile, although he recognized substantial merit in the work of some American writers like Edwin Arlington Robinson, Robert Frost, and Edna St. Vincent Millay,[83] who were not essentially different from their British counterparts, he took most interest in the writings of those poets and novelists whom he could credit with helping to cut the United States loose from the Old World. Mark Twain, for example, he regarded as more of a philistine than an artist, but also as a storyteller who by sheer vitality and irreverence toward tradition helped to create the American identity;[84] similarly, he felt that Henry James, although he "occupied a great part of his life in enriching with subtleties a life which did not seem much deeper than a wallpaper,"[85] also, through his eventual disillusion with Europe, contributed to the national task.[86]

A few months after his complaint that Whitman had had no followers, AE decided that to some extent the poet James Oppenheim (today a forgotten man) deserved to be described as such. Both Whitman and Oppenheim, he claimed, had escaped from the temptation of resorting to Europe's pagan mythologies, which Americans could not use with any degree of naturalness, both were able at times to compose truly rhythmical free verse, and both displayed a "frankness" which, he

---

[81] Review of *The Peterborough Anthology*, *Irish Homestead*, 18 August 1923, p. 524.

[82] "A Study of American Culture," *Irish Statesman*, 19 February 1927, pp. 573-74, 576.

[83] "American Poetry," *Irish Statesman*, 28 June 1924, pp. 493-95.

[84] "Social Conventions and the Freedom of the Artist," *Irish Statesman*, 12 December 1925, pp. 431-32; review of *Collected Poems*, by Vachel Lindsay, *Irish Statesman*, 5 January 1924, pp. 530, 532.

[85] Review of *The Pilgrimage of Henry James*, by Van Wyck Brooks, *Irish Statesman*, 8 August 1925, p. 696.

[86] *Letters from AE*, p. 165.

wrote, "is a poetic necessity in a land where Puritanism has ceased to be a natural austerity of the spirit and has degenerated into an unintellectual moral tyranny. . . ."[87] AE acknowledged, however, with some sadness, that Oppenheim owed too much to Whitman to be regarded as a major original voice, and he considered that the same was true of Carl Sandburg, who was content to ladle out "the raw material of poetry" without "working it up to wonder and beauty."[88] Elsewhere AE found signs of a breaking away from Europe in Vachel Lindsay, who, with a delightful but permanently immature energy, reflected the impact of the Negro on the white man's imagination,[89] and in Robinson Jeffers, who created characters driven by elemental passions, men and women belonging to an era "thousands of years before Christ was born, before any of the religions laid their rod on the spirit of man. . . ."[90] AE's final American discovery came just before the *Irish Statesman* collapsed. Reviewing Richard Eberhart's *A Bravery of Earth* in the issue for 22 March 1930, he found in his poetry "almost a continuation of the Emersonian tradition" together with something of the "bodily vitality" which was missing from Emerson's transcendentalism. The prophecy with which the review closes, that "American genius which has been going outward for so long is going to go inward," has been amply fulfilled in the age of Faulkner, Roethke, and William Carlos Williams.

AE envisioned in the United States of the future a civilization based on a mentality of unprecedented complexity, but he also hoped that the greatest phase of Ireland's culture was yet to come, and one of the ways by which he sought to help in laying the foundation for this achievement was by spreading the knowledge of literature and improving public taste through his critical articles in the *Irish Statesman*. With an enviable command of prose, he assessed the books that came his way, and his constant reader could not but be influenced by his criteria of judgment. In 1905 he wrote to Clifford Bax, "I have no interest in people who find in literature anything but an avenue to life"[91]—and to AE life that was truly human involved contact with a divine world, hence the literature which moved him most was literature which opened a window out of the material world of Newtonian physics, the Darwinian struggle for existence, and Freudian psychology; the window might be Wordsworthian revealing the Spirit through nature, or

---

[87] Review of *The Sea*, by Oppenheim, *Irish Statesman*, 31 May 1924, pp. 370, 372. See also "Free Song," *Irish Statesman*, 17 November 1923, pp. 303-04.

[88] Review of *Selected Poems*, by Sandburg, *Irish Statesman*, 3 April 1926, pp. 100, 102.

[89] Review of *Collected Poems*, by Lindsay, *Irish Statesman*, 5 January 1924, pp. 530, 532.

[90] Review of *Roan Stallion, Tamar and Other Poems*, by Robinson Jeffers, *Irish Statesman*, 24 November 1928, pp. 234, 236.

[91] *Letters from AE*, p. 56.

heroic disclosing the hidden grandeur or august destiny of the human soul. AE's greatest admiration went to the schools and periods in which such literature was the norm—those of primary epic, Greek tragedy, the Romantic Revival, and New England Transcendentalism—but he found a place in his affections, too, for the lesser literature of psychological realism, description of nature, and playful fantasy, and although Irish, Anglo-Irish, and ancient Indian literature were closest to his heart, he welcomed merit in any literature of the world.

NAKED TRUTH, FINE CLOTHES AND FINE PHRASES IN SYNGE'S *PLAYBOY OF THE WESTERN WORLD*

C. L. Innes

In his Preface to *The Playboy* Synge wrote:

> All art is collaboration; and there is little doubt that in the happy ages of literature striking and beautiful phrases were as ready to the story teller's or the playwright's hand as the rich cloaks and dresses of his time.... This matter, I think, is of importance, for in countries where the imagination of the people, and the language they use, is rich and living, it is possible for a writer to be rich and copious in his words, and at the same time to give the reality which is the root of all poetry, in a comprehensive and natural form. In the modern literature of the towns, however, richness is found only in sonnets, or prose poems, or in one or two elaborate books that are far away from the profound and common interests of life. One has, on one side, Mallarmé and Huysmans producing this literature; and on the other Ibsen and Zola dealing with the reality of life in joyless and pallid words. On the stage one must have reality, and one must have joy....[1]

The problem of reconciling joy and reality is expressed more succinctly and memorably by Pegeen Mike in her bitter rejection of the Playboy: "I'll say a strange man is a marvel with his mighty talk; but what's a squabble in your back-yard and the blow of a loy, have taught me that there's a great gap between a gallous story and a dirty deed." It is that gap between "a gallous story and a dirty deed," and, even more importantly, the relationship between them, that form the central concerns of *The Playboy of the Western World*, a play which can be perceived as a

---

[1] John M. Synge, *Collected Works*, Vol. IV, ed. Ann Saddlemyer (London, 1968), pp. 53-54. All quotations from *The Playboy of the Western World* are taken from this edition.

series of variations on the interaction between romance and reality, between fine language and the common interests of life, and between words and referents.

In the opening scene of the play, the importance of language and words as a theme is already suggested, together with the attempt to bring together romance and reality and the analogy between poetry and fine clothing. As the curtain rises, Pegeen is writing, composing a letter slowly and awkwardly, and the stiffness and labouriousness of her letter writing, with its closing ritual formula, "With the best compliments of this season," will contrast with the vitality and sharpness of her speech. Here is also suggested the gap between an alien and pallid written tradition and the oral, folk tradition, with the songs, ballads and storytelling which Pegeen will allude to throughout the play. Visually, the disorder and poverty of the public house and of Pegeen herself, "a wild-looking but fine girl . . . dressed in the usual peasant dress," is set up as a counterpoint to the wedding finery which is to come from afar: the yellow cloth, the boots with "lengthy heels on them and brassy eyes," the wedding hat and fine-tooth comb.

Synge had at one time planned to make the analogy between clothes and words a much stronger and more explicit motif in the play. In Typescript "F," he has a hamper of clothes which Pegeen tries on Christy throughout their scene together in Act I.[2] This action is changed in Typescript "G," however, to Pegeen preparing a supper of bread and milk for Christy before filling the sack for his bed. Such a change indicates a different perspective on the kind of "collaboration" between the artist and "the imagination of the people," and I will discuss the nature of that collaboration in more detail below. Nevertheless, the clothing image, while receiving much less emphasis in the final draft, is retained as a significant motif, and an analysis of its appearance suggests some of the relationships between language, poetry and reality which inform the play.

While Pegeen's first appearance suggests that for her there is a wide distance between romance and everyday reality, between fine clothes reserved for special ceremonial occasions and the usual peasant dress, in subsequent scenes clothing imagery is used in varying ways. When Shawn Keogh, terrified of Father Reilly and of what "the Holy Father and the Cardinals of Rome [would] be saying" if he stayed the night with Pegeen, tears himself away from Pegeen's father threatening "the curse of the priests . . . and of the scarlet-coated bishops of the Courts of Rome" on him, he leaves his coat in Michael's hands. Holding up the coat, Michael exclaims, "Well, there's the coat of a Christian man. Oh, there's sainted glory this day in the lonesome west. . . ." Here Shawn's coat is seen as the symbol of the "Christian man" that Shawn already is, and it is Shawn who gives the coat its

[2] Ibid., p. 78.

meaning and significance. Without it he remains the same Christian Shawn. In contrast, there is a suggestion that the relationship between the bishops and their scarlet coats is more complex; these coats, because of their colour, have a certain significance of their own, an aura of grandeur and authority which both adds to the authority of the bishops and is at the same time appropriate to, a sign of, the authority of the bishops which is already theirs as functionaries of the Courts of Rome.

Act I ends with another analogy between visible covering and heard speech:

> **Pegeen.** There's your bed now. I've put a quilt upon you I'm after quilting a while since with my own two hands, and you'd best stretch out now for your sleep, and may God give you a good rest till I call you in the morning when the cocks will crow.
> **Christy** [*as she goes to inner room*]. May God and Mary and St. Patrick bless you and reward you for your kindly talk. [*She shuts the door behind her. He settles his bed slowly, feeling the quilt with immense satisfaction.*]

Christy's response indicates that the quilt and the kindly talk are equivalent. Pegeen's talk, the romantic aura she has spread out around him made from a patchwork of traditions she has put together from Biblical phrases and folk ballads and sayings, from "Owen Roe O'Sullivan and the poets of Dingle Bay," is as yet a loose covering, which gives Christy comfort and confidence but which is not yet closely fitted to him. It is, then, very different in significance from Shawn's coat which derives its meaning only from its association with Shawn. The quilt, though made by Pegeen, can be used to cover anyone. It is also an artifact, a folk artifact, fashioned with care and bestowed upon someone as a free token of recognition. The quilt is akin to "those striking and beautiful phrases [which] were as ready to the story teller's or the playwright's hand, as the rich cloaks and dresses of his time."

The analogy between words and clothes is again made explicit in Act II. ". . . and there is Shaneen has long speeches for to tell you now," the Widow Quin tells Christy, but what the inarticulate Shawn offers, being "a poor scholar with middling faculties for to coin a lie," (in contrast to Christy who is made "a mighty man . . . by the power of a lie") is not speeches, but things, and especially clothes. In addition to a one-way ticket to America, Shawn will give his "new hat [*pulling it out of hamper*]; and my breeches with the double seat [*pulling it out*]; and my new coat is woven from the blackest sheerings for three miles around [*giving him the coat*]. . . ." When Christy takes Shawn's clothes and puts them on, the fact that he is now determined to take Shawn's place as suitor to Pegeen is underlined. As he struts around in Shawn's suit, the audience becomes aware of his likeness to Shawn, smugly content with his immediate environment: "If this is a poor place itself, I'll make myself contented to be lodging here," he tells the Widow Quin. And the confidence which up to then has marked the difference between the

Christy in Shawn's clothes and the Shawn in Shawn's clothes is quickly destroyed by the appearance of old Mahon. Both become figures of fun, one cowering before the authority of a natural father and the other before that of a Church father. What this scene suggests, then, is that the difference between Christy and Shawn is only that which Pegeen and the Mayo peasants bestow—the aura of romance, the quilt pieced together by Pegeen—and has not yet become an intrinsic property for Christy. As an outsider, Christy has no identity except that given him, whether as hero or petty property owner, identities which can be given or taken like labels. Here the Shawn-Christy identification is also reinforced by the Widow Quin, who has never perceived Christy as a hero. For her he is a possible source of security, a means of acquiring and protecting property, just as he had been for old Mahon. It makes little difference to her whether the property comes from Shawn or Christy, although she would rather have both the man and the property if she can.

Christy's triumphant appearance in the third act wearing jockey's clothes is preceded by the debate between old Mahon and Widow Quin as to whether Christy is "a dribbling idiot" or "a likely man." Old Mahon's conviction is that Christy is and always will be a stuttering fool, a looney incapable of any manly feat. The jockey suit is a reminder to the audience that he has indeed proved "a champion playboy," but it also raises the question of permanence. Is Christy's athletic prowess something that has been merely "put on" for the occasion and that will disappear when the demands of reality, of everyday living, reassert themselves in the form of old Mahon? What is the relationship between the clothes signifying "a champion playboy" and the man who wears them? As far as Pegeen and the people of the village are concerned, the appearance of old Mahon establishes that there is no relationship —Christy is nothing more than a liar, a fool, an idiot, to be beaten into submission by his father. Christy, however, asserts that he is what his clothes signify: "If I am an idiot, I'm after hearing my voice this day saying words would raise the topknot on a poet in a merchant's town. I've won your racing and your lepping and. . . ." He rejects the attempt by Widow Quin and Sara to reclothe him and "save" him by disguising him in a woman's petticoat and shawl. The play validates Christy's claim that label and referent are now properly harmonized, as old Mahon happily accepts his son's dominion and Christy blesses the villagers: "Ten thousand blessings upon all that's here, for you've turned me a likely gaffer in the end of all, the way I'll go romancing through a romping lifetime from this hour to the dawning of the judgment day."

What the clothing motif suggests throughout the play is in part analogous to the view of language and creation suggested in the preface. A series of costumes are tried on Christy just as various descriptions, poetic images and phrases are applied to him with varying degrees of incongruity or appropriateness. But what the preface does not suggest is the interaction between words and referents. Christy himself is gradually transformed by the "fine phrases" applied to him. It is he who grows and changes until he "fits" the costume of a playboy and can rightly claim it as his own. The lie which has disguised the truth and hidden it gradually becomes a new truth to which the accusation of "liar" is not so much inapplicable as irrelevant.

The counterpoint to the clothing motif is given by means of old Mahon, who is associated with nakedness and "the naked truth":

> **Christy.** It's that you'd say surely if you seen him and he after drinking for weeks, rising up in the red dawn, or before it maybe, and going out into the yard as naked as an ashtree in the moon of May, and shying clods again the visage of the stars till he'd put the fear of death into the banbhs and the screeching sows.

Christy's description of old Mahon "naked as an ashtree in the moon of May" is particularly striking because of the incongruity between the poetic quality of the image applied to him and the disgust which Christy expresses in the speech as a whole. As he indicated earlier, his reason for killing old Mahon was partly aesthetic; he was repelled by the ugliness of the man: "he was a dirty man, God forgive him, and he getting old and crusty, the way I couldn't put up with him at all." This association of old Mahon with not only the unpoetic and the unadorned but also the *anti*-poetic is emphasized by the image of him "shying clods again the visage of the stars," for both traditionally and in this play stars are connotative of transcendence of everyday reality. So at the height of Christy's triumph as Playboy, his mule is described as "kicking the stars," and, in a typically incongruous juxtaposition, old Mahon claims he'd know Christy's way of spitting "and he astride the moon."

The struggle between Christy and his father thus suggests Synge's opposition of naturalism with the imaginative transcendence of reality, of Zola with Mallarmé. Old Mahon's characteristic question, "Would you believe that?" implies the naturalist criterion of "truth to life," as does his exhibiting of his gory skull as proof of the "naked truth." Perhaps his description of himself "screeching in a straightened waist-coat with seven doctors writing out my sayings in a printed book," indicates his association with the scientific pretensions of some followers of naturalism. Similarly, old Mahon's sought response from his audience is belief in the reality of his experience, and help in righting wrongs as well as some material payment: "I'm after walking hundreds and long scores of miles, winning clean beds and the fill of my belly four times in the day, and I doing nothing but telling stories of that naked truth. [*He comes to them a little aggressively.*] Give me a supeen and I'll tell you now."

Christy's audience has also responded with bread and milk, eggs, butter, cake, chicken, and clean beds, but for Christy these are primarily tokens of admiration for the way he tells his far from unadorned story; his desire is to win his audience, and especially Pegeen, and their response is to the aesthetic qualities rather than the "reality" of his tale. "That's a grand story," Susan comments. "He tells it lovely," adds Honor.

Like the harsh reality it expresses, Mahon's speech is also joyless and anti-poetic. Christy tells of Mahon's snoring at night, and of his "raging all times the while he was waking, like a gaudy officer you'd hear cursing and damning and swearing oaths." Mahon's first appearance, which follows soon after Christy's eloquent wooing of Pegeen in Act II and his delight in "the sweetness of her voice," marks him as a gruff and plain-spoken man with no time for gracious conversation:

> **Mahon** [*gruffly*]. Did you see a young lad passing this way in the early morning or the fall of night?
> **Widow Quin**. You're a queer kind to walk in not saluting at all.
> **Mahon**. Did you see the young lad?
> **Widow Quin** [*stiffly*]. What kind was he?
> **Mahon**. An ugly young streeler with a murderous gob on him and a little switch in his hand. I met a tramper seen him coming this way at the fall of night.
> . . . .
> **Mahon**. It was my own son hit me, and he the divil a robber or anything else but a dirty, stuttering lout.

The harshness of Mahon's language corresponds to the harshness of his vision of Christy and of life, his insistence on the "naked truth" and joyless reality. In his speech, attitudes and appearance—particularly in the showing off of his bandaged skull—Mahon represents the reality half of Synge's dichotomy, and constantly threatens the survival of Christy's joyous vision built on "the power of a lie." Mahon is also connected with the anti-romantic emphasis on economic necessity, on marriage for convenience, on property and on authority. The quarrel which results in Christy's rebellion arises from Mahon's having arranged a marriage of convenience with a widow who, like Mahon himself, is for Christy most noteworthy for her ugliness of body and speech: ". . . and she a hag this day with a tongue on her has the crows and seabirds scattered, the way they wouldn't cast a shadow on her garden with the dread of her curse." Symbolically, therefore, Christy's triumph over Mahon at the end of the play represents the triumph of romance over reality. More specifically, it represents the formula advocated by Synge in his preface—the yoking together of joy and reality, with reality neither the lawgiver, nor the equal in marriage, but the servant of poetry.

This yoking together of romance and reality, of poetry and the naked truth, is also a feature of the language used by the characters in the play, and in particular by Christy and Pegeen. The language of the play has been the subject of much critical comment, ranging from the many who praise its high poetry and single out the love duets as the epitome of that poetry, to others who single out those same passages as examples of Synge's failure, due to his overreaching the level of language deemed acceptable in a semi-realistic play. As an example of Synge's succumbing to the flamboyant gesture from which "the discipline of metre" might have saved him,[3] Ronald Gaskell quotes the first half of the following speech by Christy.

> Amn't I after seeing the love-light of the star of knowledge shining from her brow, and hearing words would put you thinking of the holy Brigid speaking to the infant saints, and now she'll be turning again, and speaking hard words to me, like an old woman with a spavindy ass she'd have, urging on a hill.

That the flamboyance is characteristic of Christy at this point in the play rather than of Synge, and is to be noticed as flamboyant, might be inferred from the joining together of incongruous images—the star of knowledge, the saints, and the spavindy ass. That incongruity and flamboyance is further underlined by Widow Quin's comment: "There's poetry talk for a girl you'd see itching and scratching, and she with a stale stink of poteen on her from selling in the shop."

Like Gaskell, Ronald Peacock chides Synge for his use of an "exotic" language. But, as Peacock himself goes on to argue, the use of a distinctly strange and unfamiliar language is linked to the theme of the play:

> How much the idiom in itself has to do with Synge's art emerges from *The Playboy of the Western World*. The direct sensuous consciousness of the patently picturesque speech and way of thinking is the inspiration of the play; and the point gains in importance when we consider that this is his most ambitious work. The basis of the comic here is a delicate and fine mockery of the very idea of fine language, closely related as it is to fine ideas. Synge plays in this comedy with his own discovery. Through his mock-hero Christy Mahon he allows his instrument to elaborate its most splendid ornaments. Some have been so entranced as to take it at its high face-value as sheer poetry. Yet it is the most precise exaggeration, a distillation of his own speech material conceived in a vein of irony.[4]

The "vein of irony" is crucial, since the audience is made conscious of the "patently picturesque" and of the flamboyantly poetic, not throughout the whole play, but in the speeches which are in contrast with the norm found in other speeches. "Poetry talk" is juxtaposed with "naked truth," joy with realism, the romantic vision with the vision demanded by economic necessity including its "stale stink of poteen on her from selling in the shop." Throughout the play the two perspectives suggested in Synge's Preface—"On the stage one must have reality, and one must have joy"—are counterpointed through the attitudes

---

[3] "The Realism of J. M. Synge," *The Playboy of the Western World*, ed. H. Popkin (New York, 1967), p. 173.

[4] *The Poet in the Theatre* (New York, 1960), p. 112.

of Widow Quin and Mahon on the one hand, and Pegeen, Christy and
the girls on the other, in the struggle between the older people's irony
and youthful romanticism. And the language of individual characters
also suggests that contrast. Christy's description of Pegeen has been
quoted as one example, the play abounds in others. "That'd be a lad
with the sense of Solomon to have for a pot-boy," exclaims Pegeen
when Christy refuses to disclose the exact location of his crime; the
juxtaposition of the Biblical exemplar of wisdom with the intellectual
demands made on a dishwasher emphasizes both the rich resonances
of the phrase, "sense of Solomon," and its distance from "the common
interests of life." It also brings out the alliterative appeal of the phrase,
a phrase in which sound rather than sense joins the words together, and
it is clear that it is its sensuousness, its property as a poetic phrase, that
delights Pegeen, rather than its appropriateness to Christy. In her next
speech, Pegeen's delight in the alliterative phrase is again manifest:
"It's the truth they're saying, and if I'd that lad in the house, I wouldn't
be fearing the loosèd kharki cut-throats, or the walking dead." Here
the alliterative phrase clothes the everyday reality, the British soldiers,
endowing it with a kind of aura that does seem to make the soldiers
equivalent to those who might by nature belong in the poetic world of
"the walking dead." As the play proceeds, the joining of the poetic
phrase with the everyday reality continues to reveal these two
possibilities—the transformation of the commonplace into the poetic,
or the stressing of the distance between the two. "You should have had
great people in your family, I'm thinking, with the little small feet you
have, and with a kind of quality name, the like of what you'd find on the
great powers and potentates of France and Spain," Pegeen tells
Christy. "We were great, surely, with wide and windy acres of rich
Munster land," Christy responds. Pegeen's equation of Christy and his
name with the "powers and potentates of France and Spain" is patently
absurd and a little pathetic, while the resonance of the alliterative
phrase serves only to emphasize its distance from the referent to which
it is applied. Christy's use of alliteration, however, remains "rooted in
reality," yet endows the Munster farm with a certain breadth and
grandeur.

For Pegeen, the exotic and the poetic are identical. Just as she
savours phrases and allusions from alien traditions, she delights in
Christy because he is "a strange man," and despises Shawn both for his
familiarity and for his unquestioning acceptance of the familiar. She
can find little connection between far off places and Mayo, or between
past and present, as her *ubi sunt* lament indicates:

> **Pegeen**. . . .We're a queer lot these times to go troubling the Holy Father
> on his sacred seat.
> **Shawn** [*scandalized*]. If we are, we're as good this place as another, maybe,
> and as good these times as we were for ever.
> **Pegeen** [*with scorn*]. As good, is it? Where now will you meet the like of

> Daneen Sullivan knocked the eye from a peeler, or Marcus Quin, God
> rest him, got six months for maiming ewes, and he a great warrant to
> tell stories of holy Ireland till he'd have the old women shedding tears
> about their feet. Where will you find the like of them, I'm saying?

In her eyes, poetry is connected with those who are distant in time and
place; it is removed from ordinary events and passions, and belongs in
the realm of the epic and heroic—for the political involvement marked
by fighting police and maiming animals in the agrarian struggles are
for Pegeen examples of the extraordinary and heroic. That connection
recurs several times in the play, as when Pegeen later tells Christy, "If
you weren't destroyed travelling, you'd have as much talk and
streeleen, I'm thinking, as Owen Roe O'Sullivan or the poets of the
Dingle Bay, and I've heard all times it's the poets are your like, fine
fiery fellows with great rages when their temper's roused." She would
like to conceive of Christy "living the like of a king of Norway or the
eastern world," and is unable to see herself as belonging to the romantic or joyous world, as she reveals in her pleased amazement at Christy's
praise and her haughty response to Shawn's reminder of his "weight of
passion, and the holy dispensation, and the drift of heifers . . . and the
golden ring." "I'm thinking you're too fine for the likes of me, Shawn
Keogh of Killakeen, and let you go off till you'd find a radiant lady with
droves of bullocks on the plains of Meath, and herself bedizened in the
diamond jewelleries of Pharoah's ma." While her answer expresses her
scorn for Shawn's equal weighing of his passion, the Church's attitude,
her dowry, and his gift, the incongruity of the references to bullocks
and to "Pharoah's ma" emphasizes, as did her earlier linking of Solomon and a potboy, the disjunction between her concept of the poetic
and "the common interests of life." This association of the poetic with
the extraordinary verges often on the love of the sensational, for
instance in the delight expressed by Pegeen and the villagers in the
imagined hanging of Christy, as well as in stories of murders, strange
deaths and discoveries, the speculation about blood on the criminal's
boots, and the talk of skulls and skeletons. When Christy and his deed
lose their "outlandishness," they also lose their romantic aura for the
villagers, who are unable to poeticize the familiar and merely human.

From Christy's point of view, however, the poetic process moves in
the opposite direction. It is his own familiar self he sees transformed
into something unfamiliar. "Is it me?" he asks with wonder and delight
as he hears Pegeen describe him. His perception of himself, like his
perception of the supposed murder and of Pegeen and the public
house, begins with and is rooted in Mahon's vision, from there gradually growing toward Pegeen's perception. The passage in which Christy
recounts his night poaching and describes his father is characteristic of
Christy's speech in Act I, where his vision still derives from his father:

> . . . and there I'd be as happy as the sunshine of St. Martin's Day,
> watching the light passing the north or the patches of fog, till I'd hear a

rabbit starting to screech and I'd go running in the furze. Then when I'd my full share I'd come walking down where you'd see the ducks and the geese stretched sleeping on the highway of the road, and before I'd passed the dunghill, I'd hear himself snoring out, a loud lonesome snore he'd be making all times, the while he was sleeping; and he a man'd be raging at all times the while he was waking, like a gaudy officer you'd hear cursing and damning and swearing oaths.

By the end of Act I, however, Christy is convinced of the rightness of killing his father, and at the beginning of Act II we see him viewing himself in Pegeen's mirror and rejecting the "distortions" he saw in "the divil's own mirror we had beyond."[5] Nevertheless, it is only after Christy has knowingly become a liar and has deliberately decided to pretend that his father does not exist, that his "poetry talk" becomes both flamboyant and exotic like Pegeen's. He has accepted the crowd's acclamation of him as a poet and wonder of the Western World to-gether with their prizes for him—a poet's fiddle and a stick "to lick the scholars out of Dublin town," the latter reversing the image which Mahon portrayed earlier of Christy being beaten at school. Now he must transform Pegeen into something equally wondrous that she might be a fitting mate for him in the idyllic world of poetry: "If the mitred bishops seen you that time, they'd be the like of the holy prophets, I'm thinking, do be straining the bars of Paradise to lay eyes on the Lady Helen of Troy, and she abroad pacing back and forward with a nosegay in her golden shawl."

The extravagance of Christy's speech, its quality as "poetry talk," is emphasized by the mingling of images from Hebraic, Roman Catholic, Homeric and folk traditions. Exuberantly splashing around in a poetic sea, Christy has long since lost sight of the shore. But Mahon will not stay dead or out of sight, and Christy finally recognizes that his "romancing lifetime" must include the real; it must be fed by Mahon, not by Pegeen and the girls of Mayo, and his food will be "oatmeal and spuds," not current cake, butter and chicken. For Christy, then, the poetic will arise from making "the familiar unfamiliar" rather than making the romantic credible; his emphasis will be Wordsworthian rather than Coleridgean. The stories he will tell will be based on the real happenings and people of Mayo. For Pegeen and the girls, the romantic and the real belong to different worlds which cannot be reconciled, while for Mahon and the Widow Quin, the romantic simply does not exist, although the Widow comes closer than Mahon to in-cluding both in a kind of ironic vision.

In terms of the language of the play as a whole, it seems to me that Christy's final recognition is the dominant one. The world of the play is

---

[5] Those two mirrors recall Shelley's distinction between history and poetry in his *Defence of Poetry*: "A story of particular facts is a mirror which obscures and distorts that which should be beautiful; poetry is a mirror which makes beautiful that which is distorted."

given substance and texture through speeches which are not flamboyant or "patently picturesque," and against which the hyperboles of Pegeen and Christy do appear flamboyant and absurd. But those high-flown speeches also help to make the use of folk and natural imagery, which might otherwise appear exotic to an urban audience, seem normal in comparison. The norm for *The Playboy* is presented, perhaps in slightly heightened form, in Christy's description of his night poaching, or in his "wanderer's lament" in Act II:

> . . . It's well you know it's a lonesome thing to be passing small towns with the lights shining sideways when the night is down, or going in strange places with a dog nosing before you and a dog nosing behind, or drawn to the cities where you'd hear a voice kissing and talking deep love in every shadow of the ditch, and you passing on with an empty, hungry stomach failing from your heart.

Christy's language, when he is not being self-consciously poetic or exotic, is based on the simple and archetypal yet concrete tropes which are characteristic of folk poetry—sun and stars, night and day, "dews of dawn," birds and animals, the figure of the vagrant; in this too his impulse is Wordsworthian.[6] Unlike Wordsworth, however, Synge includes in his peasant world a rich mixture of what he himself called the Rabelaisian element, which is manifest not only in the farcical and grotesque incidents, but also in the vitality of Pegeen's invective hurled against the Widow Quin at the end of Act I, or in the language of Pegeen's father who envisages the dogs "lapping poteen from the dung-pit of the yard," and rejoices in a future with "a score of grandsons growing up little gallant swearers by the name of God." Synge's use of language is comparable to Wordsworth's also in that, though based on the language of "the common people," it is nevertheless a literary parallel carefully developed to give the illusion of a world in which the language as well as the people appear to be in touch with "the profound and common interests of life."[7] As M. Bourgeois writes, somewhat less ambivalently than Synge himself, for Synge the Irish are "born poets, the descendants of the ancient bards that were chased to the West. Hence the 'affinity between the moods of those people and

---

[6] Like the language and imagery, the structure and plot of *The Playboy* start with a "real" story taken from the peasantry, and gathers around it echoes from other more literary works and worlds. This aspect has been explored by several critics, e.g., T. R. Henn in *Twentieth Century Interpretations of The Playboy*, ed. T. Whitaker (Englewood Cliffs, New Jersey, 1969), discusses the allusions to the stories of Oedipus and Odysseus, pp. 56-57. In the same volume, Howard Pearce presents the notion of Christy as a mock-Christ, pp. 88-97.

[7] For a further description of Synge's language as "above all a stage speech, condensed and refined through many drafts in accord with the heightened dynamic relations of the theatre," see Thomas R. Whitaker's introductory essay in his edition of *Twentieth Century Interpretations of The Playboy of the Western World.*

the moods of varying rapture and dismay that are frequent in artists and in certain forms of alienation.' "[8]

Where Synge differs fundamentally from Wordsworth, however, is in his awareness, and his insistence that the audience be aware, of the artist's distance from "the common people"; the artist's perception of the common people is something which is incomprehensible to them. "All art is collaboration," Synge wrote, but as *The Playboy* suggests, the collaboration is ultimately one way. The triumph suggested by Christy's subjugation of his father, the triumph of fiction over fact, is clouded by the grief of Pegeen who has driven away and rejected the romance she herself helped to create, having decided that the truth represented by Mahon's visible appearance must banish the "lie" represented by Christy's "gallous story" of a distant deed. Moreover, Christy as artist has lost his audience, without which he would never have become a poet-hero. The final speeches of Mahon and Christy indicate the nature of the art the pair will create:

> **Mahon**. . . .my son and myself will be going our way and we'll have great times from this out telling stories of the villainy of Mayo and the fools is here.
> . . . .
> **Christy**. Ten thousand blessings upon all that's here, for you've turned me into a likely gaffer in the end of all, the way I'll go romancing through a romping lifetime from this hour to the dawning of the judgment day.

Together they will present stories of the villainy and foolishness of Mayo, with their blessings on those fools who have created the romance; they will, in short, present *The Playboy of the Western World*, with its celebration of what is "superb and wild in reality" along with its recognition of the dominion that economic necessity has in the lives of the Irish peasantry.

Like its ending, the play as a whole remains an assertion, an imposition of romance on reality, which leaves the peasantry ultimately bereft—and it is out of that very bereavement that the wild longing for romance has come. Christy is transformed by Pegeen and the villagers and their intense longing for a more poetic life, he is fed and clothed by them, but despite all his hyperbolic description of her, he fails to transform Pegeen. She is left mourning the impossibility of romance, and the villagers return philosophically to the unchanging world of reality: "By the will of God, we'll have peace now for our drinks," says Michael as Christy and his resuscitated Da depart. Thus, although the play does deal with the power of the poetic word to transform, it also deals in its tragicomic ending with the failure of poetry, a failure which relates to the narcissistic and exploitative nature of art and the artist.

---

[8] *J. M. Synge and the Irish Theatre* (London, 1913), p. 93. His quotation is from Synge's *Collected Works*, Vol. III (Dublin, 1910), p. 149.

The parallels between clothing and phrases discussed above as a motif in the play also serves to underline the contrast: Christy is given clothes which are "real" and substantial by the Mayo peasants, but he has only insubstantial words to give back. Moreover, the transformation of the real world, the joining together of reality and joy, takes place only *within* the work of art, which by that very transformation becomes alienated from the "reality" on which it is based.

There is an ironic parallel between Christy and Synge himself. Each starts off in a strange "country" where he can find neither an audience nor his true tongue. Each becomes a poet, finding his subject and his idiom among the peasants of western Ireland, and each must accept the paradox that although the substance and inspiration of his art comes from those people, he cannot remain an integral part of their lives; his art, his insistence on "the power of a lie" and on yoking together joy *and* reality, arouse the scorn of his subjects and desired audience. The rejection of *The Playboy* by Dublin and Irish-American audiences is ironically foreshadowed, and perhaps even orchestrated, by the rejection of Christy by Pegeen and the villagers.

HOPKINS, YEATS AND DUBLIN IN THE EIGHTIES

Norman H. MacKenzie

Austin Clarke, flicking a speculative penny into the clouds, once raised the question as to what would have happened if Hopkins and Yeats had become friends. "Hopkins," he observed, "in an astonishing way, anticipated the modern poetry of our century. Had Yeats been influenced by him, our literary revival might have been different."[1]

Austin Clark did not fill out the reasons behind their failure to develop a friendship. Indeed, since he described Hopkins as "The young English convert"—although he was in his forty-third year, over twice as old as Yeats when first they encountered each other—one may suspect that Clarke had delved more fully into Hopkins' verse than into his life in Ireland. In this paper, therefore, I shall attempt to direct new light upon Hopkins which will also illuminate a few facets of Dublin in the eighties. It will be largely through the eyes of Hopkins that we will catch glimpses of five literary figures: W. B. Yeats, still young and unassured; two Catholic writers, Katharine Tynan and Father Matthew Russell, S.J.; and two Trinity College graduates, Professor Edward Dowden and Mr. Yeats senior. And emerging at critical junctures from the shadows around Hopkins, like that of his predestined adversary, comes the incisive voice of Dr. William Walsh. To lend more

---

[1] *The Celtic Twilight and the Nineties* (Dublin, 1969), p. 74. The occasion he alludes to, when Hopkins and Father Russell visited J. B. Yeats and Miss Tynan, was described by (a) Katharine Tynan: *Memories* (London, 1924), pp. 155-56, cf. 276-80; also *Irish Monthly*, 40 (October 1912), 555; (b) by Father Matthew Russell, "Poets I have Known: Katharine Tynan," in the *Irish Monthly*, 31 (May 1903), 259-61; and by Hopkins in a letter to Coventry Patmore, 7 November 1886, in *Further Letters of Gerard Manley Hopkins*, ed. C. C. Abbott (Oxford, 1956), 2nd ed., pp. 372-73. I am told by Professor William M. Murphy that J. B. Yeats's unpublished *Memoirs* contains no reference to Hopkins.

form to this superabundant chaos of material I will base my story geographically on a simple axis traversing Stephen's Green, with Newman House at one end and J. B. Yeats's studio at the other. My approach will be "biocritical." And in case you hasten to the library to check the word "biocritical" in the latest *Supplement to the Oxford English Dictionary*, let me warn you that the word is unfortunately not included: I may even have invented it myself.

One memorable day in the autumn of 1886 a bustling Jesuit poet, with a smaller clerical counterpart apparently in tow, hurried across Stephen's Green from University College, Dublin, heading for the studio of Mr. John Butler Yeats: the editor of the *Irish Monthly* had at last persuaded the Professor of Greek to meet the artist and his lively young sitter, Katharine Tynan. Russell, affectionately referred to as Father Matt, always propelled himself on his errands of goodwill in a "swift, half-running walk." Yet though Russell coaxed into confidence the hesitant talents of scores of writers, he had never been shown (as far as we can gather) any of the poetry written by the man beside him, nor did he suspect that Hopkins was a literary genius who concealed beneath a mild and boyish appearance a radical disregard for all the editor's sacred prosodic rules. Hopkins did not wish his poetry to be published and discussed. Some of his Dublin sonnets were (for a priest's) embarrassingly personal. He shrank from possible acclaim with a genuinely saintly modesty and from possible blame with an all-too-human dread of being made ridiculous.

Katharine Tynan suffered less from such inhibitions. She rather enjoyed being talked about. Her first book of verse, *Louise de la Vallière*, published the previous year and promptly reprinted, had been praised (to quote Hopkins' discerning phrase) "by a wonderful, perhaps alarming unanimity of the critics." It was now October, and Katharine Tynan had already been sitting for her portrait once or twice a week for several months. But Mr. Yeats's standard definition of a gentleman—"a man not wholly occupied in getting on"—exactly described his procedure as a painter. Indeed, the most apt analogy I can find for J. B. Yeats at his easel (though the motivation was of course entirely different) is that of Homer's chaste Penelope at her loom, weaving industriously by day and as systematically unravelling her web by night. Mr. Yeats had a habit of scraping the canvas bare in order to reattempt perfection just when his sitter imagined the end could not be much longer postponed. But meanwhile this Trinity College barrister-turned-artist fascinated sitters and visitors alike with some of the most widely ranging discussions on matters mental and aesthetic to be heard anywhere in Dublin.

Hopkins has described Kate Tynan for us as a "simple brightlooking Biddy with glossy very pretty red hair."[2] Her finished

---

[2] *Further Letters of Gerard Manley Hopkins*, p. 373. Yeats in his *Memoirs*, ed. Denis Donoghue (London, 1971), p. 32, calls her "a very plain woman."

portrait (not completed and signed, let me add, till the following year) now belongs to the National Gallery of Ireland, and formed one of the most arresting pictures in that impressive array of John Butler Yeats's work which Dr. James White has recently gathered into display. We can only conjecture as to what stage of reconstruction it was in when Hopkins first saw it, but it precipitated an argument between them (still in full tide when Miss Tynan had to take her leave), on "finish or non-finish" in art.[3] Mr. Yeats's failing was more that of "never-finish" than "non-finish," a perfectionism which his son Willie demonstrated in the endless uncompleted drafts of his *Shadowy Waters*, but which, happily for his income, did not prevent Willie from publishing successive interim versions of his poems. Hopkins, on the other hand, usually made only minor adjustments to his pieces once he had, with infinite care, crafted them to finality.

The theory of finish in art which Hopkins held can be traced back to Ruskin. If in their studio debate the Jesuit actually quoted Ruskin as his authority, this is likely to have produced quite vigorous disagreement from the painter. Ruskin was one cause of those two violent quarrels between J. B. Yeats and his son Willie which W. B. Yeats selected as the significant starting point of his *Memoirs* (recently edited by Denis Donoghue).[4] Ruskin offered some admirable observations on the truest portraits being the result of moments of insight on the artist's part—a belief which is in line with J. B. Yeats's practice, and which may also have influenced Hopkins' theory of inscape.[5] But early in *Modern Painters* Ruskin emphasized his concern for a picture's peripheral details, as well as the total effect:

> Two questions the artist has . . . always to ask himself: First, "Is my whole right?" Secondly, "Can my details be added to? Is there a single space in the picture where I can crowd in another thought? Is there . . . a vacancy I can fill? . . . If so, my picture is imperfect; and if, in . . . filling the vacancy, I hurt the general effect, my art is imperfect."[6]

This typically Victorian theory of thoroughness underlies various comments on blurred details which Hopkins made during visits to Royal Academy exhibitions. And in a letter almost contemporary with this discussion (published for the first time by Fr. Anthony Bischoff)[7]

---

[3] *Further Letters*, p. 430.

[4] The quarrels were partly over Ruskin's attempts to ridicule the theories of wealth held by John Stuart Mill, whom J. B. Yeats admired. See Yeats, *Memoirs*, p. 19. The dispute is discussed by J. T. Fain, *Ruskin and the Economists* (Nashville, 1956), pp. 100-51.

[5] See my "Hopkins among the Victorians: Form in Art and Nature," *English Studies Today*, 3rd series, ed. G. I. Duthie (Edinburgh, 1964), p. 161.

[6] *Modern Painters*, in *Works*, ed. Cook and Wedderburn, Vol. III, 622. Through his Pre-Raphaelite friends J. B. Yeats may have assimilated Ruskin's advice in the same passage: "It ought to be the rule with every painter, never to let a picture leave his easel while it is yet capable of improvement."

he had criticized the sketch which his artist brother Everard had contributed to the *Graphic* because "more of the crowd shd. have been seen and it shd. have been more crowded."[8]

When eventually Hopkins viewed the completed portrait of Kate Tynan, hung in the Royal Hibernian Academy Exhibition, he conceded that it was "a faithful likeness and a pleasing picture," but added: "I do not agree with his slight method of execution in that work or in others."[9] If you examine the picture you will see that only her face is in sharp focus, and it was not until my fourth visit to the picture that I discovered that she was holding a book: in fact I might characterize all that is not flesh as in various gradations of "Old Master brown." It is therefore with some slight amusement that I read Katharine Tynan's account of that exhibition, much as I enjoy her five volumes of autobiographical reminiscences. Typical of her fictitious verisimilitude is the description in her book called *Memories* of her embarrassment on opening day at seeing strangers recognizing her as the subject simply because she was wearing the clothes she had posed in, a "Redfern coat, black with touches of brown and crimson in the alternate stripes . . . and showing the scarlet silk lining in the open sleeves and pouched bodice."[10] This, I suspect, is merely a clever little fashion note. The artist would have been less than charmed at the idea that the crowds identified his sitter only by her coat!

On the question of detail in his own art, Hopkins differed from most of his contemporaries in trying to pack every millimeter of every line with as much transmissible personal significance as a chromosome. Speaking of "a young Mr. Yeats who has written in a Trinity College publication some striking verses and who has been perhaps unduly pushed by the late Sir Samuel Ferguson," Hopkins was led aside into his most famous definition of the difference between ephemeral and durable poetry. Of most Irish poems, even Ferguson's, he remarked that they were "full of feeling, high thoughts, flow of verse, point, often fine imagery and other virtues, but the essential and only lasting thing left out—what I call *inscape*, that is species or individually-distinctive beauty of style." When Hopkins first encountered him, even Willie Yeats was not yet a distinct species, and Hopkins included him among the "odds and ends of poets and poetesses" whom he talked of meeting.[11] But before we enlarge upon his criticisms, we should inves-

---

[7] Dated 5 November 1885. See *T.L.S.*, 8 December 1972, p. 151.

[8] Cf. his criticisms of his other artist brother, Arthur, in *Further Letters*, pp. 129, 187-89; also *Journals and Papers of Gerard Manley Hopkins*, ed. House and Story (Oxford, 1959).

[9] Letter to K. Tynan, 15 September 1888, in *The Month*, N.S. 19 (May 1958), p. 269.

[10] London, 1924, pp. 279, 280, written thirty-seven years after the event.

[11] *Further Letters*, pp. 372-73.

tigate the effect which Dublin had already had on the life and work of Hopkins himself.

At the time of the celebrated meeting to which I have referred, Hopkins had been in Ireland for two-and-a-half years, responsible for teaching Greek at University College, Dublin, and for examining assorted hordes of students from every quarter of land. "There was an Irish row over my election," he wrote in a restrained postscript to Robert Bridges, leaving to his friend's experience or imagination the definition of an "Irish row" as distinct from an English one. Perhaps we might venture upon a gloss which the passage of time would have enabled Hopkins himself to supply: one characteristic of an "Irish row" is that it tends to blaze into new heat just when its ashes seem safely extinguished.

In January 1884 Hopkins had, to his diffident alarm, been unwillingly promoted from the spacious tranquility of Stonyhurst College, neighboured by carefree English cloughs and fells, into a personal prominence from which he shrank. In virtue of his brilliant Oxford degree, most warmly spoken of by Richard Nettleship, fellow of Balliol, and by the famous Benjamin Jowett, he had been elected by the Senate of the newly founded Royal University of Ireland to the post of Fellow and Examiner in Classics.

It is seldom realized that the fortunes of the young institution, as of Newman's semi-paralyzed University College at Stephen's Green, were so dubious that the Jesuit President of U.C.D. had not been able to secure the release of all the scholars he had privately placed at the top of his list for each appointment. Though men of intellectual distinction, most of those he secured, like Father Hopkins, had the reputation of being rather ineffectual schoolmasters. One cannot help suspecting that they had been offered to Dublin by their own rectors with something less than heroic self-sacrifice.[12] Stonyhurst College underestimated Hopkins—until they had to replace him, when they found that the task of preparing their "philosophers" for the University of London examinations in both Latin and Greek was one for which few were as well qualified.

---

[12] As many of the facts I am about to give are unpublished, and are followed by my own "biocritical" conclusions, it would be best to offer a general acknowledgement here, with thanks, for some of my sources: material from the archives of the Jesuit Irish Province in Dublin, in particular a manuscript on *Father William Delany and his work for Irish Education* by Father Lambert McKenna, S.J., who when a novice used to act as server in the Mass for Father Hopkins; information from Dr. Fergal McGrath, S.J., a major authority on the Irish University; *A Page of Irish History—Story of University College, Dublin, 1883-1909*, compiled by Fathers of the Society of Jesus (Dublin, 1930)—my own copy has been annotated in the margins by a former auditor of the Literary and Historical Society, John P. Doyle. Most of all I would thank the Rev. Anthony Bischoff, S.J., who has in the truest friendship allowed me to draw in advance on the unexampled knowledge of Hopkins' life which he is now composing into a biography. Naturally I remain accountable for the accuracy of the facts I have gathered from many contemporary sources, and for their interpretation.

The President of U.C.D. ran into further difficulties with the Irish Cardinal, MacCabe, who at first expressed some private hesitations because Hopkins was not an Irishman. These doubts assuaged, all seemed well until, in an eleventh hour drama, on the very evening before the election in the Senate, the Cardinal suddenly transferred his allegiance to another candidate, the Dean of Studies in a college which had proved all too successful a rival to U.C.D.— French College run by the Fathers of the Holy Ghost at Blackrock. When the Senate next day rejected his new nominee, Fr. Joseph Reffé, by twenty-three votes to three, the Cardinal resigned, and the Viceroy, Earl Spencer, was faced with the possible collapse of the whole shaky institution.[13]

Only high-powered diplomacy eventually persuaded the Cardinal to withdraw his resignation. The battle to secure some tangible recognition for the scholastic success of Blackrock was then taken up by Dr. William Walsh, the redoubtable President of Maynooth College, who himself resigned irrevocably from the Senate in May when his advocacy of Fr. Reffé's appointment, this time as Fellow in Modern Languages, failed even to raise a seconder. When Hopkins arrived in Dublin, therefore, he found himself involved in one of the recurrent turbulences of the Irish University Question, which dates back to at least the time of Charles I and which is not yet settled to universal satisfaction today. Though the dispute was neither nationalistic (Father Reffé was, after all, born in Alsace), nor directed against him personally, he could hardly help feeling that he had made an enemy of the Cardinal himself, and of Dr. Walsh, who was to become Archbishop of Dublin and Primate of Ireland on the Cardinal's death the following year. It was an unfortunate beginning to his five unhappy years in Ireland, terminated by his premature death at the age of forty-four in 1889.

Superficially viewed, the contest seems to have lessened the practical usefulness both of Hopkins the winner and Reffé the loser. The Blackrock Dean was Hopkins' antithesis in a number of respects. Reffé had no degree: like so many Catholics of his day he had not been privileged with any university education; but he was an inspiring teacher, a Dean of Studies whose praise or rebuke carried overwhelming authority, while his physique gave him immense energy as well as commanding presence. One wonders whether this failure to win for his College the distinction of a Royal University Fellowship contributed to his collapse and premature retirement a few years after this double disappointment, when he was only forty-seven. His successful rival, Fr. Hopkins, by way of contrast, was described by Katharine Tynan as "small and childish-looking, yet like a child-sage, nervous too and very

[13] Letter from Father Huvetys, Rector of Blackrock College, 13 February 1884, addressed to his Superior General, in *Blackrock Annual Centenary, 1860-1960* (Dublin, 1961); see pp. 85-98.

sensitive, with a small ivory-pale face." She mistook him for twenty rather than forty-two when first they met.[14]

Hopkins had arrived in Dublin in February 1884. The controversy in which he had caught the limelight was basically this: "Should all the Catholic Fellows of the Royal University be concentrated at Stephen's Green or distributed among the other important colleges?" Its echoes seemed to be dying away when in November Dr. Walsh brought them into full public notoriety by starting correspondence both in the London *Tablet* and the Dublin *Freeman's Journal*. No candidates' names were mentioned, but in Ireland when a spicy word-battle reaches the press it is seldom necessary to advertise identities. Day after day the hard-hitting accusations and rejoinders continued.[15]

Painful though this experience must have been, we should never forget that saying of Heraclitus so central to the thinking of Yeats: "Discord is the father of all and the king of all." Hopkins knew Heraclitus well, and accepted for himself the equivalent Hebrew-Christian saying: "Whom the Lord loveth, he chastiseth, and he scourgeth every son whom he receiveth."[16] In the very midst of the embarrassing publicity which damaged his self-confidence, Hopkins was fashioning, line by hammered line, the powerful sonnet, "Spelt from Sibyl's Leaves." Not even Ruskin could have faulted its finish. Every word in the poem has the complex suggestiveness of a whole sentence in prose. As yet some of the phrases had not come right, but even in the draft of December 1884 it was immensely moving:

> Earnest, earthless, equal, attuneable, vaulty, voluminous
> . . . stupendous
> Evening strains to be time's den, world's delf, womb-
> of-all, home-of-all, hearse-of-all night.
> Her fönd yellowy hornlight wound to the west, her wïld
> willowy hoarlight hung to the height
> Waste; her earliest stars, earlstars, stars principal,
> overbend us,
> Firefeaturing heaven. For earth unpenned her being;
> her dapple is at an end—a-
> Stray or aswarm, all throughther, in throng; self ín self
> steepèd and pashed—flush; quite
> Disremembering, dismembering all. My heart rounds me
> right
> Then: Evening is here on us, over us; our night whelms,

---

[14] Katharine Tynan, *Memories* (London, 1924), p. 155; Hopkins, *Letters to Bridges* (London, 1935), p. 250.

[15] See the *Tablet* for November, December 1884, and *Freeman's Gazette* for November 29, December 1, 3, 4, 5, 6, 8, where long letters from Dr. Walsh evoked responses from Dr. Kavanagh, F. R. Cruise, James Keating, and other Senators who opposed him.

[16] *Hebrews* 12:6; *Proverbs* 3:12.

whelms: when will it end us?
Only the crisp boughs beakèd or dragonish damask the
    toolsmooth bleak light—black
Ever so black on it. O this is our tale too![17]

He had melted and moulded his thoughts thus far when the prospect of ancestral night's devouring all things began to attract rather than repel, luring his weary mind towards its earthly counterpart, death. At the foot of the page he redrafted his opening into softer, more desirable metaphors showing the dusk as straining to be "time's hush, time's harbour world's haven." But here his longing for the peace of oblivion was sternly rebuked by his sense of Catholic duty: in the contest between them his temporary heat of inspiration was chilled. Until he had risen above the insidious deathwish, he could not create the stark vision of the ceaseless warfare of right against wrong with which the final version ends.[18]

In Yeats also, during the eighties and nineties, a submerged deathwish eddied, as we have recently been shown in the manuscript versions of *The Shadowy Waters* edited with such skill by Michael Sidnell, David Clark and George Mayhew. Aleel calls to the great reaper to "pluck out the stars / Beat down the hills and bid all be at an end." Forgael in another version urges the eagle-headed Fomor to "quench the world." So, too, when in *The Wind Among the Reeds* "Hanrahan Laments Because of his Wanderings," Yeats seems to be equating unrequited passion with existence, and making his *alter ego* "long for the day when . . . fragments of ancestral drakness . . . will overthrow the world." Was Hopkins simply following Milton, or were Yeats and Hopkins both drawing upon the same Celtic sources?[19]

Two anecdotes concerning Hopkins at University College, Dublin, call for comment and explanation. When Hopkins began teaching at Stephen's Green, young Willie Yeats was a student, first in the Metropolitan School of Art in Kildare Street, and later in the Royal Hibernian Academy School. Yeats was aware of the Jesuit's seeming eccentricities, and years later used to pooh-pooh Hopkins to Monk Gibbon "as a man of so delicate a conscience that he could not sleep at night

---

[17] Some readings from the second draft in his Dublin Notebook, composed between 22 November and 20 December 1884. See my variorum text given in *The Malahat Review* (April 1973), pp. 218-28; and my article, "The Making of a Hopkins Sonnet: 'Spelt from Sibyl's Leaves' " in the *Festschrift* in honour of Dr. E. R. Seary, ed. P. A. O'Flaherty and G. Story, Memorial University, Newfoundland.

[18] For the recurrent deathwish during his Dublin days, see e.g., G. M. Hopkins, *Poems*, 4th ed., ed. W. H. Gardner and N. H. MacKenzie (London, 1970), p. 186; and his *Sermons and Devotional Writings*, ed. C. Devlin (London, 1959), p. 262.

[19] Michael J. Sidnell, George P. Mayhew and David R. Clark, *Druid Craft* (Amherst, 1971), pp. 203, 211. Cf. also 95, 132, 182, 193, 201, 223, 290, 297. *The Wind Among the Reeds*, p. 51 and Yeats's note, p. 93. Also *The Countess Cathleen*, B. 11.277-9, in *Variorum Plays*, ed. Russell K. Alspach, p. 49. Cf. Yeats's *Memoirs*, p. 88 and note 3.

from worrying whether he had awarded his university candidates in their exam a completely just mark."[20] Since Yeats in the eighties dismissed examinations as a "great mill" set up to "destroy the imagination"—and refused to exert himself trying to turn it—he slighted any examiner who tended the machinery too seriously.[21]

Linked with Hopkins' near-collapse under the muddy tides of external examination papers, which choked him six times a year, is his often-derided announcement to his classes that in order not to show favouritism towards his own students, in setting the examination papers for candidates throughout Ireland he would carefully avoid any subjects treated in his lectures! As it stands this popular story makes little sense to me: I cannot see how a professor dealing with prescribed texts could omit everything likely to figure in the final papers. But a knowledge of another controversy fermenting at the time helps us to interpret Hopkins' attitude in the light of his scrupulous desire for right conduct.

Shortly after Hopkins' arrival in Dublin the *Second Report of the Royal University of Ireland* was published.[22] It reproduced an insensitive address delivered by the Chancellor of the University, the Duke of Abercorn, at the public ceremony in which degrees were formally awarded and prizes distributed. The Duke chose to contrast with this prize-winning the inequity with which life seems to distribute its rewards, in which self-seeking and pushful persons thrust ahead of those with more merit and modesty. But it was not so, he declaimed, with "the giving away of the prizes of University life. There you have fair contests; there you have open competitions; there you have success without insolence, and what is best of all, rivalry without heartburnings." It was a miscalculated dithyramb serving only to demonstrate how ignorant a gaudy chancellor can be of the real tensions beneath him. Aside from the inequalities in opportunity and facilities faced both by candidates and colleges, there was considerable dissatisfaction among those institutions which had no examining fellows on their staff. Dr. Walsh was once again to put this into words in an outspoken letter to the *Freeman's Journal*, 29 November 1884 (p. 5). Alluding to "what his Grace the Chancellor of the University has so oddly described as the 'fair (?) and honourable rivalry' of the University competitive examinations," he denounced the unjust advantages possessed by students who had studied under their own examiners for the whole year, especially since the highest honours depended upon a *viva voce*. A professor's predilections and quirks become quickly known to his students, and his emphases as a lecturer may unconsciously betray his intentions as an

---

[20] Monk Gibbon, *The Masterpiece and the Man—Yeats as I Knew Him* (London, 1959), p. 138.

[21] W. B. Yeats, *Letters to Katharine Tynan*, ed. Roger McHugh (Dublin, 1953), p. 95.

[22] Dated 25 March 1884.

examiner. "Monopoly is incompatible with justice" he exclaimed. If Hopkins, therefore, strove to keep his dual responsibilities as Professor and examiner separate, in the light of the inflammatory circumstances his conduct should be recognized as an idealistic gesture somewhat thrown away on very realistic students.

Hopkins' compulsion towards right conduct is revealed in a contemporary lecture which he wrote as a Christian introduction to the pagan philosophy in Cicero's *De Officiis*. This I came upon only recently in his "Dublin Note-Book." It has never been recognized nor published, possibly because it was mistaken for a translation of the Latin, as so many of the other passages in this working notebook are. I quote only one section:

> As the eye recognizes light, colour, illumination, the ear/sound; the understanding/meaning/ so the conscience recognizes a proper object of its own, viz. law, an absolutely binding law, or rather some one precept, a command, an imperative voice bidding and forbidding. Now this voice of command is absolute, which is the same as infinite, that is/ under no conceivable circumstance to be disobeyed or outweighing all possible motives and considerations to the contrary; for a weight which outweighs all possible counterpoise, a force which resists all possible countereffort, is infinite; and there is no infinite but God.

There is less contradiction than one might suspect between Hopkins' complete acceptance of the divine laws of conduct as revealed by conscience, or mediated by his superiors, and his iconoclastic disregard for the laws of meter and harmony to which contemporary poets and musicians conformed. In musical composition he was rapped over his venturesome knuckles by Sir Robert Stewart of Trinity College: "My dear Padre . . . nearly everything in your music was wrong—but you will not admit that to be the case."[23] Stewart refused to consider the new theories by which Hopkins justified his departures.

In music and poetry Hopkins relied upon the ability of his inner ear to catch the rhythms and cadences of nature. He could not respect as sacred the iambic pentameter, whose heavily shod feet in the Victorian Age had begun to ring hollow like a squad of obsolete robots crossing a plank bridge. Years after his death, Father Hopkins was recognized by some among the new generations at U.C.D. as "a rare and . . . exquisite poet"—to quote the words of Thomas MacDonagh which were still in the press when their speaker "died like a Prince" in the Rising of 1916. What a pity that MacDonagh in his M.A. thesis on *Thomas Campion and the Art of English Poetry* did not have the originator of Sprung Rhythm as his supervisor.[24] And a pity too that Hopkins,

---

[23] Hopkins, *Further Letters*, 2nd ed., p. 427. Contr. *Letters to Bridges*, p. 214, for his self-confidence in artistic matters.

[24] Thomas MacDonagh, *Literature in Ireland* (Dublin, printed June 1916), p. 229. His thesis on Campion had been published by the Talbot Press in 1913. For Hopkins' interest

instead of so receptive a student and Assistant Lecturer as Thomas MacDonagh, had a comparatively unperceptive colleague in Father Matthew Russell, editor of the *Irish Monthly*. Russell possessed no disturbing genius; his great service was in fostering those who had slightly higher poetic talents than his own. Though a shrewd connoisseur of character, he was too short of sight to relish scenery, and as unresponsive to the most maddening sounds as to the most pleasing. The same Father George O'Neill who inspired in MacDonagh his affection for Hopkins used to tell of a summer morning when Father Russell had worked away oblivious of a neighbour's lawnmower with its exasperating rattle and withdrawal. Seeing him unaware of the distraction a humorous friend remarked to him: "How persistently that wretched pigeon has been cooing!" and was rewarded with his hearty if absent-minded agreement.[25]

Father Russell was obsessed with the sonnet and its laws. He included so many instalments of "Sonnets on the Sonnet" in the *Irish Monthly* that he headed the final batch "The Last of a Hated Race."[26] He codified (even more rigidly than Hall Caine had done before him) such rules as the correct meter: "each pair of syllables, out of the ten syllables which make up the line, has the accent or stress of the voice falling on its second syllable," etc., etc. Hopkins impenitently created in "Spelt from Sibyl's Leaves" a sonnet of eight-foot lines, mostly trochaic or dactyllic, and in another sonnet written in Ireland, "That Nature is a Heraclitean Fire," he added to the sacrosanct fourteen lines three codas to make them twenty-four, each with just as many syllables as his meaning required.[27]

Indeed the two Jesuits had little in common. Hopkins was so reticent in Dublin about his poetry that none of the friends who wrote his obituaries so much as mentioned that he was a poet. Father Russell described Hopkins as an "impractical man," using the word probably in its exact sense of someone intractable, who could not be readily persuaded to go with the group. The editor remonstrated with Katharine Tynan for her "wilfulness" in including imperfect rhymes in her poems.[28] What would he have said of the final version of "Sibyl's Leaves," where for purposes of rhyme Hopkins splits "astray" between two lines, not dividing it into its true components but into "as" and "tray," intending his poetry for the resonating voice rather than the silent eye. Father Russell welcomed prosodic restrictions as he did the rules of his

in Campion's metrical experiments, see his letter to Everard, ed. Father A. Bischoff, S.J., in the *T.L.S., 8 December 1972, p. 1511.*

[25] *Irish Monthly*, 40 (October 1912), 547.

[26] *Irish Monthly*, 15, 568; 16, 366, 733; 17, 380, 615, 651; 19, 321; 20, 442.

[27] See Hopkins, *Poems*, 4th ed., pp. 97, 105.

[28] *Irish Monthly*, 31 (May 1903), 260, 264.

religious order, and quoted with approval their close identification:

> As we are told that the mere obedient observance of a rule of religious life
> contains and unfolds high, unguessed, and mystical spiritual virtues, so
> the mere obedience to the metrical laws of the sonnet implies and brings
> with it the beauties of the *crescendo*, the evolution of thought, the climax,
> the fall—and beauties more hidden and subtle than these.[29]

Among the reasons which made Hopkins conceal his poetry from his
colleagues in Ireland (I therefore venture to suggest) was this quasi-
religious conservatism on the part of the *Irish Monthly*'s editor. With
sheaves of new and unprinted poems, he risked offering Father Fussell
only two translations of Shakespeare into Latin.

One further story concerning Hopkins as a professor needs to be
neutralized by some fresh facts which have come my way. I quote
Eleanor Ruggles:

> Tradition claims that Hopkins once listened credulously while a half
> circle of unadoring youths, aware of his enthusiasm for words, plied him
> with false "Irishisms" which in his simplicity he sent to *Wright's Dialect
> Dictionary.*[30]

This may sound like a confused version of Stephen Dedalus and the
"tundish,"[31] but we have contributory evidence. Katharine Tynan
remembered that Father Hopkins conducted at least some of his lectures in an uproar.[32]

Hopkins had in 1887 tackled the philologist, Professor W. W.
Skeat (founder and President of the English Dialect Society), challenging some of his etymologies, and sending him an "Irish" word or two,
only to receive a deflating reply.[33] Skeat, who had no leisure to argue
with amateur philologists, dismissed one so-called Irishism as a common English word (like "tundish") and warned him that another scholar had wasted part of a lifetime compiling a dictionary of Irish-English
which was the worst performance Skeat had ever seen.[34] That Hopkins
was not easily browbeaten where his own intuitions were concerned is
shown by the fact that within two weeks of receiving this "put-down"
from Skeat, he wrote to his mother: "I am making a collection of Irish
words and phrases for the great *English Dialect Dictionary* and am in
correspondence with the editor."[35]

---

[29] Quoted from the *Tablet*, 18 December 1875, in *Irish Monthly*, 14 (1886), 343.

[30] *Gerard Manley Hopkins: A Life* (London, 1947 ed), p. 193.

[31] *A Portrait of the Artist as a Young Man*, ed. Richard Ellmann (London, 1968), p. 193.

[32] *Memories* (London, 1924), p. 156.

[33] See *Further Letters*, pp. 280, 284, and 431-32.

[34] Dr. Abraham Hume, D.C.L., who published *Remarks on the Irish Dialect of the English
Language* in 1878.

[35] *Further Letters*, 2nd ed., 1956, p. 184.

Joseph Wright does include the Rev. G. M. Hopkins in the "List of Unprinted Collections of Dialect Words" quoted in the *Dialect Dictionary* by the initials of the compilers. No copy has been found among Hopkins' papers. I therefore set out some years ago to discover if possible the collection which reached the editor. The search was spread over several abortive months, beginning with an investigation of Joseph Wright's will and surviving relatives, all his old friends from the *Dictionary* days such as Oliver Onions, the institutions which were his beneficiaries, and ending in an invasion of the Clarendon Press where his great work had been printed. Here, Mr. Dan Davin humoured my detective fervour by allowing me to read all the remaining files of correspondence, and to inspect every nook and cranny of the Press's ramifying buildings. When that had failed, he permitted me to spend several days, accompanied by two burly shedmen with housebreaker jemmies, in the vast acreage of their North Oxford warehouse, where together we opened every sealed crate. It was a formidable assignment.

We found huge boxes full of the original word-slips used for the *Oxford English Dictionary*, and packing cases crammed with books listed in its bibliography; but of the *Dialect Dictionary*, for which room-fulls of material had been gathered even before the first section was issued, I could find not a wisp.[36] Nor on the innumerable occasions on which I referred to the *English Dialect Dictionary* had I till recently come across the initials G.M.H. by which any of his contributions made use of would be identified.

I returned to the chase, however, with our daughter as research assistant. The six-volume dictionary contains some 9,000 columns, each citing anything up to eighty authorities. A conservative estimate would number citations at over half-a-million. I asked Catherine to work systematically through sample letters of the alphabet, switching over to another job when patience or eyesight gave out. The next day I found her subdued. She had fagged through some seven hundred columns of small print and apologized because she had found "only twenty-five quotations from Hopkins!" I, of course, was overjoyed that she had found any! The citations from Hopkins seemed to end in the letter C, and though she checked through some later letters of the alphabet, the sum total from well over 2,000 columns was not much more than double her first harvest. We must remember that Hopkins died the year after the letter telling of his correspondence with Joseph Wright.

The quotations are often very lively. Under the idiom "bloody wars," in the sense "serious consequences; also used as an exclamation of annoyance," we find an example supplied by Hopkins: "If the Pope makes Dr. X. Archbishop there'll be bloody wars." Now this statement has such an aura of authenticity about it that we can supply the context

---

[36] See Elizabeth M. Wright, *The Life of Joseph Wright*, 2 vols. (Oxford, 1932), II, 352ff.

with tolerable assurance. When Cardinal MacCabe died in 1885, it was strongly rumoured that the British government was anxious for the appointment of Dr. Moran of Sydney, Australia, and in fact he was summoned back to Rome. But the Irish press brought the government's manoeuvres into the open by publishing a secret letter which had been leaked to them, and in view of the succeeding outcry, the Papal Court appointed instead Hopkins' other opponent, Dr. William Walsh, a man who had unconcealed nationalist sympathies.[37]

It is interesting to find Hopkins and Yeats cheek by jowl in several dictionary entries. Under "boreen: a narrow lane, a byroad; a passage," for example, we have a matter-of-fact quotation from Yeats's *Fairy and Folk Tales of the Irish Peasantry*,[38] followed by a delightful idiom gathered from racy conversation by Hopkins: "He hasn't sense enough to drive a pig down a boreen."

Yet it is Hopkins rather than Yeats who is cited for two special types of fairy or hobgoblin: "bo-man" and "bugabo." From Hopkins, to my surprise, comes the definition of "Blarney-stone." I include only one further example, selected because I think I know where he may have garnered it. In Volume I of the *EDD*, among the words for which the editor felt he had as yet insufficient authority, we find a quotation under the verb "to button": "to have one's coat buttoned behind—to look like a fool." That the suspect quotation came from Hopkins is confirmed under "coat," where the illustration is his: "Here comes Paddy from Cork with his coat buttoned behind." Now curiously enough this expression is found in one of Katharine Tynan's reminiscences, which she later embedded in her *Twenty-Five Years* (1913). She used to tell of an unpleasant incident when she was a child:

> I was so very small at this time, that I remember an occasion I was allowed to put on my own coat to go home, putting it on back to front, and making the very tiny journey that was between school and home in tears, because of the derision of the street-boys, who hailed me as "Paddy from Cork with his coat buttoned behind him" (p. 22).

We might be tempted to speculate that during a visit by Hopkins to Katharine Tynan, the conversation might have turned to the lack of respect which Hopkins suffered at young Irish hands, and that the poetess tried to console him with her own mortifying experience.

Although Willie Yeats was apparently not present when Hopkins called on J. B. Yeats in his studio, the painter handed him a copy of his

---

[37] See *Annual Register*, 1885, p. 200. After Cardinal MacCabe's death, the publication in *United Ireland* of a confidential letter, which it had somehow secured, from Sir George Errington to Lord Granville made it clear that the British government was trying to persuade the Papal Court not to appoint the successor whom the Irish most wanted. This leak probably explains the rejection of Dr. Moran. See also Sir Shane Leslie, "Archbishop Walsh," *The Making of Modern Ireland*, ed. Conor Cruise O'Brien (Toronto, 1960), p. 100.

[38] 1888, p. 22, in Douglas Hyde's "Teig O'Kane and the Corpse."

son's *Mosada*—"with some emphasis of manner," as Hopkins duly noticed—a gift as it were from Trinity College to U.C.D. This dramatic poem had just been separately printed, with J. B. Yeats's pen-and-ink sketch of the gangly young poet for frontispiece. As a means of introducing his son's poetry to a Catholic priest, *Mosada* was disastrous. The epigraph had a suggestive leer about it: "And my Lord Cardinal hath had strange days in his youth." Its medieval story is of a monk with a great reputation for holiness, who resists all pleas that mercy should be shown to the beautiful Moorish maiden condemned to the stake, even when the Spanish inquisitors themselves entreat him. Yet when the monk visits her in her dungeon and finds that she is his former love Mosada, he renounces his vows in a flash, and without so much as half a line devoted to a wrestling with his conscience (unless the expression "O God!" can be so construed), he prepares forthwith to carry her off to safety and marriage through a secret route. And after this plan has been frustrated—she dies in his arms of the poison she had taken before his arrival—with equal velocity he reverts to his role as holy monk.[39]

No one could either take the plot seriously, or dislike the poetic patches (though from its natural history I would place the Moorish village of Azubia as somewhere between London and Dover). Yet the central incident, melodramatic though it is, would have brought Hopkins some distress: the recurrent sacrilege of priests abandoning their consecrated office in order to marry was one which caused him deep sorrow—as we may judge when about this time his old Oxford friend, Father William Addis, gave up the priesthood in order to wed a member of his congregation.[40]

Hopkins enters no strictures on its anti-Catholic phantasmagoria, however, perhaps remembering that his own first long poem, "The Escorial," had been critical of the Inquisiton. The modest booklet of twelve pages which Hopkins was given that morning would, if it had survived, be worth perhaps $2,000 today, in view of the reputation now accorded both to the author and the recipient. But Hopkins' copy has long since disappeared. Judging from the strictures on Yeats's work quoted in Father Stephen Brown's *Guide to Books on Ireland*, where "The Land of Heart's Desire" is referred to as a "revolting burlesque of Catholic religion,"[41] we need little imagination to interpret its fate at the hands of a Jesuit librarian in Victorian Ireland.

On the other hand, the equally slender booklet which Katharine Tynan gave Hopkins, full of adulatory extracts from reviews of that

---

[39] *The Variorum Edition of the Poems of W. B. Yeats,* ed. Peter Allt and Russell K. Alspach (New York, 1957), pp. 689-704.

[40] *Letters to Bridges,* p. 298; and *Journals,* p. 311.

[41] (Dublin, 1912), p. 248.

Catholic poet's first book, was still preserved in University College, Dublin, in 1903.[42] It was reproduced in the second impression of *Louise de la Vallière*.[43] Hopkins' shrewd comment on this chorus of praise was: "She is not exactly an original 'fountain in a shady grove' (the critics would not be standing all around her so soon if she were), but rather a sparkling town fountain in public gardens." He had a pretty good idea where her piped water came from.[44]

One Tynan poem which superficially anticipates Yeats's *Mosada*, "Vivia Perpetua in Prison," has religions and attitudes reversed. Here the Christian martyr, St. Vivia Perpetua, greets the dawn of the day when she is to be burned at the stake with lyrical enthusiasm. "O young hours, fly fast, / Bringing the time of my sweet sacrifice!" Young Miss Tynan was, fortunately for her comfort, writing way beyond her experience, but unfortunately for her art somewhat beyond her intuitions also.[45] Compare for a moment with that of Hopkins her description of the saint enduring a period of dryness of soul, when there seems no communion with God:

> Oh, sorrowing nights and days,
> When Thy love seemed far off, my soul hath known!
> Have I not suffered anguish, when mine own,
> Those whom I love, had drawn me by my love
> Back to their gods; and when to Thee above
> I cried for help, Thou didst not hear my cry,
> And Thy sweet heaven seemed brass, while wearily
> Alone I wrestled with mine anguish sore
> Through the long days and nights?[46]

The language is at once irreproachable and undisturbing: no trenchant phrase cuts unsentimentally through the mists of make-believe. And here is Hopkins, in a sonnet probably written the same year Miss Tynan's poem was published:

> I wake and feel the fell of dark, not day.
> What hours, O what black hoürs we have spent
> This night! what sights you, heart, saw; ways you went!
> And you must, in yet longer light's delay.

---

[42] Hopkins, *Further Letters*, p. 431; and *Irish Monthly*, 31, 261.

[43] I was able to discover and acquire for Queen's University library a copy of this second impression which Katharine Tynan must have given to Michael Davitt, whom she and her father used to visit during his imprisonments. In it she had copied a then unpublished sonnet by Christina Rossetti, adding "Transcribed here by Katharine Tynan, Nov. 15th 1887."

[44] *The Correspondence of G. M. Hopkins and R. W. Dixon*, ed. C. C. Abbott (London, 1935), p. 151.

[45] See *The Correspondence of G. M. Hopkins and R. W. Dixon*, p. 151, for Hopkins' embarrassment as to how best to comment on her verse. Also *Letters to Bridges*, pp. 258-59, asking for help from Bridges in finding something complimentry to say.

[46] "Vivia Perpetua in Prison," *Louise de la Vallière*, pp. 98-99.

> With witness I speak this. But where I say
> Hours I mean years, mean life. And my lament
> Is cries countless, cries like dead letters sent
> To dearest him that lives alas! away.
>
> I am gall, I am heartburn. God's most deep decree
> Bitter would have me taste: my taste was me;
> Bones built in me, flesh filled, blood brimmed the curse.
>
> Selfyeast of spirit a dull dough sours. I see
> The lost are like this, and their scourge to be
> As I am mine, their sweating selves; but worse.[47]

Hopkins is writing from sheer necessity, to clarify for himself nights when he felt spiritually deserted, abandoned among dark moors by his only possible guide and friend.

It seems clear from their correspondence that Hopkins helped Katharine Tynan towards greater independence. When she published her first collected volume of *Poems* in 1901 she had the judicious reticence, as Father Russell remarked, to include nothing from her earliest book, "in spite of all the promise it gave and all the praise it got."[48]

When Hopkins first met Willie Yeats, that young poet was still writing verse which could be described as Parnassian—to use the derogatory term for a poetic imitator which hopkins had invented when he himself was twenty.[49] His next publication after *Mosada*, for instance, was in Father Russell's *Irish Monthly*—a sonnet so derivative that he never collected or bothered to revise it:

> Remembering thee, I search out these faint flowers
> Of rhyme; remembering thee. . . .[50]

The faintness of these "flowers of rhyme," which quite rightly seems to be worrying the poet, was due to his remembering a great many poetesses besides his love—including Christina Rossetti, of course. Years later, as Dr. Helen Vendler has pointed out, Yeats was able in "Leda and the Swan" so to transform the conventional sonnet movement away from its common tidal flow and ebb that few readers recognize that poem as a sonnet.[51]

Mosada makes us think of that *tour de force* which his friend and close mentor, Professor Edward Dowden, contributed to the Trinity College *Kottabos*; supposedly an extract from a Jacobean verse play of

---

[47] Hopkins, *Poems*, p. 101.

[48] *Irish Monthly*, 31, 263. For letters between Hopkins and Miss Tynan, see *Further Letters*, 2nd ed., pp. 430-31; and "Six New Letters of Gerard Manley Hopkins," ed. Graham Storey, *The Month*, N.S. 19, No. 5 (May 1958), 263-70.

[49] *Further Letters* (to Baillie, 10 September 1864), p. 216.

[50] *Irish Monthly*, 14 (July 1886), 376.

[51] *Yeats's "Vision" and the Later Plays* (Cambridge, Mass., 1963), pp. 105-06.

1610, *'Tis Pity She's a Queen*, by a fictitious dramatist, Roger Newcombe.[52] Dowden, who used to read to Willie and his father chapters of his unpublished *Life of Shelley*, may have had through his own verse a minor influence on such early works by Yeats as *The Island of Statues*. Yeats's metrical versatility in the songs of that play, combined with pleasing Parnassian diction, are both marks of Dowden's verse too. One is tempted to find one source for Yeats's unscriptural song about Eve in the Garden of Eden happily sinning[53] in Dowden's light-hearted description of Eve as bored with her happy valley, and through eating the apple achieving "Paradise Lost and Found" simultaneously.[54] But Yeats's more obvious borrowings are from Shelley direct, from Matthew Arnold (the trick of repeated words in the opening of lines), the habit of heroic couplet narration from William Morris and Sir Edwin Arnold,[55] the rotund felicities of phrase from Tennyson. At the age of twenty-one he had not quite reached the independence of judgment achieved by Hopkins at the age of twenty when he wrote to a friend: "A horrible thing has happened to me. I have begun to *doubt* Tennyson."[56] If Hopkins failed to see in the author of *Mosada* portents of greatness, when Yeats himself re-read the play after a very long interval in 1923 he could in retrospect discern little promise either. "I . . . think rather sadly," Yeats wrote, "that when young men of that age send in like work I am not able to foresee his future or his talent."[57] Still later, in 1936, he looked back with only the vaguest memories to the times when he had encountered Hopkins, even underestimating his own age by four years. "Fifty-odd years ago I met him in my father's studio on different occasions, but remember almost nothing. A boy of seventeen, Walt Whitman in his pocket, had little interest in a querulous, sensitive scholar."[58]

Some of the other barriers between Hopkins and Yeats we can dismiss as immaterial. Religion? Hopkins preferred a Protestant poet of great ability to Catholic nonentities whose verse might be described as flowing with skim milk and honey. One of his closest friends was the Protestant, Robert Bridges: in J. B. Yeats's studio, and to Miss Tynan, he spoke lyrically of the beauties of Bridges' verse. Race? Yeats ac-

---

[52] *Kottabos*, ed. R. Y. Tyrrell, First Series (Dublin, 1874), p. 242.

[53] *Variorum Edition of the Poems of W. B. Yeats*, p. 654.

[54] This was not included in the 1st ed. of Dowden's *Poems* published in 1876. See 1914 ed., pp. 195-98. For Dowden's influence on Yeats see, e.g., *Autobiographies*, pp. 85-89.

[55] E.g., Edwin Arnold's "The Feast of Belshazzar," or "Hero and Leander."

[56] *Further Letters*, p. 215. To. A. W. M. Baillie, 10 September 1864.

[57] (*Sic.*) Quoted Allan Wade, *Bibliography of the Writings of W. B. Yeats* (London, 3rd ed. rev., 1968), p. 20.

[58] W. B. Yeats, ed., *Oxford Book of Modern Verse* (Oxford, 1936), p. v.

quired many English friends, while Hopkins could retreat from Stephen's Green to a number of delightful Irish friends who always had a welcome ready for him. Nationalism? Yeats, in the mid-eighties, had so vague a notion of literary nationalism that he inscribed a copy of his Spanish Inquisition melodrama "To Miss K. Tynan from her friend and fellow worker in Irish Poetry the Author."[59] Class allegiance? If Yeats lamented the attacks on the Great Houses, Hopkins was also made miserable by the realization that the persecution of the Irish Catholic gentry was headed by two Catholic Archbishops, one of whom was none other than the recurrent Dr. William Walsh.[60]

On the other hand, Hopkins and Yeats had shared in reverse the experience of exile. Yeats had felt himself an alien during six boyhood years spent in Hopkins' birthplace, London. Dublin, Yeats's birthplace, was the city in which Hopkins wrote, "To seem the stranger lies my lot, my life / Among strangers."[61] Yet in some peculiar way for both of them, up to 1889 Ireland was more productive of poetry than England. Hopkins' greatest pieces belong, not to his twenty-one years in his homeland, England, but to three vivid years in Celtic Wales, and to five taxing years in Celtic Ireland. Out of the ingrowing sorrows of his mental conflicts in Ireland—between loyalty to England and human sympathy for Irish wrongs, between his uniquely inquiring mind and the stultifying monotony of his drudgery as examiner where over a third of the candidates commonly failed,[62] between the consecrated purity of his devotional life and the trials of a devout man who cries to heaven in vain for reassurance—out of this strife came not only his intense Sonnets of Desolation but, in his many happy interludes, the consolations of such poems as "(Ashboughs)" and "That Nature is a Heraclitean Fire."[63] Some of them were written in Clongowes, or Dromore, or Monastereven, during holiday spells away from the confines of Newman House.

Not unexpectedly, Hopkins turned to Celtic sources for his most ambitious piece, "St. Winefred's Well."[64] And in other poems too there occurs imagery which has a curious affinity with some in the early Yeats. When Hopkins exclaims:

---

[59] Wade, *Bibliography of Yeats*, p. 20.

[60] *Letters to Bridges*, p. 223.

[61] *Poems*, p. 101. Hopkins did not attribute his nervous disorders to Ireland; see *Further Letters*, p. 251: "Out of Ireland I shd. be no better, rather worse probably."

[62] See the Annual Reports for the Royal University of Ireland, which analyse the entries and successes in each examination: e.g., in 1885, in June 42 percent of the pass level matriculation candidates failed, and 44 percent of the first year general candidates; in September and October in all the honours exams the failure rate was 34 percent.

[63] *Poems*, pp. 97-108, 185-99, 223-27.

[64] *Poems*, pp. 187-93.

> My cries heave, herds-long; huddle in a main, a chief-
> woe, world-sorrow; on an age-old anvil wince and sing—[65]

he reminds us of Dectora in the manuscript versions of *Druid Craft:*

> I lie upon the anvil of the world

as Aleel her lover is slain before her helpless gaze while she stands bound to the mast.[66] And in *The Wanderings of Oisin*, the aged hero, speaking of himself, says:

> Ay, Oisin knows, for he is of the weak,
> Blind, and nigh deaf, with withered arms he lies
> Upon the anvil of the world.[67]

I am still trying to trace these and other parallels between Hopkins and Yeats to a common Celtic source.

If Hopkins had some enemies in Dublin, the city was full of enemies for Yeats:[68] he had to go into exile to Byzantium to find singing-masters and purgation. In April 1887 he was drawn back to London by his father, and found it a foreign desert, productive of no verse;[69] but by summer again he was in Sligo, working on *The Wanderings of Oisin*. This is the first of his productions in which his individuality begins to assert itself. The book had only just been published in 1889 when Hopkins died. How much more promising would have been a friendship between the two poets if this volume rather than its predecessor had been presented to Hopkins. And because in my boyhood I thought no long poem I had come across had the rhythmic magic of *The Wanderings of Oisin*, I am going to end this paper with lines which have not lost their evocative power for me after all the intervening years:

> And I rode by the plains of the sea's edge, where all
>   is barren and gray,
> Grey sands on the green of the grasses and over the
>   dripping trees,
> Dripping and doubling landward, as though they would
>   hasten away
> Like an army of old men longing for rest from the moan
>   of the seas.
>
> And the winds made the sands on the sea's edge turning
>   and turning go,
> As my mind made the names of the Fenians. Far from the
>   hazel and oak

---

[65] *Poems,* p. 100.

[66] *Druid Craft*, pp. 119, 138, 217. The expression disappears in the printed versions.

[67] *The Wanderings of Oisin* (London, 1889), p. 30—Part II, ll. 202-04.

[68] *Autobiographies* (London, 1956), p. 83.

[69] *Letters to Katharine Tynan*, pp. 26, 29, 45, 46, 77-78, 83, 88, 89, 100.

> I rode away on the surges, where high as the saddle bow
> Fled foam underneath me, and round me a wandering and
>   milky smoke.[70]

From the end of the eighties, with this poem behind him, Yeats steadily evolved through his long life. You can outgrow many poets, but not easily Yeats. Austin Clarke's conjectures are interesting: how different the Irish Literary Revival would indeed have been if Yeats had accepted Hopkins (who was almost exactly the same age as Professor Dowden) as a friend and adviser. But it was Hopkins himself who defined the reaction of any original artist to masterpieces set before him: to "admire and do otherwise."[71] I would rather have among my closest admirations two quite different imaginative worlds: the masterpieces of Hopkins, every square millimeter of their canvas finished and packed with thought, and along with these the last gusty, turbulent, disrespectful charcoals from the studio of Mr. William Butler Yeats, who, after the inevitable apprenticeship to many predecessors in those early Dublin days, became his own master, and, to my mind, one of the four or five greatest writers in the English language.

---

[70] *The Wanderings of Oisin*, p. 46—Part III, 11. 141-48.

[71] *Letters to Bridges*, p. 291, 25 September 1888.

YEATS:
THE QUESTION OF SYMBOLISM

Denis Donoghue

From the autumn of 1895 to the following spring, W. B. Yeats shared with Arthur Symons a flat at No. 2 Fountain Court in the Middle Temple, London. Their conversations have not been recorded, except in snatches. We know they discussed Maud Gonne, and the relation between passion and poetry. We assume they talked of the trial of Oscar Wilde, and the difference it would make to the already difficult relation between artists and their audience. Yeats found in Symons an ideal conversationalist, meaning an impassioned listener. "He had the sympathetic intelligence of a woman," he reported many years later, "and was the best listener I have ever met."[1] Symons returned this handsome compliment in dedicating to Yeats *The Symbolist Movement in Literature*, first published in 1899 but already forming itself in Symons' mind in 1895. It was a Parisian book, not only because Paris was, as Walter Benjamin called it, the capital of the nineteenth century, but because Symons' mind was animated by the impressions of the city, its music halls, the anecdotes of Verhaeren and Maeterlinck which Symons brought back from Paris as gifts for Yeats.[2] "Whatever I came to know of Continental literature I learned of him," Yeats acknowledged;[3] another compliment returned when Symons in his dedication, speaking of the French Symbolists, described Yeats as "the chief representation of that movement in our country."[4]

---

[1] W. B. Yeats, *Memoirs*, ed. Denis Donoghue (London, 1972), p. 36. Cf. ibid., p. 87.

[2] W. B. Yeats, *Autobiographies* (London, 1961), p. 193.

[3] *Memoirs*, p. 36.

[4] Arthur Symons, *The Symbolist Movement in Literature* (London, 1911), p. v.

It is generally agreed that what Yeats learned of Continental literature, either from Symons or anyone else, was slight: he was a poor linguist. But it could be argued that he had very little to learn; he was already half-way toward Symbolist procedures by instinct, as the early poems show. He was writing, from desire, poems not very different from those the Symbolists were writing to a program. Conversations with Symons confirmed him in his feeling that those early poems, however fragile they might eventually appear, were notations in the spirit of the age, so far as that spirit was Parisian. Symons described Symbolism as "a literature in which the visible world is no longer a reality, and the unseen world no longer a dream."[5] The poets were attempting "to spiritualise literature, to evade the old bondage of rhetoric, the old bondage of exteriority."[6] Mallarmé's principle, according to Symons, was "to name is to destroy, to suggest is to create."[7] And the most subtle instrument of suggestion was rhythm, "which is the executive soul."[8] Bringing Yeats through the translation of Mallarmé, therefore, Symons sustained him in the belief that he was not alone in the world, that he, too, would witness the trembling of the veil. For the moment, then, it was enough. When Yeats spoke of symbols, he had French authority to associate them with the condition of trance, the ultimate liberation of mind from the pressure of will, a sense of timelessness, and the corresponding rhythms. In "The Symbolism of Poetry," asking "what change should one look for in the manner of our poetry" if readers were to accept the theory "that poetry moves us because of its symbolism," Yeats answered that in such a change the new poetry would cast out "descriptions of nature for the sake of nature," as well as vehemence, opinion, the moral law, and "energetic rhythms." "We would seek out," he said, "those wavering, meditative, organic rhythms, which are the embodiment of the imagination, that neither desires nor hates, because it has done with time, and only wishes to gaze upon some reality, some beauty."[9] It is permissible to think that the poet in this spirit is more concerned with the sensation of gazing than with the beauty or the reality upon which he gazes. Reality and beauty, in that formulation, are but the occasions of the gaze; or if that is too severe, alternative names for the condition of trance to which the gazing soul aspires. At any rate, the gazing is not for the sake of anything gazed upon; the act is internal, its value is measured by internal consequences, the concentration of consciousness as a value in itself. Reality is likely to be compromised by the attention which it

---

[5] Ibid., p. 4.

[6] Ibid., p. 8.

[7] Ibid., p. 128.

[8] Ibid., p. 129.

[9] W. B. Yeats, *Essays and Introductions* (London, 1961), p. 163.

ostensibly attracts: the mind is not really directed upon its official object.

Sartre has argued in his Preface to Mallarmé's *Poésies* that Mallarmé's devotion to the imaginary arises from his resentment against reality, and the poems written in that mood are symbolic acts of revenge: the poet's words are designed to undo the work of the first Creation, the poem being a second and higher version. Yeats's early poems do not propose to destroy reality, unless we find such a desire in their determination to escape from the given world to islands of else-where. Their happiness is always sought in another country, where the Muse's law is the only writ that runs. Hugh Kenner has remarked of Yeats's early poem, "He Remembers Forgotten Beauty" that the language proceeds, like Mallarmé's in many poems, by systematic digression from the poem's formal structure.[10] The formal structure, the sentence upon which the poem appears to depend, can indeed be disentangled from the net of subordinate clauses, but only by an effort alien to the spirit of the poem. The poem asks to be read in a more accommodating fashion, we are discouraged from enquiring how the grammar works, or what verb goes with that noun; we are to allow ourselves to be entangled, and to submit to a language in which the digressions are richer than the formal business, the sentence. I draw from this the conclusion that the sentence stands for the reality principle, and that to Yeats it is at best a necessary evil, a ball-and-chain, tolerable only to the extent to which its force is thwarted. The digressions, the subordinate clauses, are insubordinate, and they have the effect of depriving language of the nominative power in which empiricists delight; they turn the poem into a place of shadow and suggestion. The empirical world, sustained in its exorbitance by the naming power of language, the strict application of name to thing, is now made to appear blurred, rich only in the atmosphere which qualifies it: it is not allowed to assert itself. The result of reading the poem as it asks to be read is that beguiling phrases stay in the reader's mind, but the sentence is forgotten; the pleasure principle is dominant in the form of reverie, and reality must do the best it can for itself, with little acknowledgement from the poet.

I have laboured this theme only to emphasize Yeats's first notion of Symbolism, that it effects a blessed release from time, from the "malady of the quotidian," that it enables a poet to emigrate to happier lands, fictive places responsive to desire and imagination. Reality exists, like sentences and names, only to be circumvented. A symbol may be a noun, but it imposes little or no restriction upon the suggestible mind which receives it. "Rose of all Roses, Rose of all the World!" is mostly a line of nouns, but the nouns are valued only for the latitude of

---

[10] Hugh Kenner, "Some Post-Symbolist Structures," *Literary Theory and Structure*, eds. Frank Brady, John Palmer, Martin Price (New Haven, 1973), p. 388.

their associations: the one privilege they are now allowed to claim is that of setting up strict categories or demarcations to which the reader's mind is forced to confine its attention. So even if we continue to think of symbols as nouns, we think of Symbolism as a verb, a rival act of creation which subverts the original one. That is, we think of Symbolism, for the moment, in the terms in which Symons and Yeats recited it.

Left to ourselves, we would hardly approach Symbolism in this way. It is more congenial to us to think of symbols as natural forms or events which have acquired special significance, a special aura, from the ancestral feelings gathered around them. We are happy to recognize in symbols certain unconscious commonplaces, significances to which one recurs because of long association or because of kinship of feeling between one situation and another. We like to think that the symbolic aura is the result of many generations, consanguinities of feeling which enact themselves by a law entirely natural. We hope to share in those ancestral feelings, but we do not presume to invent them. It is only by courtesy and somewhat unwillingly that we allow the poet to engage in a similar enterprise from his own resources, and we are inclined to accuse him of pretentiousness, as Eliot accused Blake and Yeats, if their efforts have an air of calculation or insistence. Still, we admit that a poet may do some of the work by himself, he may resort to certain words which begin as images but which acquire a certain radiance from the largesse with which the poet uses them; as Yeats resorted to Sato's sword in "Meditations in Time of Civil War," and to the tower in several poems. With luck, these images become symbols, and we read them on the page as if they were written in italics. Perhaps I can describe the process, except for its luck, by saying that an image becomes a symbol on being touched by value or significance not attributable to its own set. For example: let us think of an event in narrative as a moment or a position along a line, straight or crooked, and then let us think of it as being crossed by another line of value from another source. Each line is a set, a paradigm. But the event which occurs at the point of intersection between two sets is an image in both; its duplicity constitutes its symbolic force. Interpreted in one set, it declares itself unrestrained by that interpretation; it is part of the other set as well. When we find an image becoming a symbol, we feel in it this double potency; its allegiance expands, as if answerable to both idioms, ready to participate in both sets of relations. This marks its freedom and its suggestiveness; we have a sense in attending to it that there is no point at which we can say for sure that its force has come to an end. We have something like this in mind on other occasions, too; when we think of a particular person, and then find in him a type of personality which he embodies without exhausting: when we think of chance or contingency, and then sense the participation of a seemingly arbitrary event in a pattern or rhythm of recurrence, so that it reverberates in time and appears fateful in its character: or when we advert to what seems a purely natural event, and then notice in it traces of human intervention in the form of consciousness. In these instances we mark a point of intersection where the individual event expands to fulfill several obligations of meaning, far beyond the call of a single duty in that respect.

This makes again something like the old-fashioned distinction between allegory and symbolism, where we say of allegory that it proceeds by parallel lines which never meet and can only be translated from one idiom into another; while we say of the symbolic event that it enfolds its meaning and cannot be translated into any other terms. Whitehead's account of Symbolism is for this reason not entirely satisfactory. "The human mind is functioning symbolically," he says, "when some components of its experience elicit consciousness, beliefs, emotions, and usages, respecting other components of its experience. The former set of components are the 'symbols,' and the latter set constitute the 'meaning' of the symbols. The organic functioning whereby there is transition from the symbol to the meaning [is] called 'symbolic reference.' "[11] To make this a more satisfactory account, one should interpret the eliciting process in such a way as to blur the otherwise too sharp distinction between a symbol and its meaning; if, for instance, one spoke of the symbol not as a thing, followed by its meaning, but as an act barely separable from its consequence. The symbolic act is unitary, it does not divide itself or set limits to its force; only by a retrospective and somewhat mechanical process can we presume to say where the act ends and its consequence begins, and even in saying so much one knows that the act is injured by the imposition of alien categories.

I would prefer to speak of Symbolism in terms of action, because the concept of meaning can be considered as dissociated from time, but action is helplessly temporal; and this is as it should be. We should not conspire too readily with a literary theory which has purity in mind. I have remarked that Symbolism plans to evade reality, and most particularly the reality of time, the inescapable Mondays and Tuesdays, but the plan acknowledges time as the governing dimension and only seeks to elude it. Indeed, thinking of Symbolism, we must hold in mind simultaneously two desires which, if taken bluntly, may appear to contradict each other. When we register the presence or the activity of a symbol, we mark a moment in time in which the world of objects is reconciled to the desires of the spirit: object and subject are folded in a single party, and this is happiness. It is true that in such a moment the subject is first among two forces only ostensibly equal, but this does not destroy the happiness of the reconciliation. The second desire must

[11] Alfred North Whitehead, *Symbolism, its Meaning and Effect* (Cambridge, 1928), p. 9.

also be registered, however, the desire that such reconciliations be prolonged, that they never end, though we know they are merely momentary and cannot be prolonged. There is no structure, according to the Symbolist aesthetic, within which they could be retained. If Symbolism appears to us today a peculiarly vulnerable form of art, and beautiful for that reason, I think the main consideration is that it exhibits a radical disaffection from time as from an alien element or an alien action. Reconciliation with time, according to such a prescription, can only be a momentary release, a stolen kiss, because such moments are surrounded by a void on each side. The Symbolist finds nothing but void in the latitude of time; it is as much as he can do to catch an instant in which an event in his imaginary set is touched by an event in the historical set, and the two events coalesce, becoming one. The "dissoci- ation of sensibility" described by Eliot, upon a hint by Remy de Gour- mont, is a condition in which the mind's reconciliation with time cannot be looked for or counted on, except in glimpses: as a general felicity, it has become impossible, according to Eliot's thesis. Hence the moral justification of living according to the imagination for all it is worth: if imagination and reality happen to join hands from time to time, that is good fortune beyond the reach of prediction.

But we must take the matter somewhat more strictly, to consider what we mean by saying, as we do, that Yeats started out as a Symbolist and ended as something else. Specifically, I want to describe the scru- ple which prevented him from making his entire art with Symons and the Symbolists, because I find the scruple present from the start, even though it was suppressed, in the early years, more often than not. So we ought to proceed more consecutively and see what happened. In "The Symbolism of Poetry" Yeats says that "all sounds, all colours, all forms, either because of their preordained energies or because of long associ- ation, evoke indefinable and yet precise emotions, or, as I prefer to think, call down among us certain disembodied powers, whose foot- steps over our hearts we call emotions."[12] And in "The Philosophy of Shelley's Poetry" he speaks of the Great Memory as "a dwelling-house of symbols, of images that are living souls."[13] The aura we feel in the symbol marks for Yeats the presence of the supernatural in the natural; if he believed in anything, he believed in reincarnation. The souls of the dead were understood as inhabiting places sacred because of that residence, mountains "along whose sides the peasant still sees enchanted fires."[14] Yeats's evidence for these fancies is not a theory of the occult, it is the fact that certain images and certain places have been

---

[12] *Essays and Introductions,* pp. 156-57. Some of the following paragraphs draw upon material published in another form in my *W. B. Yeats* (New York, 1972).

[13] Ibid., p. 79.

[14] Ibid., p. 114.

long "steeped in emotion," and sacred for that reason. In the essay on "Magic" he writes that "whatever the passions of men have gathered about becomes a symbol in the Great Memory, and in the hands of him who has the secret it is a worker of wonders, a caller-up of angels or of devils."[15] The poet is therefore a mage, an adept in secret but traditional knowledge: Yeats is hoping to establish between subjectivity and inherited symbols the kind of relation which Eliot proposed between the individual talent and tradition, a relation of discipline in the sense that if you want tradition you must work for it, if you want symbols you must attend to them. The poet must become an alchemist of the word, if he is to escape from the tautology of himself. Symbols, inherited rather than invented, mediate between the individual consciousness, which would otherwise be solipsist, and the given world, which would otherwise be, for all time, alien. Symbols are at once given and created: given, but given by creative souls not unlike our own. A race is a communion of such souls. Yeats speaks of the Symbolist poet as we might more naturally speak of the mage: "The poet of essences and pure ideas," he says, "must seek in the half-lights that glimmer from symbol to symbol as if to the ends of the earth all that the epic and dramatic poet finds of mystery and shadow in the accidental circumstances of life."[16] The Symbolist fills our minds "with the essences of things, and not with things": his instrument is rhythm, presumably because human feeling, which seeks release in words and is outraged by the poor release it finds, sways to rhythm as to music. "In art, rhythm is everything," Symons wrote in 1898, a pardonable exaggeration in a critic of Mallarméan persuasion.

With Yeats in mind, therefore, and especially the early Yeats under Symons' rhetoric, it is well for us to understand that Symbolism is the poet's form of magic, except that what the mage does consciously the poet does half consciously and half by instinct. The ancient secret is common to both disciplines. A mage believes he can do what a Symbolist does, but deliberately. Their activities are so congenial, one to the other, that their double presence in the poets of "the tragic generation" is entirely natural; two forms of the same impulse, to command a spiritual power, like an ancient art not quite lost. Cornelius Agrippa's *De Occulta Philosophia* was one of Yeats's sacred books, Shelley's *Prometheus Unbound* another: their joint presence in his mind was a choice, not an aberration. Magic was congenial to Yeats's mind for many reasons, but especially because it exerted the heuristic power of language, the common grammar of mage and poet. There is a passage in *The Philosophy of Symbolic Forms* where Cassirer says that "all word-magic and name-magic are based on the assumption that the world of things and the world of names form a single undifferentiated

---

[15] Ibid., p. 50.   [16] Ibid., p. 87.

chain of causality and hence a single reality."[17] But the names are evocations, not labels affixed peremptorily to objects. This goes some way to account for the incantatory note in Yeats's hieratic style, where his lines are more readily acceptable if we take them as rituals, prescriptions, or interdictions than as secular utterances delivered from a high horse. The basic assumption is that souls do not die and therefore may be evoked: "the dead living in their memories are, I am persuaded," Yeats says, "the source of all that we call instinct, and it is their love and their desire, all unknowing, that make us drive beyond our reason, or in defiance of our interest, it may be."[18] Correspondingly, the *anima mundi* is not merely a store of images and symbols, it is what a race dreams and remembers. The great soul may be evoked by symbols, but spirits are not mere functions of ourselves, they have their own native personalities, or so Yeats thought. The natives of the rain are rainy men. So the best reading of the *anima mundi* is that it is the subjective correlative of history, a nation's life in symbols; it is not our invention, but it may respond to our call, if like the mage we speak the right words. Yeats found in Blake's *Milton* a figure or an action to represent the process by which these symbols are engendered:

> When on the highest lift of his light pinions he arrives
> At that bright Gate, another Lark meets him and back to back
> They touch their pinions, tip tip, and each descend
> To their respective Earths and there all night consult
>   with Angels
> Of Providence and with the Eyes of God all night in slumbers
> Inspired, and at the dawn of day send out another Lark
> Into another Heaven to carry news upon his wings.[19]

This figure Yeats interpreted as meaning that man gains spiritual influence in like fashion: "He must go on perfecting earthly power and perception until they are so subtilized that divine power and divine perception descend to meet them, and the song of earth and the song of heaven mingle together."[20]

I suppose one ought to say that these songs are agreeably vague, and perhaps that they are both Songs of Myself. In the Symbolist tradition, as in the Idealist tradition for similar reasons, the exemplary act is the contemplation of one's own mind; like Mallarmé watching himself in a mirror in order to think. In Yeats, contemplation registers the mind moving within its own circle, gathering its strength in a symbolic act, purged of every impurity. Dance is its embodiment, its

---

[17] Ernst Cassirer, *The Philosophy of Symbolic Forms*, tr. Ralph Manheim (New Haven, 1953), I, 118.

[18] W. B. Yeats, *Mythologies* (London, 1962), p. 359.

[19] William Blake, *Complete Writings*, ed. Geoffrey Keynes, 1966 edition, p. 526.

[20] W. B. Yeats, *Uncollected Prose*, ed. John P. Frayne (London, 1970), I, 394.

truce with earth and time. The subtle language within a language corresponds to the self-delighting, self-appeasing gestures of the dancer, a sensuous metaphysic within the physical body. The emblem for this is Mallarmé's Hérodiade, gathering everything into the artifice of the dance, annihilating the world for the sake of her own image. To quote it in Symons' version, which Yeats recited and praised in "The Tragic Generation":

> And all about me lives but in mine own
> Image, the idolatrous mirror of my pride,
> Mirroring this Herodiade diamond-eyed.

Mallarmé's virgin is crucial in the mythology of Yeats's dance-plays and especially his Salomé-play, *A Full Moon in March*. Quoting Symons' translation, Yeats said, "Yet I am certain that there was something in myself compelling me to attempt creation of an art as separate from everything heterogeneous and casual, from all character and circumstance as some Herodiade of our theatre, dancing seemingly alone in her narrow moving luminous circle."[21] We have here an almost complete aesthetic for a Symbolist theatre: the dancer, like the mind, moves by her own sweet will, and in the climax of the play disengages her force from character and circumstance, the stage becomes a luminous circle answerable to the mind, and everything is transfigured in the dance. Yeats gave another version of this condition in *A Vision*, the perfection of subjectivity:

> The being has selected, moulded and remoulded, narrowed its circle of living, been more and more the artist, grown more and more "distinguished" in all preference. Now contemplation and desire, united into one, inhabit a world where every beloved image has bodily form, and every bodily form is loved.[22]

But Yeats has moved surreptitiously here from Mallarmé to Dante, remembering the "perfectly proportioned human body," and the admission of body and bodily motives qualifies the otherwise pure Symbolism of his theatre.

The qualification is extreme in *The Death of Cuchulain*. But for the moment it is enough if we recognize that Yeats's Symbolism, which owes much to Shelley, is turned toward the theatre by Mallarmé. Mallarmé's theatre is not Nietzsche's, and the Japanese *Noh* theatre differs from each, but for the moment Mallarmé is enough. The program outlined in "*Crise de vers*" established the procedures of Symbolism, so far as we need them in reading the early Yeats. Mallarmé is describing the modern motive, to retain nothing but suggestion, and he tells how this may be done:

---

[21] *Autobiographies*, p. 321.

[22] W. B. Yeats, *A Vision*, 2nd ed. corrected (London, 1962), pp. 135-36.

Instituer une relation entre les images exacte, et que s'en détache un tiers aspect fusible et clair présenté a la divination. (To institute an exact relation between the images, and let there stand out from it a third aspect, bright and easily absorbed, offered to divination.)[23]

In this context, the chief characteristic of a Symbolist poem is that the third aspect disables interpretation except insofar as the interpreter aspires to divination: since the images live by action rather than by knowledge, they refuse to be translated. This refusal gives them their esoteric aura, as of a secret life they live: they attract the attention of the interpreter while repelling any attempt he might make to explicate them. The poet's imagination establishes these images and the relation between them, then keeps its secret, casting out everything that is not itself. The process is described in the elegy "In Memory of Major Robert Gregory" as "our secret discipline / Wherein the gazing heart doubles her might." That is to say, the Symbolist sees not with the eye but with the mind's eye, narrowing the luminous circle for greater intensity. At a late stage in this process, the imagination is ready to transfigure the world in its own image. "Gazing" is therefore a technical term in Yeats because its visual force is internal and subjective. Yeats distinguishes between the gaze and the glance; the glance is objective, administrative, as when the eyes of a Civil Servant look upon a world to be controlled or possessed, a world in which subject and object are sharply distinguished, and names are attached, with undue confidence, to things: the gaze is internal and secret, as in Yeats's reference to "vague Grecian eyes gazing at nothing." To gaze is to set one's mind dancing in its own circle, until reverie passes into trance.

When we speak of Yeats as a Symbolist, then, we speak of him in association with Symons, Mallarmé, Shelley, Pater, and other writers for whom the mind, in its exemplary moment, hovers on the outer edge of consciousness, swaying to a rhythm which leads it toward the condition of trance. But Yeats retained a certain scruple and much misgiving even while he worked, by instinct or design, to an ostensibly Symbolist program. I think he was discontented with an aesthetic which had no hope of prolonging the reconciliation between symbol and time, consciousness and experience. He wanted the latitude of allegory, with the radiance of symbol; or that is a way of putting it. The symbol was valued for its depth, its ancient lore, its endlessness as if both above and below the finite condition. But it was not enough: one still had to live in the ordinary world among confusions of time and feeling. What Yeats sought was a dynamic relation between time and timelessness, and it is generally agreed that the majesty of such poems as "Sailing to Byzantium" and "Among School Children" depends upon the achievement of a just relation between those dimensions;

---

[23] Stéphane Mallarmé, *Oeuvres complètes*, tr. Anthony Hartley in his *Mallarmé* (Harmondsworth, 1965), p. 169.

between "the young in one another's arms" and the "artifice of eternity." The imagination mediates between the two worlds because it has the rights of a citizen in each: this is not strictly in the Symbolist program, but it is crucial in the enterprise of Yeats's art; he could not transcend the limitations of Symbolism until he had registered, with full commitment, the extent of the imagination's reach, its self-possession in both worlds. Still, the accommodation of time and eternity was not achieved in a day. I propose to say that there is a middle term between the Symbolist Yeats, at one extreme, and, at the other, the Yeats who made his art from the roughage of daily experience, chance, choice, and history. The middle term I propose is legend, which Yeats sometimes called myth, and we may think of it as situated between the unseen world of Symbolism and the indisputable world of fact and time.

The text we need for this middle term is a passage in *The Trembling of the Veil* where Yeats explains that he was not content with "an international art, picking stories and symbols where it pleased." "If Chaucer's personages," he says,

> had disengaged themselves from Chaucer's crowd, forgot their common goal and shrine, and after sundry magnifications became each in turn the centre of some Elizabethan play, and had after split into their elements and so given birth to romantic poetry, must I reverse the cinematograph? I thought that the general movement of literature must be such a reversal, men being there displayed in casual, temporary contact as at the Tabard door. I had lately read Tolstoy's *Anna Karenina* and thought that where his theoretical capacity had not awakened there was such a turning back: but a nation or an individual with great emotional intensity might follow the pilgrims, as it were, to some unknown shrine, and give to all those separated elements, and to all that abstract love and melancholy, a symbolical, a mythological coherence.

"Might I not," Yeats asks, "create some new *Prometheus Unbound*; Patrick or Columcille, Oisin or Finn, in Prometheus' stead; and, instead of Caucasus, Cro-Patrick or Ben Bulben? Have not all races had their first unity from a mythology that marries them to rock and hill?" Finally he says that "nations, races, and individual men are unified by an image, or bundle of related images, symbolical or evocative of the state of mind which is, of all states of mind not impossible, the most difficult to that man, race, or nation; because only the greatest obstacle that can be contemplated without despair rouses the will to full intensity."[24] I have quoted these sentences to show that before Yeats could incorporate in his art the rough worlds of O'Connell, Parnell, Kevin O'Higgins, "theatre business, management of men," he had to start at the beginning, with a sense of those images upon which mythological coherence is based, even if most of the images were only half-remembered if remembered at all. He could not go in a rush from the imaginary to the

---

[24] *Autobiographies*, pp. 193-94.

real; he needed a mediating term. The Celtic legends which he recited and dramatized were invoked to enforce an elaborate net of associations and fidelities corresponding to what Burke called "prejudice," the instinctual responses of a race; what Whitehead called "our vast system of inherited symbolism."

The trouble is that it is not vast enough, and that it is falling away. It is probably true that we can never have enough symbols if what we want in our lives is density and range of feeling. W. H. Auden has reflected upon the impoverishment of our symbols as one of the chief forms of our penury. So while it is easy to say that Yeats's recourse to Celtic legend as the matter of his early art was misguided, an indulgence of nostalgia and dream, since most of his audience had forgotten those legendary figures, if they had ever received them; still in such matters one never knows, there is no way of knowing for sure that a symbol is dead or that someone's spirit cannot be roused to a sense of what it shares with others by a passing cadence or a dimly remembered name. Yeats proposed to set before Irishmen not an international art but "an Irish literature which, though made by many minds, would seem the work of a single mind, and turn our places of beauty or legendary association into holy symbols."[25] In poems, plays, and stories, he put his circus animals on show: Conchubar, Cuchulain, Fergus, Caoilte, Oisin, the Fool and the Blind Man. Such figures were congenial to him for many reasons, congenial especially to his Symbolist affiliation, because their legends were suggestive but not overbearing. Legends present themselves for an interest largely intrinsic, but they do not claim to compel the reader, as fact and time compel him: they offer themselves to his feeling, but they do not make demands upon his belief; no one has ever felt himself intimidated by a legend, as he has felt himself intimidated by a fact. The stories which Yeats recited, partly received from Standish O'Grady and the nineteenth century translators, were therefore easy on his spirit, they let his mind dance while he attended to them, they did not browbeat him. They beguiled his mind as the lore of neo-Platonism and Swedenborg beguiled it, but they did not press hard upon it. In fact, the legends allowed him to apply them to his own poor case, so that when he wrote of Oisin "led by the nose through three enchanted islands," he wrote of himself and his own enslavement. In "The Circus Animals' Desertion" he confesses as much, saying of Oisin:

> But what cared I that set him on to ride,
> I, starved for the bosom of his faery bride?[26]

And in the next stanza the experience of writing *The Countess Cathleen* is intertwined with Yeats's longing for Maud Gonne, as he watched her

[25] Ibid., p. 254.

[26] W. B. Yeats, *Collected Poems* (London, 1952 reprint), p. 391.

tearing herself apart in fanaticism and hate. I am saying, then, that the legends which allowed Yeats's mind to move freely and suggestively along their margins allowed him also to find their analogies in his own life; they gave him a terminology which he was free to apply and, applying it, to move from legend into history, his own history but history nonetheless. In that sense, a mythology reflects not only its region, as Stevens said, but the experience of the mind that receives it.

This is consistent with the beliefs Yeats expressed when Magic was his theme. "I believe in three doctrines," he says, "(1) That the borders of our mind are ever shifting, and that many minds can flow into one another, as it were, and create or reveal a single mind, a single energy. (2) That the borders of our memories are as shifting, and that our memories are a part of one great memory, the memory of Nature herself. (3) That this great mind and great memory can be evoked by symbols."[27] Clearly, the great mind and the great memory are subjective equivalents of history; they are loyal to individual feeling as history is loyal to the calendar. So Edmund Wilson was right when he said in *Axel's Castle* that Yeats was intent upon discovering symbols which would stand for "the elements of his own nature" or which would seem to possess "some universal significance."[28] I would say *and* rather than *or*, because the symbols which appealed to Yeats were those which issued from a sense of his own experience and, after much wandering, flowed back into that experience. The difference between symbol and a fact is that the symbol is willing to be surrounded by an aura of personal feeling, different for each mind that contemplates it; the fact tries to insist that it be taken on its own severe terms, and remains impervious to any but the most fictive act of the mind that receives it. There is a famous passage in Pater's *Studies in the History of the Renaissance* which appears to tell against this distinction, where he says that external objects dissolve in our reflexion and analysis until they become nothing more than "impressions unstable, flickering, inconsistent, which burn and are extinguished with our consciousness of them."[29] But even if this were true, it would require the force of reflexion and analysis, the gem-like flame, to make those sensations possible, and the external objects would resist that flame, waiting for it to die. But symbols do not resist the mind, they are willing to be dispersed and re-formed, they are hospitable to our feeling, they know that they have had many lives and are not yet exhausted, they die only when there is no longer a personal feeling to receive them. This explains why Yeats hoped, as he said, to find everything in the symbol. I think he hoped also to lose himself there, committing his feelings to

---

[27] *Essays and Introductions*, p. 28.

[28] Edmund Wilson, *Axel's Castle* (New York, 1936), p. 48.

[29] Walter Pater, *Studies in the History of the Renaissance* (New York, 1919), p. 194.

their verbal fate. He was willing to live in a state of becoming, but only that he might, in the poem, achieve his being, his perfection.

I have quoted from "The Circus Animals' Desertion" and will do so again, because it is the poem in which Yeats confesses to a vulnerable relation between symbol and his own experience. We are to suppose that he begins with his own feeling—where else could be begin?—and that he sought to resolve its conflicts by recourse to some of the classic legends of Irish mythology; and in doing so he devised certain "masterful images" which, he says, "grew in pure mind." Their origin makes little difference, he comes back to that question in the last stanza. But before reaching that point he confesses that he was enchanted by the dream itself. I assume that the dream means desire, so far as it has established itself in the symbolic world to which it aspires. Or perhaps it means that desire has been transformed, given permanence and inexhaustibility, in the form of art:

> And when the Fool and Blind Man stole the bread
> Cuchulain fought the ungovernable sea;
> Heart-mysteries there, and yet when all is said
> It was the dream itself enchanted me:
> Character isolated by a deed
> To engross the present and dominate memory.
> Players and painted stage took all my love,
> And not those things that they were emblems of.[30]

We need not take this as final. I associate it with the "secret discipline" of "In Memory of Major Robert Gregory" where the gazing heart doubles her might by bringing to bear upon her experience such concentration, purely internal, that the external object is indeed virtually dissolved, and feeling is exhilarated by a sense of its own power.

It is well-known that this indulgence is a scandal to writers of a different persuasion; it is the character of Symbolism which even now constitutes an outrage, especially for writers who feel that life is tolerable only if we live, with whatever difficulty, among facts deemed indissoluble. This is what Ezra Pound had in view in Canto 83 when he asserted against Baudelaire and Yeats that Paradise is not artificial, that Baudelaire's hymn to the hieroglyphics of dream and symbol is perverse. If Paradise exists, Pound appears to say, it exists in fragments of fact, such as excellent sausage, the smell of mint, and Ladro the night cat. Pound would not deny that it exists in our sense of these facts, but he would insist that the facts come first and stay indisputable to the end. And then he teases Yeats:

> and Uncle William dawdling around Notre Dame
> in search of whatever
>   paused to admire the symbol
> with Notre Dame standing inside it[31]

---

[30] *Collected Poems*, p. 392.

[31] Ezra Pound, *The Cantos* (London, 1954), p. 563.

The point is well taken, so far as it smiles upon Yeats's tendency to dissolve the external object in favour of his Symbolist imagination, the enchanting dream: "in search of whatever," since this effect is possible only by vacancy, gazing, taking one's eye off the object. Pound is asserting that the given world, such as it appears even to common imaginations, is more durable than the artificial bronzes of Symbolism: it stands forth in its own right, bodied against the golden bird and the hieroglyphic dream of "Byzantium." Pound's position is clear; we should lay aside our dreaming and try to make sense, preferably historical sense, of the given world; we should put our house in order, rather than replace it by a castle in the Symbolist air. Perhaps this explains why Pound, hostile to Symbolism because of its collusion with subjectivity, endorsed in its stead Imagism, grateful for its ostensible objectivity: the image is newly invented, while the symbol, being old, is too tired to resist. The image, in Imagism, represents the poet's self-denial, his refusal of ancestral resonance: the image is hard, the symbol soft. This is substantially the critique which D. H. Lawrence, too, directed upon Yeats. "We are such egoistic fools," he wrote. "We see only the *symbol* as a *subjective expression*: as an expression of ourselves. That makes us so sickly when we deal with the old symbols: like Yeats."[32] Lawrence's position is given even more specifically near the end of *Women in Love*, when Ursula intervenes in the obnoxious discussion of art between Gudrun and the sculptor Loerke, denouncing their assumption that the world of art is independent of the real world. "The world of art is only the truth about the real world, that's all—but you are too far gone to see it."[33] The same aesthetic is implicit in the Lincoln Cathedral chapter of *The Rainbow*; that the Cathedral, however intensely it is seen and registered, is not to be dissolved into a sequence of impressions, or treated as a mere expression of ourselves. Cathedrals which have weathered so much ought to be able to withstand Walter Pater's attention. Stephen Dedalus knew as much, reading the "signatures of all things." "Then he was aware of them bodies before of them coloured. How? By knocking his sconce against them. . . . Open your eyes now. I will. One moment. Has all vanished since? . . . See now. There all the time without you: and ever shall be, world without end."[34] Finally, I quote a few lines from Charles Tomlinson's sequence "Antecedents," his meditation upon the joys and sorrows of Symbolism:

> The white mind holds
> An insufficiency, a style
> To contain a solitude
> And nothing more.[35]

[32] D. H. Lawrence, *Collected Letters*, ed. Harry T. Moore (London, 1962), I, 302.

[33] D. H. Lawrence, *Women in Love* (Harmondsworth, 1960), p. 485.

[34] James Joyce, *Ulysses* (London, 1947 reprint), p. 34.

[35] Charles Tomlinson, *Seeing is Believing* (New York, 1958), p. 49.

I quote these diverse passages to register variant readings of experience, in one degree or another hostile to Yeats's reading, so far as that latter reading may be described as Symbolist. Hostility to Symbolism often takes a benign form, regret that it could not succeed, reality being there all the time without you, waiting for you to tire of your excess. To Tomlinson and other poets, Symbolism in its French forms was a *cul de sac*, and the only way out was back. It is a familiar argument. But it would be wrong to present Yeats as if he were Mallarmé's pupil in all things, or merely a more robust Symons. Very few of Yeats's poems are written from a purely Symbolist mind, that mind which sets consciousness to devour the world, filling the void with itself. There are very few poems, I mean, in which Yeats is willing to let mere life die so that consciousness may reincarnate itself in the poems. We come back to his double motive: on the one hand, to give consciousness every privilege; on the other, to respect every value in life which is not attributable to consciousness. The Symbolist cannot forever escape the fear that life for him is a tautological circle, that the seer merely sees himself in everything he sees, that everything dissolves in the flow of his consciousness. The true Symbolist is content with that, but Yeats is not. There are moments in which he is satisfied with whatever the subjective will chooses to do, however destructive the result; but there are other moments in which he is satisfied with nothing short of the truth, even if it asserts itself as independent of his will. These rival allegiances are brought into a dynamic relation by the theatrical force of his imagination, its delight in conflict for the energy it creates, and there is good reason to think his poetry was saved by that pleasure.

Against symbol, therefore, we should place history, meaning by this ambiguous term, for the moment, whatever the imagination recognizes as distinct from itself and finally indissoluble. History in that old-fashioned sense means not only the past as more or less successfully resisting our sense of it, but the usual, whatever comes from the chance of things and not from the imagination's choice; in "A Dialogue of Self and Soul" Yeats calls it simply "life," and the rhetoric of that poem favours it, at the end. It may be thought that at this stage he has reneged on Symbolism entirely, forgotten his French. In 1937 he wrote to Dorothy Wellesley of these matters, saying of Mallarmé that he "escapes from history," while "you and I are in history," though he means "the history of the mind." Roger Fry's translation of Mallarmé, Yeats said, "shows me the road I and others of my time went for certain furlongs. . . . It is not the road I go now, but one of the legitimate roads."[36] But even this is not the whole story. Yeats was never willing to allow history to press upon him as a dead weight: his mind would wrestle with fact, as the dialogues and plays show, but only with live

---

[36] W. B. Yeats, *Letters on Poetry from W. B. Yeats to Dorothy Wellesley* (London, 1940), p. 135. Letter of 4 May 1937.

fact, still open to change and greater life. In his Diary of 1930 he says that "History is necessity until it takes fire in someone's head and becomes freedom or virtue."[37] This seems the right note on which to leave the question; nothing of the poet's old allegiance is disavowed, but old motives are incorporated in a stronger aesthetic, animated by the idiom of conflict and theatre. Yeats is attending to time, "the cracked tune that Chronos sings," as well as to the ethereal music of consciousness.

[37] W. B. Yeats, *Explorations* (London, 1962), p. 336.

THE POETRY OF CONFRONTATION: YEATS AND THE DIALOGUE POEM

Balachandra Rajan

The dialogue poem is a form that deserves exploration, and since there is no body of theorizing about the form we can only learn what its resources are by contemplating its products as themselves. Yeats's interest in dialogue poetry was obstinate and in the end, distinctive. Fourteen such dialogues appear in the version of the *Collected Poems* with which most of us are familiar, and to these we might add "The Fool by the Roadside." In its first printing, in the first and revised editions of *The Tower*, and in the definitive edition of 1949, the twelve line text that we know is preceded by seventeen lines of dialogue between a "Girl" and "Cuchulain" or "The Hero."[1]

Not all of Yeats's dialogue poems deserve to live, but his highest work in the form instructs us in what the form is capable of exploring and also tells us something about the substance and quality of his other poems. The earlier attempts are what we might expect of the form, before the deeper power of creativeness has touched it; in other words they are the work of a suppressed or embryonic dramatist. "Time and the Witch Vivien" with eighteen stage directions interrupting sixty-nine lines of text, is in fact described as Yeats's "first play" written for Laura Armstrong, who is thought of as a "myth and a symbol," waking the author from "the metallic sleep of science."[2] The language is that of 1889. It is a later Yeats who describes "Anashuya and Vijaya" as "meant to be the first scene of a play about a man loved by two women, who had

---

[1] *The Variorum Edition of the Poems of W. B. Yeats*, ed. Peter Allt and Russell K. Alspach (New York, 1957), pp. 447-49.

[2] *The Letters of W. B. Yeats*, ed. Allan Wade (New York, 1955), pp. 117-18.

the one soul between them, the one woman waking when the other slept." The note proceeds characteristically, to hammer Yeats's work into unity. "I am now once more in *A Vision* busy with that thought, the antitheses of day and of night and of moon and of sun."[3] The poem would be more of an accomplishment if something in it succeeded in teaching out to this awareness of man divided in the depths of his being. We are conscious rather of a slight misunderstanding between a petulant priestess and an absent-minded suitor. Even the borrowing of a notorious image from Milton's "Nativity Ode" fails to lift the poem into the higher mood.[4]

Steady attention is needed to perceive that "The Wanderings of Usheen" is actually a dialogue poem, since St. Patrick has less than twenty-one lines of routine remonstrance in 891 lines of text. But Yeats saw the poem as establishing an opposition which was to continue creatively to the end of his life. "The swordsman throughout repudiates the saint but not without vacillation. Is that perhaps the sole theme—Usheen and Patrick?"[5] Repudiation is a key word, for Yeats does not write a poetry of synthesis. He writes instead a poetry in which the energy of rejection is shaped to some degree by what it rejects. Given the final stance, it is necessary that the swordsman should also be the dreamer, that the hero should also be the poet, that the life-choice should be a clear-eyed, yet compulsive preference for a road that leads to tragedy rather than comedy. These recognitions are in Usheen's mind but a considerable distance must be travelled before St. Patrick turns into Von Hugel. Until that happens we cannot have a dialogue. It is not clear that we even have an exchange of views.

Yeats's next volume, as we know, is symbolically symmetrical, with both the opening and closing poems looking out in opposite directions from that precarious middle ground between the rose and the world which is one day to become the dolphin-torn sea of Byzantium.[6] Fergus and the Druid meet similarly in a common area of disappointment. A crown is dreamed of by those who do not possess it, but if the dream of the crown is empty, so too is the dream beyond the crown. To be something is to fail to be something else and to pass through everything is to dwindle to nothing. The shape of the *oeuvre* enables us to discern how the protean Druid looks forward to Mohini Chatterjee and how weariness can transform itself into the contrary gyre of lust for life. Time is not "burnt" but is

---

[3] *Collected Poems* (London, 1960), pp. 523-24.

[4] "Anashuya and Vijaya," *Collected Poems*, pp. 24-25; "On the Morning of Christ's Nativity," *The Complete English Poetry of John Milton*, ed. John T. Shawcross (New York, 1963), p. 40.

[5] *Letters*, p. 798.

[6] Balachandra Rajan, *W. B. Yeats: A Critical Introduction* (London, 1969), pp. 28-29.

"bundled" and "thundered" away.[7] Marvell, we may remember, called on his coy mistress to "devour" time, reversing the traditional image which begins Shakespeare's nineteenth sonnet. This is not Yeats's only point of contact with Marvell but at this stage the resonances of Yeats's poem are needed only to tell us that basic oppositions are being adumbrated. "Adumbrated" rather than "penetrated" is the right word, and ironically it is the pseudo-dramatic incitements of the dialogue, the rudimentary needs for characterization and a "story," which obscure attainment of the real drama of self-discovery.

Yeats's desire to dine "With Landor and with Donne"[8] is intriguing and there can be no doubt that he would have relished the imaginary conversation between them. But Landor also wrote several dialogue poems of the type which Yeats was to supersede in himself. Donne wrote no dialogues, but what Helen Gardner deprecates as the histrionic note in the Holy Sonnets[9] may well have appealed to a man who was beginning to recognize that reality cannot be known but only experienced, and that it is perhaps most adequately experienced as "theatre." By the time the imaginary dinner ended Yeats, as Mohini Chatterjee, could have assured his guests that, in a certain sense, he had succeeded in becoming both of them.

Yeats wrote no dialogue poems between *Crossways* and *The Wild Swans at Coole*. When he took up the form again the theoretical basis had been laid for the poetry of confrontation which the form now strikes us as designed to embody. Theory can precede practice in the writing of Yeats's poetry—*A Vision* looms as the unavoidable example—and the progression is not necessarily as dangerous as horror of the abstract can make it seem. Often the theorizing gathers together what has been insufficiently possessed, providing the encouragement and the proof of coherence for a decisive advance into the precision of passion. Behind *The Wild Swans* there lies the doctrine of the mask, a doctrine which is not so much the sanction for a poetry of posing, as a recognition that the style of the mind is creative of its life. But to know itself the mind must defend itself, and to discover itself fully through its defence it must find that true enemy which is ultimately its ally. "We make out of the quarrel with others, rhetoric, but of the quarrel with ourselves, poetry" is a thought which Yeats took from his father. It is more than a louder version of Mills's remark that rhetoric is heard but poetry overheard. Much turns upon the quality of the quarrel and if "the poet finds and makes his mask in

---

[7] *Collected Poems*, pp. 62, 75, 140, 280.

[8] Ibid., p. 157.

[9] John Donne, *The Divine Poems*, ed. Helen Gardner (Oxford, 1952), pp. xxx-xxxi.

disappointment"[10] the disappointment must be capable of bearing the weight, the momentum, and the mockery of poetry. By 1919 Yeats had made his mistakes and it was not simply with his mistake in love that he quarrelled. In turning on himself he found himself.

"Ego Dominus Tuus" was written two years before "Tradition and the Individual Talent," and the two works form an intriguing juxtaposition if we are not asked to decide which one is right. As might be expected from the context which led up to it, Yeats's poem is an aesthetic dialogue with existential overtones. Precedents are not lacking. We think of Suckling's dialogue with Carew and of the more elaborate exchange between Crashaw and Cowley, but to make the comparisons is only to register the extent of Yeats's advance. "Conoisseur of Chaos" is a better companion piece, and Yeats and Stevens join in awareness of a physical world in which the supreme fictions of poetry find their substantiation. It is Yeats, however, who is the more biting in the self-born mockery of his enterprise and in the capacity of the poem to live through and be strengthened by that mockery.

A dialogue between principles can be designed to end in an ironic stalemate, but Yeats does not seek the symmetry of what might be called a balanced understanding. *Ille* clearly has the honours, and the tone of *Hic*'s "A style is formed by sedentary toil / And the imitation of great masters" is close to an admission of defeat. Yet *Ille* does not so much defeat as reanimate in a new context the propositions for which his adversary stands. The road from the self leads back into the self. The man who seeks an image not a book is destined to find both a book and a series of images. The "mysterious one" who walks the wet sands by the edge of the stream (and whose brother probably wears grey Connemara cloth)[11] is both one's double and one's anti-self. Impulsive men, according to *Hic*, look for happiness, and sing spontaneously when they have found it. But wise men who, according to *Ille*, own nothing but their blind stupefied hearts, also sing "luxuriantly" out of the tragic war with themselves. The deserted tower will be occupied two poems later. The characters traced upon the sand prefigure the sacred book of the system and the coming into being of characters that will remain "When all is ruin once again." Sedentary toil will be recovered as "blear-eyed wisdom."[12] The self-conquest of a writer, which is style, will involve the imitation of great masters, not so much in externals, as in their way of knowing reality. We could go on but the evidence is sufficient to outline a strategy which is not limited to this particular poem. Without compromising the adequacy and fullness of the

[10] "Per Amica Silentia Lunae," *Mythologies* (London, 1959), pp. 331, 337.

[11] *Collected Poems*, pp. 166, 183, 222.

[12] Ibid., pp. 214, 245.

dialogue, it helps to make possible a poetry of commitment rather than one of ironic equilibrium.

If "Ego Dominus Tuus" is about the making of the poem, "The Phases of the Moon" is about the making of the soul. The two poems, taken together, put it to us that the dialogue form is well-suited to esoteric discussion. Two men in the know expound the system and contemplate with amusement the ignorance of a third man who actually knows more than both of them put together. The mysterious ones are not at the edge of the stream but on a bridge which can be taken as joining the worlds of *Hic* and *Ille*. The poet, in a nicely judged reminiscence, has now assumed *Hic*'s posture and is seeking "mysterious wisdom" won by toil. Much of the effect of "The Phases of the Moon" turns not on the exposition itself (which does not lack its moments of eloquence), but on the dramatic contrivance which makes the poet a citizen of his world as well as the creator of the world in which he is a citizen. Living within a myth is one way of assuring us that the myth has been authentically made.

A form acquires a patina when it can be shown to have a classical origin. The dialogue-poem can fortunately be traced back to the pastoral, and particularly to its convention of the singing match. MacNeice uses the Eclogue for social comment and in his "Eclogue for Christmas," A and B representing town and country, and differentiated accordingly in the timbre of their voices, harmonize with each other in concern and in self-consolation. In "Shepherd and Goatherd," Yeats avoids commenting on the state of the nation and even avoids those comments on land reform which Vergil sanctions[13] and which the situation in Ireland might seem to invite. His two speakers inhabit the valley of the natural life and the barren ridges of a higher but more desolate understanding. One speaks of a man who excelled in skill and courtesy but who knew himself to be a bird of passage and left no memorial of himself in his brief sojourn. The other sings of a man who made music out of loneliness and of a life "dreamed back" so that knowledge unwinds into a higher ignorance. Without being too fanciful it can be said that the shepherd's interventions extend the mood of "In Memory of Major Robert Gregory," and that the Goatherd's bleaker understanding has affinities with that clear, cold light in which the Irish airman foresees his death. The three poems must be taken together in their responses and we must ask ourselves what a man's death means to his friends, what it means to the man, and what it means apart from the friends and the man. The fullness of the design can only be respected, and we can now see how the distancing effect of the pastoral convention is meant to contribute to the final objectivity. If the

---

[13] See the Ninth Eclogue.

result is not entirely convincing it is only because not all of us can accept *A Vision* as final.

Yeats's next volume includes two poems in the dialogue style. "Michael Robartes and the Dancer" is dominated by Robartes' guidance on the thinking of the body to a dancer who has not gone to the right school and is unprepared to play Sheba to his Solomon. The dragon of the abstract is destroyed when a woman accepts the reality in her looking glass. Athene who took Achilles by the hair is now to be given similar treatment. Sinew can rule by supernatural right without ceasing to be sinew. Blest souls are not composite, the union of love promises uncomposite blessedness and unity of beauty leads to unity of being. But to achieve perfection a woman must exclude the irrelevance of what the body is unable to think. There is a point in having Robartes deliver this lecture which gives the poem more than gaiety and makes it more than a masculine declaration that a woman's place is in front of her dressing table. But what is involved (and no more is pretended) is a piquancy rather than a major accomplishment. "An Image from a Past Life" is more compelling partly because of the extraordinarily evocative stanza form, in which the four outer lines, linked as a quatrain, enclose three central lines rhyming with each other, that can be thought of as floating into the stanza, with the gradual lengthening of the lines settling them down into the stanza frame. We have both propriety and disturbance, and to create this sense is part of the poem's larger effort. Yeats's extremely long note on the poem in the 1921 edition[14] does not quite dissipate this effect, but it was the better part of wisdom to omit it. There is a necessary uncertainty about what is seen, and "Overshadower, or Ideal Form, whichever it is" unduly confines the possibilities.

In "The Hero, The Girl and the Fool" (known to us as "The Fool by the Roadside") the sum of frustration is made by the unlikely elements of strength and beauty. Michael Robartes' advice to concentrate on what the body can think and the looking glass reflect is now seen as a betrayal. A woman is loved not for herself, but for her image in the mirror, and a man for his image in the glass of heroic action. A nunnery can dispose of the looking glass but a woman is then reverenced for her holiness and not for herself. Only God can love us as we are, yet what we are can only find its fulfillment in the frustration of love by another person. The Fool adds that when the dreaming back is over, when the thread wound on the bobbin of life has been unwound, and when that life has been dissolved because its content is understood, the disembodied self may find a faithful love. The road by which the Fool stands is, of course, the thread of life, and the Fool himself, as *A*

---

[14] *Variorum Poems*, pp. 821-23.

Vision tells us, brings us escape from the wheel.[15] But fidelity to insubstantiality is scarcely a solution that recommends itself. On the other hand, to be alive is also to be betrayed. The issues raised are certainly meaningful, though some sense of the Yeatsian infrastructure is called for if the meaningfulness is to be released into the poem. Yeats's reasons for omitting the first seventeen lines are not clear since they provide at least some of the activation that is necessary. Moreover, their absence leaves *The Tower* without a poem in the dialogue form.

A further consequence of the longer version is that the commitment to the world at the end of the bobbin is even more tentative than it would otherwise be. It is not that life is presented as worth living —there is simply no alternative that is self-evidently worth more. This embittered understanding keeps its connection with the fury and the mire of human veins, that gong-tormented sea in which the dialogue poems so often find their anchorage. Whether it is the emptiness of a bag of dreams, the thinking of the body, or the creation of poetry from tragic war in the self, the dialogues bear witness not so much to the triumph of life, as to its inescapable givenness. Even in "The Phases of the Moon" the wheel turns, the light goes out, and the bats that haunt the last phase of the moon rise from the hazels where Cuchulain sought the magic waters, not to deliver the man in the tower from time, but to enable him to write the poetry which is time's monument. "Men dance on deathless feet" and the dance at any moment includes both elation in what it achieves and frustration in what it omits. "All could be known or shown / If Time were but gone." Being haunts becoming, yet achieves substantiality only in the haunting. "And, ever pacing on the verge of things, / The phantom, Beauty, in a mist of tears" is Yeats's rather mannered way of putting it in his first dialogue.[16] The latter poems, even when they are not saying quite the same thing, are persistently reconnoitering the same area.

"A Dialogue of Self and Soul," therefore, stands in a personal tradition. It is Yeats's highest achievement in a form the resources of which he himself had worked out and deepened. The philosophy behind it (and we speak of more than *A Vision*) has been hammered into unity by the years of his life. The ingredients of debate are his home and his possessions. The contending principles are the forces in his own mind drawn up for the warfare that is the ground of creativeness.

Beyond the personal context, lie the literary precedents. Marvell's two dialogues are an obvious affiliation, and behind Marvell in turn, is Jacopone da Todi's *Dialogue of the Body with the Soul, leading it*

---

[15] See also *Collected Poems*, p. 188.

[16] *Collected Poems*, pp. 280, 292, 12.

to the Last Judgment. Herbert Read's dialogue, in *The End of a War*, between the body and soul of a murdered girl is a poem that may have been influenced by Yeats's practice. While Marvell is certainly instructive in telling us how to read Yeats, his poems are less "embattled" than Yeats's "Dialogue." The word used is taken not from Yeats, but surprisingly, from Ben Jonson.[17] Perhaps it is Milton rather than Marvell who looks forward most strongly to Yeats in his sense of man as a battleground and in those crises of confrontation which lie at the heart of each of his major poems. One consequence of "embattlement," of warfare raised beyond a certain intensity, is to rule out the possibility of an ironic truce. Yeats, as much as Milton, involves us in a poetry of commitment.

"A Dialogue of Self and Soul" is carefully designed, both in the expectation of symmetry which it sets up and in the manner in which it breaks through that expectation. The combatants address each other almost ritualistically in heavily-cadenced double quatrains. Even if the positions are opposed, the rhythms of declamation are strikingly similar, keeping us aware that both self and soul are factions in a war within the whole man, and that the objective of that warfare is not division but a recreation of the sense of wholeness. Because of this, the repetitions do more than simply present us with the left and right sides of a common entity. *Soul*, for example, repeats the word "upon" five times in his first statement, suggesting, as it were, the pivot and the still center. *Self* responds by repeating the word "still" four times, suggesting in the repetition not the state beyond motion, but the prolongation of motion, time and life. *Soul*'s repetition of the word "thought" in lines 6 and 7 of his intervention is countered by *Self*'s interweaving (also in lines 6 and 7) of "round," "bound," and "wound." Fixity and sinuosity, the tower and the stair, are immediately suggested, but we surely should not forget that both structures are part of the same building. They lead us upwards into the night of being but in another form they are also the sword and its winding, emblematic of the day as well as of the darkness. The looking-glass of the blade is the mirror of art and of reality, and the blade itself the cutting edge of action. "Unspotted by the centuries" it can be thought of as potentially timeless. Yet is is the embodiment of tradition and human time, fashioned by the third scion of a family, with five hundred years of history about it and with the flowers of an unknown embroiderer joining art, nature and passion in their workmanship. The winding stair, we are now reminded, is significantly "ancient." In another poem it is the stairway of tradition. It ascends into a night which is "ancestral," promising both escape and generation.

---

[17] "De Malignatate Studentium," *Timber or Discoveries made Upon Men and Matter*.

Enough has been said to indicate how the interplay of rhetoric in the dialogue undercuts the declamatory statements. So far, the insinuations are typically Marvellian, with each position not only defined by reference to the other, but stating itself partially in the other's language. Above the crosscurrents, the symmetries of debate maintain themselves, with equal rights carefully given to both parties. Thus, after *Soul's* third intervention we have every reason to expect a third response by *Self* in double quatrains. Instead, we have four double quatrains presented in a separate section of the poem, making it clear that what is taking place is a commitment and not a counterstatement. As a commitment it must be conceded to be singular, since three-fourths of *Self's* intervention is devoted to a vehement and embittered appraisal of the very principle to which commitment is made.

To those who have looked behind the set exchanges, the rage of affirmation will not be wholly surprising. When *Soul* refers to the crime of death and birth *Self* does not, as we might expect him to do, pounce on the exaggeration. Instead, he demands a "charter to commit the crime once more." It is not a debate we are looking at but rather a confrontation in which the intensified statement calls forth an intensified response. Behind the movement is a familiar Yeatsian paradox: if hatred of God can bring the soul to God, the same can presumably be said of hatred of life. But behind the movement there is also a familiar Yeatsian strategy. It is to accept the situation at its worst and to drive the affirmation through by the sheer force of poetry against a resistance that is deliberately maximized.

The sheer force of poetry is a phrase that once would have brought reproachful glances from higher critical circles. It is partly thanks to Yeats that we are able to use the phrase without shame. Nevertheless, vehemence can be uncomfortably close to a boundary on the other side of which lies rant. The second part of the "Dialogue" is not usually accused of ranting—frustration is accepted as alive in the movement and language—but the conclusion is sometimes regarded as a mere declaration, thrown in against the tide of the evidence. "What matter" and "I am content," even if repeated, cannot achieve the transition from bitterness to blessedness.

To grasp *Self's* intervention and its climax adequately, we must realize that the poetry of confrontation cannot admit a negotiated compromise. One of the principles must prevail and prevail by taking over the poem in its name. But the prevailing principle ought to be able to find itself in combat and to proclaim itself more fully and inclusively because of the challenge that is made to its being. Instead of whittling down the opposition's arguments it should annex them to the laws of its own life. The alternative can only lead to statements and counterstatements of mounting stridency, declaimed from positions that are progressively sealed off from each other. It is in order to take over rather than meet his opponent's strictures that *Self*, in bearing witness to the anguish of life, goes far beyond anything that *Soul* has said or implied. In doing so, he puts before us a familiar Yeatsian awareness—the inextricable entanglement of man's humiliation with his dignity. Because this entanglement is part of the texture of life it is *Self*'s privilege to speak of a wholeness from which *Soul*, in its nature, can only stand aloof.

Self's statement is woven upon repetitions, but the cadences are now those of impassioned speech rather than significant gesture and the repetitions are no longer the anvil for the hammer of polemic. The movement from "boyhood" through "unfinished man" to "finished man" gives substance to "the toil of growing up," superseding each stage of frustration by another that is more fully evolved and therefore all the more difficult to escape from. The climax is the finished man (the pun is surely intentional) besieged by his enemies and imprisoned in a "shape" which is not what he was made for but what he will inexorably be made into. Repetition joins alliteration here, so that the walls of the imprisonment seem to reflect into each other. Sato's sword can be more than one kind of mirror.

Escape scarcely seems possible, and even if it is possible it serves no purpose if a man's honour calls on him to stand and suffer in the "wintry blast." The impure ditches have become the fecund ditches, with misdirected love as the worst fecundity. The blind batter the blind in spawning energy. For over thirty lines the vehement bitterness has surged forward, building up a momentum that seems almost impossible to reverse. Yet in eight more lines we are brought to the conclusion that "Everything we look upon is blest." The transformation is startling enough to lead to the suspicion that no transformation has taken place at all. The Old Master, we are advised, has simply unnerved us with yet another of his conjuring tricks.

Shouting into the wind is one of Yeats's more constructive occupations. Defiance replies to mockery, and the emotional exchange is thought of (and felt through) as part of the health of the whole man. The heroic cry in the midst of despair and the cry that mocks Plotinus's thought are not answers but refusals—the refusal to lie down and die when we are called on to do so by the cold consistency of circumstance. The final lines of the "Dialogue" are this, but more than this. Under the apparently simple statement—the transparency of awareness that could come at the end of the struggle for understanding—*Soul*'s propositions are being comprehensively taken over. If darkness is the condition of the *Soul*, blindness is the condition of the *Self*. If the former refers everything to Pound's "unwobbling pivot," the "hidden pole" that coordinates understanding, the latter follows all action and thought to its source. In *Soul*'s world, imagination scorns the earth and intellect ceases its wandering. In *Self*'s world, it is "remorse" that is cast out. "Only the dead can be forgiven," *Soul* declares. *Self*'s reply is that he can "measure the lot" and forgive himself the lot. A living man may be blind but we are also rendered blind in the presence of infinity. In "that quarter where all thought is done" the fullness of the ultimate overflows into the basin of the mind. In the world below, "Sweetness" flows into the breasts of the living. Finally, those who are taken into infinity have to be "stricken deaf and dumb and blind." In the ditches below, those who have cast out remorse are able to laugh and sing and to discover something of that happiness that is only made possible by the impurity of passion.

A creative mind is marked by certain distinctive habits, and what unifies the work is the style of the mind. It is entirely to be expected that *Self* should deal with *Soul* as *Ille* deals with *Hic*. The strategy is the same. What differs and by differing marks the extent of progress, is the depth and intensity of the dramatic engagement. As we proceed from the making of poetry to the finished man rejoicing in the midst of tragedy, we see both a style discovering itself and a form opening out and offering its resources to the style.

In "Ego Dominus Tuus," *Hic* who sought the self, was taken over by *Ille* who found the self in the poetic image. In the "Dialogue," the expanded *Self* confronted the *Soul* and was able to find in involvement, with its bitterness and happiness, much of what *Soul* offered in the name of deliverance. In "Vacillation," the antagonists are Soul and Heart—the heart where the holy tree grows, the heart of "heart's purple," the "aching heart" in which a work of art is conceived, and the "blind stupefied" heart which is the only possession of the truly wise.[18] The battlefield has been narrowed, partly because the issues have already been fought over and partly, perhaps, because Crazy Jane is round the corner waiting to play *Heart* in her fashion, to the Bishop's version of *Soul*.

The thrust and parry of stichomythia are right for this late stage in the interior confrontation when positions can be taken as if in a ballet. Six lines of riddling exchanges put to work a remarkable number of contraries—reality versus appearance, simplicity versus complexity, fire versus earth, salvation versus immersion, the sage against the singer. But to state the polarizations is also to subvert them—the poet deals with reality as well as with appearance, Isaiah's coal has been used as a symbol of poetic inspiration and salvation can only be achieved when sin is recognized. The meaning of song is that all things pass away, but the singer must celebrate the complexity of the passing rather than resign himself to the simplicity beyond. When he does so, the holy fire of eternity turns into the gold mosaic of art. The tree in the heart is at the same time night and day, blood and the moon, purgation

---

[18] *Collected Poems*, pp. 54, 266, 228, 182.

and generation, the fury's clear-eyed destructiveness and the leaf blind
in the lushness of its hunger for life. With Attis's image hung between
these extremeties, it is no wonder that Von Hugel should be dismissed
with blessings on his head and that the *Heart*, pleading predestination
and invoking Samson's riddle, should find both theology and scripture
to its purpose.

The end of the dialogue's progress is the monologue. As the
turmoil of warfare in the mind subsides, we hear the sound of silence
and realize that silence is the last antagonist. One third of the poems in
"Last Poems" have refrains, and the refrain in many cases provides the
static rejoinder around which the poem circles, seeking to read its
meaning or its menace. There is one formal dialogue in the "Last
Poems," and, significantly, it is between Man and his Echo. We can ask
what the answers are and what the meaning will be. A bodkin brings no
release, but will the end be more significant than the end that a bodkin
makes? The cleft looms and all that we hear in response are the
decaying cadences of ourselves. The "Dialogue" inches up to the fron-
tier and is distracted touchingly, by the cry of a rabbit, from a line which
poetry cannot avoid but also cannot pass.

It is academic, but at this point not entirely useless, to say that
Yeats's achievement in the dialogue form is singular and rewarding.
More pertinent is the question of how the dramatic imagination makes
use of the form within the lyric theatre. It does not achieve drama by
the mimicry of drama or by the kind of debate which is the problem
play writ smaller. Rather, it achieves it by discovering the style of the
mind through the fundamental antagonisms which give the mind its
character. As early as 1901 Yeats knew that "among the kingdoms of
poetry" there was "no battle that does not give life instead of death."[19]
It is in the dialogue poems that the creative battles are most explicitly
joined.

---

[19] *Variorum Poems*, p. 847.

YEATS AS AN AUTOBIOGRAPHICAL POET

Joseph Ronsley

All poetry is autobiographical one way or another: poets express feelings and thoughts arising out of their experience, and often allude more tangibly to their lives. Recognizable allusion to tangible personal experience is, in fact, commonplace in twentieth-century poetry, even well before what M. L. Rosenthal has called the "confessional" manner came into prominence. The autobiographical element in the work of Frost, Pound, and Auden, for instance, is readily apparent. More striking is the pattern of T. S. Eliot's developing autobiographical mode, reflected partly in the contrast of the youthful poet hiding diffidently behind Prufrock, with the later personal directness of *Four Quartets*. This contrast actually suggests a similarity with Yeats's development, from Oisin—Yeats's own Prufrock as it were—to the unabashed personal presence in the volumes beginning with *The Tower*. And Eliot himself has remarked the "triumph" of Yeats's first "naming of his age" after "more than half a lifetime" in the prologue to *Responsibilities*.[1] Dylan Thomas, too, celebrated his birthdays poetically as a means toward reflection on the human condition, made his familiar Welsh landscape prominent in his poems both as atmosphere and symbol, and explored the universal implications of his relationships with members of his family. Yet the autobiographical element in the poems of both Eliot and Thomas, each displaying quite clearly as it does a personal, spiritual growth, is overall more generalized than that in the poems of Yeats, where there is a special danger for the student, and for the teacher for that matter, in the temptation to reduce the poetic experience by using the poems for the purpose of illuminating

---

[1] "Yeats," *On Poetry and Poets* (New York, 1957), p. 300.

the poet's life. Inclusion in his poems of the external facts of his life—people, places, possessions, incidents—in a way that at times almost coerces the reader to link his poetry with his life, whether or not he has the inclination to do so, carries Yeats's autobiographical mode considerably beyond that of his contemporaries, and thereby characterizes him as a more distinctively "autobiographical" poet.

Notwithstanding the general acceptance of obscure allusions, exotic languages, esoteric images, and eccentric constructions since the advent of the figures who wrote what now represents the canon of early twentieth-century poetry, Yeats's autobiographical allusiveness demands a special kind of tolerance because of its strictly personal, or private, reference. We can, after all, deal with problems of language or cultural allusion either by concentrated study of the poem itself, or by consultation of other works of literature, or of philosophy, psychology, history, myth, and so on, works which make up a shared cultural heritage. But the private reference is not necessarily part of this bond. While there is certainly an abundance of scholarly material uncovering these references in Yeats's poems, and at least from one point of view the excellence of the poems themselves may be said to justify ultimately any difficulties they initially present, whether autobiographical or otherwise, the questions still remain as to what extent he actually demands that we consult his personal life in order to gain insight into some of his most important poems, and to what extent he developed his distinctive manner with the aid of autobiographical reference. Both questions can be answered through examination of Yeats's expanding autobiographical mode, from his youthful diffidence to the bold self-assertiveness of his mature work.

I

In the poems Yeats wrote before the turn of the century he either obscured personal references to the point of virtual irrelevancy, or refrained from using them entirely. Whatever autobiographical elements exist in "The Wanderings of Oisin" are carefully and elaborately concealed behind an esoteric symbolism, the key to which he meant, as he told his friend Katharine Tynan, to be kept secret. In his first group of lyric poems, *Crossways*, he disguises his youthfully romantic world-weariness, and feelings of love, or love-sickness, by giving them a pastoral or fairy setting, by making use of various personae, and by use of dramatic and ballad forms. No biographical information is very helpful in reading these poems. There is an added interest, it is true, for the reader of "The Song of the Happy Shepherd" who is familiar with Yeats's description of his dreamy and romantic boyhood temperament, but this self-portrait, presented (though ambiguously) in the first part of his *Autobiography*, is itself only half true factually, and is one assumed pose among many which both prose and poetry help to enforce. There is an added interest, too, when reading "The Stolen

Child," in being familiar with Sleuth Wood, Lough Gill, Innisfree, Rosses Point, and Glen-Car as landmarks in County Sligo, and in knowing something of Yeats's boyhood in this region, but such knowledge is essentially of non-literary interest. Nor are these details, as they occur in the poems, very compelling as objects of biographical curiosity: the poems stand distinctly detached from the facts of the poet's life.

Likewise, Yeats's love of Maud Gonne inspired the love poems of *The Rose*, but his personal love is obscured either by its submersion in the eternal beauty symbolized by the rose, or in the image of a girl seen as "the greatness of the world in tears,"[2] a symbol of "The Sorrow of Love" which lies at the center of the human condition and informs all nature. Even in poems like "When You are Old," "The White Birds," and "A Dream of Death," where lover and beloved are referred to in the first and second persons, the absence of personal details evokes a kind of impersonal Petrarchan artificiality. And while many of the love poems in *The Wind Among the Reeds* are considerably more passionate than those in *The Rose*, they do not in themselves for the most part make clear whether they arose out of Yeats's love for Maud Gonne or for Olivia Shakespear. Even our curiosity is piqued only after we know something about Yeats's life. His mask at this time is that of the universal lover, and the poems deal, initially and ultimately, with love and not with a specific love affair.

For Yeats, however, neither love nor any other emotion could be conjured up abstractly, but had to be rooted in living experience in order to be raised authoritatively to symbolic power. If the feeling and imagery of his early love poems are often artificial and stylized, he would subsume artifice and style within the intensity of the poem's life force as soon as he acquired the skill to do so. But artificiality and stylization aside, the love poems of *The Wind Among the Reeds* contain a sensual imagery which is far from abstract. Yeats had himself experienced love, and while he did not embark on his love affairs, as he accused his friend Arthur Symons of doing, simply for the sake of experience as subject matter for poetry, he too sought experience with his poetry in mind. His experience gave him the substance of his poems, even if he had no compunction about manipulating the record to suit his artistic purposes. Since childhood he had heard his father insist that "some actual man" be palpable behind the "elaboration of beauty" in a poem;[3] as in many other things, this was a precept of his

---

[2] This phrase is actually the product of a late revision, but the basic image remains the same as in the original version. See W. B. Yeats, *The Variorum Edition of the Poems*, ed. Peter Allt and Russell K. Alspach (New York, 1957), p. 120. Such revisions will be taken into account only when Yeats's original version differs from the final one in a way which would affect the argument of this essay. Quotations from his poetry, therefore, are taken from *The Collected Poems* (New York, 1951). This quotation, p. 40.

[3] *The Autobiography* (New York, 1953), p. 39.

father's with which he was to agree more emphatically during the course of his life. Moreover, while he himself had important reservations, the Rhymers' Club in the 1890s took one absolute philosophical stand (probably the only one), that there was no place for generalization and abstraction in poetry, that poetry must consist solely of uninhibited personal expression. The personal expression in the poetry of Yeats's friends is, in fact, highly romanticized. The directly autobiographical traces in his own early poems, as we have seen, are plainly visible to any reader who wants to uncover them, but carefully obscured from those who do not.

With the 1903 volume *In the Seven Woods* Yeats's reticence to use openly autobiographical allusions begins to break down. Compared with later poems, considerable restraint is still in evidence, and most of the poems in the little volume actually continue the pastoral-romantic mode of earlier poems. But there are enough overt references to specific places and people important to him personally to indicate a shift in attitude. The Seven Woods of Coole Park, for instance, comprise a much more personal reference than do the County Sligo landmarks in "The Stolen Child" of *Crossways*, if for no other reason than that they are in the private rather than the public domain. And while most of the love poems are still in the impersonal vein of *The Rose* and *The Wind Among the Reeds*, there is something a little more specific about the reference in "The Arrow" to ". . . your beauty . . . Tall and noble but the face and bosom / Delicate in colour as apple blossom"; Maud Gonne was nearly six feet tall, Yeats always saw great nobility in her stature, and he associated her youthful complexion with apple blossom because when he first met her she was standing before a vase of the flowers. These physical details in the poem at least tempt the reader to conceive a specific, identifiable woman. More compelling because of a more immediate personal allusiveness embodied in a confiding conversational tone are the identities of "one that is ever kind" (Lady Gregory) in "The Folly of Being Comforted," and the conversationalists (Maud Gonne and her sister) in "Adam's Curse." A peculiar power is given to both poems by the poet's tacitly inviting the reader into the intimate circle of his friends, and this is an intimacy that is different and in a way more complete than that of overhearing an expression of romantic love.

It is generally agreed that this shift toward Yeats's tangible experience may have been stimulated by his new involvement beginning in 1899 with the more concrete artistic medium of the theatre, and strengthened in his ongoing work by the sobering effect on him of Maud Gonne's marriage in 1903 to John MacBride. His passion for Maud Gonne was renewed when she separated from her husband only a few years later, with the result that love poems inspired by her nearly dominate the next volume of poetry published in 1910, *The Green Helmet and Other Poems*. Still he does not actually identify her, but her consistently heroic nature—associated with that of Helen of Troy in "A Woman Homer Sung" and "No Second Troy," and less definitely in the poem "Peace"—and the apparently stormy nature of the love affair, as suggested in these poems and two others, "Words" and "Reconciliation," bring into clearer focus the woman who had begun to emerge in the poems of *In the Seven Woods*. In another autobiographical context in this volume, Yeats's friend and colleague, Douglas Hyde, is addressed directly in the poem, "At the Abbey Theatre," in which the title itself presupposes a knowledge of Yeats's theatrical involvement. And Yeats does not hesitate to devote important lines in the poem "The Fascination of What's Difficult" to his own difficulties connected with the writing of plays and the management of the Irish theatre, assuming the reader's familiarity with his activities there:

> My curse on plays
> That have to be set up in fifty ways,
> On the day's war with every knave and dolt,
> Theatre business, management of men.

Yeats's purpose in using autobiographical allusion in all these poems is not to recount episodes in his life, but to express universal human truths with the authority and emotional impact that actual personal experience can give them.

Finally, several short, cryptic poems in this volume draw on events in the poet's life in order to express his rage over middle-class values. Most of these poems grew out of his confrontation with a public morally, religiously, and patriotically hostile to the plays performed at the theatre, but "Upon a House Shaken by the Land Agitation" speaks in reaction to a different social controversy. An important catalyst for the intense feeling expressed in this poem was Yeats's affection for Lady Gregory and for Coole, where he had been enjoying an aristocratically gracious hospitality for over ten years. Coole had come to represent for him an advanced culture threatened by the barbarians of modern democracy. The house of the poem is raised clearly to symbolic power even in the second and third lines which speak of it as a place "Where passion and precision have been one / Time out of mind. . . ." But the specificity of the reference in the first line to "This house" undoubtedly helps to make the biographically uninformed reader feel a little removed from the total poetic experience, and the emotions (especially the indignation) which inform many of the poems written during those years have less meaning if we know nothing of the current circumstances of the poet's life. Despite Yeats's desire for universality, the infusion of this material makes the reader's familiarity with Yeats's biography in a rather wide variety of its aspects increasingly useful in the reading of his poems.

This tendency—since the first years of the twentieth century —toward outspoken personal allusion was far from unconscious. Yeats had relied, as we have been, on concrete experience rather than abstract theory for the raw material of his poetry before the turn of the century, but now he was moving more deliberately to re-create his own image. Toward this end he began in 1908 to keep his diary; in giving his thoughts and feelings concreteness and form by the objectifying process of writing them down, and in thereby clarifying his personal image, he made all more useful as the substance of a poetry that he was now more than ever convinced had to find its power in its evocation of the living man. "I find myself at moments desiring a more modern, a more aggressive art," he wrote in 1908, "an art of my own day. I am not happy in this mood unless I can see precisely how each poem or play goes to build up an image of myself, of my likes and dislikes as a man alive today."[4] And to his father he wrote in 1913, "Of recent years instead of 'vision' . . . I have tried to make my work convincing with a speech so natural and dramatic that the hearer would feel the presence of a man thinking and feeling."[5]

II

With the prologue to his next volume of poems, *Responsibilities*, Yeats introduces a new, outspoken autobiographical mode—"a more aggressive art," a "triumph" of self-assertion according to Eliot. Although the prologue to this volume was not his first such poem—others in the same volume had been written earlier—it forcefully clarifies in the final arrangement of poems his intention to set aside any diffidence he might have felt concerning an open self-portraiture. He begins by portraying himself as the descendant of distinguished, even heroic, ancestors. He does not use names at first, but the references to individuals—the seventeenth-century Jervis Yeats and Yeats's great-grandfather, John Yeats, rector of Drumcliffe in the first half of the nineteenth century—are unmistakable. He then makes more general references to Butlers and Armstrongs, ancestors who were merchants, scholars, and soldiers; and most important, he devotes the last part of the poem to his half legendary maternal grandfather, William Pollexfen, whose forceful personality he knew as a boy. In the end he accuses himself, not so modestly as he pretends, of being unworthy of his heritage because, having become nearly forty-nine years old, his accomplishment consists only of a book. The poem is a response to George Moore's accusation that Yeats was ashamed of his bourgeois ancestors, but no knowledge of this argument is needed to understand its most significant theme. Nor, in fact, is it necessary to know anything about Jervis or John Yeats, or William Pollexfen: the quality of Yeats's ancestors is clear, and they are collectively made into a symbol of a

[4] "Discoveries: Second Series," ed. Curtis Bradford, *The Massachusetts Review*, V (Winter 1964), 301.

[5] *The Letters of W. B. Yeats*, ed. Allan Wade (London, 1954), p. 583.

noble heritage that is inseparable from that of Ireland. Yet there is a definite void for the reader who is not more specifically familiar with the references, and that part of the poem devoted to William Pollexfen, especially, does require a biographical knowledge if the reader is to have more than a general notion of what the poet is talking about. As in some of the earlier poems that are autobiographically oriented, the power gained by the personal voice is slightly weakened by the poem's lack of total autonomy—a shortcoming Yeats would overcome in his later work. Most important in terms of his growing tendency toward outspoken self-portraiture, however, is the fact that for the first time the poet is speaking directly about himself and his family, without the use of any distancing device whatsoever.

"The Grey Rock"—the first poem in the volume proper—is perhaps more biographically demanding than the prologue. The poem alternates Irish myth with reverently nostalgic glances at the poet's friends of the nineties who are now dead, and ultimately gives these friends themselves a mythical stature.

The prologue to *Responsibilities*, then, focuses on Yeats's ancestral background, the opening poem on his youthful friends; together they direct our attention obliquely toward a personal image of the poet which in effect absorbs by association the admirable qualities of both relatives and friends that he has been celebrating—a composite image which is partly factual and partly of his own creation, and which embodies definite human values.

This personal image, distinctly evoking an antipathy toward human mediocrity, is enhanced by a series of poems imbued with a caustic bitterness generated by Yeats's disillusionment with the Irish people for failing to live up to the ideals he had envisioned for them. The specific event upon which he draws is their failure to respond as he thought they ought to Hugh Lane's generosity in offering to donate his valuable collection of Impressionist paintings to Dublin, on the condition that the city build a gallery suitable to house them. Although Yeats calls attention in a rather lengthy note to the event upon which they are based, however, the Lane incident itself is in most of the poems obscured in a more universal expression of dissatisfaction with the mediocrity of the age. "September 1913" and "Paudeen" are exemplary. "September 1913" was originally titled "Romance in Ireland (on reading much of the correspondence against the Art Gallery)." The revision of the title, aside from making it less cumbersome, places the poem directly in a more universal context. Referring to a different but related matter, the poem "On Those that Hated 'The Playboy of the Western World,' 1907" is inextricably tied to the event with which it deals, but the reference is made clear in the title. And in another related matter, the poem "To a Shade" is obscure until it is known that it addresses itself to Charles Stewart Parnell, certainly a public enough figure. While Parnell's identity is needed for the symbolic weight it

carries, it is not really important to know that the "old foul mouth" in
this poem, and

> one
> Who, were it proved he lies,
> Were neither shamed in his own
> Nor in his neighbors' eyes

in the poem "To a Friend whose Work has Come to Nothing" are
references to William Martin Murphy, owner of two Dublin newspapers and a major antagonist both of Parnell and Hugh Lane; the importance of Murphy's identity is quickly minimized as he becomes a symbol
of middle-class philistinism, ingratitude, and dishonesty. But the identity of Lady Gregory—an aunt of Hugh Lane who had worked hard for
the gallery—as the "Friend" in the latter poem whom Yeats describes as
"Bred to a harder thing / Than triumph," is much more compelling. It
is true that she too becomes a symbol—of Yeats's aristocratic ideal—but
the entire poem is directed toward her as a specific friend, much as "To
a Shade" is directed specifically toward Parnell, with the difference that
Parnell's heroic image had already become public property; there is in
consequence a personal quality to this poem which dominates. Both
Parnell and Lady Gregory, moreover, provide Yeats with foils which,
by spiritual and personal association, enforce his own image as being in
conflict with a mean and uncultured age.

The theme shifts away from the poet's disenchantment with Ireland in the love poems that make up the central portion of the volume.
Yeats's long, unsuccessful love affair with Maud Gonne has so fascinated even those readers with the sketchiest knowledge of his life or
poetry that it is difficult not to focus on the obvious personal allusions
in poems like "A Memory of Youth" and "Fallen Majesty." Yet, if they
did not concern Maud Gonne the only thing in these poems about past
love that would be more personally compelling than the love poems of
The Rose and *The Wind Among the Reeds* is the fact that they bring to light
the fuller course of the love affair, thereby giving it a more definite
particularity. An aggressively personal note is asserted, however, in the
next poem, "Friends," where Yeats sets out to praise three specific
friends, "Three women that have wrought / What joy is in my days."
And "The Cold Heaven" follows with an obvious allusion in a "love
crossed long ago." In all these poems the speaker could, if the reader
were not so preoccupied with Maud Gonne, be any middle-aged man
thinking back on the love of his youth. "That the Night Come," opening with the line "She lived in storm and strife," again depersonalizes
Maud Gonne by making her a feminine symbol of the heroic spirit, but
allusions to the same subject, even though they are deliberately kept
vague, become decidedly less vague if reiterated often enough, and the
reader soon cannot help but begin to see the love poems collectively as
well as individually. It is not by chance that Yeats's agonizing love affair
became so famous: by this time all the love poems begin to focus on the

personal reference through the cumulative effect of the constant and by now almost readily identifiable object. Yeats is subtly raising Maud Gonne's image to mythical proportions in order to serve the myth he is building of his own life: the lover, even the disappointed one, of a magnificent women must share that magnificence and become something of a hero for it.

The volume's epilogue, like the prologue, is inspired by George Moore, especially in the closing lines, ". . . till all my priceless things / Are but a post the passing dogs defile." It thereby supplements in its offensive tone the more defensive prologue as a response to Moore's derision. "A Coat" is still more self-assertive. It proclaims the poet's resolve to set aside those poetic devices which had in the past tended to obscure his personal image; he will now, he says, make his poetry express himself more directly, "For there's more enterprise / In walking naked." He is overstating his intention because the poet never really "walks naked": the very poetic artifice provides a covering. The nakedness of which he speaks, though, will provide him with a new mask, that of the uninhibited, outspoken protagonist. In the *Responsibilities* volume which this poem closes he has already utilized it, and the new openness with which he treats his own life—his experience, his family, and his friends as well as his thoughts and feelings —provides him with one important means of doing so.

Several poems in the 1914 *Responsibilities*, then, indicate that Yeats had arrived at a willingness, even a desire, to treat his own life more openly, to display in full view the facts of his life when such a display seemed useful for his poetic purpose. This autobiographical mode continues in the next two volumes, *The Wild Swans at Coole* and *Michael Robartes and the Dancer*, but they contain nothing quite so aggressively self-assertive as some of the poems in the preceding volume. Yeats's autobiographical prose writing very likely contributed heavily to his sense of freedom to use his autobiography in his poetry. First his diary of 1908 to 1913, then, more publicly, "Reveries Over Childhood and Youth" must have helped him to overcome any feelings of self-consciousness or inhibition he might have had in so exposing himself. The somewhat traumatic breakthrough having once been negotiated, however, he could proceed without qualms both in his prose and his poetry—and not feel the need apparent in his most outspoken *Responsibilities* poems of a kind of personally defensive hostility. Even before "Reveries" was completed he had planned to continue his autobiography, and late in 1915 he began his "Memoirs" of 1916-17 which is among the most candid and intimate of all his writings, and ultimately serves as a first draft for "The Trembling of the Veil" and for a small part of "Dramatis Personae." Virtually for the rest of his life Yeats was engaged in writing *The Autobiography*, although he was to move in it beyond the simple objectification—and perhaps catharsis —of his diary and "Memoirs," and even to a lesser extent of the first version of "Reveries," toward the formulation of a design or pattern in which he wished to see his life evolving.

Within this design Lady Gregory's estate, Coole, would come to symbolize an ideal culture uniting the best qualities drawn from all elements of Irish life, and ultimately the symbol would be operative in the poetry as well. It is doubtful whether Yeats in 1919 had fully formulated this symbolic function for Coole, although he was certainly thinking about it generally in these terms.[6] An especially personal atmosphere is generated throughout *The Wild Swans at Coole* in the poet's preoccupation with his impending old age. The preoccupation is not new—there are signs of it as early as "The Wanderings of Oisin"—but now, Yeats having reached fifty years, the theme becomes prominent in his work for the first time, and more convincing.

The thematic movement in the title poem quickly leaves the actual man and surroundings behind in an expression of the universal human condition, but this expression rests upon the evocation of a concrete presence: the naming of Coole in the title, the specificity of the setting—even to the number of swans—the recalling of nineteen autumns (the poem was written in 1916; Yeats's first extended stay at Coole was in 1897), and a precise delineation of the image in which the swans mount into flight (an actual event, according to Jeffares).[7] The realistically transcribed detail in this poem is notable when compared with the earlier "In the Seven Woods." Then the speaker heard "the pigeons of the Seven Woods / Make their faint thunder"; now, much more precisely, "Upon the brimming water among the stones / Are nine-and-fifty swans." In the earlier poem the experience recounted is general: the speaker opens with "I have heard . . ."; in the later poem, beginning with the tangibly present "The trees are in their autumn beauty," there is a personal immediacy that is almost Wordsworthian and that coincides with the actual experience that inspired and pervades the poem. The voice of intense personal experience validates and fortifies the universal statement.

Yeats speaks of his own fifty years in the little poem, "Lines Written in Dejection," but most of the poems dealing with his advancing years do not so much center on his age as evoke its poignant presence through his reminiscing in a variety of nostalgic moods about people who were important to him. The second poem in the volume,

---

[6] The reference to Lady Gregory's estate by name both in the title of the 1919 volume and in the title poem which opens it is reminiscent of the earlier *In the Seven Woods*, with the difference that by this time the estate, having become a center for the Irish cultural movement, was far less private a reference than it had been in 1903. Allusion to the "seven woods," of course, suggests a more personal association than does the simple allusion to Coole. Yeats had also recounted each of the seven woods by name and with a sense of intimate familiarity in the 1900 prologue to "The shadowy Waters."

[7] A. Norman Jeffares, *A commentary on the Collected Poems of W. B. Yeats* (Stanford, California, 1968), p. 155.

"In Memory of Major Robert Gregory," is exemplary. It is an elegy for Lady Gregory's son, but in addition to Gregory, who is eulogized at length with a specific—if heightened—account of his natural gifts, a stanza is devoted to each of three other close friends who had died earlier—Lionel Johnson, John Synge, and Yeats's uncle George Pollexfen. All are mentioned by name and made into vivid portraits through Yeats's drawing together what were for him their most telling personal qualities; the portraiture of friends in this poem goes into considerably more detail than that in "The Grey Rock." The elegy, too, contains the first allusion to Thoor Ballylee with its "narrow winding stairs," which Yeats had purchased the year before. His intention, he says, had been to seek Robert Gregory's counsel in rennovating it; the suitability of the man for the task has, within the context of the poem, the effect of promoting the symbolic role of both the tower and the dead man. W. H. Auden, perhaps seeing a relationship with his own elegy for Yeats, had said that the elegy for Robert Gregory "never loses the personal note of a man speaking about his personal friends in a particular setting—in *Adonais*, for instance, both Shelley and Keats disappear as people—and at the same time the occasion and the characters acquire a symbolic public significance."[8] The very personal nature of the poetic experience comes to a climax at the poem's close, when the speaker—undisguisedly Yeats—is left speechless by the power of his emotion.[9]

More disguised are three poems based on Yeats's infatuation with Maud Gonne's daughter, Iseult Gonne—"Men Improve with the Years," "To a Young Beauty," and "To a Young Girl"—and one on his recent marriage—"Solomon to Sheba." And there are eight late love poems to Maud Gonne, mostly in a vein of nostalgic sadness recalling a past youthful love; while they are rather more biographically open than those on Iseult and on his marriage, and than the love poems in *The Rose* and *The Wind Among the Reeds*, they are generally less so than surrounding poems based on other experience—the Robert Gregory elegies, for instance, and the poems which follow, on Alfred Pollexfen and Mabel Beardsley. Again, approaching the collected poems sequentially, the numerous, consistent characterizations of Maud Gonne throughout the love poems has come to make her image strikingly, and purposefully, recognizable, but evidently Yeats still felt some restraint in sharing the intimacy of his love life with the world.

"In Memory of Alfred Pollexfen" is really an elegy for the entire Pollexfen family. As in the prologue to *Responsibilities*, Yeats refers to

---

[8] "Yeats as an Example," *Kenyon Review* (Spring 1948), p. 193.

[9] Two other elegies for Robert Gregory, "An Irish Airman Foresees His Death" and the pastoral "Shepherd and Goatherd," make specific and unmistakable allusions to Gregory and his milieu, but neither deals so extensively with the poet's personal experience as does the first.

members of his family individually, and transforms them collectively into a symbol—in the earlier poem of a heroic temperament, in the later one of a warmly human quality. The motivation in the prologue had been largely polemical; in this poem it is the expression of personal sadness at the passing of a generation strong in personality of a kind disappearing from the world. Mabel Beardsley, sister of Yeats's friend Aubrey Beardsley, is the subject of "Upon a Dying Lady." While she is not identified by name, the poem is comprised almost entirely of private anecdotes which nearly demand an acquaintance with the generating autobiographical experience. Nevertheless, the dying lady is a lady in the most exalted and heroic sense, raised to symbolic power equal almost to that of Robert Gregory, and as in the elegies for him, the symbol is evolved within the poem itself.

Aside from "A Prayer on Going into My House"—which mentions Yeats's "tower and cottage" but is otherwise quite universal in its imagery—most of the remaining poems in this volume are directed toward Yeats's philosophical-mythical system. Michael Robartes, the persona taken from occult tradition and used to represent "the pride of the imagination brooding upon the greatness of its possessions"[10] in several poems in early editions of *The Wind Among the Reeds*—hence in a sense a figure out of Yeats's past—appears in several poems, as do the "old wind-beaten tower," the "shallow stream" which runs beside it, the bridge over the stream and the light in Yeats's study on the top floor of the tower as well. Even Yeats himself appears, hard at work trying to evolve the system of *A Vision*. But in the poem "The Phases of the Moon" Yeats has Robartes convert this very personal imagery into an ideogram which effectively obscures, though it does not eliminate, the presence of the actual poet:

> He has found, after the manner of his kind,
> Mere images; chosen this place to live in
> Because, it may be, of the candle-light
> From the far tower where Milton's Platonist
> Sat late, or Shelley's visionary prince:
> The lonely light that Samuel Palmer engraved,
> An image of mysterious wisdom won by toil. . . .

Theme and imagery from this point on are recurrently interwoven with the symbolism of *A Vision*, but not to the exclusion of autobiographical allusion. Opening the volume *Michael Robartes and the Dancer*, the title poem represents a conversation between Yeats and Iseult Gonne, and "Solomon and the Witch" and "An Image from a Past Life" conversations between him and his wife,[11] although none of the poems in itself indicates this directly. In "An Image from a Past Life" as in other instances, and largely as a consequence of them, the slightest

---

[10] W. B. Yeats, *The Variorum Edition of the Poems*, p. 803.

[11] See Jeffares, *A Commentary*, pp. 217, 218, 220-21.

acquaintance with Yeats's developing method of autobiographical portrayal will suggest to the reader that the poem is concerned with the
haunting of the early days of his marriage by Maud Gonne's image.
"Under Saturn" is much more openly personal, and because it is a kind
of extension of "An Image from a Past Life," it opens up the biographical reference in that poem. Maud Gonne is again the disturbing presence, and Yeats attempts to restore peace by assigning her a role in his
inescapable youth, which also embraces his Sligo childhood among the
Pollexfens, Middletons, and Yeatses who were, he suggests, his earliest
sources of inspiration.

Five poems based on the 1916 Easter Rising contain allusions to
various friends and acquaintances, but all these people, because of
their parts in the event, had become public figures. The references to
John MacBride, Maud Gonne's husband and "A drunken, vainglori-
ous lout," in "Easter 1916," and to Constance (Gore-Booth) Markievicz
in "On a Political Prisoner" are in fact more personal, but these are
exceptional instances, and the images are generalized. "A Prayer for
my Daughter," on the other hand, dwells on universalized ideals, but
they are embodied in personal hopes which Yeats cherishes for his
newborn daughter. The setting for his reflections, moreover, is con-
cretely factual: it is a stormy night in the tower, "Gregory's wood" is
almost the only barrier against the storm "Bred on the Atlantic," the
bridge and stream are mentioned. And finally, Maud Gonne serves as
an example of the greatest danger besetting the achievement of Yeats's
feminine ideal.

The final poem in the volume consists almost entirely of a statement of simple autobiographical fact, and while not hostile, it is, especially in its opening line and uncompromisingly declarative stance, one
of the most brashly self-assertive poems Yeats ever wrote:

TO BE CARVED ON A STONE AT THOOR BALLYLEE

> I, the poet William Yeats,
> With old mill boards and sea-green slates,
> And smithy work from the Gort Forge,
> Restored this tower for my wife George;
> And may these characters remain
> When all is ruin once again.

Yet the forcefulness of rhetorical simplicity combines with the wish
articulated, without such absolute confidence, in the last two lines to
express a value judgement about the permanence of art which goes
well beyond personal autobiography.

Looking back over Yeats's use of autobiography since
Responsibilities, when he first significantly set aside his reluctance to use
it, the tone of self-portraiture appears to shift from belligerent self-
assertiveness to strong introspective sobriety. To inform a universal
theme he comes imperturbably to employ his own experience for the

sake of concreteness, vitality, and the mythologizing of his life. It is true that the atmosphere of *Responsibilities* generally is one of disenchantment with Ireland, of bitter disappointment and hostile response to what seemed the failure of all his dreams and ambitions, in contrast with a preoccupation with impending old age expressed—in *The Wild Swans at Coole* if not so much later—with sadness and nostalgia. This volume and *Michael Robartes and the Dancer* manifest, in fact, a kind of emotional calm between the social and political invective of the relatively youthful volume of 1914, and the more profoundly powerful raging of old age with which the poet felt afflicted in the volumes beginning with *The Tower*. The very nature of the emotional charge, then, is different in the two periods of his life, with the later tending to direct a sharper focus on himself as symbol of universal man.

Beyond this, a worldly confidence—or seeming arrogance—that can be natural to old age zealously claiming superior wisdom as the product of long and varied experience, seems to have made Yeats more at ease in the open use of the facts of his life: the aggressiveness in the earlier self-portraiture at least in part reflects a personal self-consciousness, whereas later his family and friends, and himself, are used with a certain freedom—a casualness, even, or nonchalance —absent from the earlier work. He is even willing to use his personal image and experience tangentially in order to serve some other poetic purpose, a willingness consistent with the more fully developed insouciance which, as he originally learned from Castiglione, was a highly desirable aristocratic quality.

One outgrowth of this new sophistication was the intensifying of his urge to continue his autobiographical publication. During the time he was writing the poems of *The Tower*, most of *The Autobiography* was published for the first time, some of it newly written, some revised from earlier writings. Yeats was obviously growing accustomed to seeing large portions of his personal life displayed to the world, and the freedom he felt to draw upon it, either pointedly or casually, is increasingly apparent. The prose writing, moreover, would elucidate many of the autobiographical allusions in the poems; in effect, Yeats was drawing his life and his art together more closely into the kind of unity he sought. And, just as facets of his life are converted into symbol in *The Autobiography*, so in the poetry candid autobiography is, even moreso, far from the point, the alchemical process being achieved with greatest success in the late poems.

III

Aside from references to mythical towers in early poems, Yeats refers to his own tower, Thoor Ballylee, six times prior to the 1928 volume called *The Tower*. It is not surprising, therefore, that the structure will have already assumed some symbolical significance: it represents the home with all its ramifications of security, family traditions, and hospitality; it is associated with art; it evokes a sense of Irish history and of racial and cultural aristocracy; and it is the place of solitary pursuit of subjective wisdom and the anti-self. There is an implication of permanence, of unchanging other-worldliness, attached to the tower, despite the fact that in each reference the image of the tower built of actual stone and in which Yeats actually lived is unmistakably present.

Although the image of Yeats's tower appears in only two poems of *The Tower* volume, all these symbolic functions are operative, and that involving the pursuit of subjective wisdom and the anti-self is heightened by the recurrent assertion throughout the volume of the existence and power of the world of the imagination, discovered only through this subjective pursuit. In major poems like "Sailing to Byzantium" and "Among School Children," where the tower itself does not appear, the symbol is implied thematically, through the affirmation of an imaginative or spiritual world separate from but tied inextricably to the physical one. The tower, having its foundation in the earth but reaching into the sky, is a fit symbol for the human condition partaking of both worlds: man is limited physically by his body but able to probe the infinite with his imagination. When the speaker in the title poem paces "upon the battlements," then, reflecting on his old age and then transcending this mortal affliction through the imaginative creation of an ideal world around him, the tower provides at once a physical setting for the musing poet and a symbolic base for the reality of the imaginatively created world which compensates for the limitations of the ordinary one. Autobiographically, Yeats recalls the legendary figures that have captured his imagination in the past, as well as his own creation Hanrahan and the "ancient bankrupt master" of the tower; all have escaped mortality by being transformed into, or simply existing as images. The images are themselves, like Yeats's very real agony over old age, clearly transfigured from the poet's personal experience into artistic entities. The product of imaginative rather than physical engendering, the work of art inhabits the immortal world of the imagination and is capable of eclipsing the often harsh mortal one of our physical habitation.

The tower image is again prominent in the next poem, "Meditations in Time of Civil War," where in the second section, called "My House," Yeats recounts the personal surroundings which he has made into his favorite symbols: the ancient bridge and tower, "acre of stony ground," "symbolic rose," "Old ragged elms, old thorns," the rain and wind, "stilted water-hen," stream, "winding stair," "chamber arched with stone," "open hearth," "A candle and written page." The passage is autobiographical both because the objects belong to Yeats's actual experience and because they are images evoked from his earlier poetry. Due especially to the symbolic weight given the tower in the preceding poem, the references to the "symbolic rose," and the fact that the last images (winding stair, arched chamber, hearth, book and candle) are followed by the statement, "*Il Penseroso*'s Platonist toiled on / In some like chamber . . ." the symbolic implications of all the images are brought to bear. Moreover, the first section, "Ancestral Houses," places all the individual symbols within a single larger symbolic perspective—that of ancestral, cultural, and artistic traditions, and the values they impose upon life. In subsequent sections of the poem other personal images are called up to function similarly: Yeats's rustic table, the ancient Japanese sword, his ancestors and children, Lady Gregory and his wife, the beehives and stare's nest in the lossening masonry, "the tower-top" and "broken stone" upon which he leans during his musings. All together the images evoke an extraordinarily intimate view of the poet contemplating his most important values from within his own world, but in the context of what appears a larger hostile world which—itself crumbling—is bent on destroying him. Much of the poem's poignance rests in the conflict of the two juxtaposed worlds, one filled with personally meaningful and life-enriching objects, the other with destructive violence growing out of the very absence of such vital images which are replaced by inhuman abstract principle.

Several other poems in the volume make use of autobiographical factors in a variety of ways. "All Souls' Night" is another poem among several that invoke the spirits of Yeats's friends who had died. The three portrayed here all had shared his occult interests and, like him, were mocked for doing so. The poem, consistent with *The Tower*'s dominant symbolism, closes the volume by lamenting the incompleteness of human life, and by memorializing Yeats's friends—who were aware of this incompleteness and so sought fulfillment in the spiritual world—along the way.

While not necessarily asserting the superiority of the imaginative or spiritual world over the physical one, merely affirming its existence and power in *The Tower* results in an emphasis that might give this impression. The next volume, *The Winding Stair*, is corrective in reasserting with new forcefulness the attraction for the poet of a sentient existence. The winding stair of the title is the winding stair in Yeats's tower, but by now made, as a gyre image, into one of his most important symbols. The opening poem, "In Memory of Eva Gore-Booth and Con Markiewicz," does not contain the image but is strongly autobiographical, contrasting the Gore-Booth sisters as Yeats knew them in their youth—beautiful girls who with their very presence contributed to the aristocratic elegance of their ancestral home—and as they later became (perhaps, disturbingly, because of advice Yeats gave them)—images of grubby revolutionary politics. In the poetic process the girls become symbols of two eras with sadly differing values, and of the destructiveness of time itself, which is implicitly identified with the gyre image (the winding stair) representing an historical pattern. But the extremely personal references both in this volume's title and in its opening poem suggest the distance Yeats has come in the autobiographical manner of his mature years from the relatively coy hinting of 1903.

"A Dialogue of Self and Soul" opens with the soul proclaiming the images of winding stair and tower:

> I summon to the winding ancient stair;
> Set all your mind upon the steep ascent,
> Upon the broken, crumbling battlement. . . .

But whereas the soul celebrates the imaginative and spiritual world approached by the "steep ascent" and contemplated from the "broken, crumbling battlement," Yeats sides in this poem with the self, who prefers the sentient, mortal world of "love and war" symbolized by Sato's sword with its silk binding. Yeats, in fact, directly declares his personal possessions to be symbols:

> . . . and all these I set
> For emblems of the day against the tower
> Emblematical of the night. . . .

If the tower in "A Dialogue of Self and Soul" symbolizes the ascent out of the physical world, in "Blood and the Moon" it is the more complete symbol of unity of being, conjoining sentient mortality with spiritual permanence. Hence, the tower in this poem is more closely associated with physicality:

> Blessed be this place,
> More blessed still this tower;
> A bloody, arrogant power
> Rose out of the race
> Uttering, mastering it,
> Rose like these walls from these
> Storm-beaten cottages—

The image represents a fusion of mortal power and immortal spirit, and Yeats is just as emphatic as in the preceding poem in declaring his deliberate transfiguration of his concrete possession into an emblem or symbol that embraces both body and spirit. He is even more insistent in the next section where, after noting that towers have been used as symbols many times before, he says, "I declare this tower is my symbol; I declare / This winding, gyring, spiring treadmill of a stair is my ancestral stair. . . ." Proudly proclaiming his Anglo-Irish heritage, he offers in the last two sections the powerful image of the tower reaching from the blood-stained earth toward the "purity of the unclouded moon"; giving at the same time credence to the myth and mythical proportions to his own life, the tower symbolism is perfected as an ideogram of unity of being.

While the tone in the two poems on Coole Park suggests the poet's intimacy with the estate and with the hostess who presided there, and a close friendship with the visiting guests, none of these—Coole, Lady

Gregory, or the guests mentioned—could by 1929 still be considered a private reference; all had become part of public knowledge through their roles in the Irish cultural revival, and in some cases through Yeats's poetic mythologizing. Yeats by this time obviously saw Coole clearly as a microcosm of the unity of culture he desired for all of Ireland.[12] At the same time the now famous Lady Gregory, who was also Yeats's closest and most cherished friend, is the dominating personality in both poems, and although written before her death, they have served as her elegies since.

Several other poems in *The Winding Stair* and in the next volume, *A Full Moon in March*, as well as some among the "Last Poems," stem from specific personal experience, but do not rely very extensively on the generating elements. The love relationship of "After Long Silence," for example, emerges out of a combination of personal experiences, "Lapis Lazuli" moves directly from the actual carved stone that inspired the poem to its symbolic form, and two other poems make Margot Ruddock into a symbol of youth, feminine beauty, grace, and sensitivity—qualities always much appreciated by Yeats and which he now declares, having gathered them into a single image, "A beautiful lofty thing."

The poem which takes this phrase as its title, "Beautiful Lofty Things," is one of five poems, distributed over four volumes, which look back nostalgically on the poet's life and memorialize some of the friends who he felt contributed to the dignity and meaning of his life. Each figure in this poem is presented in a particularly exalted moment in his memory, and made into an image which transcends the original living mortal: "O'Leary's noble head," J. B. Yeats answering a hostile crowd from the Abbey stage, Standish O'Grady in a moment of divine—or drunken—madness, Lady Gregory displaying her courage and aristocratic insouciance, Maud Gonne appearing as a goddess. All, as it were, are transfigured into gods, "Olympians"—or into works of art. Of the five poems, however, "The Municipal Gallery Revisited" is the one most highly charged with personal emotion. The dramatic circumstance—the aged poet wandering through the gallery viewing pictures that depict both the important public events in his life and his close friends all of whom are now dead—would be justification enough. Yeats is now willing to set aside all reserve, to forego the use of any persona, and to display openly the intensity of his own emotion; the poem in this regard goes considerably beyond even the conclusion of the Robert Gregory elegy. Nevertheless, it succeeds in achieving the public symbol—and without sacrificing the tone of personal intimacy—because out of the collection of pictures Yeats not only re-creates much of his own life, but an important chapter in the history

---

[12] *Dramatis Personae*, written a few years later—in 1935—deals with the theme in prose.

of Ireland as well, and out of them both evokes a powerful myth of universal human nobility. The poem is exemplary of some of Yeats's most compelling ideals: to see his own life unified with that of Ireland; to create the universal symbol out of the concrete experience, thereby eliminating abstraction and expressing truth by making the reader "feel the presence of a man thinking and feeling"; and to bring his life and art into unity.

A far lesser poem, certainly, is the little one called "Are You Content?" but it is the last of several to treat his ancestors as the others had his friends.[13] As in the prologue to *Responsibilities*, written more than twenty years earlier, he is captivated by mental images of those men of action, and seems uncertain that his own contemplative life as a poet is worthy of them. The conflict of values between the contemplative and the active life remains always for him a cogent issue. And if Yeats in these last poems takes final leave both of his friends and his ancestors, he also feels the need to look back once more on this work. This he does in "The Circus Animals' Desertion," recounting his old images upon discoveing that now in old age no new ones would come to mind, and that he has to make do with the objects and emotions out of which those images had grown, to revert to the raw material out of which his imagination had constructed a higher reality. Thus, again in a personal voice speaking with universal implication, he affirms his need for the sentient world even after having constructed an elaborate edifice of art.

The "Last Poems" have a recurring atmosphere of impending death and a thematic apprehension of the desirably heroic way to meet it. Appropriately enough for the aged poet, Yeats concludes his final volume with his own elegy.[14] In the first two sections of "Under Ben

---

[13] And the last poem of a volume published by the Cuala Press in 1938, called *New Poems*. According to Yeats's intentions, and the Cuala Press volume published in July 1939, *Last Poems and Two Plays*, as well as *New Poems*, "Last Poems" should properly include only those poems subsequent to "Are You Content?" See Curtis Bradford, "Yeats's *Last Poems* Again," *The Dolmen Press Yeats Centenary Papers MCMLXV*, ed. Liam Miller (Dublin, 1968), pp. 259-88, and Allan Wade, *A Bibliography of the Writings of W. B. Yeats* (London, 1958), pp. 193-95, 197-99.

[14] "Under Ben Bulben" is the opening poem of *Last Poems and Two Plays*. Ibid. The ultimate decision to conclude the volume with "Under Ben Bulben" appears more appropriate, however, although by concluding *Last Poems and Two Plays* with the play "Purgatory"—as Yeats originally intended—the book achieved, as Curtis Bradford says, "a grim and desperately earnest book recording Yeats's response to the mounting crisis in Western culture and asserting the values of that culture as opposed to all 'Asiatic vague immensities' "(p. 260). But a volume containing only the poems and hence eliminating "Purgatory," could not very well conclude with the poignant but minor poem "Politics." Yeats, of course, never had the opportunity to supervise the publication of his *Collected Poems*, which is a very different kind of volume from *Last Poems and Two Plays*. In fact, though, the order of the poems had already been altered in the 1940 volume, *Last Poems and Plays* (Macmillan, London), and Senator Michael B. Yeats, the poet's son, has assured me in conversation that the alteration, placing "Under Ben Bulben" at the end, was

Bulben" he demands of his legatees allegiance to his two-fold faith: in the occult tradition rooted in ancient prophecy, and in the ideals of the Irish mythical heroes. In succeeding sections he proclaims the need for conflict as a means to transcendence, and elaborates on the ideals of art, of tradition, and of an aristocratic demeanor in life. Then, figuratively descending from the top of Ben Bulben where the mythical horsemen ride to the Sligo earth that helped to form him, he dictates his own epitaph to be cut into his gravestone in the Drumcliff churchyard. And at the last he engages in ambiguity that partakes of both the physical and spiritual worlds between which he had always been torn, for the horsemen ordered to "pass by" in the epitaph might be either the mythical horsemen—the Irish heroes—of the poem's opening stanza, or noble men who consider matters of life and death coldly and move on to the business of living and creating their own truths. The transfiguration of private values into public symbol is self-evident.

Looking back over Yeats's collected poetry, it is clear that for a complete or at times simply a specific understanding, a rather detailed biographical knowledge of the poet is quite useful. So compelling, in fact, is the personal quality of some of the poems that uninformed of their biographical bases we may come away frustrated or dissatisfied. But at the same time it is clear that in the largest sense we can participate in the poetic experience without knowing anything of the poet's life whatsoever: in every poem that alludes to Yeats's personal life —either in a catalogue of friends or ancestors, in reference to his love life, his children, or his work, or in the imagery of his tower or Japanese sword—the friend, relative, possession or experience is transfigured, given universality in symbolic power. If this process is not quite so complete in the volumes where Yeats first became an openly "autobiographical" poet, he appears to have achieved virtually total success in the late poems. Even more striking is the fact that bears out Yeats's own abiding poetic principle—that rooting his themes in his concrete, personal experience, even to the inclusion of the experience itself in his poems, has enabled him to speak in a special voice, uniquely intimate and authoritative, which contributes effectively to a general strengthening of his verse, and, ironically, to the achievement of a universality of meaning and relevance beyond that of almost any other poet.

---

clearly set out by the poet himself before his death, and that Mrs. Yeats would never have permitted an alteration by the publisher in the manner Professor Bradford has suggested. Certainly, with his capacity to recover repeatedly from states of extreme depression, bitterness, and even despair over his sentient existence, Yeats would ultimately have preferred to conclude on the powerfully affirmative note expressed in his own, self-written, epitaph.

AFTER "SILENCE,"
THE "SUPREME THEME":
EIGHT LINES OF YEATS

David R. Clark

For Fred Benjamin Millett, 1890-1975, in whose class at Wesleyan, in 1946, I first wrote on this poem.

I

Yeats's little poem "After Long Silence," from the series "Words for Music Perhaps," has been much admired and much discussed. Two questions still bother me about it, however, one interpretative and one biographical.

AFTER LONG SILENCE

Speech after long silence; it is right,
All other lovers being estranged or dead,
Unfriendly lamplight hid under its shade,
The curtains drawn upon unfriendly night,
That we descant and yet again descant
Upon the supreme theme of Art and Song:
Bodily decrepitude is wisdom; young
We loved each other and were ignorant.[1]

The interpretative question is, What is the "supreme theme"? The biographical question is, What, if any, was the "long silence" in Yeats's life which may have suggested the first line of the poem? Light on the second question may cast a glimmer on the vexed first as well. I shall start with the interpretative question.

Six years after the poem was first published—in *Words for Music Perhaps and Other Poems* (Dublin: The Cuala Press, 1932)—Brooks and

---

[1] *The Variorum Edition of the Poems of W. B. Yeats*, ed. Peter Allt and Russell K. Alspach (New York, 1957), p. 523.

Warren gave what has been a standard, though not unchallenged, interpretation:

> ... The two lovers are in a shadowed room alone, the lamplight being almost hidden by the shade. One of the lovers is speaking to the other. . . . The lovers are evidently old. The relationship has not been a constant one, for we are told that all other lovers are "estranged or dead." . . .
>
> The speaker says, in effect, this: one lover can no longer take pleasure in the physical beauty of the other. . . . Furthermore, the outside world has no more use for them. . . . It is right that, having passed through the other phases of their lives, they should now talk of the "theme of Art and Song," which is "supreme" because it involves the interpretation of their own previous experience. Wisdom, the power to reach an interpretation, comes only as the body decays. The poet sees the wisdom as a positive gain, but at the same time he can regret the time of beauty and youth when the lovers could dispense with wisdom. The basic point of the poem is the recognition, with its attendant pathos, of the fact that man cannot ever be complete—cannot, that is, possess beauty and wisdom together.[2]

Thomas Parkinson rejects the Brooks and Warren interpretation or at least his understanding of that interpretation which he rephrases thus: ". . . Brooks and Warren have read the line as 'Art and song *are* the supreme theme,' only art and song matter in view of the inevitable loss of bodily force, and the ignorance of the young is wasteful."[3] I do not think, however, that this is what Brooks and Warren wrote. Parkinson is thrown off by the statement, "It is right that . . . they should now talk of the 'theme of Art and Song..' . . ." That theme is that age brings wisdom as we "wither into the truth" (*Variorum Poems*, p. 261), although our triumphant sense of "positive gain" is tainted by "regret" at the loss of "beauty and youth." "Man cannot ever be complete." To put it more extremely than Brooks and Warren do, if you want wisdom you have to die for it.

Parkinson's own interpretation is based on a study of the manuscripts:

> ... The supreme theme of art and song is love. The variants of the line bear this out:
>
>> Come let us talk of love
>> What other theme do we know
>>
>> On love descant

[2] Cleanth Brooks and Robert Penn Warren, *Understanding Poetry* (New York, 1947, first published 1938), pp. 224-25. This edition contains an impressive analysis of the metrics. For John Unterecker also the poem makes a "precise statement of man's ironic anguish—impotent wisdom succeeding youth's ignorant passion." *A Reader's Guide to William Butler Yeats* (New York, 1965, first published 1959), pp. 232-33. Fred B. Millett, to whom this essay is dedicated, discusses student analyses of this poem in *The Rebirth of Liberal Education* (New York, 1945), pp. 166-68.

[3] Thomas Parkinson, *W. B. Yeats: The Later Poetry* (Berkeley and Los Angeles, 1964), p. 90.

Upon the sole theme of art and song

Upon that theme so fitting for the aged; young
We loved each other and were ignorant.

And though it might be argued that he changed his mind in the midst of composition, this seems to me extremely doubtful.[4]

Earlier John E. Parish, too, had found that the supreme theme "is not *wisdom*, as the critics suggest, but *love*." His interpretation of the tone of the poem differs from Parkinson's however, as it does from that of other critics. "The tone is almost as sour as that in Rochester's *The Maimed Debauchee*, where the incapacitated rake wryly announces that he will, 'being good for nothing else, be wise.' " His paraphrase reads: "Now that we are too old to experience love, we can talk owlishly and interminably on every aspect of the subject. We are wonderfully wise about love now that we are incapable of loving. When we were young we knew nothing about it—except that we were in love." Parish's challenging brief note seems to me to go wrong in making a minor qualification into a major emphasis. For example there may be a minor suggestion of the "long-winded pomposity" and "weary repetition"[5] of an old man's talk in the verb "descant." But to me the line "That we descant and yet again descant" is triumphant song.

Here, then, are four possible "supreme themes": (1) "Art and Song" (2) "Bodily decrepitude is wisdom" (3) "Bodily decrepitude is wisdom," *but* it is also decrepitude. "Man cannot ever be complete." (4) "Love." Before debating among these four, let us turn, for light, from the interpretative question to the biographical one. What, if any, was the "long silence" in Yeats's life which may have suggested the first line of the poem?

Before I can move outside of the poem, however, I must correct what seems to me a misreading of one line by Brooks and Warren: "The first line suggests that there has been a long silence after [the lovers] have 'descanted' upon the 'supreme theme of Art and Song.' . . . This silence has been broken by more talk on the same subject, apparently now the only subject left to them, and one of the lovers makes the comment which constitutes the poem itself."[6] Rejecting this reading, I feel that the "long silence" must be one of years, not of minutes. Perhaps Brooks and Warren feel that the break in the lovers' talk

[4] Parkinson, pp. 90-91.

[5] John E. Parish, "The Tone of Yeats' *After Long Silence*," *Western Humanities Review*, 16, No. 4 (Autumn 1962), 377-79.

[6] Brooks and Warren, p. 225. Parish is mistaken to think that there is a printer's error in Brooks and Warren's text and that "*which* should be inserted between *after* and *they*. . . ." Brooks and Warren think that the lovers descant for a while, then, after a long silence, descant some more. But I agree with Parish that "There is no long silence immediately preceding the eight-line monologue" and that "the 'descanting' takes place after long years of silence between the man and woman who were once in love." Parish, p. 378.

reveals that they have no subject left but the one "supreme theme." Such a natural break could also be a vehicle for the symbolic significance of their long parting. But I do not feel such a break in the talk. The lovers seem to me to "descant and yet again descant" without interruption. There seems no place in the argument of the poem for any significant pause in the conversation. The significant silence is the silence of the years since they have last seen each other, the years during which other lovers have died or become estranged, the long years during which their bodies have changed so drastically that they must be hidden from the eyes that last saw them young and beautiful. The title, "After Long Silence," surely refers to this gap of years, not to a lag in the conversation. The "long silence" measures the gap between youth and "bodily decrepitude," between ignorance and "wisdom." I hold that the internal structure of the poem demands that the primary meaning of "long silence" is a silence of many years.

Was there such a silence in Yeats's life which may have suggested the line? I suppose there were many, as there are in any life. A reunion with Mrs. Olivia Shakespear, his mistress during a brief period of the nineties, apparently seems a sufficient explanation to other critics. But I cannot think that the intensity of the line is sufficiently explained by the fact that Yeats had not seen Mrs. Shakespear for the duration of an entire summer in 1929!

Richard Ellmann tells us that "Yeats had Mrs. Shakespear in mind when he wrote this poem. . . ."[7] Parkinson, probably legitimately, strengthens this to "The poem takes its origin in a visit to Olivia Shakespear in October, 1929."[8] I presume that he bases this statement on the evidence of the letters that Yeats did visit Mrs. Shakespear in London in late October or early November of 1929[9] and that on December 16 he sent her from Rapallo the substantially finished poem "of which I showed you the prose draft."[10] (From London Yeats had left for Rapallo "on the morning of the 21st"[11] of November, and he had written "After Long Silence" "when I first got here,"[12] in other words in Rapallo soon after November 21st. He had been ill since then and unable to write letters in his own hand. He had dictated a December 12 letter to Mrs. Shakespear but did not send the poem to her until he could write it in his own hand on December 16.)

The only "prose draft" of the poem extant has been transcribed by

---

[7] Richard Ellmann, *The Identity of Yeats* (New York, 1964, first published in 1954), p. 279.

[8] Parkinson, p. 83.

[9] *The Letters of W. B. Yeats*, ed. Allan Wade (London, 1954), pp. 770-72.

[10] *Letters*, p. 772.

[11] *Letters*, p. 771.

[12] *Letters*, p. 772.

Ellmann, by Jon Stallworthy, and, with a variation, by Parkinson.
Ellmann and Stallworthy agree on the following transcription:

> Subject
>
> Your hair is white
> My hair is white
> Come let us talk of love
> What other theme do we know
> When we were young
> We were in love with one another
> And therefore ignorant

(Parkinson transcribes the last line, wrongly I think, as "And then were
ignorant.")[13]

There is nothing about a "long silence" in this draft, and that is not
surprising if this is the draft which Yeats showed to Mrs. Shakespear on
his October/November visit. There had been no "long silence." He had
seen her before the summer, early in May 1929,[14] and, earlier, in
October 1928[15] and in June 1928.[16]

Furthermore, if "speech" can include letters, there certainly had
been no "long silence" in Yeats's converse with Mrs. Shakespear. In the
volume of Yeats's *Letters*, there are more letters to her than to any other
person except Lady Gregory. The usual tone of these letters may be
indicated by a sentence from one postmarked September 15, 1928: "It
is always a delight to see you for as you have grown older you have
grown into the essence of yourself."[17] Age is not a shock to the former
lover here.

---

[13] Ellmann, p. 280; Jon Stallworthy, *Between the Lines: Yeats's Poetry in the Making*
(Oxford, 1963), p. 209; Parkinson, p. 83.

[14] *Letters*, p. 763.

[15] *Letters*, pp. 747-48.

[16] *Letters*, pp. 742-46. On April 25, 1928, Yeats wrote to Mrs. Shakespear, "Will you be
in London in June? I want to see you. . . ." *Letters*, p. 742. He did go to London as planned
(cf. letter of July 9 [Postmark July 11, 1928], *Letters*, p. 744, "I was very tired after
London"), and although one cannot say for sure that he saw Mrs. Shakespear, a following
letter [Postmark September 15, 1928] sounds as if he had. *Letters*, p. 746. On October 11
[Postmark 1928] he writes from Dublin that he will be in London October 17 and asks
"Where shall we meet and when?" *Letters*, p. 747. There is no indication in his November
23 [1928] letter from Rapallo that they failed to meet. *Letters*, p. 748. On March 2 [1929]
he writes again, "I shall be in London on May 1 and stay perhaps a fortnight, so keep
some hours for me." *Letters*, p. 759. A letter of April 10 [1929] confirms his plan to stay in
London. *Letters*, pp. 761-62. Letters of April 26 [1929] and May 4 [Postmark May 6,
1929?] show him confirming plans to meet Mrs. Shakespear. *Letters*, p. 763. His letter of
Sunday May 19 [Postmark 1929] to Lady Gregory mentions being in London and
mentions seeing the "usual round of friends, Sturge Moore, Ricketts, Lady Ottoline and
so on." *Letters*, 764. Was it tact that made him fail to mention Mrs. Shakespear? There is
no other evidence that he did not see her "Tuesday 7:30." *Letters*, p. 763. His next visit to
her in London was the one in October or November 1929 which, Parkinson believes,
precipitated "After Long Silence."

[17] *Letters*, p. 746.

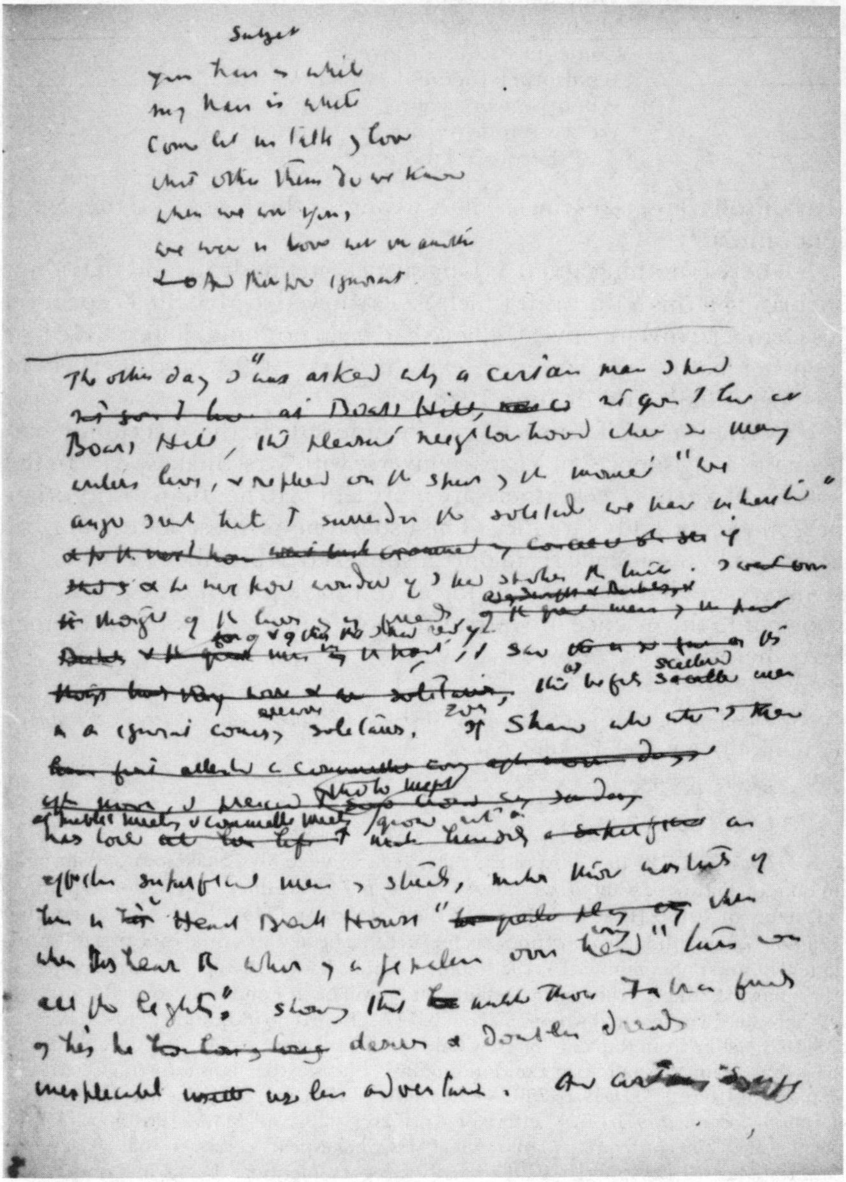
Subject

Your hair is white
My hair is white
Come let us talk of love
What other theme do we know
When we were young
We were in love with one another
And therefore ignorant

The manuscripts show that "Speech after long silence" was the last idea to enter the poem. The phrase appears first in what Stallworthy gives as "the final version . . . dated 'Nov 1929.' "[18] And I do not believe that it was primarily the meeting with Olivia Shakespear that suggested it. An idea like that would probably have gotten into the first draft if it had been an important part of the occasioning experience.

To what other external influence was Yeats subject at this time which might have suggested the "Speech after long silence" situation? None that applies directly, so far as I know. But I do observe that Yeats was actively involved with his revision of the 1925 *A Vision*. I agree with Marjorie G. Perloff that "the reader must be wary" of concluding from Yeats's own extreme statements that there is a "pervasive presence of the sexual theme in the later poetry."[19] I agree with Andy P. Antippas that it is important, in reading the Crazy Jane poems, "to shift the emphasis from Jane's anarchism and sensuality to Jane's sense of the *Vision*'s history,"[20] and certainly it is just as important to do that in reading the other poems in *Words for Music Perhaps*. If the letters are any evidence Yeats was more preoccupied with wisdom and the immortality of the soul than with physical love in the months September through November 1929.

On September 13 (Postmark 1929) Yeats wrote to Mrs. Shakespear explaining the purpose of his *A Packet for Ezra Pound* (her son-in-law):

> The essay in the *Packet* will be the introduction of a new edition of the *Vision* under the name of 'The Great Wheel.' But this new edition will be a new book, all I hope clear and as simple as the subject permits. Four or five years' reading has given me some knowledge of metaphysics and time to clear up endless errors in my understanding of the script. My conviction of the truth of it all has grown also and that makes one clear. I am taking to Rapallo what will be I hope a clear typed script of the whole book. I will work at it here and there free at last, now that all is constructive, to sharpen definitions and enrich descriptions. I should go to press with it next spring. I shall begin also I hope the new version of the Robartes stories. Having proved, by undescribed process, the immortality of the soul to a little group of typical followers, he will discuss the deductions with an energy and a dogmatism and a cruelty I am not capable of in my own person. I have a very amusing setting thought out. I shall also finish the book of thirty poems for music I am more than half through. 'For Music' is only a name, nobody will sing them.[21]

There are further references to his work on *A Vision* in letters of

---

[18] Stallworthy, p. 210.

[19] Marjorie G. Perloff, " 'Heart Mysteries': The Later Love Lyrics of W. B. Yeats," *Contemporary Literature*, 10, No. 2 (1969), 267.

[20] Andy P. Antippas, "A Note on Yeats's 'Crazy Jane' Poems," *English Studies*, 49 (1968), 557.

[21] *Letters*, p. 769.

October 13 (Postmark Oct 14, 1929), and November 16, 1929.[22]

It is important to bear *A Vision* in mind when interpreting any of Yeats's later poems. However, what interests me at the moment is the relevance of Yeats's work on *A Vision* at this time to the biographical question, not the interpretative one. In order to use *A Packet for Ezra Pound* as the introductory section of *A Vision*, Yeats removed not only the old "Introduction" by "Owen Aherne" but also the "Dedication" to "Vestigia."

The woman to whom the first edition of *A Vision* was dedicated was a close friend of Yeats's middle and later twenties, "the young and beautiful wife" of MacGregor Mathers (the author of *The Kabbalah Unveiled*) and "the sister of the philosopher, Henri Bergson."[23] The Mathers were married shortly after MacGregor initiated Yeats into the Order of the Golden Dawn,[24] and Yeats's deep involvement with that Hermetical society was also a deep involvement with the Mathers. It may help to review some of the events of that time. Joseph Hone tells how Yeats stayed with the Mathers while in Paris, scenes which must have made pleasant memories:

> As a rule, though he evidently lived under a great strain, Mathers was a gay and companionable man. In the evenings he made his wife and Yeats play chess with him, a curious form of chess with four players. Yeats' partner was Mrs. Mathers, Mathers' a spirit. Mathers would shade his eyes with his hands and gaze at the empty chair at the opposite corner of the board before moving his partner's piece.[25]

For a brief time, Maud Gonne was a member of the Golden Dawn until she decided it was tainted with British free-masonry and resigned. Yeats was very much in love with her, and I think it is important that Mrs. Mathers was not a mere spectator but a minor actor in the emotional drama of their relationship. Maud Gonne had seen "an apparition, a woman in grey, remembered from her infancy," and Yeats "was persuaded that he must make this woman visible, for he believed it was an evil spirit troubling his friend's life, weakening affections and creating a desire for power and excitement. If it were made visible, it would put the temptation into words and could be faced." Mrs. Mathers "made a symbol for him accord.ng to the rules of the Order . . . and almost at once it became visible." The resulting vision "showed Miss Gonne going off into the desert to die alone, and also connected her with someone who lived in the desert and bore a curious relationship to Yeats himself. . . ."[26]

---

[22] *Letters*, p. 770.

[23] *The Autobiography of William Butler Yeats* (New York, 1953), p. 113.

[24] Joseph Hone, *W. B. Yeats, 1865-1939* (New York, 1943), p. 75.

[25] Hone, p. 113.

[26] Hone, p. 89.

The Mathers were also involved in Yeats's plan, with Maud Gonne, to found an Order of Celtic Mysteries.[27] However, Mathers' "restless conduct and extreme spiritual pretensions"[28] resulted in a schism in the Golden Dawn in 1900, and Yeats arraigned him before a chapter of the Order, but without forgetting "the past and the honour that one owes even to a fallen idol."[29] Yeats saw little of the Mathers after that. Mathers died at the end of World War I.

Here follows the episode which I think may have given Yeats the idea of the line "Speech after long silence." Hone writes that "After the death of Mathers his widow came to London, where she read with great displeasure the statements about 'S.R.M.D.' [Mathers] in Yeats's *Autobiographies*, such as that 'he was to die of melancholia' and that he was 'self-educated, unscholarly, though learned,' whereas he had received one of the best English educations at Bedford Grammar School. Yeats visited Mrs. Mathers—[after long silence]—and they were reconciled. . . ."[30] This visit probably took place after the publication of *The Trembling of the Veil* (in which the offending passages occur) in 1922 and before Yeats wrote the "Dedication" to the 1925 edition of *A Vision*.

This "Dedication" is echoed in "After Long Silence" in both words and substance.

To Vestigia

It is a constant thought of mine that what we write is often a commendation of, or expostulation with the friends of our youth, and that even if we survive all our friends we continue to prolong or to amend conversations that took place before our five-and-twentieth year. Perhaps this book has been written because a number of young men and women, you and I among the number, met nearly forty years ago in London and in Paris to discuss mystical philosophy. You with your beauty and your learning and your mysterious gifts were held by all in affection, and though, when the first draft of this dedication was written, I had not seen you for more than thirty years, nor knew where you were nor what you were doing, and though much had happened since we copied the Jewish Schemahamphorasch with its seventy-two Names of God in Hebrew characters, it was plain that I must dedicate my book to you. All other students who were once friends or friends' friends were dead or estranged.[31]

The quoted passage begins with a reference to conversations of youth interrupted by the passage of time yet continued in one's own writing. Yeats has in mind "All Souls' Night" with which he ends the volume. Yet from the ghosts he calls up there, "to prolong or amend

---

[27] Hone, p. 140.

[28] Hone, p. 179.

[29] *Letters*, p. 340.

[30] Hone, p. 516.

[31] William Butler Yeats, *A Vision: An Explanation of Life Founded upon the Writings of Giraldus and upon Certain Doctrines Attributed to Kusta Ben Luka* (London, 1925), p. ix.

conversations that took place before our five-and-twentieth year," it is not a far cry to the ancient lover met "after long silence" who is but a ghost of her youthful self. "After Long Silence" continues the conversation with the aged living as "All Souls' Night" does with the dead. They seem companion poems thus. In both there is "a marvellous thing to say" or a "supreme theme" to descant upon. The "marvellous thing" is mocked by "None but the living"[32] the "supreme theme" misunderstood by "ignorant" youth. In both, "Bodily decrepitude is wisdom."

The last sentence quoted from the "Dedication" needs but little editing to turn it from "All other . . . friends were dead or estranged" to the second line of our poem: "All other lovers being estranged or dead." It is a clear echo.

Now what is more natural than that Yeats while revising *A Vision* in the autumn of 1929, while planning to put *A Packet for Ezra Pound* in and to take out the old "Dedication" and "Introduction," should find himself rereading or rethinking that "Dedication" and remembering the meeting which led to its writing? I am not, certainly, claiming that Mrs. Mathers was ever one of Yeats's "lovers," merely that she had been a beautiful woman who was deeply associated in his mind with the love experiences of his young manhood. I believe that Yeats reread the "Dedication" to Vestigia at a time when he was also working on his poem to Olivia Shakespear and saw that he could borrow and alter the sentence "All other . . . friends were dead or estranged." The train of association once started continued. My answer to the biographical question raised above is that Yeats got the idea for the line "Speech after long silence" from his own account of his meeting of reconciliation with Mrs. MacGregor Mathers after not having seen her for "more than thirty years."

II

But if this answer to the biographical question is correct, how does such an accidental detail help to clarify the "supreme theme"? The possibility that Yeats was recalling his reconciliation with Mrs. Mathers while writing a poem occasioned by a visit to Mrs. Shakespear enlarges the context in which we read the poem, reminding us that when Yeats wrote a poem for one woman he may very well have brought in experiences which he had had with others, in other words that the process of universalizing the unique experience may involve melding it with other unique experiences. In this case the unique experience of visiting Olivia Shakespear, an old friend and former mistress, the woman who was for "more than forty years . . . the centre" of his life in London and of whom he was to write painfully after her death, "She was not more lovely than distinguished—no matter what happened she

---

[32] Cf. *Variorum Poems*, pp. 470-74, for "All Souls' Night."

never lost her solitude,"[33] may have melded with the unique experience of being reconciled with Mrs. Mathers, the wife of an old friend with whom he had quarreled, a woman with whom he had never had a love experience.

One value of the larger context for me, as I have said, is that it leads me to think of "After Long Silence" in connection with "All Souls' Night," on which the "Dedication" to Vestigia is a gloss. The dead taste "ecstasy / No living man can drink from the whole wine" (*Variorum Poems*, p. 474), but the old man and old woman have become so refined in palate through bodily decrepitude that they can almost equal the dead. They can "laugh and weep an hour upon the clock" or "descant and yet again descant" on "mummy truths" that sober youth ignorantly act out. It is not the physical possession of love but the mental or spiritual possession of it that is valuable. And this spiritual possession is impossible without physical loss.

The pattern is basic to *A Vision* (cf. the man of phase 17) and to Yeats's concept of the life of the great artist in the *Autobiography*. If love is a "supreme theme of Art and Song" it is because of the loss of love by poets who then had to try to regain it in another sense through their art.

> Had not Dante and Villon understood that their fate wrecked what life could not rebuild, had they lacked their Vision of Evil, had they cherished any species of optimism, they could but have found a false beauty, or some momentary instinctive beauty, and suffered no change at all, or but changed as do the wild creatures, or from devil well to devil sick, and so round the clock.
>   They and their sort alone learn contemplation, for it is only when the intellect has wrought the whole of life to drama, to crisis, that we may live for contemplation, and yet keep our intensity.[34]

This widening of the reference accords with the abandonment, in revision, of specific sensual data—"Your hair is white / My hair is white"; "Once more I have kissed your hand"—and with the change from "love"—"Come let us talk of love"; "on love descant"—to "the sole theme of art and song" and finally to "the supreme theme of Art and Song." Anyone knows that love is not "the sole theme of art and song," nor is limited human love the "supreme theme," as a quick run-down of some supreme masterpieces would quickly show: *King Lear, Hamlet, The Last Supper, The Last Judgment*, etc. "Come let us talk of love" might lead to conversation on the following subjects:

> How such a man pleased women most
> Of all that are gone,
> How such a pair loved many years
> And such a pair but one,

---

[33] *Letters*, p. 916.

[34] *Autobiography*, p. 165.

>   Stories of the bed of straw
>   Or the bed of down (*Variorum Poems*, p. 458).

For such matters, "The Secrets of the Old" is a better designation than "the supreme theme of Art and Song."

Think how much weaker the line would be if it read "on love, the supreme theme of Art and Song." As it is, the reader's mind soars supremely, looking for the "supreme theme" and following the "high talk" of the old couple as it too soars—descanting: playing variations, or expatiating—on the highest conceptions of great art. In the context of "lovers," "supreme theme" allows us to associate their descant not only with Paris and Helen, Romeo and Juliet, Antony and Cleopatra, and Tristan and Isolde, but also with Dante and Beatrice and thus with Love in its highest state as in Plato's *Symposium* or St. John of the Cross's "The Living Flame of Love." Certainly, "Bodily decrepitude is wisdom" could be straight out of the *Phaedo*:

> And the true philosophers, Simmias, are always occupied in the practice of dying, wherefore also to them least of all men is death terrible. Look at the matter thus: if they have been in every way the enemies of the body, and are wanting to be alone with the soul, when this desire of theirs is granted, how inconsistent would they be if they trembled and repined, instead of rejoicing at their departure to that place where, when they arrive, they hope to gain that which in life they desired—and this was wisdom—and at the same time to be rid of the company of their enemy. . . . [35]

For Plato, "Bodily decrepitude is wisdom." Earlier in Yeats's manuscripts the line read "Decrepitude increases wisdom," but "bodily decrepitude" is a process already, a breaking down or cracking up, the release of the soul from the chains of the body. The word "increases" is redundant. The decrepitude of the body *is* wisdom.

Two of the three "dead or estranged" friends whom Yeats mentions in his "Dedication: To Vestigia" were "lovers" who exemplified that "Bodily decrepitude is wisdom." Horton, who "knew that sweet extremity of pride / That's called platonic love" (*Variorum Poems*, p. 471), survived the object of this love "but a little time during which he saw her in apparition and attained through her certain of the traditional experiences of the saint."[36] There was in Horton's love an ambiguity like the one which we find in the "supreme theme." The "supreme theme" cannot be limited to ordinary human love, and Horton's love cannot be for God alone:

> Two thoughts were so mixed up I could not tell
> Whether of her or God he thought the most,

---

[35] *Plato*, trans. B. Jowett, ed. Louise Ropes Loomis (Toronto, New York, London, 1942), p. 97.

[36] *A Vision* (1925), p. x.

> But think that his mind's eye,
> When upward turned, on one sole image fell. . . .
>   (*Variorum Poems*, p. 471)

Florence Farr Emery made the best of her "bodily decrepitude" by attempting to use it to rise to ecstasy:

> On Florence Emery I call the next,
> Who finding the first wrinkles on a face
> Admired and beautiful,
> And knowing that the future would be vexed
> With 'minished beauty, multiplied commonplace,
> Preferred to teach a school
> Away from neighbour or friend,
> Among dark skins, and there
> Permit foul years to wear
> Hidden from eyesight to the unnoticed end.
>
> Before that end much had she ravelled out
> From a discourse in figurative speech
> By some learned Indian
> On the soul's journey. How it is whirled about,
> Wherever the orbit of the moon can reach,
> Until it plunge into the sun;
> And there, free and yet fast,
> Being both Chance and Choice
> Forget its broken toys
> And sink into its own delight at last.
>   (*Variorum Poems*, pp. 472-73)

Her " 'minished beauty" is "hidden from eyesight" as the "Unfriendly lamplight [is] hid under its shade." "Chance" and "Choice" are almost one in the sexual act according to "Solomon and the Witch" (*Variorum Poems*, p. 387), and in "All Souls' Night," through "bodily decrepitude," chance and choice are united, as above, at the end of the soul's journey. The link with "All Souls' Night" clearly pulls the "supreme theme" from "love" towards "bodily decrepitude is wisdom."

III

Now the reader may find it a bit far-fetched to use "All Souls' Night" to prove an interpretation of "After Long Silence." A new look at the manuscripts, however, will show that beyond a doubt at a certain point in writing the poem Yeats began to think about the book he was revising—*A Vision*—and specifically about the dedication "To Vestigia" which begins that book (in the 1925 edition) and about "All Souls' Night" which ends it (in all editions).

The first draft that we have of "After Long Silence" is extremely direct and personal.

[Draft 1]

>   Subject
>   Your hair is white
>   My hair is white
>   Come let us talk of love
>   What other themes do we know
>   When we were young
>   We were in love with one another
>   A̶ ̶O̶[?] And therefore ignorant[37]

The second draft, too, begins with a very direct, personal line:

>   Your other lover being dead & gone

Yeats thought of his widowed mistress's late husband. This line is
revised, however, into the more general and impersonal "Those other
lovers being dead & gone." Then, when he came to versify the prose
"Come let us talk of love," perhaps this general reminiscence brought
"All Souls' Night" to his mind. The process could have gone something
like this: Draft 1 had given him one rhyme sound in "white" and two
rhyme words "young" and "ignorant." In draft 2 he spreads these out
on the page, making a sort of map which will guide him in filling in new
lines and rhymes.

[Draft 2]

>   Those   rs
>   Y̶o̶u̶r̶ other lover being dead & gone *
>
>   friendly[?]   light
>   hair is white

---

[37] From National Library Manuscript 13,581; Manuscript Book B, p. 69.

Transcribing Yeats is a tricky business, and in what follows I have nothing but
admiration for the work of the pioneer editors of these manuscripts. Parkinson's trans-
criptions differ from Stallworthy's at various points. Moreover I have found that both are
incomplete. Another look is needed. I have therefore re-transcribed the manuscripts
from the photographs in the Yeats Archives at the State University of New York at Stony
Brook, and although I have not yet had a chance to check the original manuscripts, the
items which I have noted are clear on film. The versions are all in Yeats's hand.

Cancellations within a line are reproduced. Cancellation of an entire line is indicated
by an X at the left. Cancellation of several consecutive lines is indicated by a line down the
left side. An illegible letter is indicated by an asterisk. Spelling is silently corrected, but
punctuation is as in the manuscript. Anything added by me is in square brackets.

Ellmann, Stallworthy and Parkinson all read "theme" where I read "themes."
Though Yeats's spelling and handwriting are unpredictable, he almost always indicates
an "e" ending by an up-stroke, an "s" ending by a down-stroke, as here. For the last line
Parkinson has "And then were ignorant." Although the two syllables of "therefore" are
separated, the first seems to me to end with "re," the second to begin with "f." The second
syllable is unlike the other appearances of "were" in the draft.

All previously unpublished material by W. B. Yeats copyright © 1976 by Anne Yeats
and Michael Butler Yeats. Thanks are due to them, to A. P. Watt & Son, to the National
Library of Ireland, to the W. B. Yeats Archives, Center for Contemporary Arts and
Letters, State University of New York at Stony Brook, and to the Macmillan Company,
for permission to publish these manuscripts.

~~on love descant~~   descant
Upon the ~~sole theme~~ supreme theme of art &   song
Wherein their [=there's?] theme so fitting for the aged   ; young
We loved each other & were ignorant   [ignorant][38]

In order to line up the rhyme words as Yeats did I have had to greatly exaggerate the spaces before them, but the spaces are there. Yeats has already decided—or the poem has decided—what the rhyme scheme will be: abbacddc. He has the beginning of a first line

> Those other lovers being dead & gone

but he leaves a space for an end rhyme (even though he already has five beats and will have to cut back the line later). Then at the extreme right he puts in the middle rhymes of the quatrain:

> friendly light
> hair is white.

Then he leaves a space for a fourth line to rhyme with the first.

Moving to the second quatrain, he has found "descant" to rhyme with "ignorant" and "song" to rhyme with "young." He lines these up under "light" and "white."

> _____
> light
> white
> _____
> descant
> song
> young
> [ignorant]

(He does not add "ignorant" under "young" as I have because he already has secured his final line by a slight revision of "We were in love with one another / And therefore ignorant" from draft 1.)

---

[38] From Manuscript Book B, p. 73.

Although Stallworthy does not print these "preliminary jottings" (p. 209) and Parkinson treats them as "very tentative notes" (p. 87), I find in them one important biographical detail and, in the last four lines, not a series of interchangeable possibilities (listed _a_, _b_, and _c_ by Parkinson), but a very revealing transitional version of the final four lines of the poem. Parkinson misses the fact that "lovers" was at first "lover." In this poem for this widowed former mistress Yeats began by writing "Your other lover being dead and gone," surely a bow in the direction of Olivia Shakespear's deceased husband. The line which Parkinson prints as "Your other lovers being dead and gone" probably never existed. It would indeed, as Parkinson says, have had "the tone of accusation." But I think that the line went directly from "Your other lover being dead & gone" to "Those other lovers being dead & gone." The latter line as Parkinson says, establishes "equality and community between the two aged lovers."

Parkinson's transcription of the next to last line above is "Upon that theme so fitting for the aged; young." "Upon that" is certainly an incorrect reading. The words are longer than these. I believe that, as the rhyme scheme shows, Yeats was not trying out variants here but was composing a verse paragraph.

Next he fills in some of the spaces:

~~on love descant~~   descant
Upon the ~~sole theme~~ supreme theme of art &   song
Wherein theirs [there's?] theme so fitting for the aged   ; young

"Descant" he wants and keeps, though he eliminates the repetition of it.
"On love" must go, however, as the poem has moved towards the "All
Soul's Night" pattern. In "All Soul's Night" he sought a ghost

> Wound in mind's pondering
> As mummies in the mummy-cloth are wound;
> Because I have a marvelous thing to say,
> A certain marvelous thing
> None but the living mock. . . .
> (*Variorum Poems*, p. 471)

Here the lovers

                                                                        descant
Upon the supreme theme of art & song
Wherein there's theme so fitting for the aged. . . .

With the cancellation of "on love" the subject of the poem is changing
or is being defined. "Wherein" can refer either to "theme" or to "art &
song." The awkward repetition of "theme" makes "art & song" a more
likely referent. It makes more sense to say that there is a fitting theme
in art and song than that there is a fitting theme in the supreme theme.
The poem is getting away from saying "Come let us talk of love" and is
feeling for a higher subject which has something to do with art and
song.

Perhaps Yeats remembered the familiar and beautiful "Conclusion" of Pater's *The Renaissance*, in which the "poetic passion," as
compared to other "great passions" such as "ecstasy and sorrow of
love," is said to give most of wisdom and "the highest quality to your
moments as they pass." Pater quotes Victor Hugo, "We are all under
sentence of death, but with a sort of indefinite reprieve," and goes on,
"Some spend this interval in listlessness, some in high passions, the
wisest . . . in art and song."[39] Since the interval diminishes as one grows
older, it is a short step from Pater's assertion to Yeats's thought that in
art and song "there's theme so fitting for the aged." And implicit in that
phrase is the further thought, which will emerge in the next draft, that
"Decrepitude increases wisdom." The direction is toward making
"Bodily decrepitude is wisdom" the "supreme theme." Definite echoes
of "To Vestigia" and "All Souls' Night," also in the next draft, will
demonstrate this probability.

In draft 3 Yeats has abandoned "hair is white" and found another
rhyme for "light" which will allow him to make a complete sentence of

---

[39] Walter Pater, *The Renaissance: Studies in Art and Poetry* (London, 1925; first published 1873), pp. 251-52. As the subtitle suggests, the supreme theme of Pater's book, at
any rate, is "art and song."

the whole poem.

[Draft 3]

I h
Once more I have kissed your hand[?] & it is right—
All other lovers being estranged or dead
The heavy curtain drawn—the candle light
Waging[?] a doubtful battle[?] with the shade

                                   descant
We call ~~our wisdom~~ up upon our wisdom & ~~descant~~
Upon the supreme theme of art & song—
Decrepitude increases wisdom—young
We loved each other & were ~~ignorant~~ ~~ignorant~~ ignorant[40]

The sentence structure is now set, though the rhyme scheme is askew: ababcddc instead of the more symmetrical abbacddc. A third line has been perfected: "All other lovers being estranged or dead." This line is a direct echo of Yeats's dedication of *A Vision* "To Vestigia" whom he "had not seen . . . for more than thirty years": "All other students who were once friends or friends' friends were dead or estranged" (*A Vision*, 1925, p. ix). The scene which follows recalls "All Souls' Night":

    Midnight has come, and the great Christ Church Bell
    And many a lesser bell sound through the room;
    And it is All Souls' Night,
    And two long glasses brimmed with muscatel
    Bubble upon the table. A ghost may come. . . .

                       (*Variorum Poems*, p. 470)

    The heavy curtain drawn—the candle light
    Waging a doubtful battle with the shade
    We call our wisdom up. . . .

In connection with this draft Parkinson excellently says that " 'shade' entered the poem in association with its rhyme word 'dead,' and that at first it came to [Yeats's] mind because of its suggestion of shadow and spirit. The candle at this stage was the spark of life, the light asserted

---

[40] From Manuscript Book B, p. 73, bottom of page. Parkinson (p. 88) does not transcribe the dash after "song." The dash is there, though no more than a hyphen in length. It separates off "Decrepitude increases wisdom" and strengths the likelihood that this interpolation is there to define the "supreme theme."

Stallworthy has "hair" rather than "hand" in the second line, and "hair" seems more natural. But the end of the word goes up, not down, and cannot be an "r." (Compare the "And's" in the "Byzantium" manuscript which is the frontispiece to Stallworthy's book.) If Yeats meant to write "hair," he failed to do so. Parkinson reads "hand" and remarks that Yeats's "courtly manner of greeting came directly into the poem (Parkinson, p. 88).

Parkinson's reading "Waging a doubtful battle with the shade" is brilliant! Stallworthy has "Bringing a doubtful (   ) with the shade," which is exactly what I came up with myself, misreading the first word and not being able to read the fourth. The first word has a line which makes "b" unlikely and "w" a possibility as a first letter.

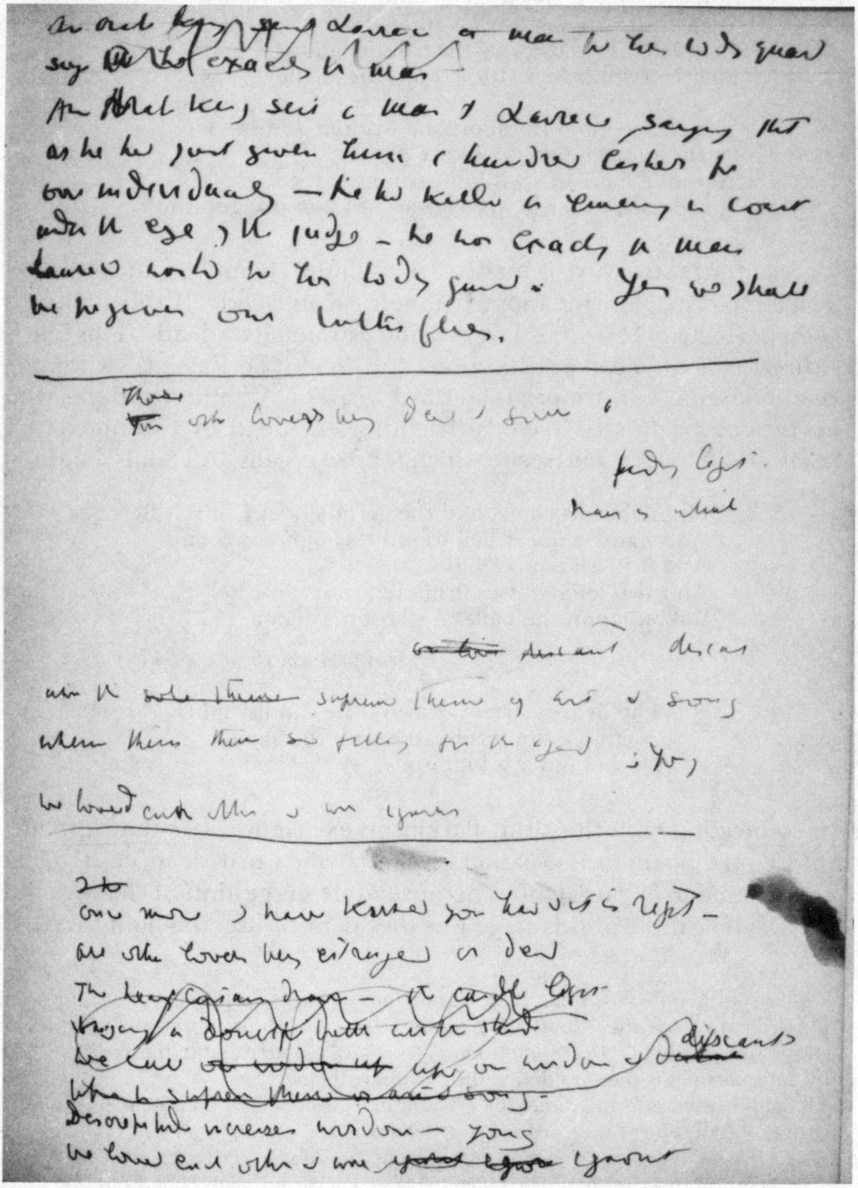

against the deepening surrounding dark, night, death" (Parkinson, p. 91). The lovers are to call their wisdom up as the speaker of "All Souls' Night" called up ghosts: "Horton's the first I call"; "On Florence Emery I call the next"; "And I call up MacGregor from the grave . . ." (*Variorum Poems*, pp. 471-73). "Decrepitude increases wisdom" in "All Souls' Night," though not in "The Tower"—"dull decrepitude / Or what worse evil" (*Variorum Poems*, p. 416)—nor in James Clarence Mangan's "Lament for the Princes of Tyrone and Tyrconnell" from which Yeats probably got the word.[41]

In draft 4 Yeats restores the abbacddc rhyme scheme and in the process is forced—in order to find an immediate rhyme for "dead"—to put "the candle light" and "the shade" in the same line, thus losing "light" as a rhyme.

> X The candle hidden by its friendly shade
> X The curtains drawn on the unfriendly night
>   That we descant & yet again descant
>   Upon the supreme theme of art & song.

"The heavy curtain drawn" of the previous draft suggests "night" as a rhyme for "right" and with "The curtains drawn on the unfriendly night" we have another line nearly perfected. Then the line, "That we descant and yet again descant" is completed because Yeats must get rid of the awkward repetition of wisdom in the previous draft:

>   descant
> We call ~~our wisdom up~~ upon our wisdom & ~~descant~~
> Upon the supreme theme of art & song—
> Decrepitude increases wisdom. . . .

At this point Yeats went over the original four lines of draft 4 with a purple pencil, adding the lines which I have indented below.

[Draft 4]

>   Un
>   ~~The~~ friendly lamplight hidden by its shade
> X   And shutters clapped upon the deeping night
> X The candle hidden by its friendly shade
>   Those curtains drawn upon the deepening night—
>   s
> X The curtains drawn on the unfriendly night

---

[41] In W. B. Yeats, *A Book of Irish Verse* (London, 1911; first published 1895), p. 34:

> Theirs were not souls wherein dull Time
>   Could domicile Decay or house
>   Decrepitude!
> They passed from Earth ere Manhood's prime,
>   Ere years had power to dim their brows
>   Or chill their blood.

Cf. "Out of a People to a People," in David R. Clark, *Lyric Resonance* (Amherst, 1972), pp. 26-27.

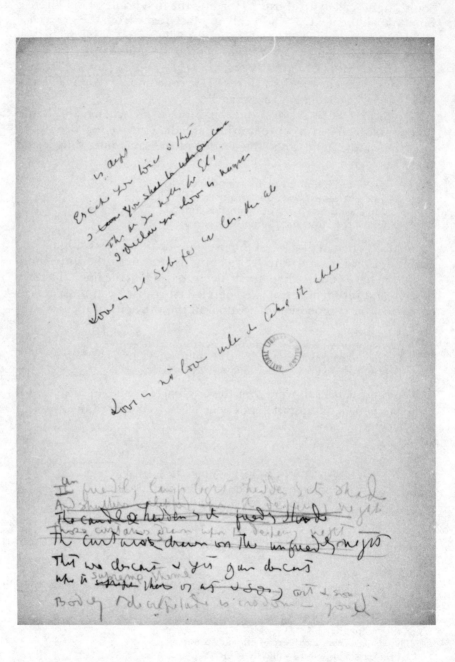

> That we descant & yet again descant
>   supreme theme   art & song—
> Upon the ~~supreme theme~~ of ~~art & song~~
>   Bodily decrepitude is wisdom—young[42]

As Parkinson eloquently puts it:

> Then suddenly the candle became a lamp, and with this act it was possible
> to see it not as the analogue of life but, with its persistent electric
> revealing glare, as the enemy to the illusive memory of youth, the harper
> on bodily decrepitude. So the shade became friendly to the lovers and the
> lamplight unfriendly, a reminder of death as surely as was the night.
> Once this was seen, it was possible to effect the startling balance of the
> equal unfriendliness of night and light (Parkinson, pp. 91-92).

The idea of the "Unfriendly lamplight" may well have been suggested by the references to Florence Emery in "To Vestigia" and "All
Souls' Night." "Dreading old age and fading beauty" (*A Vision*, 1925, p.
ix), she

> Preferred to teach a school
> Away from neighbour or friend,
> Among dark skins, and there
> Permit foul years to wear
> Hidden from eyesight to the unnoticed end.
>   (*Variorum Poems*, p. 472)

The "deepening shades" that end "The Tower"—in the same passage
as "dull decrepitude" (*Variorum Poems*, p. 416)—may have suggested
the "deepening night." In both poems the speaker is making his soul,
"Compelling it to study / In a learned school" (*Variorum Poems*, p. 416)
as the darkness deepens toward death. This association perhaps facili-
tated the perfecting of the phrase "Bodily decrepitude is wisdom." ". . .
Wisdom is the property of the dead" we learn in "Bood and the Moon"
(*Variorum Poems*, p. 482). Whereas "Decrepitude increases wisdom"
seems to describe some mortal attainment, "Bodily decrepitude is
wisdom" describes the condition of knowledge toward which the aged
descend as they pass through deepening shades out of the mortal
condition of power.

The revisions in draft 4 are incorporated in a fair copy (which I
shall call draft 5, although I have seen only Parkinson's transcription of
it on page 89). Draft 6 is, except for punctuation changes, the completed poem:

[Draft 6]

> Speech after long silence; ~~*~~ it is right—

---

[42] From Manuscript Book B, p. 72 (indented lines added after the others; that is,
Yeats superimposes a new attempt on the old). Parkinson has "clipped" rather than
"clapped" and may well be right, although there is no dot for the "i." It is significant that
Yeats has been careful again to add the dash after "song."

Speech after long silence; it is right —
all other lovers being estranged or dead,
Unfriendly lamp-light hid under its shade,
The curtains drawn upon unfriendly night —
That we descant and yet again descant
Upon the supreme theme of art and song:
Bodily decrepitude is wisdom; young
We loved each other and were ignorant

                              Nov 1929

When I wrote this poem, I had clearly been ill for two or three weeks or so — I had just arrived in Rapallo & stopped into complete sleepiness — the first sign I suppose of Malta fever. Now it is the end of March & for the last ten days I have begun to work again, reading "The Vision". I am at Porto Fino Vetta & can look from my windows out over a very tranquil sea & a coast dotted with sunlight houses as far as Genoa. I know seven or eight hotels at Rapallo & have stage-fright in any hotels if a few hundred yards. Here I can slip in & out either a word & unperceived hourly. It is now four months since my [recovery] from the flu, in London & I have written nothing, but one poem as I dick say I will again for another three months, about even I suppose not able to write verse

or

All other lovers being estranged ~~*~~ dead,
hid
Unfriendly lamp-light ~~hid~~ under its shade,
upon
The curtain's drawn ~~upon~~ unfriendly night—
That we descant & yet again descant
Upon the supreme theme of art & song/ :
Bodily decrepitude is wisdom~~*~~ ; young
We loved each other & were ignorant

Nov
~~Oct~~ 1929[43]

The striking new phrase "Speech after long silence" is one more and the final borrowing of an idea from "To Vestigia." The opening line of the poem is reminiscent of the opening sentence of the dedication: "It is a constant thought of mine that what we write is often a commendation of, or expostulation with the friends of our youth, and that even if we survive all our friends we continue to prolong or to amend conversations that took place before our five-and-twentieth year. Perhaps this book has been written because a number of young men and women, you and I among the number, met nearly forty years ago in London and in Paris to discuss mystical philosophy" (*A Vision*, 1925, p. ix). The dedication itself is "Speech after long silence."

The echoes and reminiscences of the 1925 *A Vision* in the manuscripts of "After Long Silence" show that Yeats's revision of the book had a substantial effect on the development of the poem. This development was towards presenting "Bodily decrepitude is wisdom" as the "supreme theme of art and song." Other manuscript changes support this conclusion.

The most revealing items in draft 6 are the revisions of the punctuation in lines 6 and 7, which neither Stallworthy nor Parkinson takes note of. In line 6 Yeats first uses a semi-colon after "song" (replacing the dash of the previous version). This he then changes to a colon. In line 7 he perhaps first used a dash after "wisdom" as in the previous version, then superimposed a colon on the dash, then cancelled both and added a semi-colon. He must have made these punctuation changes as he wrote or there would not have been room for the semi-colon before "young." Although Yeats's use of the colon is not consistent throughout his poetry, over half of those in *The Winding Stair* (in the definitive edition) indicate that an elaboration or summation follow. Here, the fact that he distinguishes so carefully between colon and semi-colon leads me to believe that he means the colon to introduce the "supreme theme," which is therefore "Bodily decrepitude is wisdom." These changes are incorporated into drafts 7 and 8.

---

[43] From Manuscript Book B, p. 75. The illegible cancelled items represented by the asterisks in lines 1 and 2 may be ampersands, although the one in line 1 may be a two-letter word.

From a December 16, 1929, letter to Olivia Shakespear:
[Draft 7]

> Speech after long silence; it is right—
> All other lovers being estranged or dead,
> Unfriendly lamp-light hid under its shade
> The curtains drawn upon unfriendly night|—
> That we descant, & yet again descant
> Upon the supreme theme of art & song:
> Bodily decrepitude is wisdom; young
> We loved each other & were ignorant.

A fair copy for the typist, some time after August 14, 1931:
[Draft 8]

XVII

After Long Silence

> Speech after long silence; it is right~~××~~
> All other lovers being estranged or dead
> Unfriendly lamplight hid under its shade
> The curtains drawn upon unfriendly night,~~××~~
> That we descant & yet again descant
> Upon the supreme theme of art & song:
> Bodily decrepitude is wisdom; young
> We loved each other & were ignorant.

(I assume that what is cancelled in lines 1 and 4 is the dash after "right" and the dash after "night" which appeared in the previous version.)

The first printed version, in *Words for Music Perhaps and Other Poems* (Dublin: The Cuala Press, 1932), differs from the above only as follows: lines 2 and 3 end with commas; "Art" and "Song" are capitalized; and "and" is substituted for each ampersand. The capitalization of "Art" and "Song" testifies to the importance of these arts but does not help us determine the "supreme theme."[44]

To summarize, in my view the evidence shows that the subject of the old lovers' conversation evolved in the manuscripts from love

> Come let us talk of love
> X On love descant

towards art and song themselves

> ... descant
> Upon the ~~sole theme~~ supreme theme of art & song
> Wherein theirs [there's?] theme so fitting for the aged

to "Bodily decrepitude is wisdom":

> ... the supreme theme of art & song—
> Decrepitude increases wisdom—

---

[44] Parkinson states that "the title was, for one printing, 'Words After Long Silence'" (Parkinson, p. 90). This seems to be a mistaken reading of *Variorum Poems*, p. 523. I find no instance of such a title.

> ... the supreme theme of art & song—
> Bodily decrepitude is wisdom—

> ... the supreme theme of art & song/ :
> Bodily decrepitude is wisdom⧸ ; young
> We loved each other & were ignorant.

The colon announces the "supreme theme": "Bodily decrepitude is wisdom."Thus the manuscripts lead me to reject Parkinson's argument, based on his own reading of them, that love is the "supreme theme." In this poem the only love that can be the "supreme theme" is a love won through bodily decrepitude, a love inseparable from wisdom. The two persons of the poem are "lovers" but no longer "love each other." This is a meaningful paradox. If they descant of love it can only be of a love which is non-exclusive and which outlasts strength and beauty. No other love could be the supreme (highest, utmost, ultimate) theme of art and song. Logically, bodily decrepitude is necessary before one can know a love that outlasts strength and beauty. Therefore, to declare knowledge of such a love is to sing that "Bodily decrepitude is wisdom." Only in this sense can love be the "supreme theme."

IV

Because of illness, this was the only poem which Yeats finished during a period of five months. Has anyone ever transcribed the poignant note which he added in March 1930 under the November 1929 version of the poem? Let me use it for a conclusion:

> When I wrote this poem, I had already been ill for three weeks or so—I had just arrived at Rapallo & struggled with constant sleepiness—the first stages of suffer[ing] of Malta fever. Now it is the end of March & for the last five days I have begun to write again revising "The Vision." I am at Portofina Vetta and can look from my windows out over a vast tranquil sea & a coast dotted with sunlight houses as far as Genoa. I know seven or eight people at Rapallo & had stage-fright in my walks of a few hundred yards. Here I can slip in or out without a word & improve hourly. It is now five months since my hemorrhage from the lung in London & I have written nothing but one poem & the doctor says I will not be well again for another three months, which means I suppose not able to write verse.[45]

"Bodily decrepitude. . . ."

---

[45] This passage is somewhat similar to the April 7 entry which opens *Pages from a Diary Written in Nineteen Hundred and Thirty* (Dublin, 1944), p. 1. There, no mention is made of the poem.

BETWEEN SHAPES AND SHADOWS

Shotaro Oshima

I am going to speak about Japanese classical dramas *Noh* and *Kabuki* as
an expression of the aesthetic sense of the Japanese people, not about
the minor details of technique. The *Noh* Drama, which was greatly
appreciated by W. B. Yeats, Padraic Colum and Ezra Pound, has many
technical terms unfamiliar to outsiders, but such terms as *hana*
(flower)[1] and *yūgen*[2] will not be so difficult to understand if they are
taken as mere literary expressions.

Motokiyo Zeami (1363-1443),[3] who brought the *Noh* to artistic
completion, and Monzaemon Chikamatsu (1653-1725),[4] the greatest
playwright of *Kabuki* Drama, each had his own unique views of dramatic art, but the two men seem to be in accord in finding the essence of art
in the subtle boundary between the real and the unreal, and in recognizing the need of art to provide pleasure. Zeami attached great impor-

---

[1] Zeami thinks that *Hana* (flower) is a very important element in the *Noh* drama.
According to him, *Hana* is the mind, technique is *Tane* (the seed). The seed is exercise
and *Hana* is the result of the seed. *Hana* may be said to produce at once freshness and
freedom.

[2] The term *yūgen* has no exact equivalent in English; literally it means "profound
and mysterious," and "obscure and dark," but as used by Zeami, it carries the connotation of half-revealed or suggested beauty, at once elusive and meaningful, tinged with
wistful sadness.

[3] Motokiyo Zeami (1363-1443?) is known as an excellent player and writer of the
Noh drama. He is also famous as a theorizer of the *Noh*. Manuscripts of his essays on art
were published in 1910 under the title *Zeami Jūrokubushū* (Sixteen Essays by Zeami).

[4] In the period of *Joruri*, Monzaemon Chikamatsu (1653-1725) wrote such plays of
contemporary life as "*Sonezaki Shinju*" (Lovers' Suicide at Sonezaki), "*On'nagoroshi Abura
no Jigoku*" (Murder of the Wife of an Oil Dealer), etc., and historical dramas like
"*Kokusenya Gassen*" (Kokusenya's Battle) and others. His *Kabuki* dramas number about
forty.

tance, then, to the pleasure which theatrical performances afford to the audience: "The purpose of all art," said Zeami, "is to bring pleasure to the hearts of all people" (*Fūshi-Kwaden*). And Chikamatsu implies as much when he says that "the pleasure of art exists between the fictitious which is not fictitious and the real which is not real."[5] Both Zeami and Chikamatsu thought that in order to please the audience there must be something more than mere realistic expression, as, of course, did William Butler Yeats, who tells us that "the reciter must be made exciting and wonderful in himself, apart from what he has to tell."[6]

The emphasis these classical dramatists placed upon the pleasant emotion stimulated by theatrical performances seems to have been handed down to modern artists such as Michio Ito.[7] And Michio Ito presents an interesting artistic problem. The first dancer to perform in Yeats's "*Noh*" play *At the Hawk's Well* with great success, Ito refers to the subtle connection between the realistic expression of the body and the creative emotional expression of the mind. "Dancing is an expression of one's own feelings through the medium of the movement, the body must be free and capable of expressing the idea in the mind of the dancer," Ito says. And he continues, "the dance uses the body as the medium of expression of the Art."[8] These words indicate, as it were, his understanding that art is more than mere imitation and must contain something idealistic.

But Zeami had said as much five hundred years before. Zeami wrote many books, including *Zeami Jūrokubushū*, as well as many *Noh* plays, such as *Yoro, Oimatsu, Takasago, Kiyotsune, Sanemori, Izutsu, Kinuta, Toru,* and others. But his most important book is *Kwadensho*, written in the seventh year of the Oei Era (1400). This book deals with the basic problems of the *Noh* Drama, and as a book of art theory it may be compared to Aristotle's *Poetics*. In this book Zeami considers that the actor must first of all learn *Monomane*, or faithful imitation of reality, but finally what is most important for him is to attain such grace as does not exist in reality. "In *Monomane* there must be *kurai* [grace] which

---

[5] Chikamatsu, *Naniwa Miyage*, ed. Ikwan Hozumi (1738). Ikwan Hozumi (1713?-1768 or 1769) was a Confucian scholar and a friend of Monzaemon Chikamatsu. He wrote down Chikamatsu's talks about his own works and published them under the title *Naniwa-Miyage*. This book was revised and published by Man'nen Ueda in 1904.

[6] "The Irish Dramatic Movement," *Explorations* (London, 1962), p. 215.

[7] At the age of eighteen Michio Ito (1893-1961) received the *natori* degree of the *Mizuki Ryu* (Mizuki School of Japanese Dancing). In his nineteenth year he left Japan for Europe where he soon established himself as a modern stage dancer. In London after World War I, Ito won the friendship of William Butler Yeats who wrote his "*Noh*" drama *At the Hawk's Well* in 1916. Ito then went to the U.S.A., where he taught dancing for 27 years ("Michio Ito's School of Dancing at Carnegie Hall," New York), turning out 4,000-odd dancers, including such big names as Ruth St. Dennis, Doris Niles, and Martha Graham.

[8] From the private papers of Michio Ito.

cannot be found in nature," he says. "If *Monomane* reaches perfection and the actor can become the real person himself, he will forget the necessity of imitation. Then if he tries to express only the artistic aspect of reality, the *hana* [flower] needs must be produced" (*Fūshi-Kwaden*). These words may be understood to mean that the highest degree of imitation is unconscious, and when this unconscious imitation is attained the beauty of art is born of itself. W. B. Yeats must have had something similar in mind when he talked of "the great realist," meaning "a realist more than a realist." Like Zeami, Yeats considered it important to produce great art which can deeply move the audience by giving it artistic pleasure. His "great artist" does not try merely to imitate the "living speech" or to wear the "garment of life." It is when more delicate movements and speeches are given on the stage that the great realist is born.

Zeami lived to be eighty years old, and when a man is really old he does not feel that he is imitating the carriage of an old man, because he is himself an old man. He needs only to identify himself with the nature of the character. From this state of mind grace is born of itself. And this state was for him the highest reach of art.

Thus Zeami made it the end of his art to establish the world of *yūgen* upon the basis of imitation. *Yūgen* was advocated as early as the twelfth century in *Senzai Wakashū*, compiled by Shunzei Fujiwara,[9] and gave profound feeling to the literature of the Heian period. And by Zeami it was placed at the pinnacle of dramatic art.

In short, imitation, for Zeami, is ultimately to grasp the artistic truth of the object and to express it as the actor's own. Yeats may be said to express the same idea of the theatrical performance when he says, "Speak that language which is his and nobody else's, and speak it with so much of emotional subtlety that the hearer may find it hard to know whether it is the thought or the word that has moved him."[10]

I have traced chiefly Zeami's view of imitation and *yūgen*. After him greater importance began to be attached to realistic expression than to that aiming at *yūgen*, and by the time of Motomasa, the eldest son of Zeami, the audience was already attracted to plays which contained more reality than vision in them. People wanted to weep and laugh at the realistic performance on the stage. This was perhaps the main object of disagreement between Zeami and Motomasa in their attitudes toward the *Noh* Drama. There is an interesting episode in *Sarugaku Dangi* which typically shows this difference of attitudes. It

---

[9] (1114-1204). From the end of the twelfth century to the seventeenth and the concept of *yūgen* prevailed in the fields of poetry, painting, drama and tea ceremony. In editing *Senzai Wakashū* (1188-89) Shunzei considered it his task to give importance to the mode of *yūgen* in the poetic expression in *Waka* poems written during 200 years since the tenth century.

[10] "The Irish Dramatic Movement," *Explorations*, p. 108.

concerns the performance of a *Noh* play, *Sumida Gawa*, or *The Sumida River*.

In this play a distracted woman comes wandering to a village by the side of the Sumida River, and is told by a ferryman that there is a burial mound of a boy on the bank of the river. This boy was kidnapped, and on his way to a distant country to be sold, died of illness at this place. The woman knows that it is the very grave of her boy for which she has been searching so long. And she sings songs of sorrow, and dances, singing. Then she falls upon her knees before the mound and chants the prayer "*Namu-Amidabutsu*," which means "May his soul rest in peace!" And even the rippling waters and whistling winds join in her prayer.

It will be expected that the ghost of the dead boy will naturally appear to see his mother again. But on this very point Zeami disagreed with his son Motomasa, the author of this play. Motomasa insisted that the preceding development of the play made it inevitable that the ghost of the dead boy should appear in answer to his mother's prayer, and that it would achieve a great dramatic effect as the climax of the play. But Zeami said it would be far more effective that the boy should not appear on the stage, for in this play the boy was not a real being but a phantom which the mother saw in a vision. And he advised his son to produce the play with this point in mind. But Motomasa replied he could not produce the play without letting the ghost appear on the stage. Then Zeami gently remonstrated with him and told him that he should try both ways and choose the one he found better, for it would be impossible for him to decide which was better unless both were tried.

To Motomasa the appearance of the ghost seemed so dramatic that it could not be omitted, but to Zeami it was enough if the prayer "*Namu-Amidabutsu*" was heard from within the burial mound joining the mother's prayer. The audience's imagination would be excited by visualizing the ghost of the unfortunate boy, and it would appeal to them far more strongly than to see the ghost actually on the stage. The sight of the mother staggering after the phantom of her boy to the mound would also serve to stimulate their imaginations. Thus Zeami thought it better to impress the audience by appealing to their imaginations than by showing them too realistic a ghost.

Even today opinion is divided about the production of this play, and it is left to the producer's judgment to decide whether the boy should not appear on the stage but remain the phantom the mother sees in a vision, or he should make his appearance on the stage as a visible being to the audience.

Just for information, let me quote the last part of the text of this play. It runs as follows:

> **Mother:** Surely just now (among them) I heard my child's voice. He seems to be playing inside this mound.

> **Ferryman:** We too have heard your child. We shall keep silent; say your prayer alone.
> **Mother:** O that I might hear his voice but once again! *Namu Amida!*
> **Ghost:** *Namu Amidabutsu! Namu Amidabutsu!*
> **Chorus:** See, his voice and shape!
> **Mother:** Is it you, my child?
> **Ghost:** Is it you, my mother?
> **Chorus:** And as she seeks to grasp it by the hand, while the visage or phantom of her boy seems to fade and reappear, first streaks of light begin to glimmer in the east, effacing the vision. And what a pity it is that she finds what seemed to be her boy is but a grass upon the mound overgrown with rash weeds! Oh, what a pity it is!

It will be interesting to suppose here which position Yeats would have taken, that of Zeami or that of Motomasa. I think he would perhaps have sided with Zeami, for he expresses a view similar to Zeami's in an essay published in *Samhain*:

> We must . . . substitute for the movements that the eye sees the nobler movements that the heart sees, the rhythmical movements that seem to flow up into the imagination from some deeper life than that of the individual soul.[11]

Now let us turn from Zeami to Chikamatsu. Chikamatsu was, as I said before, a leading Kabuki playwright in the Genroku era, and from his long experience as a playwright he held a unique view of art. The following words are famous as his art theory:

> Art holds an unstable position in the filmy boundary between the real and the fictitious. It is true that because realistic expressions are preferred today, an actor who plays the part of a minister of a *daimyo* [a feudal lord] faithfully imitates the miens and ways of talking of a real minister. But does a real minister of a *daimyo* apply rouge and powder like an actor? Or if an actor plays on the stage with his beard unshaven and his bald head uncovered because a real minister does not adorn himself, will it give pleasure to the audience? This is what I mean by saying that art exists in the filmy boundary between the real and the fictitious. The pleasure of art exists between the fictitious which is not fictitious and the real which is not real.[12]

Here Chikamatsu refuted the view that actors who are faithful in every point to reality are good actors, and warned against the too realistic tendency of his time. The essence of art lies in the vague boundary where it is difficult to tell where the real ends and where the fictitious begins. It is when the real merges into the imaginary that art can give pleasure to the audience. We may say after the example of Chikamatsu that the essence of art exists between shapes and shadows.

Tojuro Sakata (1647-1709),[13] a celebrated *Kabuki* actor who lived

---

[11] Ibid., p. 109.

[12] *Naniwa-Miyage*, ed. Hozumi.

[13] During the Genroku era he was the leading *Kabuki* actor both nominally and

about the same time as Chikamatsu, expressed a view to the same
effect:

> A *Kabuki* actor, whatever part he may play, must first of all take care to
> imitate the real person faithfully. But when he plays the part of a beggar,
> he should refrain from too faithful realism in everything including
> make-up and costume. The part of a beggar is an exception and must not
> be played according to the general rule. The reason is that the audience
> comes to see the play for pleasure, so that everything on the stage must be
> given a gay appearance. A real beggar is nasty and unpleasant to the eye.
> So too faithful representation of a beggar cannot afford pleasure.[14]

Thus Chikamatsu and Sakata, as well as Zeami, gave warning against
too faithful a realism and insisted upon the importance of imagination.
They considered it the essence of artistic expression to adjust the
oscillation between the real and the unreal. Zeami and Chikamatsu,
especially, may be said to have tried as dramatists to create a world of
vision in their dramas.

Yeats was able to penetrate a central principle of Japanese art
when he discussed Japanese *Noh* Drama and painting, saying:

> In the painting that decorated their walls and in the poetry they recited
> one discovers the only sign of a great age that cannot deceive us, the most
> vivid and subtle discrimination of sense and the invention of images
> more powerful than sense; the continual presence of reality.[15]

It is not surprising, then, that Yeats expressed a heartfelt sympathy
with the stage effects of Gordon Craig at a very early time, saying that
Craig did not want to imitate nature, but to create a noble artificiality.[16]
We must pay attention to the fact that it was in his youth, long before he
developed an interest in the *Noh*, that he considered it important both
for the actor and the dramatist to keep a certain distance from things in
the outer world. J. M. Synge, too, consciously tried to take an objective
view of things, even when he dealt with materials in which he was much
interested, but the superficial realities of Irish life were not important
to him, for he, like Yeats, tried to grasp the artistic truth. Both men

---

virtually in Kyoto and Osaka. Rejecting exaggeration, he mastered realistic acting and
was praised as the first great player of the lover's role in love scenes.

[14] *Kengai-shū, Yakusha-Rongo*, ed. Kenji Shuzui (1954), pp. 129-30. *Kengai-shū* is a
collection of talks of Jurobei Somekawa, a *Kabuki* actor (born ?, died in the first year of
the Shotoku era), written down by Azuma Sampachi, a *Kabuki* playwright. Jurobei had
the pen name of "Kangai" as a Haiku poet and the title of this book was derived from his
pen name. This book contains various words Jurobei heard from many leading actors of
the Genroku era, including Tojuro Sakata, as well as various anecdotes concerning their
acting, and was intended as a guide book for actors.

[15] "Certain Noble Plays of Japan," *Essays and Introductions* (New York, 1961), p. 235.

[16] "Mr. Gordon Craig has done wonderful things with the lighting, but he is not
greatly interested in the actor, and his streams of coloured direct light, beautiful as they
are, will always seem, apart from certain exceptional moments, a new externality." "The
Irish Dramatic Movement," *Explorations*, p. 179.

endeavoured to penetrate the fundamental truth of Irish folk life and to express it vividly on the stage. And in order to create vivid images they considered it necessary to simplify realities. To produce an artistic effect the most impressive aspect of the material had to be emphasized. The essential parts had to be set off from unimportant incidentals. Such simplification can be found in many works of Irish dramatists. And it was also the traditional technique of Japanese classical arts. In all ages and countries the artist aims at vividness and intensity of expression, and here we must remember the words of Yeats: "Just as it is necessary to simplify gesture that it may accompany speech without being its rival, it is necessary to simplify both the form and colour of scenery and costume."[17] Knowing that these words had been uttered before Yeats knew the *Noh*, we cannot but be impressed at discovering what a profound community of aesthetic sensibility there is between the Irish and the Japanese people.

The love of simplicity, which was one of the essential characteristics of Japanese classical arts, is still alive among Japanese people. I will end my essay by quoting the words of Michio Ito, who succeeded in creating impressive visual and auditory images by simplified dancing and singing. "Civilization," he said, "was divided between the East and the West. In Europe they developed and intensified material civilization, but we Japanese have directed our efforts to the establishment of oriental, spiritual civilization. To what should our next efforts be directed? We should endeavour to produce an artistic balance between simple being and beautiful being, for it is only when this balance is established that the condition under which people can live happily is prepared."[18]

---

[17] Ibid., p. 109.

[18] *Utsukushiku naru Kyoshitsu* ("A Room for Those who Wish to Become Beautiful") (Tokyo, 1956), pp. 80-81.

TWO PLAYWRIGHTS:
YEATS AND BECKETT

Thomas Kilroy

I have always looked upon he play written to be read only as an imperfect
form, even for the reader who would find it the more exciting for the
vigorous structure, the working to a climax, that had made it hold some
fitting audience.

W. B. Yeats, 1912[1]

I say that the stage is a concrete physical place which asks to be filled, and
to be given its own concrete language to speak. I say that this concrete
language, intended for the senses and independent of speech, has first to
satisfy the senses, that there is a poetry of the senses as there is a poetry of
language, and that this concrete, physical language to which I refer is
truly theatrical only to the degree that the thoughts it expresses are
beyond the reach of the spoken language.

Antonin Artaud, 1938[2]

I

The first dramatic gesture is the draping of the human figure. With it
comes the first illusion of the stage, the illusion of identity. The second
dramatic gesture is processional, the finding of place, the movement of
the figure from a station that is merely of the occasion to one which
anticipates what is to follow, which, in generous circumstances, helps to
define what is to follow. With it comes the second illusion of the stage,
the illusion of motive, the illusion of an action. And what follows from
these two may or may not include speech. To acknowledge the pre-
verbal, the pre-literary, in the drama is to acknowledge not simply a
history but a constant, a continuous claim of silence upon the spoken

---

[1] W. B. Yeats, *The Poetical Works*, Vol. II (London, 1912), p. v.

[2] Antonin Artaud, *The Theater and its Double* (New York, 1958), p. 37.

word in the life of the drama. What this offers us, if we are so disposed to accept it, is a scale from silence to speech to silence that allows description not only of the historical development of the drama but also of the internal process of the individual play. It offers us the context of language in drama, that peculiar, moderating circumstance in which the language of plays is composed, the way in which theatrical language becomes responsible to a publicity beyond the literal statement.

For centuries speech has been the most accessible entry into the life of plays; dialogue being more accessible than other stage activity to the vocabulary of literary criticism. In overhearing speech we assume, often without warrant, that the mere efficiency of language will carry us to valid conclusions about that moment which speech has encapsulated for us. Above all we read language and hence assume that plays are readable. The problem is obviously most acute with the poet who writes plays and it is only in our century that we have begun to assemble a morphology of poetic drama, notably in Shakespearean studies, which would account for its poetry by recourse to the nature of drama itself. There is a duality in the writings of plays, two different but inextricable obligations, one towards the creature life of the play, the other, often a concealed writing, ascription rather than description, directed towards the mechanization of the stage. We may read plays only if we are literate in both languages, or rather if we are responsive to the extra-literary context which operates at all times on the printed words of the play.

Happily, most commentators on Beckett's plays seem to arrive with a sense of the theatricalism behind them. It seems to me that most readers of Yeats's plays come equipped with the experience of the poems, the prose, the *Vision*. And it is not enough.

Yeats, relatively remote from the theatre outside Ireland and alienated from his own theatre at home, is to be found at one of the centers of the modern dramatic tradition. It is a center that subscribes to the integrity, the wholeness, the autonomy of stage-practice, one which undermines the idea of humanist imitation which had long dominated the European theatre, that web of Occidental preconceptions, verbal, psychological, social which Artaud rages against. As a revolutionary movement it is extensive but it would include, for example, *The Dream Play* and Expressionism, the various kinds of Orientalism in the twentieth-century European theatre, the work of someone like Peter Brook; it includes the theatre of Beckett. The society or image of human collectivism in this theatre is "cold," to use a relevant anthropological term, static, enclosed in a severe formalism the structure of which is determined by the limits of stage-space. How can one speak of a "sovereignty of words" in a theatre of this kind? The theatrical coherence of a play like *The Herne's Egg* or *Endgame* is not linguistic, or not primarily so. Since this is one of Beckett's subjects, the gap between precision of word and predication in action, one may accept this in his play. In the Yeats play what is at risk is not the verbal system of *A Vision* or Indian mysticism, but a theatrical ceremony that draws attention to its own stage artifice, which relies upon the exclusiveness of its stage-action and the capacity of stage-presence to yield an experience which exists for its own sake and that alone.

The student of theatrical history is quite aware of the uneasy authority of language in the drama, a competitiveness between the information of speech and the information of action. He finally comes to understand dramatic form as the operation of one upon the other. As a student of theatre he is conscious of those periodic fluctuations in taste by which the visual, the eurhythmic, the musical, obtrude upon and even eliminate the speaking voice on the stage at certain points in theatrical history. As a student of theatre he is, or ought to be, profoundly interested in such a phenomenon. But if he is a student of literature he may turn aside from it, from something that seems of marginal interest to his discipline, something that is conspicuously intractable to the kind of analysis available to him, something which constantly defeats the kind of expectations which he brings to literary narrative.

To become precise for a moment: when we think of the seventeenth century masque, the eighteenth century opera, the nineteenth century melodrama, we tend to think of them, as far as the drama is concerned, as sterile withdrawals from the central tradition. Such plays of substance that owe something of their existence to these forms, *The Tempest, The Beggar's Opera, Arms and the Man, The Plough and the Stars*, these, we feel, survive despite rather than because of their association with non-literary, sub-literary or quasi-literary forms. When we reinforce this view we refer to language. We say the plays are plays because language has been restored to us. Yet, in each of these four plays that I mention, language is suspended in a strict, modifying context, a style of action, a conventional way of indicating behaviour on the stage without which, in each case, the language itself may tend to lose plausibility, shrinking or inflating, as the case may be, on the printed page.

Whenever language ceases to be the central mode of communication on the stage we have inevitably reached a point of ripeness, a high degree of self-consciousness, self-sufficiency by which the theatre finds its own imagery within the confines, the possibilities of the stage. There is something else at stake, then, in the retreat or partial retreat from language other than the primacy of language itself. In the first place the retreat is to some well of independence, even narcissism, within stage action, a contemplation of its own virtuosity. What is thereby being asserted is the exclusiveness, the histrionics of performance, common alike to the splendid vulgarities of Boucicault and the devices, the figures of Jonsonian masque.

Our interest, as I take it, is the effect of such theatricalism upon plays that engage our attention as literature. As we re-emerge to the drama of complex language on the perimeter of extreme theatricality we bring back with us indispensible terms of description, categorization and judgment that are not to be had or not to be had with the same connotation in the criticism of non-dramatic literature. I believe that this exercise is crucial to a reading of the plays of Yeats and Beckett.

But what in fact is this extreme theatricality behind these plays and can one really speak of it as a base common to such individualistic playwrights? Grotowski, a director whose work, theatrically if not ideologically, is very pertinent to the theatre of both Yeats and Beckett, talks of the evolution of the modern theatre in terms of "the Great Reform of the theatre from Stanislavski to Dullin and from Meyerhold to Artaud."[3] Each of us might have his own way of putting this, his own litany: of playwrights, perhaps, rather than directors, Ibsen, Chekhov, Strindberg, Shaw, Pirandello and so on. Or of documentation: Zola's dramatic criticism of the 1870s, the writings of Adolphe Appia or Gordon Craig, *The Quintessence of Ibsenism* or Eisenstein or Kabuki Theatre. Yet, however we try to bring the field into focus we are inevitably conscious that this is a period, unique in the history of the theatre, in which two rival conceptions of what the stage should be, meet and converge, compete and fall apart but are at all times obliged to acknowledge the existence, the claim of the other.

I refrain from using the words "Naturalism" and "reaction against Naturalism" but I will substitute an equally inadequate simplicity. We characterize a play according to the kind of stage image of human experience which the playwright creates and this, in turn, is related to the kind of expectation which it excites in the audience and is intended to fulfill. The essential difference has to do with the bridging of that distance, spatial and experiential, between audience and the stage. Stage imagery which relies, to one degree or another, upon the imported pre-conceptions, the subjective luggage of the audience, is of one kind; playwright and audience rely upon a complicity of knowledge. Stage imagery which demands a subjection of the audience's expectation to the severe legislation, the severe mathematics, of the stage is of another kind; the imagery is, in a sense, explicit, authoritarian and its immediate authority is that of the stage. The stage imagery of Yeats and Beckett is of this second kind.

I am aware of the looseness of these categories but I am also aware that some such polarity is active in the modern theatre giving it its distinctive tension and dialectic. When Brecht, in his Scandanavian lecture "On Experimental Theatre" of 1939-40, speaks of experiment "defined by the two functions of entertainment and instruction" he is

---

[3] Jerzy Grotowski, "Towards a Poor Theater," *Tulane Drama Review*, 2, No. 3 (Spring 1967), 65.

making this kind of observation but with a radically different emphasis. He is exercised in cementing the break in the Neo-Classical unity of profit and pleasure in the drama, lost since the eighteenth century but his motives would hardly appeal to Diderot or Lessing or Jonson. When he goes on to talk about the inhibiting effects of Naturalism on "the imagination, the sense of play and elements of pure poetry," he might be describing a threat to the private, asocial theatre of Yeats and Beckett. When he goes further and laments the solipsism of Expressionism, whatever its technical success, its incapability, as Brecht puts it, "of shedding light on the world as an object of human activity," he might be summarizing one type of discomfort with the plays of Yeats and Beckett. Neither Yeats nor Beckett is expressionist, of course, but as users of the stage they belong to the same stable. Brecht's scathing summary of the Expressionist image of human existence comes from a disillusion with a theatre which appears to owe no social obligation to its audience, a theatre which makes no concessions beyond the provenance of its own territory. The argument is proceeding elsewhere but one will recognize, I think, one characteristic view of the kind of theatre that I am trying to describe. "It represented art's revolt against life; here the world existed purely as a vision, strangely disturbed, a monster conjured up by a perturbed soul."[4]

II

To return, however, to the two playwrights themselves. If we expand upon what Yeats means by "simplicity" in the theatre or for that matter what he calls "distance from life," or when we consider what Beckett means by "shape" in the plays, we eventually become involved in a set of claims that are being made on behalf of the stage itself. These claims arise out of the circumstance, central to the idea of theatre of both dramatists, that stage-space is given meaning by what is enacted there, hence becoming part of the meaning of the action itself. The stage as sanctuary in two senses in *Endgame*. The stage as place of sacrifice in *A Full Moon in March* or *The King of the Great Clock Tower*. The stage as tomb in *Happy Days*. The stage as free space defined by its action in *Godot* or *The Dreaming of the Bones*. The numina of place in a Yeats or Beckett play, its hallowed quality, derives not from an image of human history or myth, human architecture or occupation, but from the conscious retention of a theatrical setting with its accommodation, its propagation of the irreducible event, that which has no obligation of fidelity to anything outside itself.

In the beginning is space; the stage-direction occupies space, gives it location, a particularity and so at least a partial meaning. To replace the available space with a graphic reproduction of an external image of

---

[4] Eric Bentley, ed., *The Theory of the Modern Stage* (Harmondsworth, England, 1968), pp. 97 f.

the world, of drawing-room or street-scene or whatever, is to annihilate the potential freedom of space, that is, its freedom to continue to exist, to be accounted for as an element which surrounds, isolates the action, suspending it within its own structure.

To say that simplicity in a Yeats or Beckett play is a simplicity in staging is but to begin to say something about the plays themselves. The props, the items, the objects on the stage, like stage props at all times, begin by communicating through familiarity. Although at this point one might well remember Molloy's grim injunction: "To restore silence is the role of objects."[5] Painted screens, a wild rocky place, steps, chairs, trees, mounds, a wall, the selected fragments of a world beyond the stage become vital things in themselves. "The danger," as Beckett reminds us again but in another context, "is in the neatness of identifications."[6] We identify objects on a Yeats or Beckett stage only at the expense of memory, or to put it another way, by surrender to the economy of action within the play, the only system in which the objects are usable.

Something similar may be said of the human figure in both playwrights since in each case what arises is the usable figure, the figure that conforms to a strict stage utility. The figures retain reflections, echoes, manners of an external order of human history, myth, commerce, but such reflection is subordinated, ironically or dogmatically, to the life of performance, of histrionics. There is an analogy which I do not find altogether far-fetched, between the dramatization of myth in Yeats and the use of vaudeville-type routines in Beckett. Each is a received structure in itself and what is retained in the play is the fixity, the enclosure of that structure. We know from the turbulent history of the Futurists, for example, that what Marinetti called The Theatre of Variety—circus, burlesque, music-hall—became more than an intellectual flirtation with exotic anarchy, quite the reverse, the highly disciplined choreography of low theatre came to support the relentless mechanization of the human figure, the search for absolute stage structures in the theatre of the first half of this century. In Yeats and Beckett the acting out of a situation depends upon the narrowest field of options: in each the play is modular in shape rather than linear in its action, in each the absurdity of human endeavor is temporal, enclosed within a perfect, harmonious temporality of stage-life.

III

The world of the Beckett plays is pre-social, pre-tribal, pre-communal, but one might as easily describe it as post-social, post-tribal, post-communal. We are all aware of the disturbing conjunction of begin-

---

[5] *Molloy* (New York, 1965), p. 16.

[6] *Our Examination Round his Factification of Work in Progress* (New York, 1962), p. 3.

nings and endings in Beckett's work, the disposable journey, the elision of histories. Yet the appropriate adjective is residual—a primitive stage, yes, but one which has been earned out of the excess, the waste of human culture.

The human figures on the Beckett stage are bound by a few persistent but scarcely rewarding connections: paternity, maternity, mastership and slavery, the cord of feeling that unites Didi and Gogo, Winnie and Willie, the more tenuous cord of memory. As relationships they simply are; they do not have that profuseness, that spread and growth that is our reassurance in most of life and most of art. "What happened?" asks the blind Pozzo, and Vladimir screams in the pain of relating, "Will you stop it, you! Pest! He can think of nothing but himself." "You could hang on to my legs," says Estragon in the hapless effort at hanging. "And who'd hang on to mine?" asks Vladimir, the joke floating, like so many Beckett jokes, in a space empty of connections.[7]

What is pronounced in Beckett is the self, a self whose physical station, physical motion, incarceration, debilitation, is recorded time and time again and is given striking visual emphasis as in the opening tableau of *Endgame*. The frontal effect of a Beckett play, then, is decidedly physical, a constant evocation of presence, of comfort and discomfort, of flagging endurance in which distance is measured by the demands on the body. The surface of a Metaphysical poem, too, teems with a physical life, the movement of the poem is a penetration through the physical, a transformation of language by which sensation becomes the mode of passage to the preternatural. I believe that this is the kind of movement which occupies a Beckett play. The pre-occupation with movement and speech on this stage is rooted in the awesome certainty of immobility and silence. The dramatization of this is wholly dependent upon an acute sensitivity to the character of the automonous stage. As the variety of Beckett's narrative fiction reduces itself to the monologue in the novels, the variety of his stage narrows to mime in the plays. Beckett's turn to the theatre out of the diminishing possibilities of the trilogy is the finding of an alternative space, an alternative model with an intense and highly ambiguous physical definition. In the Trinity College Beckett manuscripts what strikes one at once in the unfinished or unpublished mimes and plays is this obsession with the geometry of the stage. Form arises out of what is physically possible in the given space. Stage-action is what is measurable.

Formalism in art is a mark of maturity so that we frequently understand the development of an individual writer as progression from informal or less formal to formal fictions. As playwrights both Yeats and Beckett capitalize upon a body of mature stage-practice at the turn of this century which began by freeing the stage of facile

---

[7] *Waiting for Godot* (New York, 1954), pp. 53, 60.

imitation and went on to release the possibilities of a free stage as an element of dramatic action, in effect denuding the stage of its cultural paraphernalia and returning it to a state of elementary usefullness. The formalism of Yeats and Beckett is a model of freedom, the one assured consolation offered by the plays. To attend to it is to submit oneself to a symmetry, a shape that cannot be described simply in terms of what is said.

Whether a specific myth is recognized or not, the formalism of Yeats is an attempt to reproduce the multilevelled communication of the mythic, as he put it, "the little limited life of the fable, which is always better the simpler it is, and the rich, far-wandering, many-imaged life of the half seen world beyond it."[8] The characteristic mode of stage-craft for Yeats was the illumination of the singular event, remembering his early interest in creating what he called miracle plays. And the singular event, whether it be the early faery-abduction of Mary Bruin or the dance of the Queen in *A Full Moon in March*, is the final moment in the creation of a role which becomes progressively more theatrical as Yeats proceeds. The language of symmetrical action has both a liberating and a discriminatory force in Yeats. The compartmentalization of stage-figures goes beyond the choric musicians or attendants and from the beginning has the arrangement of a social hierarchy and this continues to be part of its meaning to the end. There is another hierarchy, however, a hierarchy in the system of knowledge of the plays by which the primary figures are isolated in the central moments of the plays. In the mature Yeats, and I could single out *The Resurrection, The Herne's Egg* and *Purgatory*, the stage ceases to be a miniature of some external ground of human activity; it becomes the sole ground of the action, it is what shapes the play as it is.

The symmetry of a Beckett play is both a defiance against meaninglessness and a recepticale of an action that is meaningless. The structure is allowed to stand, a perfect theatrical shape while the human enactment within it seethes with anguish, the intolerable, the unnamable. The incidental staginess of *Waiting for Godot*, the "little canters," the clown routines of Vladimir and Estragon, their contempt of the ever-present audience, their playing of parts, this histrionic quality of the play is self-evident. But the whole play is structured about the ancient theatrical device of the reprise, conventionally a way of reassuring an audience in its first impressions. For Beckett, stage repetition, its extreme artifice, its simulation of zero, its formal excellence, is a way of total organization and therefore elimination of human choice. It is very appropriate that the stating of this should be given to Vladimir with his weary aestheticism, his self-mocking literary style. He is the one who wilts before the insult of "critic," he is the one who recognizes the failure of language even as it says exactly what has

---

[8] *Essays and Introductions* (New York, 1961), p. 216.

to be said:

> It's evening, Sir, it's evening, night is drawing nigh. My friend here
> would have me doubt it and I must confess he shook me for a moment.
> But it is not for nothing I have lived through this long day and I can
> assure you it is very near the end of its repertory.[9]

IV

I know that I should speak of some of these things with specific
reference to one or two plays. I can at least suggest a provisional
approach. I would choose *The Countess Cathleen, the Player Queen* and
The Herne's Egg. I choose these plays partly out of eccentric determination to avoid those plays or motifs in plays that strikingly remind one of
Beckett—*Purgatory*, very obviously, or the beggar and fool figures,
such as the tyranical camaraderie of the beggars in *The Cat and the
Moon*.

These three plays provide one fairly coherent line in Yeats, versions of his mystique of the female figure, a kind of cult, you might say,
with its attendant liturgy, a female hierocracy in situations of power
that have political, social, religious or quasi-religious implications. The
struggle in each play is for domination of the scene and the woman
emerges triumphant in scenes that continue to bother readers of the
plays as to what exactly Yeats was up to.

I would try to categorize each play according to the kind of stage
for which it was written. We begin with drama as episodic pageant, that
naïve genre of early Abbey nationalism, the kind of play which fulfills
its debt to history or it is nothing. *The Countess Cathleen* has many
weaknesses, as Yeats was the first to admit. But its fundamental weakness as theatre is that two radically different kinds of drama and two
different styles compete within it, one a half-hearted historicism, an
awkward play of peasant and Big House in famine Ireland, the other, a
drama of epiphany, of the singular event, the mediation of the woman
between the human and the divine. The mature Yeats is the playwright
who effects the spread of this singular event so that it operates not as
climax, like the Faustian climax of *The Countess Cathleen*, but as the
controlling element in the whole life of the play.

If The Player Queen is transitional and the fruit of much labour, it is
transitional in this sense, a groping towards an integrity of structure,
towards a stage which would adequately convey through all its activities, the kind and quality of that final event. The freedom which
Yeats is pursuing is a freedom from the local, the particular associations of his theme, "some No-man's-land"[10] and he confuses this freedom with a freedom from nationality, a matter of setting. What he
finally achieves in *The Herne's Egg* is the absolute freedom of stage-

---

[9] *Waiting for Godot*, p. 55.

[10] R. K. Alspach, ed., *The Variorum Edition of the Plays* (New York, 1966), p. 1306.

space, a freedom by which the nexus of physical violence, sexuality and knowledge, the bare, partially obscured idea of the other two plays, is finally, totally revealed in its essentials and given organic theatrical form. As carriers of such an idea the folk-tale structure of *The Countess Cathleen*, the pantomime artifice of *The Player Queen,* are digressive and fussy, leading to imbalances such as that between scene one and two of *The Player Queen*. In the perfect formalism of *The Herne's Egg* each has his place in a diagram of clarity, "of clean outline,"[11] of which the sufficiency, the controlled energy of the language, the perfect stylization, grouping of scenes, the logic of the action, are integral factors. It has always been a mystery to me why admirers of "Leda and the Swan" cannot always admire *The Herne's Egg* and for similar reasons. Of course, it means a transference from one dimension to another, from one kind of mastery to another, but poem and play have this in common: apart from ideas, each completes and exhausts its own form and the form, in retrospect, appears imperative.

The Herne's Egg, neglected as it may be, brings Yeats back into that area of the modern theatre that I've been trying to talk about. It seems to be a more substantial work—and the comparison is interesting —than anything of Genet. We must all be accustomed to the respectability, the inevitability even, of farce in the theatre of our time. For Yeats, as for Beckett and Ionesco, the farcical is a kind of finality, the final mechanization of human action, human impotence, a final moderator of human speech and in itself a model of subversive freedom in circumstances of ultimate risk.

Before trying to describe the ending of *The Herne's Egg*, I would like to bring together, by way of these three plays, that complex of feelings of which I think this is the final, brutal image in Yeats.

At the center of each play, then, is a female figure whose physical allure is crucial but who is agent of an action that transcends the physical while remaining rooted in it. She is, whether saint, actress or priestess or a combination of all three, invulnerable before the surrounding catastrophes. One of the achieved perceptions of Yeats in the treatment of the figure is precisely this, that she finally emerges as responsible for these catastrophes, developing from intermediary, iconic saviour to active violator of the material order about her. In each play she is confronted by a male lover-figure, and although Yeats added the love-scene between Aleel and Cathleen after the 1899 production of the first play, it is simply a move towards what I consider the plays to be about. Each is very much about the frustration of sexual concord between man and woman, and the type of energies, ethical, mystical, political, which this releases in the imagination of Yeats. In seeing the plays in this way we are seeing them, I think, with the initial response of an audience. When we proceed from this basic level of

---

[11] *Poems*, 1899-1905 (London, 1906), p. xii.

feeling we do so from the floor of the plays to their superstructure of ideas, from impact to reverie, from a spring of agitation to the plays' "stillness."

The accomplished action of the plays is in this capacity by which the woman converts her human, sexual nature into a role, a performance, of imminent, transcendental proportions. And whatever identity we afford Cathleen, Decima or Attracta, we cannot be unaware that as Yeats progressed he came to rely more and more upon the theatricality of the role, its self-attention, its dependence upon the persuasiveness of theatre, its need of an impressionable audience.

One ought to add that each play has a rudimentary social image, ranging from an aristocratic or courtly apex down through attendants, citizens, merchants, peasants, to the curiously compensated dispossessed of Yeats—fools and beggars and old men. To retain this framework as a scale of power and yet level it to the urgency of a single style is one of the achievements of *The Herne's Egg*. This style, in language, is staccato, thrusting, masculine in the actual process of being subsumed into its opposite, the languid, feminine rhythms of the scene between Attracta and the three girls, the language of the play's triumph which asserts its own kind of fitness to match the savage god of the play. This style, in stage movement, is rigid, ritualistic, with the joints showing, broken by the violence of Congal's death, coterminous with the absurd sexual coupling with which the play ends.

Finally, each of these plays arises out of a disturbed order, a state of flux of varying intensity from play to play but alike, so that, in each play, it allows, even demands the suspension of conventional authority. The simplest account of this is in Mary's retort to the First Merchant's hypocrisy in *The Countess Cathleen*. The words that she uses are more appropriate to Shakespeare or Donne, quite incongruous in the speech of a forty-year-old peasant woman, but they are definitive of the situation which continued to haunt Yeats as that fracture in human institutions which admitted the irrational, the immaterial, the superhuman, the essential dramatic event:

> These scruples may befit a common time,
> I had thought there was a pushing to and fro,
> At times like this, that overset the scale
> And trampled measure down.[12]

The Herne's Egg is not, to paraphrase Beckett, about something; it is that something itself. Its aim is not the elucidation, the corroboration, of Yeatsian ideas, but the immediate experience of such ideas in an action, and this action, however awkward it may be for rational discourse, is theatrically harmonious and complete.

The first scene of the play, like the first scene of a Beckett play, is an invitation to consider the distance which separates us from it. The

---

[12] *Plays and Controversies* (New York, 1924), p. 237.

mechanical fight of the kings is remarkable for the confidence with
which Yeats uses the stage as an enclosed world of balanced rhythms, a
theatrically perfect encounter but also an encounter of absurdity. To
enter into this play is to yield to the effects of such meticulous arrangement on the stage, to pay the price of initiation into a kind of theatre
that undermines the rational, the logical, the claim of language that all
experience is expressible in words. A primitive stage again, yes, but one
which is supremely confident of its alternative, mythical modes of
structuring experience. The narrative line of the play is very simple but
this has little to do with its impact as drama. For one thing there is this
elusiveness with which action escapes the reported version of it, the
rape of Attracta, for example, the apparition of the great bird, the true
significance of Congal's death. There is also this immediacy in the play,
the immediacy of performance by which the figures seem to generate
each movement as a unique, unrepeatable event:

> This is Tara; in a moment
> Men must come out of the gate.[13]

It is in this sense that I described *The Herne's Egg* as a ceremony, a
celebration, that having accepted what is begun and accepting the
dynamism of the play we rise with it to the kind of realease with which it
ends. The experience is profoundly theatrical and cannot be understood in any other terms. But the play is a celebration too in the sense of
Freud's description as an excess that has been allowed, a solemn viola-
tion of a prohibition. The imaginative scope of Yeats's final image of
sexuality and violence in this play is extremely painful, an outrage of
ordinary humanist sensibilities, a test of our resilience. This is scarcely
unusual in Yeats, or in any major artist for that matter; I mention it
because it seems to trouble many readers of this play.

The Herne's Egg has many familiar Yeatsian motifs, the symbolic
bird, the woman, the dying hero before the Fool, the dying cycle, and
yet it is felt, and I think this is true, that the play has a literal incoher-
ence. It is as if the units of the play are separated by spaces, as it were
composed in a kind of laconic shorthand with three or four speeches of
obvious beauty but lacking connective tissue. Everything about the play
has this impetuosity of presentation, this elimination of everything but
the experience itself. The myth of *The Herne's Egg* becomes an active
stage-event, a point at which narrative has given way to the immediacy
of its action. The play's motto is "the imperfection of a man,"[14] and
given the kind of theatricality of the piece its logic is that of farce. Our
misgivings, if we have them, with this type of stage-text are almost
entirely literary; we lament the displacement of language as the main
mode of communication. It is not a happy experience to speak of a

---

[13] *The Herne's Egg and Other Plays* (New York, 1938), p. 33.

[14] Ibid., p. 84.

poet's work in this way but it is the only way in which I can describe this dramatic effect. The true neighbourhood of this theatre that I've been talking about, although one has to go beyond Yeats to see this clearly, is not literature at all, but music, the symbolism of numbers, non-representational painting or sculpture, certain forms of architecture, perhaps, a range of human activity in this century which has consistently challenged the possibility of linguistic description.

It is for this reason that one returns to Artaud, who understood exactly what this theatre was about and who in his own demented way went closer than anyone else to communicate its environment, its impact, in written words. "Here," he says of Balinese theatre, "is a whole collection of ritual gestures to which we do not have the key and which seem to obey extremely precise musical indications, with something more that does not generally belong to music and seems intended to encircle thought, to hound it down and lead it into an inextricable and certain system. In fact everything in this theatre is calculated with an enchanting mathematical meticulousness."[15] And since this paper ought really to end on an expletive there is the word to hand in Artaud, a word compounded of anarchic humour and deadly serious motivation which cannot describe anything concrete of this theatre; it is merely a signal. The word is Danger.[16]

---

[15] *The Theater and its Double*, p. 57.

[16] Ibid., p. 42.

MYTHOLOGIZED PRESENCES:
MURPHY IN ITS TIME

J. C. C. Mays

Sinclair v Gogarty—as reported in [1937] I.R. 377,382 or as summarized in the Digest of Irish Reported Cases, 1929-1938, col. 172—is well-known to students of Irish law. In May 1937, the plaintiff obtained an injunction restraining the publication of *As I Was Going Down Sackville Street* pending a trial for alleged libel on himself, his deceased brother and his deceased grandfather. Then, in the following month, the defendant appealed to the Supreme Court on the grounds, *inter alia*, that, even assuming the publication was libellous, there was no evidence that he was publishing it; and that the order should not be allowed to stand, as it had no legal effect if he were not the publisher. The Supreme Court nevertheless upheld the injunction and the appeal was dismissed. The plaintiff was awarded £900 damages plus costs, which amounted to some £2,000. The book was withdrawn and subsequent re-issues do not contain the offending paragraphs.

Sinclair v Gogarty is studied because of the legal principle it involves—of the circumstances in which an interlocutory injunction will be granted to restrain further publication of a libel pending trial. The action in the Supreme Court is of no more legal interest than the initial hearing before Hanna J., whose outcome it merely confirms, but at the time, inevitably, it attracted greater attention. Notoriety is not too strong a word. There were queues for seats in the gallery, the case was given full coverage in the English and Irish press. "Only the *Pickwick Papers* rewritten by James Joyce," Charles Graves wrote for the *Daily Express*, "could really recapture the atmosphere of this trial."[1] It in-

---

[1] Quoted by Ulick O'Connor, *Oliver St. John Gogarty* (London, 1964), p. 279.

volved two of the most celebrated Dublin lawyers of the time, a suit for
obscene libel against a celebrated wit, politician and surgeon, and a
writer of banned books from Paris. Beckett's aunt was married to the
plaintiff's twin brother, and Beckett had filed the second affadavit on
the plaintiff's behalf at the initial hearing. He appeared as principle
witness for the plaintiff in the courtroom, where he was treated very
badly in cross-examination. The defending counsel, Fitzgerald, ran his
defence along lines calculated to discredit the publication witnesses in
the minds of the Dublin jury. Mr. Justice O'Byrne, addressing the jury,
summed up the impression Beckett had made in deprecatory terms:
"He did not strike me as a witness on whose word I personally would
place a great deal of reliance."[2] Friends of Beckett like Arland Ussher
and the late Owen Sheehy Skeffington were convinced that the
humiliating experience of the courtroom confirmed his commitment
to Paris. As he later said, "I preferred France in war to Ireland in
peace."[3]

Gogarty's reaction to the proceedings was equally bitter but it was
very much less fruitful. Though the Palace Bar had been almost
unanimously behind him and though literary figures like F. R. Higgins
had testified on his behalf, his pretensions had been deeply hurt by
Beckett's giving evidence against him. Dublin's view was that Beckett
was Joyce's secretary, and Gogarty undoubtedly felt the victim of a
conspiracy. A month later, he too left Dublin. Then, still smarting from
his defeat, he sought relief at the expense of an unsuspecting Patrick
Kavanagh and his publisher, Michael Joseph, in the King's Bench
Division, London.

In *The Green Fool*, Patrick Kavanagh had described his first visit to
Dublin and how he had gone to the National Library hoping to discover AE's address. No one knew where AE lived, so he asked if he
could have the address of some other poet. After much research, he
was given the address of Gogarty. " 'Is that the best you can do?' I
queried. And that was the best they could do." Kavanagh had then
described his reception at Ely Place, where he had mistaken "Gogarty's
white-robed maid for his wife—or his mistress. I expected every poet to
have a spare wife." Gogarty seized on these last sentences. "Are you
seriously inviting the jury to believe that the passages of which you
complain meant that you were a person who might keep a mistress?"
Counsel asked. "I did not like the word 'mistress' being associated with
my wife," was the reply. The special jury returned a verdict in

[2] *The Irish Times*, 24 November 1937, p. 5; *Irish Independent*, 24 November 1937, p.
13; *The Irish Press*, 24 November 1937, p. 12.

[3] To Israel Shenker: cf. "Moody Man of Letters," *New York Times*, 6 May 1956,
Section 2, p. 1.

Gogarty's favour, assessed damages at £100 and the book was withdrawn. This was in the spring of 1938.[4] Less well-known is that when
Murphy was published, at the same time, Gogarty urged Austin Clarke
to bring a libel action against Beckett.

I have no legal training, but it seems to me that the case for legal
proceedings against Beckett's *Murphy* is at least as strong as against *As I
Was Going Down Sackville Street* and *The Green Fool.* If anything, the case
seems stronger. A number of characteristics associate Ticklepenny,
"Pot Poet / From the County of Dublin," with Clarke. They begin with
names. " 'Call me Austin,' said Ticklepenny, 'or even Augustin.' He felt
the time was hardly ripe for Gussy, or even Gus" (67).[5] " 'Do you know
what it is?' said Ticklepenny, 'no offence meant, you had a great look of
Clarke there a minute ago' " (133). They continue with the sort of
poetry written by the real-life and the fictional character. The "class of
pentameter that Ticklepenny felt it his duty to Erin to compose, as free
as a canary in the fifth foot (a cruel sacrifice, for Ticklepenny hiccuped
in end rimes) and at the caesura as hard and fast as his own divine flatus
and otherwise bulging with as many minor beauties from the gaelic
prosodoturfy as could be sucked out of a mug of Beamish's porter"
(63)—this inevitably recalls a well-known note in Clarke's *Pilgrimage*
(1929) that Beckett had already referred to in his essay on recent Irish
poetry:

> Assonance ... takes the clapper from the bell of rhyme. ... The natural
> lack of double rhymes in English leads to an avoidance of words of more
> than one syllable at the end of the lyric line. ... But by cross-rhymes or
> vowel-rhyming, separately, one or more of the syllables of longer words,
> on or off accent, the difficulty may be turned: lovely and neglected words
> are advanced to the tonic place and divide their echoes.

Even Ticklepenny's attachment to the Magdalen Mental Mer-
cyseat reflects Clarke's experience when he was a few years younger
than Beckett, at the time of the writing of the novel, as an inmate of St.
Patrick's Hospital. The experience of grey-padded rooms with their
judasses, in which the sense of ordered time is lost and with it the sense
of self, was made fully public with *Mnemosyne Lay in Dust* in 1966.
Clarke's descriptions are often startlingly close to *Murphy's:*

> Fists hushed on a wall of inward-outness.
> Knees crept along a floor that stirred
> As softly. All was the same chill.

---

[4] *The Irish Times*, 21 March 1939, p. 8.

[5] Bracketted figures refer to page numbers in the most recent Calder/Faber/Minuit
editions. Unless obviously otherwise, they refer to page numbers in the Calder *Murphy.*
The uncollected pieces mentioned and quoted from in this essay may be traced through
Federman and Fletcher's Beckett bibliography.

> He knew the wall was circular
> And air was catchcry in the stillness
> For reason had returned to tell him
> That he was in a padded cell.

"Clarke had been for three weeks in a catatonic stupor," Beckett wrote, as Murphy prepares to succeed Ticklepenny. " 'You want to take a pull on yourself,' said Ticklepenny. 'Good night' " (133).

The correspondences between Ticklepenny and Clarke are extensive and deliberately contrived. To recognize them is to acknowledge an incidental but obtrusive feature of the book's interest. The portrayal of Ticklepenny as a fawning homosexual, on the other hand, brings one up short because it seems like a gratuitously introduced slur. As far as there are justifications for it, in Clarke's character and writing and in the logic of Beckett's book, they are inadequate.

Clarke undeniably had problems of sexual adjustment. He discussed them in his two volumes of autobiography and with researchers such as Maurice Harmon.[6] It is common knowledge that his adolescence was tormented by guilt and shame and that his first marriage, which lasted ten days, was unconsummated. It can also be argued that a coy and mawkish strain disfigures his writing, from the subdued eroticism of the earlier poems and *The Bright Temptation* to the less restrained proclamations of sexual freedom in late poems like *Tiresias*, where licentiousness is no more than prurience—"more a giggle than a delight."[7] It is also undeniable that if Ticklepenny shares similar characteristics, and if they are taken farther, they are necessary in terms of his place in the book's argument; his homosexuality has a thematic significance related to the image of Narcissus in *Echo's Bones*.[8] Mr. Endon represents for Murphy "a psychosis so limpid and imperturbable that [he] felt drawn to it as Narcissus to his fountain" (128). As Murphy plunges towards Mr. Endon, "his lips, nose and forehead almost touching Mr. Endon's," he discovers in Mr. Endon's eyes, "horribly reduced, obscured and distorted, his own image." The closed circle of meanings alternating between *eye* and *I* is given an explicitly homosexual dimension as Beckett describes the lips "all set . . . for a butterfly kiss" (170). Ticklepenny's reduction of a condition to a perversion—to work in the MMM for his profit but not for his loss—is necessary to his role as foil as well as precursor to Murphy.

---

[6] "Notes Towards a Biography," *Irish University Review* (Special Austin Clarke Issue), IV (Spring 1974), 13 *et seq.*

[7] The reviewer's phrase in "The Irelands of Austin Clarke," *TLS*, 1 December 1972, p. 1460.

[8] Jean-Jacques Mayoux offers some pertinent comments in his introduction to *Paroles et Musique, Comédie, Dis Joe* (Paris, 1972), p. 26.

The logic of the book in this way comes near to justifying the view of Clarke that it implies. Ticklepenny's "pretentious fear of going mad" matches the movement of *Mnemosyne Lay in Dust* towards recovery and relationships and "rememorizing"—a movement the exact reverse of *Murphy*'s. The compulsive working of Ticklepenny's knees under the table, in the Archaic Room before the Harpy Tomb, like a fowl writhing "long after its head has been removed, on a void place and a spacious nothing," (67) just translates into bizarre visual terms Beckett's critique of Clarke's ingenious metrical operations: "the need for formal justifications, more acute in Mr. Clarke than in Mr. Higgins, serves to screen the deeper need that must not be avowed."[9] Ticklepenny's preparedness to compromise for the sake of a drink or a favour or an easier time, owed or anticipated, expresses Beckett's view of the journalistic career Clarke had embarked upon. "The Olympian sot had reverted to the temperate potboy." So it must have seemed as the poet hailed in 1917 as successor to Yeats put in a stint as assistant editor of *Argosy* and strove to placate editors and publishers, as Ticklepenny whinges before the clownish Bim and Bom. "He accepted. He no longer had the spirit to refuse" (64).

These are literary explanations, nonetheless. It seems to me unlikely that an action for libel could be answered with the argument that an identifiable character is rendered as an exploitative homosexual because the book's themes require it so. But Austin Clarke decided not to accept Gogarty's urging: "When I glanced through it, I found it so heavy-going that I decided that few here would get through it and I did not bother about the matter."[10] Few people in Dublin did read it. It was never reviewed in *The Irish Times*: R. M. Smyllie, the editor, had testified on Gogarty's behalf in the *Sackville Street* trial and most likely declined to give it space. It was never listed as a good seller by the Dublin bookshops. Only Niall Montgomery, as far as I know, has mentioned that the book entertains with "secret jeers at a Dublin poet,"[11] and admirers of Clarke's work who have also read *Murphy* have seemed oblivious of the identification. Austin Clarke's good sense was probably the best answer. He was bewildered, but not resentful.

* * * * *

Austin Clarke assumed *Murphy* was a *roman à clef*, and the obvious and integral way in which he is incorporated makes such a possibility seem,

[9] Andrew Belis [Samuel Beckett], "Recent Irish Poetry," *The Bookman*, LXXXVI (August 1934), 235. This essay, which continues onto p. 236, is the one cited and drawn upon a few paragraphs further on. It is not included in the Federman and Fletcher bibliography.

[10] Letter to me, 19 September 1972.

[11] "No Symbols Where None Intended," *New World Writing*, No. 5 (April 1954), 325.

at first, unarguably real. If *Murphy* clearly does not maintain a series of exact identifications, like *Point Counter Point* or *Nightmare Abbey*, it might still be expected to incorporate looser equations between life and fiction, such as one finds in *At Swim-Two-Birds* or even in *A la recherche du temps perdu*. There is evidence that Beckett was at least conscious of the matter of libel during the composition of the book: he has Miss Counihan sit on Wylie's knees but "*not* in Wynn's Hotel lest an action for libel should lie" (83). In fact, Austin Clarke was wrong, and as far as *Murphy* incorporates references to writers other than himself it is in a different way. They are most certainly present, but they are less specific and consistent. Characters approximate to "reality" in different ways and to differing extents to make up a range of references which has only a general significance. It is no less important for that, however, for if the book is not at all the tissue of particular, consistently evolved allusions that Clarke supposed, its fabric depends on a specific and idiosyncratic view of Anglo-Irish writing at large.

The staking out of critical principles and of a relationship to the traditions he inherits or is aware of is an almost inevitable preliminary to any Irish writer's career, and one that at the same time involves him in predicaments of national and personal identity. Beckett's first occasional and uncollected writing is of this sort, and, as in the case of Joyce, it defines his position as much in terms of what he emphatically opposed as of what in general he stood for. His position is stated at most length in the pseudonymous *Bookman* essay of 1934 on "Recent Irish Poetry," in which he makes the distinction between "antiquarians and others." He sets the poets of the Revival, "delivering with the altitudinous complacency of the Victorian Gael the Ossianic goods," against those who looked to European models in various ways to write about themselves, here and now.

Beckett's distinction is, fundamentally, between the different examples of Yeats and Joyce. One has to recall Yeats in a tall silk hat and frock coat, reciting the thirty-nine articles in the Free State Senate; not the Yeats who spoke against censorship or divorce, but Yeats by tradition the opponent of Dowden and by current repute a lecherous old man. It then becomes clearer why Beckett criticizes Yeats for leading the "flight from self-awareness." The tradition for which Yeats stands, Beckett argues, assumes "that the first condition of any poem is an accredited theme, and that in self-perception there is no theme, but at best sufficient *vis a tergo* to land the practitioner into the correct scenery, where the self is either most happily obliterated or else so improved and enlarged that it can be mistaken for part of the décor." "What, be a singer born and lack a theme!" is the question that skewers Yeats' assumptions. The montage of conventionally derived components offers the sole opportunity for freedom and individuality to enter in, "and it is very often in virtue of this, when the tics of mere form are in abeyance, that attributions are to be made." This is the only real ground for discriminating among Padraic Colum, James Stephens, AE, "the Rev. Monk Gibbon," Beckett claims. Though Joyce is not mentioned in this 1934 essay, his example is the implied alternative to Yeats's. In this respect, it is significant that Beckett has consistently acknowledged a moral rather than a literary debt. As he said later of Jack Yeats, whom he does cite in the essay: "*L'artiste qui joue son être est de nulle part. Et il n'a pas de frères.*"[12]

Such an argument is not, in outline, so unusual as may at first appear. For example, while English and American criticism of the 1930s was concerned to answer the "problem of belief" in Yeats's poetry, that is, to accommodate Yeats's commitment to the occult without losing the poetry in the process, Irish readers have never had such problems. What concerns Beckett is what has always occupied Anglo-Irish poetry, and derives from the Celtic Revival phase of Yeats's career. The more usual view of Anglo-Irish writing in the 1920s and 1930s sets the tradition of myth and folklore deriving from and surrounding Yeats against the realism and satire that succeeded it in writers like O'Flaherty and Clarke: the romanticism of turn-of-the-century Ireland as opposed to the succeeding period of political and artistic disillusionment. The view was propounded at the time by John Eglinton in *The Dial* and by AE in *The Irish Statesman*; it has been repeated down to the present in such books as Frank O'Connor's *Backward Look* (1967). Even so, Beckett's analysis has its counterparts. He is very much of his generation in his understanding of the situation in more than national terms, in feeling the alternative to Yeats lies not in realism but, following the example of Joyce, in European writers of a quite different ambience.

Mervyn Wall has spoken of how "even [he], an indifferent playwright, never thought of studying an Abbey Theatre play, but read every word of Ibsen, Hauptmann and Hasenclever."[13] Niall Montgomery has recorded his great joy not in Yeats but in discovering Rimbaud, Apollinaire and Valéry.[14] Denis Devlin became the translator of René Char and St. John Perse, and Thomas McGreevy had already been the translator of the Spanish Machado, Jiménez, Raphael Alberti, Jorge Guillén, Lorca, as well as of Valéry and Montherlant. Beckett's experiments in troubador verse forms in *Echo's Bones* are accountable, no

---

[12] "Hommage à Jack B. Yeats," *Les lettres nouvelles*, No. 14 (April 1954), 619. This tribute to Yeats' *oeuvre*, with its talk of "*son insistance à renvoyer au plus secret de l'esprit qui la soulève*" and so on, makes a good deal more sense when read alongside Beckett's 1934 essay.

[13] In an interview with Michael Smith in *The Lace Curtain*, No. 4 (Summer 1971), 83.

[14] "Bird Lives! (D'Alembert, go home!)," *The Lace Curtain*, No. 5 (Spring 1974), 45.

doubt, to T. B. Rudmose-Brown's particular interest in all things Provençal, but it should be noted that it was shared by others whose associations with Rudmose-Brown were at most slight. Sean O'Faolain, for example, took the relations that exist between Provençal love poetry and the Gaelic to illustrate the one perfect synthesis literary history has to offer of creative interchange between Ireland and Europe.[15] Beckett's argument is idiosyncratic not in its broad outlines, therefore, but in the terms in which it is apprehended and developed.

What does distinguish Beckett's *Bookman* essay is less its arguments than the way they are put—that is, the coherence and forthrightness of the analysis and, even more, its being couched in negative terms. Such qualities are related: the clarity of the analysis depends on the same image that makes it intransigent. Yeats's edict of "Irish poets, learn your trade!" is thus presented as condemnation to an art of the circumference; "the circumference is an iridescence of themes—Oisin, Cuchulain, Maeve, Tir-nan-og, the Táin Bo Cuailgne, Yoga, the Crone of Beare—segment after segment of cut-and-dried sanctity and loveliness." "At the centre there is no theme. Why not? Because the centre is simply not that kind of girl, and no more about it."

In his 1928-29 *Exagmination* essay, Beckett had seen Joyce's art as of the center, desophisticating language to the extent that form is a concretion of content and "all humanity [circles] with fatal monotony about the Providential fulcrum—the 'the convoy wheeling encirculing abound the gigantig's lifetree' " (9). In the 1934 essay, he is more impressed by the space that intervenes between the artist and the world of objects: "breakdown of the object" or "breakdown of the subject." "It comes to the same thing—rupture of the lines of communication." It is for their awareness of this bankrupt relationship that he praises the poetry of Devlin and Coffey, though the principle is better illustrated in his comments on O'Casey and Jack Yeats in the same and in a later year. O'Casey's achievement is seen to rest on an art of knock-about disintegration:

> If "Juno and the Paycock," as seems likely, is his best work so far, it is because it communicates most fully this dramatic dehiscence, mind and world come asunder in irreparable dissociation—'chassis.'[16]

The same discontinuity sustains the more delicate ironies of Jack Yeats:

> The irony is Ariotesque, as slight and as fitful and struck from the same impact, between the reality of the imagined and reminiscence of its elements. The face remains grave, but the mind has smiled. The profound *risolino* that does not destroy.[17]

---

[15] *The Irish* (Harmondsworth, Middlesex, 1947, revd. ed. 1969), pp. 66-67.

[16] "The Essential and the Incidental," *The Bookman*, LXXXVII (Christmas 1934), 111.

[17] "An Imaginative Work!" *The Dublin Magazine*, 11 (July-September 1936), 80.

Literary analysis thereby merges with themes closer to Beckett's own personal concerns while its statement becomes more assured and objective. The analysis is so integral to Beckett's thinking about literature that its incorporation into the ordering of events in *Murphy* causes no surprise. The plot involving Neary, Wylie and Cooper is a plot described by surfaces and circumferences. "Remember there is no triangle, however obtuse, but the circumference of some circle passes through its wretched vertices" (146). Such characters inhabit a Newtonian world where the quantum of wantum cannot vary (43, 137), or so they think. Their medians meet in Murphy only in the sense that they follow one another, and Miss Counihan, round the rim of cause and effect in a way described by Beckett's comments on O'Casey's burlesque. They are puppets that mock the plausible concatenations of conventional fiction, and their gyrations achieve nothing more than a rearrangement of the already known. "*Le pou est mort. Vive le pou!*" (138). These comically and quite literally incongruous characters on the circumference receive the most attention, but their fate hangs on Murphy and Murphy's failure mirrors theirs. At the center of the book he, too, suffers from "this—er—psychomatic fistula" (149), caught between the irreconcilable contraries of Celia and Mr. Endon as body against mind. Only Mr. Kelly appears to establish a *modus vivendi*, but his poor triumph is filled with a sense of other days and places.

Various strands of *Murphy's* plot overlap, and situations are contrived to echo one another. Murphy's garret is matched by Celia's move upstairs and in turn by Mr. Endon's pad; Celia's sitting on Mr. Kelly's bed is recalled when she sits on Murphy's and on Neary's; the close of Chapter 2 mirrors the close of Chapter 3; Miss Counihan leaning out of the window after Wylie anticipates Celia's looking out after Murphy in the following chapter; Miss Carridge swears by "my rump," "Just like Mr. Kelly" (102); Neary and Wylie in the restaurant in their way anticipate Murphy in the same situation; Neary's eyelids share the same property (of being "not teartight") as Mr. Kelly's. Symmetries pervade the book and, in Chapters 10 and 11, they culminate in a double climax. The absurdity of the conclusions reached one after another by Neary, Wylie and Miss Counihan, as each of them speaks "to the best of his ability the truth to the best of his knowledge" (146), is topped by Wylie passing silk handkerchiefs into his mouth and out of his ear (154). Most important of all, Celia's final statements are contrived carefully to match the conclusion reached by Murphy in his confrontation with Mr. Endon:

> "At first I thought I had lost him because I could not take him as he was. Now I do not flatter myself."

Beckett uses similar terms in "Henri Hayden, homme-peintre," *Les Cahiers d'Art—Documents*, No. 22 (November 1955), [2].

A rest.

"I was a piece out of him that he could not go on without, no matter what I did."

A rest.

"He had to leave me to be what he was before he met me, only worse, or better, no matter what I did."

A long rest.

"I was the last exile" (159).

> "the last at last seen of him
> himself unseen by him
> and of himself"

A rest.

"The last Mr. Murphy saw of Mr. Endon was Mr. Murphy unseen by Mr. Endon. This was also the last Murphy saw of Murphy."

A rest.

"The relation between Mr. Murphy and Mr. Endon could not have been better summed up than by the former's sorrow at seeing himself in the latter's immunity from seeing anything but himself."

A long rest.

"Mr. Murphy is a speck in Mr. Endon's unseen" (171).

The world of objects, being what it is, and the world of self, being what it is, are irreconcilable; the bankrupcy is hilarious and bitter. Only with the rounding out of the book—the book as distinct from the book's argument—does a different mood succeed.

The two plots of *Murphy*, on the circumference and at the center, are thus related to one another by way of the critical ideas Beckett was refining upon while the novel came into being. What may also be suggested is that the two plots are related not only in broad structural terms to Beckett's thinking about literature but in shadowy coincidences of detail. It is difficult not to see those figures chasing each other and Miss Counihan round the circumference as those twilighters in pursuit of Cathleen ni Houlihan, just as it is difficult not to identify Celia with a parodied purer muse, if such a one exists—"Heaven. Helen. Celia" (122). *"Celia, s'il y a, Celia, s'il y a"* (82). In turn, the two sets of characters, on the rim and at the center, frequently call to mind, in various ways, particular persons.

It is as well to be clear what I am suggesting. The organization of *Murphy* reflects ideas Beckett was evolving, at the time the book was gestated and composed, concerning the scope and possibilities of literature. In particular, the book's structural principle repeats the terms in which Beckett conceived of his alienation from Yeats and Dublin literary coteries and his admiration for Joyce, which was also qualified: fiction and criticism coincide in the controlling image of circumference and centre. If a number of incidental identifications are now suggested, they are to be understood with caution. They are shadowy, opportunistic, of varying degrees of obviousness and involvement. They are alternatively specific and by implication in a way that is confusing unless the overall context is properly understood. They are as often likely to be unconscious as intended. Who is to say if Murphy's game of chess deliberately mocks the game so often played in Irish legend, as by Cuchulain and Fionn?

The Newtonians recall a number of real-life admirers of Cathleen ni Houlihan. Neary is closer to AE than to James Stephens or Stiéfan MacEnna, whom his particular mystical interests also resemble, and Wylie to a parody of Yeats. The attributions—shadow possibilities is perhaps a better term—are suggested by a number of details: their names, their interests, the different degrees of sympathy with which they are perceived. AE is described in Beckett's *Bookman* essay as one who, "when thoroughly galvanised by the protracted apathies, rigidities and abstractions, enters his heart's desire with such precipitation as positively to protrude into the void:" Wylie's "way of looking was as different as a *voyeur*'s from a *voyant*'s, though Wylie was no more the one in the indecent sense than Murphy was the other in the supradecent sense. The terms are only taken to distinguish between the vision that depends on light, object, viewpoint, etc., and the vision that all those things embarrass" (64). Cooper, their shared and rebellious man-of-all-work, suggests a number of possibilities: Colum? Higgins? O'Flaherty? One recalls Beckett's comment in the *Bookman* essay on Higgins' "entire Celtic drill of extraversion" or O'Flaherty's restless travelling. Cooper is not unlike O'Flaherty's own Gypo the informer, and his dumb stupid relation to Celia resembles Gypo's to Katie fox, just as his whole mode of fictional being is the equivalent of O'Flaherty's flat plain rough style—"as though it had been written by a cave-man for cave-men."[18]

In a different way, Rosie Dew cruelly recalls that twilighter of mediumistic inclination and friend of Yeats, Hester Travers Smith, whose *Psychic Messages from Oscar Wilde* [1924] had included the message that Oscar Wilde did not like *Ulysses* and in whose Chelsea house Beckett's friend Thomas McGreevy was living at the time Beckett was writing the novel nearby. In a different way yet again, the allusions to Cork—to Neary's Cork origins, the references to F. S. Mahony and Shandon churchyard, Neary's chauvinistic assault on Cuchulain at the G.P.O. ("That Red Branch bum was the camel's back" [36])—mock the narrow literary nationalism emanating from Munster and upheld by Daniel Corkery.

The identifications I am suggesting are partial and not at all consistent; they are only one aspect of Beckett's characters, and they do not preclude alternative possibilities. Cooper not only shares attributes of a writer like O'Flaherty in Beckett's understanding of Irish writing,

---

[18] L. P. Hartley reviewing *The Black Soul* in *The Spectator*, CXXXII (17 May 1924), 809.

he also has a separate meaning in the world of the novel that makes him a progenitor, or distant ancestor, of Lucky and of Clov. There is no suggestion that Beckett ever sat at AE's feet, as Murphy did at Neary's, though they did meet,[19] nor that the sage of Rathgar was a drunk or would shave off his whiskers, nor even that AE's Armagh accent disguised a Corkman. (The suggestions are joke enough in themselves.) Cork is laughable in the way that every second city is from the vantage of the first: " 'I say you know what women are,' said Wylie impatiently, 'or has your entire life been spent in Cork?' " (141). It has its place alongside Dublin and London, also, to complete one of the many triangles that figure in the book's world. The literary implication is only one element in a spectrum, and the satire is at random at the expense of all things Irish, from Junior Fellows to Irish virgins, as well as at life at large.

One dimension of the satire reflects one very particular view of the Irish literary situation, accompanies and, of course, does not replace other possibilities. It enriches the texture of allusion and meaning, and only the point of view is consistent as Beckett undercuts the more than slightly ridiculous. To take one other example: Murphy's will, that his ashes be flushed down the w.c. of the Abbey Theatre, is simultaneously a joke at the expense of the swirling movement of the Cartesian vortex and the famously noisy convenience of an "antiquarian" monument. At the same time, it picks up the book's controlling image of center and circumference and, whereas the true artist shrinks "from the nullity of extracircumferential phenomena, drawn in to the core of the eddy," even at the last Murphy's will is denied. As Beckett says in *Proust* (90—cf. 65-66), the will is "a servant of intelligence and habit [*sc.* it] is not a condition of the artistic experience." This is one level of meaning, which is very funny and very serious. It is, even so, surely more than a coincidence that the actual fate of Murphy's ashes is not unlike that of George Moore's, who willed his body to be cremated and his ashes spread over Hampstead Heath, "where donkeys graze," again to have his will frustrated.[20] The similarity between Murphy's end and that of George Moore a few years earlier is indeed appropriate, in that Beckett's distanced and demeaning attitude towards the Revival most resembles Moore's. One is not surprised to learn that *Hail and Farewell* is enjoyed by Beckett, nor that the passage concerning the disposal of Murphy's remains was one committed to memory by James Joyce.

---

[19] Cf. A. J. Leventhal, "Seumas O'Sullivan" in *Retrospect: The Work of Seumas O'Sullivan and Estalla F. Solomons*, ed. Liam Miller (Dublin, 1973), p. 12.

[20] Moore's will and what happened to his ashes is described by O. St. J. Gogarty in "George Moore's Ultimate Joke," *Intimations* (New York, 1950), pp. 25-40; cited by Sigle Kennedy, *Murphy's Bed* (Lewisburg, Pa., 1971), p. 270.

Fortuitous coincidences reflect consistently held assumptions. And the same varying distance between life and art, and the same contradictory mingling of apparently intended and perhaps not wholly conscious identification, exists in the case of those characters at the book's center. In the case of those two, who define the alternatives between which Murphy is caught, the allusions are most private almost inevitably, because most meaningful. Lawrence Harvey has written of the real girl who shared a number of characteristics with Celia, and there is no need to say any more. Something may be said about Mr. Endon, however, if only because he is more relevant to the matter being discussed.

It seems to me that a number of characteristics associate Mr. Endon with Thomas McGreevy, and whether or not this was intended is beside the point. McGreevy was far from lunatic, and he remained one of Beckett's closest friends from the time they met in Paris in 1928 until his death in 1967. What suggests the names be associated is nothing on the gross level of the penny-a-line vulgarity of a literature of notations, but that the sort of poetry McGreevy wrote represented for Beckett a similar sort of hypnotic narcissistic attraction. This is a theme that deserves fuller treatment than I can give it here. It involves the coincidence of theme and manner between McGreevy's poems and very early poems by Beckett which have never been collected, and the two poets' subsequent statement of differences. "Calvary by Night," for instance, carried over from "Dream of Fair to Middling Women" to *More Pricks Than Kicks* (65), or the close of *Whoroscope*—"and grant me my second / starless inscrutable hour"—reflect in style and attitude (even if the body of the latter poem most decidedly does not) the influence of McGreevy. McGreevy's poem "Fragment" turns on that same line of Dante which Beckett alludes to, differently, in a contemporaneous poem in his own, "Text," published in *The European Caravan* and later in *The New Review*, and with greater assurance and control in "Dante and the Lobster": *Qui vive la pietà quand'è ben morta* (*Inf.* xx.28). It is a theme that McGreevy returns to in the poem which rounds out his 1934 volume, called "Swan Song": he continues his plea that Beckett should realize "that the first virtue does not necessarily / Contradict the greatest."

In this dialogue in verse between McGreevy and Beckett, intelligence and logic are met by an irrepressible will to believe, and McGreevy sounds the same note as those later critics who read *Imagination Dead Imagine* as a positive affirmation of the human spirit:

> Song is dead. Yes. Song
> Is dead. Long live song!

Against such an attitude Beckett cannot win. Indeed, when every contradiction becomes merely the occasion for affirming faith, he cannot even begin to engage. From his point of view, the McGreevy poems are like solitaire or like Mr. Endon's game of chess. Their characteristic movement traces a *Zweispringerspott* towards the oblivion of Mr. Endon's sightless gaze:

> In the darkness
> I close my eyes
> To the German sadism on the screen
> And the recessionalist lovers
> Around me.
>
> I recede too,
> Alone ("Giorgionismo").

Even the terms in which Beckett reviewed these poems for *The Dublin Magazine* evoke the novel he wrote in the following year: their self-absorption into light, their rapt obliteration of the squalid and the ordinary, "this blaze of prayer creating its object." Even the form of what Mr. Endon means to Murphy is set out in Chapter 11 in a way not unlike the syntax of a McGreevy poem, originating from the same nucleus of "endopsychic clarity." And this same "light, calm and finality" Beckett makes clear, in the review and in the novel, cannot be his.

So much for Mr. Endon. Mr. Kelly is an equally intriguing figure, and he shares with Mr. Endon the distinction of the respectful prefatory title. However, whereas Mr. Endon represents a hypnotic narcissistic evaporation of selfhood, at the very center of the novel, Mr. Kelly stands a little to one side. Any understanding of the book must reckon with the special, indeed familial, relationship he bears to Celia. He lives off her earnings but he also ends the book with her, in a magnificent and memorable chapter beyond the point where the plot concerning Murphy has been completed. He shares Celia, the book's modern muse, with its titular hero. At the close he remains the only poet for this shining whore.

A number of aspects of Mr. Kelly, some large and some incidental, suggest the figure of Joyce. Various details link them, like the yachting cap, the endless work in progress (in bed), the Icaran kite-flying and the attempt to join heaven and earth. But, more importantly, Murphy's divergences from Mr. Kelly coincide with Beckett's divergences from Joyce. Mr. Kelly's Christian name is Willoughby, which sets him against Murphy's will-less ideal of *Ubi nihil vales, ibi nihil velis* (124—cf. 79-80). Though his attention is described as "dispersed"—"parts would wander away and get lost if he did not keep a sharp lookout" (17, 81)—he works continually to bring these parts into a relationship—"to know the who, what, where, by what means, why, in what way and when. Scratch an old man and find a Quintilian" (15). Beckett's comment in his *Exagmination* essay comes to mind, on Joyce's concern with correspondences and interrelationship:

> Why should the Armistice be celebrated at the eleventh hour of the eleventh month? He cannot tell you because he is not God Almighty, but in a thousand years he will tell you, and in the meantime must be content to know why horses have not five legs, nor three (21).

His comments to Israel Shenker on Joyce's art of omniscience and omnipotence—"The more Joyce knew the more he could"[21]—as opposed to his own art of the non-knower, the non-can-er, are also clearly relevant.

At the close, Mr. Kelly sits in his chair, less like Murphy off his rocker than as a visual equivalent of Joyce off on his "wholemole millwheeling vicocyclometer." The excitement, pleasure and lyrical pathos of his long-prepared attempt to "determine the point at which seen and unseen met" (190) brilliantly transposes Joyce's attempt to tunnel through his *Work in Progress* from both ends ("Doublends Jined"); or, as Beckett put it to Richard Ellmann, to demonstrate that reality is a paradigm, an illustration of a possibly unstatable rule.[22] As in the poem "Home Olga," Beckett celebrates the "Swoops and loops of love and silence in the eye of the Sun and view of the mew," but with detachment. And though Mr. Kelly finishes the novel and even though his eye has been also on Celia's customers, he closes it in failure suffused with enormous regret. The book's form is rounded out—art's promise is allowed—only on the basis of a premise the book itself has destroyed. Fittingly it bears the title of Joyce's false Ulysses from "Eumaeus" (W. B. Murphy): Beckett's art of inadequacy, besides masquerading under the title of the Irish everyman, trails memories of an episode of linguistic erosion and undermining, of doubleness and shifting ambiguity, of inevitable letdown as art gives way to life. It is characteristic of Beckett that if there is to be an allusion to Joyce, it should be to this, one of the least "Joycean" sections of *Ulysses*.

I hope it is not necessary to repeat again that these possibilities add to but in no way usurp Beckett's more obvious meanings. Mr. Endon is no more Thomas McGreevy, nor is Mr. Kelly Joyce, than Murphy himself is Beckett. But it is true to say that each of the first two characters in the novel embodies values coincident with Beckett's estimation of the two writers, as well as embodying a number of curious shared details. The important thing is that these embodyings, or reflections or whatever one elects to call them, confirm and extend meanings and that their authority is not of the sort that changes or cancels. Because their significance is dependent on the novel's themes, they do indeed sometimes cross or contradict one another at the level of anecdote. For example, the description of Murphy's third zone owes some-

---

[21] Ibid., p. 3.

[22] *James Joyce* (New York, 1959), p. 562.

thing to the purgatorial self-cancelling flux described in Beckett's essay on Joyce: "an endless verbal germination, maturation, putrefaction . . . a step forward is, by definition, a step back" (16, 22). This in its turn owes something to the discussions of Joyce's "sweet noo style" in *The Irish Statesman*, at the time and before.[23] All Beckett has done in putting together this part of his essay is to take over their descriptions of Bedlamite language and to reverse their judgment. Neary's "pretentious fear of going mad" (64) and his "curious feeling . . . that he would not get through the night" of Murphy's death (152-53), as well as Murphy's etymology of gas as chaos (121-22), are to be recalled. The apparent contradiction between Murphy's approach to his third zone—"Matrix of Surds"—and his ultimate recoil from Mr. Endon is thereby explained. Though in the novel they appear as almost identical states, in a way that some readers find confusing, the one derives from an earlier and accidental source and the other from a recent and vividly experienced visit to the Bethlehem Hospital. The complication of other patterns I have described is quite irrelevant.

The nature of Beckett's allusions in *Murphy* might finally be clarified in a brief comparison with Brian O'Nolan's *At Swim-Two-Birds*. Joyce yoked the two books together as "*Jean qui pleure*" against "*Jean qui rit*,"[24] and at first they would seem strikingly similar in subject matter and treatment. The starting point of each of them is the pretension of Joyce's achievement; each includes a satiric portrait of the artist as a Joycean figure, employing the same motifs of yachting cap, highflying folly and the osmosis of form: the Joycean trellis of three narratives in a fluid circular relation matches Beckett's structure of circumference and center and echoed situations. Against these coincidence, the assumptions that develop the shared techniques and themes are strikingly different. Brian O'Nolan's imagination is essentially conservative; Beckett's divergence from Joyce is critical and not moral; literary allusions in the two books are developed in opposite ways. Brian O'Nolan is situated within the literary context his book describes, which is mirrored not only in his attitude towards Joyce (which is harder) and towards Finn (which is softer) but in the specificity of his references. The echoing of Joycean sentences and motifs is exact, and the references to friends and acquaintances is similarly literal: Cecil French Salkeld appears as Michael Byrne, for instance, because Byrne was his mother's maiden name. Literary references, to Keats or to Huxley, are

---

[23] For instance, by Y. O. [AE], "New Languages," *The Irish Statesman*, 10 (25 August 1928), 492-93 (part reprinted in *The Living Torch*, ed. Monk Gibbon (London, 1937), pp. 139-40) and by James P. O'Reilly, "Literature and Life: Joyce and Beyond Joyce," ibid., V (12 September 1925), 17-18.

[24] Letter from Beckett to James Knowlson, 8 January 1971, quoted in *Samuel Beckett: An Exhibition*, ed. James Knowlson (London, 1971), p. 29.

of the same kind: cowboy stories and pub poetry are isolable quantities. To be aware of this is at once to be conscious that literary echoes in Murphy are of a different kind. Beckett's references to psychologists and theologians and especially to philosophers are specific but generally curtailed and often offer a joke for the initiated, unlike his literary allusions, which are glancing and possibly involuntary. They are traces of working assumptions and stages in a half-private process of clarification. They are never included for a knowing Dublin audience to seize on and to react to, and the single specified allusion in the range under discussion is revised out in the French translation. Miss Carridge ceases to be a reader of AE's *Candle of Vision* (108) and takes up instead "*roses de Décembre*, par Madame Rosa Caroline Mackworth Praed" (114). Every difference is of the same kind. If each book is in its own way cruel, Brian O'Nolan's is more often at the level of personality (at the expense of others), Beckett's at the level of theme (to himself).

*   *   *   *   *

Austin Clarke as Austin Ticklepenny is therefore an aberration in Murphy. No other identification is so specific or so uncomplicated. Clarke's reasoning that *Murphy* is a *roman à clef* seems based not on the book itself—which he liked much less than the "gay and spirited" *More Pricks Than Kicks*—but on the assumption that what Beckett had done for him must somehow be the method of the whole. After all, they had met occasionally in a bar in Grafton Street (or off it) when Beckett was lecturing at Trinity, and talked about Proust and other matters, and he could not in all humility understand why Beckett should have singled him out for special treatment. The manner of the portrait is in fact adventitious. It is as if Beckett had been led astray by the neatness of the identification and by a bitter opportunism into what may perhaps be admitted to be a lapse of taste, not consistent with the book's methods as they have been discussed. What is finally worth considering is this aberration in terms of Beckett's early fiction at large. The early fiction is, in an important sense, an attempt to resolve the problem of characters who get out of hand.

It is important that *Murphy* is the beginning of Beckett's *oeuvre*, his first satisfactory large piece of writing for the common reader and for himself. It was the first of his out-of-print works to be reissued. He has only recently and under pressure from an importunate academic industry allowed the general recirculation of *More Pricks Than Kicks*. At a time when the money would have been welcome, he declined to act on suggestions that he collect his early reviews, essays and stories. He has no intention of allowing the publication of *Proust* in French. *Murphy's* claim to mark the beginning of Beckett's *oeuvre* is indubitable. "If you want to find the origins of *En attendant Godot*," he told Colin Duck-

worth, "look at Murphy."[25] Again, to Sigle Kennedy: "If I were in the
unenviable position of having to study my work my points of departure
would be the 'Naught is more real . . .' and the 'Ubi nihil vales . . .' both
already in *Murphy* and neither very rational."[26] The proof of Beckett's
assumptions is his own practice. Ruby Cohn remarks that the references to Murphy in the subsequent novels, and not to Belacqua, suggests that Beckett himself views *Murphy* as his first significant
creation.[27] Even so, the sense in which the book is his first significant
creation needs to be defined.

   Murphy is continuous with the writing that precedes it at the level of
allusion, motif, and theme. Its specific allusions are to writers who had
engaged Beckett for a number of years—St. Augustine, Descartes,
Job.[28] It incorporates motifs pervasive in the earlier stories and poems,
so that Murphy's music MUSIC *MUSIC* has a background in the
Schopenhauer of *Proust* and the uncollected "A Case in a Thousand";
and when Lawrence Harvey asks of the title of Beckett's earlier poem,
"Why should the précis of life in the horoscope reading have anything
to do with a prostitute? . . ."[29] the answer is elaborated in Celia. Descartes' secrecy over the date of his birth is inherited, with equal
unsuccess, by Murphy; and Murphy's chair is not only a visual pun
anticipating his fascination with going off his rocker, but it repeats the
interest in self-cancelling boomerang movement differently embodied
in "Enueg I," "Ding-Dong" and *Whoroscope*'s "That's not moving, that's
moving." The novel picks up and develops themes that had held
Beckett's interest for some time already: the double claim on Murphy
of Celia and Mr. Endon merely transposes the two sorts of time that
confront Descartes—that which opens towards Christina of Sweden
and death, and that of memory, love and childhood.[30] The oppositions
of *Proust*, "of Habit and the brief suspension of its vigilance" (23),
describe exactly the *modus operandi* of the characters at circumference
and center in *Murphy*, as do the oppositions of piety and pity, habit and
individual feeling, in *More Pricks Than Kicks*.

   Even the resolution of these themes is similar—the only research is
excavatory and yet the center of the onion is not reached—together
with the form in which they are stated. Murphy's death is matched by

---

[25] *En attendant Godot*, ed. Colin Duckworth (London, 1966), p. xlvi.

[26] Letter dated 14 June 1967, included in Kennedy, *Murphy's Bed*, p. 300.

[27] *Samuel Beckett: The Comic Gamut* (New Brunswick, N.J., 1962), p. 64.

[28] For instance, "This grisly relic from the days of nuts, balls and sparrows" (30)
echoes Augustine's comment on "truckery among boys, for nuts and balls and sparrows,"
about two-thirds of the way through the final chapter of Book I of the *Confessions*.

[29] *Samuel Beckett: Poet and Critic* (Princeton, N.J., 1970), p. 57.

[30] Cf. Mayoux, *Paroles et Musique, Comédie, Dis Joe*, p. 17.

Belacqua's equally accidental death in "Yellow," the shared colour symbolism having a significance pointed out in "Gnome":

> Spend the years of learning squandering
> Courage for the years of wandering
> Through the world politely turning
> From the loutishness of learning.

Both Belacqua's and Murphy's deaths are set back from the close, and each book is completed by an episode bearing a similar emotional relation to those that come before. Cooper is able to remove his hat and to sit down, just as Hairy (Capper) Quin is able to take on a new lease of life:

> Perhaps the explanation of this was that while Belacqua was alive Hairy could not be himself, or, if you prefer, could be nothing else. Whereas now the defunct, such of his parts at least as might be made to fit, could be pressed into service, incorporated in the daily ellipses of Capper Quin without his having to face the risk of exposure. Already Balacqua was not wholly dead, but merely mutilated (200-01).

Cooper derives from Capper, which—Cappoquin being the location of a Trappist monastery in Munster—gives yet another twist to the Cork joke in *Murphy*. Celia dies in part along with Murphy, and does the Smeraldina along with Belacqua, and the resolution of novel and stories is structurally approximate, even if it is set in a different key.

The difference in key is what is finally important, however, because it determines the other real differences that in every case distinguish *Murphy*. Though the novel incorporates themes and allusions endemic in the writing or the five or so years that preceded its composition, it establishes a new attitude towards them and thereby a new relationship between them. The actually geometrical principle of its structure is an index of its firmer grasp. Murphy is not more ironically conceived than Belacqua, but differently and in a way that formalizes his relationships and in turn holds them in more steady focus. Episodes are more patterned and concerted. The humour is more controlled, and it derives from an involvement on the author's part that leaves room for more even exploitation of emotions like savagery and tenderness. Lawrence Harvey observes that the early prose seems to be an attempt to exorcise the Beckett who was or might have been Belacqua, to move his art out of the realm of detached play and into a world taken to be more "real," more "serious."[31] The essential achievement of *Murphy* is to articulate this tension successfully and at length. The timidity and abruptness, the shyness and offensiveness which had broken into and taken over the earlier writing, are for the first time subordinated to a mastering literary purpose.

---

[31] Ibid., pp. 332-33.

This is the real significance of the Irish literary dimension of the novel. Any footnotes it supplies are likely to be misleading because the identifications are so shadowy and contradictory, but it does make clear that the novel's achievement is closely involved with Beckett's view, from the outside, of the literary context he had separated from. His consideration of what he himself was trying to do, against other possibilities open to him, as an artist, became in turn the means of control. The reviewing he did for money may not have been as irrelevant as is sometimes suggested, in that it appears to have made firm his grasp of his own intentions in the way that his writing about Bram Van Velde was to do after the war. It provided the structural metaphor in which philosophical and psychological diagnosis coincided in a literary solution—Cartesian dualism and the psychology of schizophrenia stated, if not solved, as the situation of the Irish writer.

Murphy is Beckett's first satisfactory large piece of writing for the reason that it articulates with a degree of coherence themes and moods which concerned him. At the same time, these things are not wholly under control, as the intrusion of Ticklepenny shows. The book is more restless and diverse than some of its better-known critics allow. It is not the altogether "genial" book that Hugh Kenner describes:[32] for instance, in the portrayal of Miss Rosie Dew's duck's disease and Miss Carridge's body odor, of weekend lechers sprawling in their eczema and Wyllie's mollusc kisses, Beckett's humour is wilfully gruesome. Nor is it the "*Andromaque jouée par les* Marx Brothers" described by Ludovic Janvier:[33] There is venemous cruelty in this vision that foreshortens people to puppets. The Old Boy cuts his throat and then expires in an ambulance, at his own expense.[34] Within the schematically contrived form, as in Joyce's *Dubliners*, the author's relation to his material oscillates, in a way that is not under control, between denunciation and tenderness. Dylan Thomas described this variability of tone, and what is disturbing about it, when he said that while the book's humour has energy, hilarity, invention, it is still too involved in the Belacqua manner.[35] The book is not rightly what it should be, that is, what Beckett intended it to be, because he has tried to sell his bluffs over the double counter.

Dylan Thomas' review is perceptive because it recognizes that *Murphy* presents not just the problems of a pervasive dualism but the spectacle of its author caught up in the cognate problem of psychological and aesthetic distance or balance. The two associations of the book's

---

[32] *Samuel Beckett: A Critical Study* (London, 1962), p. 48.

[33] *Pour Samuel Beckett* (Paris, 1966), p. 27.

[34] Ruby Cohn, *Back to Beckett* (Princeton, N.J., 1973), pp. 61-62 lists examples.

[35] In his review in the *New English Weekly*, 12 (17 March 1938), 454-55.

title are emblematic. On the one hand the association through the Greek with form, on the other through the Latin with dreams and shifting lights and perspectives. The book displays Beckett's discovery of a satisfactory form, but also that he had still to resolve the question of a stable tone: this is what occupied him thereafter. "Cascando," which was published in *The Dublin Magazine* in 1936, repeats in personal terms the same tension between being alone and needing another, and attains a fragile equipoise. It is hardly a coincidence that in the next year Beckett began writing in French, and the French pre-war poems continue the theme: *non che la speme, il desiderio è spento* is Leopardi's answer (quoted in *Proust* 18), and Schopenhauer's, that they severally approach. Essentially and in its literary aspect, Beckett's effort was to attain to a neutrality, to prevent things getting out of hand and taking on a life of their own. *Murphy* was translated into French before the outbreak of war, and Beckett was to comment on the supposed "weakening effect" of such a transposition.[36] In this reading of Beckett's fiction after *Murphy*, *Watt* is significant largely as a workshop in which the tools are constantly called into question, and the *nouvelles* largely as an attempt to hit off a style of controlled neutrality. The main line is resumed in *Molloy* and *Malone meurt*, which restate and enlarge upon the same theme of a double-failed quest on the circumference and an investigation into the writer at the center. It is the theme of "*l'empêchement-objet et l'empêchement oeil*": "*Je ne peux voir l'object, pour le représenter, parce qu'il est ce qu'il est. . . . Je ne peux voir l'objet, pour le représenter, parce que je suis que je suis.*"[37] But this time the attempt will be neutral and inert:

> *Sans rien exagérer bien sûr, en pleurant et en riant tranquillement, sans m'exalter. Oui, je vais enfin être naturel, je soufrirai davantage, puis moins, sans en tirer de conclusions, je m'écouterai moins, je ne serai plus ni froid ni chaud, je serai tiède, je mourrai tiède, sans enthousiasme. Je ne me regarderai pas mourir, ça fausserait tout (Malone meurt 8).*

Malone's monologue may seem a long way from Austin Clarke's intrusion into the world of *Murphy*, but it should now be clear why it is not. The intrusion embodies most clearly the problems facing Beckett in the first phase of his career as a writer, problems which he attempted to solve by techniques aspiring towards neutrality and demythologization. In the end the solutions were to fail—Malone's monologue continues to become increasingly burdened with emotion, as had the third written of the *nouvelles*, the recently published *Premier Amour*—and the

---

[36] To Herbert Blau: Cf. "Meanwhile, Follow the Bright Angels," *Tulane Drama Review*, V (September 1960), 90-91. Beckett's comments on the shift to French are brought together by Cohn, *Back to Beckett*, pp. 58-59.

[37] "Peintres de l'empêchement," *Derrière le miroir*, No. 11-12 (June 1948), 7.

failure inaugurated, in its turn, a new phase in Beckett's writing and the beginnings of a new mythology in *L'innommable*. Austin Clarke's intrusion is not fortuitous at all. It is opportunistic, certainly, but Murphy's sudden closeness to Ticklepenny is Beckett's motivation. The sentence, "You had a great look of Clarke there a moment ago" (133) is integral as well as unexpected. Confusion of identity, and self-consciousness in an everyday as well as strict sense, underlies Beckett's oscillation between bitterness and burlesque, the wilful besmirching and the peculiar brilliance. The coupling of commitment and indecision, which Clarke reflects in only the most obvious way, is an aberration integral to this early fiction. It sets the limits of an imaginative world.

BECKETT, THE CAMERA, AND JACK MacGOWRAN

Alec Reid

Many commentators have remarked on Beckett's artistic versatility, but few, if any, have paused to consider the reasons for it, or its possible implications. They marvel at the uncanny ease with which he masters each new medium—*Godot* was his first full-length play; *Embers*, his second radio drama, won the *Prix Italia; Film,* his first venture into cinema, was awarded the *Prix Filmcritice*—yet they seem content to accept this as an arbitrary phenomenon, a kind of cultural Act of God, even as we all take it as normal that Beckett should write now in English, now in French.[1] But why should a writer who has already shown an almost pedantic elegance in his own tongue suddenly take to writing violently disruptive work in a foreign language? Why should an author whose novels have earned distinguished, if rather specialized, acclaim, and whose first play has been professionally shown in Paris, London, Dublin, Berlin and New York, within a period of five years, feel driven to investigate mime, radio, cinema and television?

Beckett himself has provided one clue: he is essentially an explorer. As far back as 1956 he described his post-war writing as so many attempts to chart areas of human experience hitherto deliberately neglected by the traditional Apollonean artists anxious to achieve a statement.[2] These explorations into ignorance, impotence, anguish,

---

[1] See the review of *Eh Joe* in the London *Times*, 5 July 1966: "Whatever Mr. Samuel Beckett does is more surprising than it should be because it always, if somewhat paradoxically, belongs entirely to whatever medium he has chosen for it." Quoted by Alec Reid in *All I can Manage, More than I Could* (Dublin and New York, 1968), p. 20.

[2] See a "Profile" of Samuel Beckett by Michael George (i.e., Alec Reid) in the *Irish Tatler and Sketch*, February 1956.

needed new equipment, something more than the static sentence on the silent page. Even as Beckett was writing himself into an *impasse* with the trilogy of novels, he had broken fresh ground with *Godot*, coming into a whole new world where eye and ear are involved as much, if not more, than intellect. As George Devine, who directed *Endgame, Happy Days,* and *Play* for the English National Theatre has well said, "When working as a director on a Beckett play . . . one has to think of the text as something like a musical score wherein the 'notes,' the sights, the sounds, the pauses, have their own special inter-related rhythms, and out of their composition comes the dramatic impact."[3]

Once Beckett had convinced himself that he could write plays which "worked" on a stage, it was a natural step to radio drama where the limitations imposed by the visible no longer apply. In *Godot* he had shown us two men waiting; in *Embers* he takes us inside a man's skull. In a similar way the limitations on physical movement and changes of scene which operate on the stage do not restrict the film; it seems only logical, then, that Beckett should have explored the additional possibilities offered by the camera, both in cinema and television.

A second clue to Beckett's versatility is to be found in the stimuli to which he will respond. Abstract philosophies, disembodied principles of any sort, have never struck him as valid causes for action; concrete situations, personal involvements, frequently have. Here life serves admirably to illustrate art. When war broke out in September, 1939, Beckett, on holiday in Ireland, hurried back to his Paris flat remarking that he preferred France at war to Ireland at peace, but he then took no part in the hostilities until the fall of Paris. What had a war between Germany, England, and France got to do with a neutral Irishman like himself? Soon after the Germans arrived, however, he joined the Resistance, angered by the day-to-day humiliations inflicted by the Germans on the local Jews, among whom he had many friends, and by the arbitrary executions of innocent civilian hostages.[4] "The Germans were making life hell for my friends," he explained some years later,[5] and on another occasion he remarked, "I couldn't stand with my arms folded."[6] In a similar way, a great deal of his work has been written for specific people. *Acte Sans Paroles I* was devised for the dancer Deryk Mendel.[7] *All That Fall* came at the suggestion of an acquaintance

---

[3] In a program note to his production of *Play* at the Old Vic, London, April 1964. Quoted by Reid in *Irish Tatler and Sketch*, February 1956.

[4] See Israel Shenker, "Moody Man of Letters," *New York Times*, 6 May 1956, sec. 2, p. 1.

[5] To Alan Simpson who directed the Dublin premiere of *Godot*. See Simpson, *Beckett, Behan and a Theatre in Dublin* (London, 1962), p. 64.

[6] See Reid, *Irish Tatler and Sketch*, February 1956, p. 14.

[7] Ibid., p. 74.

working in the BBC.[8] *Krapp's Last Tape* was called into existence by the voice of the actor Patrick Magee.[9] *Film* was part of a project conceived by his American publisher Barney Rosset.[10] *Cascando* was written for his friend the composer Marcel Mihalovici to complement his score for "*une invention pour musique et voix.*"[11] The TV piece, *Eh Joe*, was for Jack MacGowran.[12] In short, Mendel's dancing, Magee's voice, Mihalovici's music, MacGowran's theatrical genius had each led Beckett into a new artistic world, just as the Yellow Star of David which every Jew in occupied Paris was forced to wear as a mark of infamy had led Beckett into the world of the Resistance.

More interesting still, it would seem that even inanimate objects have led Beckett to extend his operations beyond the written word. To practice his craft the author needs only paper and some kind of writing instrument—pen, pencil, or typewriter, all of which are but means to an end and will not appear in the finished product. As Beckett moved from one medium to another, however, he soon became aware of other men's professional paraphernalia which he could use just as effectively in the finished work as he could use men and women, or words. This process began in the theatre, with scenery. The tree in *Godot* is no more than a stage prop, an addition to the work, and if, for any reason, the tree were unavailable, a production could still be staged after only slight alterations in the dialogue. But then look at the mound in *Happy Days*, which literally defines the action—no mound, no play. Next consider that familiar theatrical machine, the spotlight. Its normal use is to focus the attention of the audience onto the actors: in *Play*, it has become a character in its own right, directing the actors, making them speak or fall silent, and it is placed not at the back of the auditorium, but between the audience and the players. More spectacular still, and involving a strange kind of cross-fertilization, is Beckett's association with the tape recorder. Beckett's first broadcast play *All That Fall* had drawn heavily on sound effects—indeed it taxed the BBC's technical resources to the full—and most of these sounds were recorded on tape for the radio production. In just over a year Beckett had finished a stage play in which a similar recording machine plays a leading part, is in fact one of the two protagonists. The audience in the theatre is

---

[8] Ibid., p. 68.

[9] Magee had played Mr. Slocum in the premiere of *All That Fall*. Beckett's manuscript is headed "Magee Monologue." See James Knowlson, *A Beckett Exhibition*, p. 80. This catalogue of an exhibition at Reading University, England, from May to July 1971 was published by Turret Books, Kensington Church Walk, London.

[10] See *Film*: complete scenario, illustrations, production shots with an essay "On Directing *Film*" by Allan Schneider (New York, 1969).

[11] See Knowlson, *A Beckett Exhibition*, p. 104.

[12] Ibid., p. 105.

present at a confrontation between Krapp at 69, as he is, and at 39, as he was. The confrontation, though entirely verbal, is none-the-less real for that. Without the tape recorder *Krapp's Last Tape*, as we know it, could not have been created. The play, however, has nothing to do with retrospection or memory; it takes us into the area of rejection—here the rejection of love and life.

And now, what of the camera? At the 1973 conference of the Canadian Association for Irish Studies in Montreal, four items were screened: *The Goad, Film, Eh Joe,* and *From Beginning to End.*[13] In all of these the central idea is Beckett's, but while the second and third pieces were created by him for a specifically chosen medium, the first and the last might best be described as transplants. *The Goad*, a film treatment of the mime *Acte Sans Paroles II*, was undertaken without the author's knowledge by a young director called Paul Joyce, and then shown to a delighted Beckett who sold him the world rights of the film for ten shillings. Joyce had grasped the fact that the impact of a film is quite different from that of a live presentation, and that if you are purporting to show a film you must offer something more than a photographic record of a stage production. Perhaps he had seen films of opera or ballet and had drawn his own conclusions. What Joyce did was to take Beckett's text and have it performed absolutely to the letter, not however as prescribed, "on a low platform at the back of the stage, violently lit in its entire length; the rest of the stage being in darkness,"[14] but out of doors on a vast dumping ground, with lorries coming and going, loading and discharging. The transplant "takes" because for Beckett's purpose the background is totally unimportant. In the theatre the platform does not shape the mime as the mound shapes the action in *Happy Days*; it is there simply because you cannot perform a piece *in vacuo*. In the same way, while providing us with a photogenically acceptable background, the rubbish heap and the lorries do not affect or impinge upon the mime either; nor does the fact that what we see is much larger than life size. We might describe the piece as Beckett *plus* camera *plus* executants—a mixture, not a compound.

With *Film* and *Eh Joe* things are radically different, for each was created especially for the medium chosen; here we have Beckett *cum* camera, a compound, not a mixture. In *Film*, indeed, we find the process that we noticed with the spotlight in *Play* and with the recording machine in *Krapp's Last Tape*. The camera, instead of being a recording instrument and nothing more, becomes a character influencing the human protagonist, being in one sense his very *raison*

---

[13] All hired from Grove Press, New York.

[14] Beckett's stage direction. Samuel Beckett, *Eh Joe and Other Writings* (London, 1967), p. 25.

d'être. In *Krapp* we watched an old man fumbling with keys, bananas, boxes of spools, and in *Film* we see a stumbling, heavily muffled figure fleeing through the streets of a town, shutting himself in a room in a shabby lodging house, taking fantastic precautions to avoid being seen—turning out the pets, covering a bird-cage and a gold-fish bowl—then rocking himself back and forth in a rocking chair till he almost drops off to sleep, only to be aroused twice. As in *Krapp* the recording machine was the second protagonist, so here it is the camera. It is the eye which sees the victim as he flees from all other eyes, and which in the end must be seen by him. It is the self who recognizes that as long as we live we can never get away from ourselves. In *Krapp*, as we suggested, Beckett was exploring rejection; here it is the philosophical proposition *esse est percipi*. But we do not need to know this. Beckett may have explored areas hitherto only investigated in the words of the philosophers, may have formulated a knotty little academic problem, but, by his use of silent-film conventions, familiar situations (the cops and robbers chase), and recognizable characters (the Chaplinesque clown), he has produced a gripping, disturbingly obsessive little piece of cinema.

In his television piece *Eh Joe* Beckett restores the camera to its familiar role of simple recording instrument, but now we are in a new medium since, though both use a camera and screen, cinema and television are as different as prose and verse, even though each of these relies on words and a writing instrument. In the cinema we sit in a public auditorium looking at a sequence of moving pictures projected from behind us onto a screen, where they appear larger than life. Television, by contrast, we watch usually in the privacy of our own homes, looking at a sequence of moving pictures projected at us through a tube behind a screen that compresses the images to a tenth of life size. Movement is the essence of a movie, but concentration is the essence of a television piece, which is what Beckett has created. The dimension is depth, not size. To transplant such a work to a cinema screen in a large hall is inevitably to dissipate it, as if we were to hang a miniature in complete isolation on one wall of an exhibition gallery. That is what happened at Montreal and explains why this writer—and he strongly suspects almost everyone else present—found *Eh Joe* the weakest of the four items. It simply did not work. The head and shoulders of one man—which was all we saw for over twenty minutes—could not rivet our attention to the screen for that long. The changes in expression were slight and therefore out of scale in the large area before us. The voice, low and insidious in a small room, here was nigh inaudible and merely irritating. In fact we did not see Beckett's television piece at all, but only a film of it, which had about as much chance of registering as a prose paraphrase of "The Ode to a Nightingale," or a versified Discourse on Eating Roast Pig.

A narrative, or at least a sequence of movements, is essential in the cinema, but in *Eh Joe* this is minimal. We watch Joe, a man in his middle fifties, in dressing gown and slippers, seal himself up in his room, much as the man in *Film* had done, and reassure himself he is alone. He then sits on his bed where, for the next twenty minutes or more he will remain, the camera making only nine slight moves and covering a total distance of thirty-six inches.[15] At once the voice begins. It is not Joe's, but belongs to a former mistress who, after mockingly solicitous enquiries about Joe's health, describes at great length the last hours and suicide of another girl whom Joe has seduced and rejected. Since we have seen that Joe is alone, this voice can exist only in his mind, but, as it gleefully reminds him, he can no longer by an act of will throttle it into silence as he had done to the voices of earlier victims. The process which he used to call "mental thuggee," will no longer serve him and he can no more escape the voice of conscience than the fugitive in *Film* can escape perception of himself self-perceived. All Joe can do is to sit on his bed, head cocked, face impassive save when it registers the mounting tension of listening, or registers varying degrees of relaxation as the voice pauses and he thinks that it "may have relented for the evening." During the voice's narrative the camera has been moving imperceptibly in on Joe until, with the climax of the story, it "achieves maximum close-up of his face," whereupon image and voice are simultaneously extinguished.

An inner voice implies an "outer" ear, and to bring this home we must *see* Joe and know that he is alone. Further, the voice is not under Joe's control, is not his own, and so, to establish this point, Beckett makes it that of a woman. Voice without image would have been ambiguous, while image without voice would have been complete nonsense. By fusing them Beckett takes us into a man's very soul, even as with sound alone in *Embers* he had taken us into his skull.

But for his tragic death a few weeks before the Montreal conference, Jack MacGowran would have been there to present his *From Beginning to End*. This was not the conventional anthology style program: MacGowran's purpose was to present the Beckett Man, an opposed to a series of individuals—Murphy, Watt, Krapp, or even Worm. In this he had succeeded so brilliantly that he had, in effect, brought another dimension to Beckett's work. To use Beckett's own verb for a play on stage as distinct from the text on paper, MacGowran had "realised" the Beckett Man in every shambling movement, every helpless gesture, in his gravel-like lower-class Dublin voice, in his sardonic laughter, even in his occasional howls. MacGowran had realized, too, the pathos, the irreverence, the compassion, the unbreakable stoicism; not to speak profanely, through MacGowran the Beckett word had

---

[15] Beckett's stage direction. Ibid.

become flesh. Providence has ordained that before leaving us Mac-Gowran should have made a record for Claddagh Records of Dublin, under Beckett's personal supervision, and that Beckett should have directed the definitive version of the stage program in Paris. This is what MacGowran brought to America and committed to film.

In this we find that process of transplanting noted in *The Goad*. The Beckett content is left untouched but the sequence is presented against a new background, the Nevada desert, and it is filmed in brilliant technicolor. The settings are magnificent, and as McGowran clambers onto some craggy eminence or trudges across great wastes of shale we feel all Man's littleness before Nature, yet his indomitable refusal to be overwhelmed by it. This is a totally different, perhaps more exhilarating, impact from that of the stage performance, where, by the inescapable reality of MacGowran's presence in the same room, we felt more directly involved with him as a human being, more conscious of his anguish, yet of his ultimate triumph.

MacGowran had played in the premiere of *All That Fall* in 1957, and in the English premieres of *Godot* and *Endgame*. Gradually, a remarkable sympathy developed between author and actor until in some uncanny way MacGowran seemed to become Beckett's representative; it was as though Sam himself were there. Indeed MacGowran would confess that at times he was not sure of his own identity.

Rational explanations of this closeness are easy enough to find. Both were Dubliners with the same ironic derogatory twist; both took their artistic work with a fine high seriousness, valuing it far more than themselves; both had a remarkably imaginative intelligence and a deep sense of compassion. Both rejected the domination of the word. When MacGowran decided to make the stage his life work he, of all the actors then in Dublin, alone felt it a necessary part of his training to go to Paris to learn something of mime and of ballet. Both, in their day, were noteworthy athletes. Yet reason does not quite tell all.

A BBC director, Michael Bakewell, has described rehearsing MacGowran for a radio production of *From Beginning to End*, with Beckett in attendance. "They were like conspirators," he said, "fellow conspirators who were brothers." Brothers they were in their understanding of art, and in their vision of life, the tragicomic angry yet compassionate vision of the clown. We are fortunate, indeed, to have MacGowran in Beckett preserved on disc and film; the machines have made a valuable contribution to the future.

THE ITALIAN SOURCES FOR *EXILES*: GIACOSA, PRAGA, ORIANI AND JOYCE

Dominic Manganiello

(I would like to thank David Thomas of the Taylor Institution Library, Oxford, for helping me to obtain many of Praga's works.)

Much of the criticism dealing with *Exiles* has centered on the influence exerted on Joyce by Ibsen. This tendency, though understandable in view of Joyce's manifest devotion to the Norwegian playwright, has diverted attention from other relevant areas of enquiry. In Trieste Joyce profited by the exposure to Italian culture, and he interested himself particularly in the native drama. The Italian theatre appealed to Joyce's penchant for raising relatively unknown names from obscurity. The themes of the plays also proved congenial to him, as he assimilated and transformed them to suit his art. Joyce himself indicated the undercurrent of Italian drama in his preliminary notes to *Exiles*; namely, Giacosa's *Tristi amori* and Praga's *La Crisi*.[1]

Although he was the leading Italian dramatist in the latter part of the nineteenth century, the Piedmontese Guiseppe Giacosa (1847-1906) is perhaps best remembered for the libretti he wrote in collaboration with Luigi Illica for Puccini's *La Bohème* (1896), *Tosca* (1899), and *Madame Butterfly* (1903). Stanislaus Joyce claims that his brother once told Alessandro Francini-Bruni that Giacosa was "a paunchy vulgarian whose highest ideal in life is a bellyful of *pasta asciutta*."[2] The only difficulty with this account is that Joyce is purported to have uttered this derogatory remark after attending *Il Can-*

---

[1] *Exiles* (Harmondsworth, 1973), p. 150.

[2] *My Brother's Keeper* (London, 1958), p. 252.

tico dei Cantici, which Stanislaus mistakenly attributes to Giacosa. In fact, *Il Cantico dei Cantici* (1881) was written by the Milanese Felice Cavalotti (1842-1898) and Joyce coached some non-professional Italian actors for the play in Zurich in 1918.[3] As early as 1901 Joyce described Giacosa along with Sudermann and Björnson in "The Day of the Rabblement" as "earnest dramatists of the second rank" who, at any rate, "can write very much better plays than the Irish Literary Theatre has staged."[4] And as late as 1939 Joyce, in a letter to Livia Svevo, alluded to *Come le foglie* (1900),[5] considered by some critics to be Giacosa's masterpiece.

In *Tristi amori* (1888), Fabrizio Arcieri is in love with Emma, the wife of Giulio Scarli, a fellow lawyer and friend. He has no money and finds it difficult to maintain his father, the Count Ettore, who wallows in heavy debts which Fabrizio is in the process of repaying. Giulio, ignorant of his friend's passion for his wife, seeks to aid him by securing clients. But when he discovers his wife's adultery, Giulio takes custody of his daughter and leaves, thereby tacitly giving his wife her freedom. Emma momentarily chooses to flee with Fabrizio but, catching sight of her daughter's doll, decides against it. On his return Giulio finds that his wife has remained and, for the sake of their child, their former relationship is restored.

In its presentation of the perennial "triangle," *Tristi amori* stands out from the great mass of similar plays because of the treatment of the husband. To this simple, kindhearted, sympathetic country lawyer everything even remotely connected with his wife is of necessity perfection. This admiration for Emma gives to his discovery of the truth a special poignancy. Some critics have argued that Giacosa is too didactic by having the wife and the disillusioned husband agree to remain together for the welfare of the child. Joyce avoids this pitfall in *Exiles* by not making Archie a stepping-stone towards reconciliation, but also by leaving the very nature of the reunion in doubt. Giulio does not resort to violent action in vindication of his wife's adultery, just as Richard or Bloom do not rely on physical retaliation. More importantly, Giulio's implicit offer of liberty to his wife strikes a "modern" note which Joyce detected and transformed into Richard's express invitation to Bertha.

If the fact that Joyce used *Tristi amori* as a model for the "triangle" theme in *Exiles* is not evident except through the preliminary notes, this does not hold true for *Ulysses*. Molly states at one point that "I wont forget the wife of Scarli in a hurry supposed to be a fast play about

---

[3] Richard Ellmann, *James Joyce* (London, 1966), p. 460.

[4] *The Critical Writings of James Joyce*, eds. Ellsworth Mason and Richard Ellmann (New York, 1959), p. 70.

[5] *Letters of James Joyce*, ed. Richard Ellmann (London, 1966), III, 439.

adultery" and remembers that someone in the gallery hissed Emma during the performance.[6] *The Wife of Scarli* (1897) has been identified as an English version by G. A. Greene of Giacosa's play.[7] That Joyce used Emma as a prototype for Molly is borne out by Molly's claim that "its all his own fault if I am an adulteress as the thing in the gallery said."[8] This is a reference to Giulio's indirect admission of his own guilt in his final speech where he proposes to give his daughter a rich dowry so that she may be free to marry a man of leisure and not one like himself who, in being so busy at earning a living, neglects his wife.[9] Moreover, Molly echoes the reconciliation scene of *Tristi amori* when she says, "Why cant we remain friends over it instead of quarrelling."[10]

Joyce thought so highly of the Milanese dramatist Marco Praga (1862-1929) that he expressed the wish that the latter would sign the *Ulysses* protest,[11] but Praga refused to do so. Joyce's library, in fact, included many of Praga's works.[12] This interest may be explained by the dramatic method and basic theme employed by Praga in his plays. He treated the theme of adultery, central to Joyce's work, in the aristocratic milieu of Milan. His primary interest was an objective representation of life, not a moral judgment of it. In this attitude Praga could be assured of finding an ally in Joyce. For this reason Joyce says of Praga's *La Crisi* that it is one of the most "characteristic works we possess" in the recently discovered papers in Padua.

The most amoral character of Praga's theatre, however, is Giulia, first performed by Eleonora Duse, in *La Moglie ideale* (1890). She is described ironically as the "ideal wife" by the lawyer Costanzo Monticelli because she contrives to make her husband, Andrea Campiani, happy, while at the same time deceiving him. As the "modern women" she is able to maintain a "strange but benevolent equilibrium between love for a man and affection for her domestic life."[13] But her demeanor disturbs the audience because she seems to be living a double existence without indicating which is her true domain. In *Exiles*, when Richard encourages Bertha to fulfill the assignation with Robert the potential of an "ideal wife" situation is present, but the audience is made aware of Bertha's choice in the final scene.

---

[6] *Ulysses* (Harmondsworth, 1968), p. 690.

[7] Don Gifford and Robert J. Seidman, *Notes for Joyce: An Annotation of James Joyce's Ulysses* (New York, 1974), p. 511.

[8] *Ulysses*, p. 702.

[9] *Tristi amori*, eds. R. Altrocchi and B. M. Woodbridge (Chicago, 1920), p. 98.

[10] *Ulysses*, p. 698.

[11] *Letters of James Joyce*, III, 149.

[12] *James Joyce*, p. 794.

[13] *La Moglie ideale* (Milan, 1920), pp. 69-71 and 137 (my translation).

The situation presented in *La Moglie ideale*, however, could not suit Joyce's purposes entirely, for it did not adhere to what he termed the "modern" tendency in drama:

> Since the publication of the lost pages of *Madame Bovary* the centre of sympathy appears to have been esthetically shifted from the lover or fancyman to the husband or cuckold. This displacement is also rendered more stable by the gradual growth of a collective practical realism due to changed economic conditions in the mass of the people who are called to hear and feel a work of art relating to their lives. This change is utilized in *Exiles* although the union of Richard and Bertha is irregular to the extent that the spiritual revolt of Richard would be strange and ill-welcomed otherwise can enter into combat with Robert's decrepit prudence with some chance of fighting before the public a drawn battle. Praga in *La Crisi* and Giacosa in *Tristi amori* have understood and profited by this change but have not used it, as is done here, as a technical shield for the protection of a delicate, strange, and highly sensitive conscience.[14]

La Crisi, then, according to Joyce, effected this transition into the "modern" field more adequately.

In *La Crisi* (1901), considered Praga's masterpiece, the focus of attention is on the suffering of the husband, Piero Donati. His brother, Raimondo, recently returned to his country after an absence of four years, suspects Piero's wife, Nicoletta, is having an affair with Pucci. Raimondo challenges Pucci to a duel on a trumped up pretext. On the eve of the encounter, he presses for a colloquy with his sister-in-law. Nicoletta, on hearing Raimondo's accusation, frankly acknowledges that she has never loved her husband, even though she remains grateful that he married her against the censures of public opinion because of her unvirtuous past. Meanwhile, word of the impending duel reaches Piero, who is not deceived by the pretext. He intimates to Raimondo that he knows of the affair, yet prefers complaisance to losing her. Raimondo, in any case, is convinced that all is not lost for his brother. He believes that Nicoletta, once the "crisis" is surmounted, can still be a good wife. He endeavors to conceal the fact of adultery by persuading Piero that he had been mistaken in his suspicions. Nicoletta wishes to confess her fault but Raimondo implores her to remain silent. The duel ends without injury to either contestant and Nicoletta decides to tell her husband the truth, and presumably they are reconciled.

Praga's influence on Joyce can be witnessed in the apparent similarities that exist between *Exiles* and *La Crisi*. Richard Rowan resembles Piero Donati, the acquiescent cuckold, but he encourages the affair in a way that Donati does not. Richard and Piero both marry women not approved of by the society in which they live, although in Richard's case it is because Bertha is not considered his "equal." Joyce also felt free to refine other points in order to forge "a technical shield

---

[14] *Exiles*, p. 150.

for the protection of a delicate, strange, and highly sensitive conscience." Although Nicoletta will eventually confess her fault to Piero,
Bertha's desire to reveal what transpired between her and Robert is
thwarted by Richard in the final act. Similarly, Nocoletta is ignorant of
the fact that Piero suspects her infidelity, whereas Bertha keeps
Richard informed of her every movement. As a result, Piero's reluctant
yielding of his wife's favours to another by force of habit is transformed
into Richard's wish "to feel the thrill of adultery vicariously,"[15] even
though it is not clear whether he does. This leads in *Exiles* to what is
called a battle of "souls" between Richard and Robert, as opposed to the
harmless physical combat enacted by Raimondo in Piero's stead. The
material discovered in *La Crisi*, therefore, had to be altered to compose
Joyce's "naked" drama.

Joyce, nonetheless, retained some distant verbal echoes from
Praga's play. Nicoletta's view that it is impossible for some women to
live with one man,[16] is also held by Robert.[17] At one point in the final act
of *La Crisi*, Nicoletta tells Piero that even if she denied having a lover,
"*ti rimarrà sempre un dubbio nell'anima*" ("there will always remain a
doubt in your soul").[18] In the same scene Piero also refers to the
attempt of an unknown person to "wound" his love: "*da mesi e mesi, un
ignoto s'incaricava di ferirmi nel mio amore*" ("for months and months, an
unknown person took it upon himself to wound me in my love").[19]
These remarks are transferred to Richard in the final scene of *Exiles*,
where he tells Bertha "I am wounded . . . I have a deep, deep wound of
doubt in my soul."[20]

In addition to Giacosa and Praga, Joyce relied on another Italian
source as background for his play. He mentions the historian Alfredo
Oriani (1852-1909),[21] a complex personality who was almost ignored
by his contemporaries and then labelled a precursor, and major
prophet, of Fascism. Oriani also wrote novels on sexual themes, but he
incorporated his views on these matters into his general philosophy in
his last work, *La Rivolta ideale* (1908). When Robert likens Bertha to the
moon because of her dress, Joyce's gloss on the passage reveals that her
age, 28, "is the completion of a lunar rhythm." Joyce then bids the
reader to consult "Oriani on menstrual flow—*la malattia sacra che in un*

---

[15] Ibid., p. 158.

[16] *La Crisi* (Milan, 1907), pp. 218-19.

[17] *Exiles*, p. 82.

[18] *La Crisi*, p. 198 (my translation).

[19] Ibid., p. 204 (my translation).

[20] *Exiles*, p. 146.

[21] Ibid., p. 148.

ritmo lunare prepara la donna per il sacrificio[22] ("a sacred malady seems within a lunar rhythm to prepare her for the sacrifice"). Robert M. Adams has pointed out that Joyce is here referring to *La Rivolta ideale.*[23]

The "revolt" is aimed against the general skepticism of the times in Italy, and it is to be "ideal" because, in Oriani's opinion, great changes in history must first be ripe for thought before being enacted. It is curious, indeed, that Joyce should have been attracted to a book based on conservative-reactionary sympathies. But Joyce, although a revolutionary in politics, still held conservative notions about woman's intellectual capacities.

The excerpt Joyce refers us to is taken from the chapter entitled "Femminismo," where Oriani claims that the family lies at the center of all cultures. The argument put forward by Oriani is introduced by remarks on the rivalry of the sexes which provide the necessary context to the extract in Joyce's notes. The irreconcilable differences that nature bestows upon man and woman are illustrated by what Oriani calls the "immutable" human picture. A woman's body, for instance, seems to be moulded for her maternal duties, as when

> she remains seated with an infant on her abdomen, her breasts suspended over his small mouth. The growth of her hips and lap is enormous, and that of the rest of her anatomy even more so. . . . Her breasts cannot be a hindrance, her arms rest involuntarily on her lap, and her head bends toward her shoulder in a maternal pose. She feels weak and it is imperative that her beauty strengthens her. She must not work, for her vices as well as her virtues are repelled by work. Misery, ancient and modern slavery may compel her to, though leaving at least the more difficult tasks, now and then, to man. But a woman's body gets spoiled without changing either the features or the posture because her maternal instincts absorb her whole life and all her physical and spiritual energies. A sacred malady seems within a lunar rhythm to prepare her for the sacrifice. A still more sacred seal guarantees her virginity as the first or only prize to man, who, possessing woman in his lifetime, cannot ask of her any other guarantee of paternity. It takes nine months for a woman to give birth, then eighteen to nurse her child, and in all this time even while generating her energies toward unforeseen miracles in strength and endurance, she is like a sick person. Everything upsets her, anything may harm her: every spiritual crisis may become a physical illness for her or for the more delicate constitution of her baby. . . . For twenty years a woman's life is caught in this cycle, almost always fecund due to man's work. . . . Considering the different roles of the sexes in those twenty years of fecundity, one involuntarily smiles at those who maintain that woman is man's social equal. In those twenty years of fecundity, of nursing, the male would not have employed but a few minutes between sleep and toil: a call of blood and of soul. As a breeder

---

[22] Ibid., p. 148 (my translation).

[23] *Surface and Symbol* (New York, 1967), p. 99 footnote.

he will not succeed the mother, at least not until the child is six or seven years old, when it is necessary to bring out his masculine sentiments. The son then becomes the father's companion: the mother, on the other hand, bends towards the latest child.[24]

Needless to say, Oriani's picture would not meet with the approval of the women's liberation movement. Joyce indicates, however, that Richard must not appear as a champion of woman's rights and that his language must approximate that of Schopenhauer against women and "he must show at times a deep contempt for the long-haired, short-legged sex." Richard, in fact, is fighting "for his own hand, for his own emotional dignity and liberation in which Bertha, no less and no more than Beatrice or any other woman is coinvolved."[25] The liberation brought to pass, then, is to be male rather than female.

Joyce generally approved of Oriani's views. Budgen reports that on occasions Joyce surprised him with bitter comments like these on women: "You have never heard of a woman who was the author of a complete philosophical system. No, and I don't think you ever will."[26] He also surprised Mary Colum by saying "I hate intellectual women."[27] And in a lecture delivered in Trieste, Joyce noted that "Like many other men of great genius, Blake was not attracted to cultured and refined women."[28] This view, borne out by his own love for Nora, he shared with Oriani who argued similarly that "great men never loved any but simple women."[29]

This general appraisal might, at first glance, seem idle and ordinary. But Joyce's view that the realm of philosophy remains inaccessible to the female mind is one that he clearly borrowed from Oriani. Although Joyce concedes the point that women have excelled in the field of scientific research, which the Italian historian does not, the gist of his remarks echoes those made in *La Rivolta ideale*:

> Women never leaves mediocrity behind. . . . Philosophy does not owe to her any system, science any discovery, art any monument: the genius is male. Woman learnt and repeated at times the work of men, but she did not anticipate or resume it; the highest achievements in feeling and thought remained inaccessible to woman, metaphysics and music are masculine arts. What woman can emulate Hegel or Beethoven? . . . Science and philosophy are scarcely a dilettantism for women: in art they only achieve sentiment and cleverness . . . women have failed and will

[24] *La Rivolta ideale* (Bologna, 1912), pp. 277-79 (my translation).

[25] *Exiles*, p. 154.

[26] *James Joyce and the Making of Ulysses* (London, 1972), p. 354.

[27] *James Joyce*, p. 543.

[28] *Critical Writings*, p. 217.

[29] *La Rivolta ideale*, p. 289.

continue to fail in all fields which demand the subordination of feeling to thought.[30]

Oriani, in fact, goes a step further than Joyce by claiming that women will never be judges (a view no longer true), because this involves greater moral speculation than either philosophy or music.[31] This context may also help to explain why the characterization of Molly Bloom does not stress the "intellectual."

The ideas expressed on "*Femminismo*" also permeate a crucial aspect of the paternity theme in *Ulysses*, where Bloom and Stephen share a "spiritual" affinity as father and son. Stephen, at one stage during the exposition of his theory on Hamlet, argues in the following manner:

> Boccaccio's Calandrino was the first and last man who felt himself with child. Fatherhood, in the sense of conscious begetting, is unknown to man. It is a mystical estate, an apostolic succession, from only begetter to only begotten. On that mystery and not on the madonna which the running Italian intellect flung to the mob of Europe the church is founded and founded irremovably because founded, like the world, macro- and microcosm, upon the void. Upon incertitude, upon unlikelihood. *Amor matris*, subjective and objective genitive, may be the only true thing in life. Paternity may be a legal fiction. Who is the father of any son that any son should love him or he any son?[32]

In his notes to *Exiles* Joyce speaks of Richard's "spiritual affection for his son" as opposed to the biologically-inspired motherly love of Bertha.[33] Oriani had also argued that fatherhood is a spiritual estate, unlike that of motherhood, entailing its own set of mysteries:

> Man holds dominion over the family, not because he is the strongest physically, but rather on account of his paternity which is a purely spiritual belief. Masculine sovereignty has no other foundation: nature did not accord man either the joy or the pain to actually feel himself a father. Instead he loves, or even not loving, weds a woman, she gives birth to a child, and he, out of faith in the woman, out of compassion for the child, or better still out of a deep-rooted sense of the human race, accepts being a father. But is he really? His knowledge, his consciousness does not go beyond this: the voluptuousness which seduced him is a curtain drawn in mystery; only the woman can say to the child the fond and haughty words: you are my own flesh and blood!
>
> Every quest for paternity beyond the limits indicated by the ancient law as regards abduction and rape is wrong and fruitless: the law can never know that which nature conceals as her own dark secret and, in

---

[30] Ibid., pp. 281-83 (my translation).

[31] Ibid., p. 283.

[32] *Ulysses*, p. 207.

[33] *Exiles*, p. 159.

allowing woman to proclaim a father in the lover, consecrates feminine deception in the most tyrannical of irresponsibilities.[34]

Hence it appears that "Paternity is a legal fiction," since only the ancient law was realistic in such matters, and Stephen's thesis corroborates Oriani's views.

Joyce's notes on the subject of jealousy indicate that he also made use of another work of the Italian historian. Joyce possessed a copy of Oriani's novel, *Gelosia* (1894),[35] which treated a lover's jealousy of his mistress's husband. Mario Zanetti, an apprentice in the office of the lawyer Filippo Buonconti, seduces his employer's wife, Annetta. Although this intrigue becomes the dominant passion of his youthful existence, for Annetta, who senses her husband's moral and social superiority, it remains a game of sensuality. In vain Mario is consumed with anger and jealousy at not being able to possess Annetta totally. Buonconti rises in fame and wealth, takes possession of the girl born out of wedlock, thinking he is the father. In the end he is elected a deputy and takes his wife, who welcomes the turn of events, with him to Rome. Mario, who has sacrificed for that transitory passion his career, is unable to make his way in the world and is forced to retire dejectedly in utter failure.

Joyce rejected the analysis of jealousy found in *Othello* and in Spinoza as being made from the "sensationalist" point of view, and therefore incomplete. He then divulged the treatment of the subject in his own play:

> In this play Richard's jealousy is carried one step nearer to its own heart. Separated from hatred and having its baffled lust converted into an erotic stimulus and moreover holding in its own power the hindrance, the difficulty which has excited it, it must reveal itself as the very immola-tion of the pleasure of possession on the altar of love. He is jealous, wills and knows his own dishonour and the dishonour of her, to be united with every phase of whose being is love's end, as to achieve that union in the region of the difficult, the void and the impossible is its necessary tendency.[36]

Joyce's comments are, to a great extent, inspired by Mario's medita-tions on the topic. At one point, he describes his passion in vague, metaphysical terms as the claim to dominate Annetta totally "from the vertex of her own individuality to the region where not even passion may reach."[37] On another occasion Mario affords a literary allusion:

---

[34] *La Rivolta ideale*, pp. 279-80 (my translation).

[35] *James Joyce*, p. 788.

[36] *Exiles*, pp. 148-49.

[37] *Gelosia: Vortice*, ed. Giulio Cattaneo (Firenze, 1971), p. 105 (my translation).

The great jealousies, in which the passion of an Othello or a Hamlet holds all the dominion that a soul can have in the world, so that it becomes impossible not to die from them at the first outburst arising from the catastrophe, remained incomprehensible to the vulgarity of their spirit. They ignored the supreme holocaust of hearts, that interpenetration of consciousness, which makes out of love a rock red-hot by the sun in the middle of the ocean, on which two ship-wrecked persons forget the tempest from which they emerge, and the death which awaits them.[38]

Eliminating the "hatred" found in Spinoza's definition, Joyce proceeds to conceive of jealousy as involving an "immolation" similar to what Mario calls a "holocaust of hearts." Moreover, Richard's desire to achieve a union with Bertha "in the region of the difficult" recalls Mario's willful determination in possessing Annetta beyond the limits of "passion."

Joyce, then, learned from Oriani's handling of the same theme and deftly utilized the usings of Mario, the lover, as a model for the jealousy of Richard, the husband. Admittedly, Richard's jealousy is not as active as Mario's, nor does it evince the ferocious drive which informs the lover's passion. But as Joyce himself pointed out to Frank Budgen, in stressing the affinity between *Exiles* and Fernand Crommelynck's *Le Cocu Magnifique*, the people in his play "act with a certain reserve."[39] *Gelosia*, like *Exiles*, does not incite any tumultuous scene such as the one in *Le Cocu Magnifique* where Bruno offers his wife to all the men of the neighbourhood so as to avoid being gnawed at by jealousy about her unknown lovers. The "crisis" brought to the fore in Praga's play and in *Exiles* is here notably absent. Oriani concentrates, on the other hand, on the contrast between sensuality and the spiritual values of talent, character, paternity and political prestige. Buonconti's thoughts are not delved into, and the unity of the family is preserved by his "spiritual" virtues. Although Richard's feelings are disclosed in the final scene, the passive nature of Buonconti is akin to Richard's wish not "to know, or to believe" the truth about his wife's conduct.

The influence of Italian drama and thought on Joyce proves crucial, then, to the understanding of his only play. At times it may also illuminate some aspects of *Ulysses*. Joyce profited by what he termed the "esthetic shift" in modern literature and which he first detected in the dramas of Giacosa and Praga. He extended the range of possibilities of this "change" in accordance with his own refined sensibility. But *La Moglie ideale, La Crisi*, and *Tristi amori* enabled Joyce better to focus on his task. In addition, Oriani's *La Rivolta ideale* developed a psychology of "*Femminismo*" which Joyce generally accepted. At the

---

[38] Ibid., p. 128 (my translation).

[39] *James Joyce and the Making of Ulysses*, p. 350.

same time, what he considered to be the inadequacy of the sensationalist standpoint on jealousy led him to supplement his reading of Shakespeare and Spinoza with Oriani's *Gelosia*. All these works provided the necessary ingredients for Joyce's art to enable him to become the third minister, after Hauptmann, in the tradition of his Norwegian master.

JOYCE, EROS, AND "ARRAY! SURRECTION"

Donald F. Theall

As the intricacies of interpretation which Joyce himself invited multiply, there is a tendency to lose sight of just how very basic the ingredients of his major works really are. If we think of *Finnegans Wake*, for example, it is a book first about sex, family and dreams, and then religion, history and politics. To have said this is not to have said anything especially remarkable except that we seldom remind ourselves that the complex symbolism which goes to form the fabric of the *Wake* is woven out of such very basic ingredients. The problem arises because we get lost in language (just as Joyce seems to have intended to have his readers do) and when we escape from language we become enmeshed in symbolism. Certainly no one will deny the centrality of language and symbol to *Finnegans Wake*, but it might be worth exploring whether they operate in terms of some very specific development of the other basic ingredients. So, in the terms of the *Wake*, let's for a few moments be basic.

The book is about an Irish working-class male, who is an innkeeper (H.C.E.—Humphrey Chimpden Earwicker) who dreams a dream while he is in bed at night with his wife, Anna. As an Irish male, or for that matter any male, he is interested in his sexual life, his body, his women, his family and the way these shape the goals of his life. He is also interested in eating and drinking and generally enjoying a life of the senses. His sexual success is apparent in spite of the dream complexities, in that he has two sons and a daughter and he still wakes during the night with enough sexual excitement to want to have relations with his wife. The action of the book, therefore, refines on that of *Ulysses*; for instead of taking place on one day in one town about the life of one alienated man, the *Wake* takes place in one bed in one night in the dreams of one man. Or, if we want immediately to get more complex, is it really one man or one man and his family? Or, as we may see by the end, is such a question significant if we understand the keys to Joyce's dreamland?

In any case, like Joyce's other books, the *Wake* is a book about the family. *The Portrait of the Artist* is partly about the family and *Ulysses* is constantly about the family. To an even greater extent the *Wake*, too, is about family. But just as *Ulysses* is a book which places the family against (or, perhaps much better, within) a social context, a city, so too the *Wake* uses a social context which is the city and its environs, and also the psychological consciousness generated by that social environ. Sex, family and city, these are the stuff that novels, psychology and sociology are made of. The family, in fact, is, because of its nuclear nature in the society within which Joyce is writing, the source of both our super-biological-psychological development as well as the first and most immediate source of our social development. In the family, we first learn language, and mores and inhibitions and the patterns from which the world constructs its social reality. If the hero-dreamer of Joyce's *Wake* is what Joyce describes him as being, "that patternmind, that paradigmatic ear, receptoretentive as his of Dionysus . . .",[1] the patterns, the paradigm and the memory related to the Dionysiac life force rise out of the very heart of human existence, and are the very means of human understanding through sensuous encounter with reality.

Consequently, if we begin discussing the *Wake* in terms of language pattern and concepts of form, we are not necessarily establishing Joyce as a writer who was indulging in some mode of philosophical idealism, but tracing the way the dream of his dreamer re-discovers the world of matter, "the very stuff that dreams are made of," through the transformation of the words and forms which are intrinsic parts of the everyday reality in which the process of the dreamer's life (which is the life of his dream) takes place. What Joyce tries to achieve is most basically exemplified by the way in which he adapts the technique of Lewis Carroll's Jabberwocky from *Alice in Wonderland*. The way in which he develops a new language along lines similar to those of Carroll (which Kenner and others have illustrated) is central to the way in which he adapts the materials of his everyday world to his artistic form:

> Twas brillig, and the slithy toves
> Did gyre and gimble in the wabe:
> All mimsy were the borogoves
> And the mome raths outgrabe.

---

[1] *Finnegans Wake* (New York, 1939), p. 70.

From this, as we all know, evolves Joyce's "punny" language in which, by using the device of playing with the patterns of syntax and changing chiefly the nouns, verbs and adjectives, he can create his own dance of words. Although his technique of pun differs from Jabberwocky, in that the elements combined in his portmanteau words are concrete, recognizable, and contain a high degree of rational control, he combines word forms themselves with the paradigmatic nature of language itself to create the effect which is meant to reassess the individual's consciousness of the everyday things and phenomena to which the words refer. In a sentence such as "that grene ray of earong it waves us to yonder as the red, blue and yellow flogs time on the domisole, with a blewy blow and a windigo" (*Wake*, p. 267), the grammatical processes and forms are characteristically English (or English with an Irish-like rhythm) but the process takes on a new consciousness. So, too, in a passage such as:

> And the message she braught belaw from the missus she bragged abouve that had her agony stays outsize her sari chemise, blancking her shifts for to keep up the fascion since the king of all dronnings kissed her bees-wixed hand, fang (pierce me, hunky, I'm full of meunders!), her fize like a tubtail of mondayne clothes, fed to the chaps with working medicals and her birthright pang that would split an atam like the forty pins in her hood, was to fader huncher a howdydowdy, to mountainy mots in her amnest plein language, from his fain a wan, his hot and tot lass, to pierce his ropeloop ear, how, Podushka be prayhasd, now the sowns of his loins were awinking and waking and his dorter of the hush lillabilla lullaby (lead us not into reformication with the poors in your thingdom of gory, O moan!), once after males, nonce at a time, with them Murphy's puffs she dursted with gnockmeggs and the bramborry cake for dour dorty dompling obayre Mattom Beetom and epsut the pfot and if he was whishtful to licture her caudal with chesty chach from his dauberg den and noviny news from Naul or toplots talks from morrienbaths or a parrotsprate's cure for ensevelised lethurgies, spick's my spoon and the veriblest spoon, 'twas her hour for the chamber's ensallycopodium with love to melost Panny Kostello from X.Y. Zid for to folly billybobbis gibits porzy punzy and she was a wanton for De Marera to take her genial glow to bed (*Wake*, p. 333).

So *Finnegans Wake*, as he describes it, becomes a vision that has a rhythmic movement which is a mime, a game, a play, and particularly a dance,

> ... when a man that means a mountain barring his distance wades a lymph that plays the lazy winning she likes yet that pride that bogs the party begs the glory of a wake while the scheme is like your rumba round me garden ... (*Wake*, p. 309).

In this combination of mime, game, play and dance, Joyce can transform the apparently banal everyday language, the clichés of his world, into a language which reveals the roots of reality involved in those clichés, so that when, for example, he describes Alice of *Alice in*

Wonderland, he can speak of her as being "yung and easily freudened" (*Wake*, p. 115).

This is by no means a mere device, for it is deeply involved with the conceptions of language as a code and calculus as well as providing a means by which a form can be given to the vast content which involves the everyday life of the average man, in this case, the average Irishman. To underline this formal aspect of his work, Joyce played on the analogy between *Finnegans Wake* and the mediaeval illuminated gospel, the *Book of Kells*. A section of *Finnegans Wake* concerned with the writing of a letter about the guilt of the central dream event, the motif of the *Book of Kells*, is associated with motifs surrounding various manuscripts. Hieroglyphics as a sensuous form of picture writing are a part of this manuscript theme as well, for the letter is composed of runes or Morse Code or alphabetic letters or oghamic script or hieroglyphics, depending on how we are looking at it. This famous letter in *Finnegans Wake*, which may be just a litter (in fact, it is found in a litter)—a mound of living museum ("Museyroom") is a "proteiform graph," a "polyhedron of scripture" (*Wake*, p. 107). A proteiform graph exhibits a movement through transformation of formal structures. This is surprisingly close to the way that Foçillon, in his *Life of Forms*, discusses the nature of form in mediaeval illuminations such as the *Book of Kells*: "Forms are always tending toward the realization; they do, in fact, realize themselves and create a world which acts and reacts."[2] The form of *Finnegans Wake*, which moves through the night of dreaming towards the light of day, which will be its completion, is achieving, as Joyce puts it, a "trancefixureashone." This ties up with Joyce's view of the sacramental nature of arts as transsubstantiating the bread of everyday life through the forms of art.

Now while it may seem that this is moving rather far from the simple concerns of sexual life, eating, drinking, and the family mentioned earlier, it is interesting to realize that this transformation or metamorphosis of forms, as Foçillon observes, rises out of nature and the human person:

> ... the models of nature may themselves be regarded as the stem and support of metamorphoses. The body of man and the body of woman can remain virtually constant, but the ciphers capable of being written with the bodies of men and women are inexhaustibly various and this variety works upon, activates and inspires all the works of art, from the most elaborate to the most simple.

Joyce's book, therefore, creates a verbal equivalent to the strategy of the *Book of Kells*. One of the two sons in *Finnegans Wake*, Shem the Penman, who is presumably writing the *Wake*, is described as having a

---

[2] Henri Foçillon, *Life of Forms in Art*, tr. Hogan and Kubler (New York, 2nd. ed. 1948), p. 58.

"lovom of labaryntos," which obviously refers to the intricate weaving and interlacing of verbal language as the dream unfolds. Interestingly enough, the *Book of Kells*, according to Foçillon's analysis, shares this labyrinthine character:

> ... what I may call the "system of the series"—a system composed of discontinuous elements sharply outlined, strongly rhythmical, and defining a stable and symmetrical space that protects them against unforeseen accidents of metamorphosis—eventually becomes "the system of the labyrinth," which by means of mobile synthesis stretches itself out into a reel of glittering movement and colour.[3]

The Celtic Gospels provide an ideal example of this "system of the labyrinth," for the ornament "which is constantly overlayering itself and melting into itself, even though it is fixed fast within compartments of letters and panels, appears to be shifting among different panels at different speeds."[4] The "counterpoint" that is described here—"constant overlayering and melting in"—is paralleled by the "counterpoint words" that take part in the intrasensory transformations in Joyce's work of art. The "labyrinth" also is an important Joycean symbol from the days of Stephen Dedalus, with the obvious labyrinthine connotations, to the labyrinth or troia-type dance motif in the *Wake*. The dance motif reminds us, as Curt Sachs has observed, that:

> The essence of the labyrinth is movement. The building has no meaning by itself. It only takes on meaning when people walk through it. . . . The movement can exist without the building and actually does in places where nothing is known about a labyrinth.[5]

In the children's play scene, Glugg performs a serpentine round, and is in certain perspectives seen as the devil figure, so Glugg, a Shem type, follows the same patterns of movement. Foçillon comments on the movement involved in looking at the *Book of Kells*:

> As the eye moves across the labyrinth in confusion misled by a linear caprice that is perpetually sliding away to a secret objective of its own, a new dimension suddenly emerges which is a dimension neither of motion nor of depth, but which still gives us the illusion of being so.[6]

At one level, this phenomenon can be explained in terms of a theory of style based on expectancy and surprise emanating from cybernetic structuralists' descriptions of style. The forms of the *Book of Kells*, like

---

[3] Ibid., p. 8.

[4] Ibid., p. 20.

[5] Curt Sachs, *World History of the Dance*, tr. Bessie Schönberg (New York, 1903), p. 152.

[6] Foçillon, *Life of Forms in Art*, p. 20.

the *Wake*, can be seen as taking on meaning through the operation of *gestalt*, the laws of closure and good continuation. The message of the words in the *Wake* go through the "post office" of the human mind to be reassembled in the acts of perception in intellection. The senses and mind of the reader-listener recreate the work by retracing the labyrinth of creation.

Joyce's theory in the *Wake* is closely related to the conception of form that has evolved into theories of such writers as Herbert Marcuse in *Eros and Civilization*, which should hardly be surprising if we remember that Joyce's contemporaries were writers such as Wilhelm Reich, whose *Sexpol* writings appeared in the late twenties. The movements are based and rooted in the very life form of human individuals in their most natural or mundane interactions. These interactions are paralleled to natural processes in nature itself and to processes existing in that second nature, civilization, which man has created from nature. Consequently, Joyce can move from the sex play of H.C.E. and his wife in their bed to the shape of the Christian liturgical year within the same formal structure. This may seem initially to be a kind of typical idealism in which everything is reduced to everything else by the application of archetypal patterns, but, in fact, Joyce employs it in such a way as to make it specific and concrete to the society of his time and place in Ireland and Europe. Perhaps the most central formal pattern in the *Wake* that might be examined from this point of view is that of its liturgical theological orientation.

If one were to attempt to identify the night of *Finnegans Wake*, there are a number of references within the work which would be of assistance. The word "wake" is associated with the funeral rites before the burial, because in another sense, it means vigil, or watch. At one level, the *Wake* in Earwicker's dream is the celebration of the funeral rites for an Irish bricklayer named Tim Finnegan about whom the famous ballad of "Finnegan's Wake" was written. But at another level, it is the vigil of the feast of the Ressurection, Easter, of which Tim Finnegan's famous resurrection after whiskey pours on his casket is a kind of comic symbol. In other words, the night of *Finnegans Wake* is the vigil of Easter and the tripartite structure of the work relates to the triduum, that is, the three days preceeding Easter: Holy Thursday, Good Friday, and Holy Saturday. There are references in the work to "ténèbres," "tenebrous" and "tonebrass" referring to the Tenebrae services of Holy Week and the end of the work refers to the "triduum before Our Larry's own day" (*Wake*, p. 517). In addition to such specific references, the themes of Baptism, of water, of fire, and of *felix culpa* (the fortunate fall) all of which are interwoven elements of the liturgy and of the Easter vigil, run as refrains throughout the work.

By this step, we certainly seem to have moved far from innkeepers or bricklayers, Irish pubs or brawling brats, or for that matter, whatever activities may occur during the night in Irish bedrooms, but it is interesting to realize that one of Joyce's other major preoccupations in the *Wake*, Sigmund Freud, had an intense fascination with the psychological import and social function of the Holy Week period, and naturally of its relationship to the Jewish Passover. Consequently, it is possibly useful to keep in mind, as we explore *Finnegans Wake*, the suggestion that Joyce's brother, Stanislaus, made about the "Circe" section of *Ulysses* (Bella Cohen's Dublin whorehouse): "The relation or at least the analogy between the imagination and the intellect and the sexual instinct in the body . . . is worked out with a fantastic horror. . . . It is undoubtedly catholic in temperament. . . ."[7] While not sharing Stanislaus's puritanical evaluation of the paralleling of the sexual instinct and the operation of the imagination or its close relationship with the rich liturgical traditions of Catholicism, Joyce appears to have used precisely this pattern in working out the vision of *Finnegans Wake* and in relating the everyday life of a working-class family to a secular sacramental vision of nature.

There is a very close parallel between the resolution in *Finnegans Wake* on a religious level and its resolution on a sexual level. The dreamer, that is, the innkeeper-husband, H.C.E., Humphrey Chimpden Earwicker (sometimes better known as Here Comes Everybody), and his wife, Anna Livia Plurabelle (named as we know after the River Liffey), mate in bed towards the end of the dream in a scene which is treated as an imaginary film projection against a lighted window shade seen by an imaginary voyeur in the street. Their coming together, whether in the dream or in a brief moment of waking, precedes the breaking of dawn, which is presented in the dream as the rising of the sunlight through a triptych stained-glass window in the chapel at Chapelizod. Ironically, however, the acronyms H.C.E. and A.L.P., when joined together, as they are in bed, spell chapel, so that the bursting through the chapel is parallel to the light bursting from the union of the dream couple. This also parallels one of the other crucial closing scenes of the work (in fact the first that Joyce composed) which is a philosophical debate between St. Patrick and the archdruid, Balkelly, about the nature of light. This debate is of interest in a variety of ways in that Patrick presumably landed in Ireland and appeared before the druids on the Easter vigil, lighting the first paschal fire that Ireland had known. The figure of the druid is carefully interwoven with that of the Anglo-Irish philosopher, Berkeley, who expounded an early version of an idealistic theory of vision. In the dream, the figure of Berkeley and St. Patrick form a dialectical pair of opposites representing appearance and reality, a mundane faith and prophetic vision,

---

[7] Richard Ellman, *James Joyce* (New York, 1959), p. 562.

the dull black and white world of everyday activity and the multi-chromatic world of the aesthetic vision. But most important, they summarize what is one central movement in *Finnegans Wake*, that of the pattern of dialectical oppositions. I have often wondered if Joyce might not have liked to have used Hegel's phrase from the introduction to the *Phenomenology of Mind* as an epigraph for *Finnegans Wake*; that is, "truth is a bacchanalian revel where not a soul is sober"[8] which neatly parallels one of H.C.E.'s constant by-words as an innkeeper "*in vino veritas.*" Joyce's use of dialectical movement in the *Wake* involves references ranging from Plato and Nicolas Cusa, through Giordano Bruno, to Hegel and Marx. But ultimately the intention of his dialectical movement is deeply based in material reality and in the same realization that Marx developed from Feuerbach, that religion is rooted in the sensuous everyday reality of the life of man.

In fact, in developing his patterns, Joyce weaves the insights of Hegel and his dialectic into the cyclical patterns of the Neapolitan philosopher, Giambatista Vico, whose *Nuova Scienza* propounded the theory that civil societies were the creation of man's imagination and not divinely ordained. It was not unusual during the period during which *Finnegans Wake* was being written, to find European Marxist philosophers such as Gyorgy Lukács and Gramisci exegeting the works of Marx using Hegel and Vico.

So Joyce is very characteristic of his time in Europe, but also of his time in Ireland in creating a structure which is an interplay between a dialectic movement and coupling that ranges from the union of male and female in the marriage bed to the debate between idealist and realist with a cyclical theory of history in which man's imagination generates in an ever-spiralling evolution a series of evolving societies.

But since at the beginning I had suggested that we should keep our inquiry somewhat down to earth, it is important to realize that all of this is embedded in most Rabelaisian forms of humour:

> The Gracehoper was always jigging ajog, hoppy on akkant of his joyicity, (he had a partner pair of findlestilts to supplant him), or, if not, he was always making ungraceful overtures to Floh and Luse and Bienie and Vespatilla to play pupa-pupa and pulicy-pulicy and langtennas and pushpygyddyum and to commence insects with him, there mouthparts to his orefice and his gambills to there airy processes, even if only in chaste, ameng the everlistings, behond a waspering pot (*Wake*, p. 414).

But such wit also involves the intricate linguistic technique mentioned earlier, for a phrase such as "hoppy on akkant of his joyicity" involves the stock phrase "happy on account" and the overlayerings of "hop" with the stem "hap-," of "cant" and "Kant" with "count." It works for

---

[8] Tr. J. B. Baillie (London, 1931), p. 105.

the obvious reason that "_____ on account" is an expected collocation and because the overlayerings create close phonetic associations.
The word "joyicity," of course, is formed on analogy with "felicity,"
"specificity," and the like. Apart from the rhythmical effect, the new-
ness of the word calls attention to the state—joy—and intensifies it as
well as calling attention to the components in the new form "joy-" and
"-city." The creation of the compound "Grace + hope + er" over-
layered with "grasshopper" is obvious. The graduated wordplay of the
sex games "pupa-pupa," "pulicy-pulicy," "langtennae" and "pushpygyddyum" lead from actual words to the extreme Carroll type of
Jabberwocky. If *pulicy* contains the overlayering with *policy*, and
langtenna, the fusing of long and the stem of *languid* with *antenna*,
"pushpygyddyum" is a Jabberwock portmanteau working by complex
phonoaesthetic suggestivity.

As the Rabelaisian elements such as gourmandizing sex play,
polymorphous perversions and general licentiousness run through the
Wake they make of it an even richer handbook of bawdry than Gargan-
tua and Pantagruel. The father and mother, sisters and brothers combined and recombined in a wide variety of kaleidoscopic encounters
suggest everything from the creative sexuality of marriage through
homosexuality to the perversities of de Sade. The major point, as in
Rabelais, however, is to mesh the intellectual and spiritual world into
the material world of the lower and more natural activities of the
average human person so that the banal linguistic collocation "young
and easily frightened" becomes "yung and easily freudened" which
parallels the way in which the everyday sensuosities of human individuals come to be at one with the content of the rituals of the triduum.

As Mikhail Bakhtin demonstrated in his study of Rabelais' use of
carnivalesque and market place materials in the development of his
Renaissance humanistic vision of the new world of the 16th century,
Joyce has similarly applied the humor and wit and everyday Irish life to
a transformation of the social relations involved in Church and State to
expound a new vision of socialist humanism. Immediately following
the climactic debate between the archdruid and St. Patrick concerning
the nature of light, there appears a passage which summarizes the form
and movement of the entire work:

> What has gone? How it ends?
> Begin to forget it. It will remember itself from every sides, with all
> gestures, in each our word. Today's truth, tomorrow's trend.
> Forget, remember!
> Have we cherished expectations? Are we for liberty of perusiveness?
> Whyafter what forewhere? A plainplanned liffeyism assemblements
> Eblania's conglomerate horde. By dim delty Deva.
> Forget!
> Our wholemole millwheeling vicociclometer, a tetradomational
> gazebocroticon (the "Mamma Lujah" known to every schoolboy scandal-

ler, be he Matty, Marky, Lukey or John-a-Donk), autokinatonetically preprovided with a clappercoupling smeltingworks exprogressive process, (for the farmer, his son and their homely codes, known as eggburst, eggblend, eggburial and hatch-as-hatch can) receives through a portal vein the dialytically separated elements of precedent decomposition for the verypetpurpose of subsequent recombination so that the heroticisms, catastrophes and eccentricities transmitted by the ancient legacy of the past, type by tope, letter from litter, word at ward, with sendence of sundance, since the days of Plooney and Columcellas when Giacinta, Pervenche and Margaret swayed over the all-too-ghoulish and illyrical and innumantic in our mutter nation, all, anastomosically assimilated and preteridentified paraidiotically, in fact, the sameold gamebold adomic structure of our Finnius the old One, as highly charged with electrons as hophazards can effective it, may be there for you, Cockalooralooraloomenos, when cup, platter and pot come piping hot, as sure as herself pits hen to paper and there's scribings scrawled on eggs.
        Of cause, so! And in effect, as? (*Wake*, p. 614).

This passage on forgetting and remembering reminds the reader that memory occurs "from every sides, with all gestures, in each our word." The pattern will communicate—the pattern of the play of H.C.E. and A.L.P.— for as the text queries: "have we cherished expectations? Are we for liberty of perusiveness?" and therefore suggests that the freedom to peruse in such a way as to alter the "cherished expectations" allows the reader to grasp the "plainplanned liffeyism" which rise out of the way that the "conglomerate hordes" form an "assemblement." The "assemblement" concerns Man, as H.C.E. or Finn and therefore deals with that movement by which "the heroticisms, catastrophes and eccentricities" are "anastomosically assimilated and preteridentified paraidiotically" revealing the "sameold gamebold adomic structure of our Finnius the old One, as highly charged with electrons as hophazards can effective it." This process is "paraidiotic" to the degree that the dialectical process of learned ignorance of Cusa is necessary to achieve the anastomosaic assimilation.

The passage continues to present a process by which the author communicates with the world through his daily contact and weaves from the "dialytically separated elements" his "subsequent recombination." The "wholemole millwheeling vicociclometer, a tetradomational gazebocroticon" is literally a "dome" or home of the person. The "Vicociclometer" plays on the rhythm of the Viconian cycles which themselves are four sided—"tetradomational." The "vicociclometer" squares the circle as Joyce said he was doing in the work, for it creates a four-part structure, which through its repetitions is circular. But the tetral or four-sided structure is that of theme-time-habit-reburn, which if it were set forth as imagination-memory-habit-return to intellection—"to flame anew" would be an un-Viconian Viconian inspired account of learning and intelligence as processes. The word, "gazebocroticon," refers to the concepts of sight (gaze), writing (or making a book), custom and memory (rote), and image or metaphor or representation (icon). This emphasis on image or icon, though, is paralleled by an insistence on intersensory function, for the "gazeboc-roticon" is "autokinatonetically preprovided with a clappercoupling smeltingworks exprogressive process." This refers to the momentary arresting of motion in the operation of the intellect which performs its "clappercoupling smeltingwork" by drawing the "dialytically separated elements" into "subsequent recombinations." In this way creative activity binds time and space into formal structures for it permits the "heroticisms, catastrophes and eccentricities transmitted by the ancient legacy of the past" to be preserved in new forms. Light, speech, writing, artifacts, the dance, and systems of classification are all related to this process of transmission in the phrase, "type by tope, letter from litter, word at ward, sendence of sundance."

The results of intellection through symbolic processes are types, topes, letters, words, and "sendence." The "tips" and "taps" of the *Wake* are the "types" and the "topes," the topics or places by which we classify reality. The "letters" provide a form for preserving the "litter," the mound of history; the "word" acts as a guardian of the past, creating a pattern of the future, the "sundance" of the code being the mode of preservation related back to the bodily motif of dance and the role of light in the *Wake*.

The nature of light in modern physics is closely bound up with the whole problem of atomic structure. If the whole of the world of the *Wake* is to be "anastomosically assimilated" to the "sameold gamebold adomic structure" this can occur only through a coming to terms with the nature of light and the way that it is perceived by man. As dawn approaches, the use of light as a symbol and actual discussions of the quality of light play an increasingly important role in the *Wake*. The last section unfolds as the light of day enters the chapel at Chapelizod through the stained-glass windows and especially through the stained-glass window containing a triptych, one of the elements of which is St. Patrick debating with an archdruid. The chapel is the symbol of the "coupling" of H.C.E. + A.L.P. The debate between Patrick and the archdruid provides only a limited perspective, because it forms only a part of the total illumination that comes with dawn. The triptych not only has the usual religious symbolism, but also refers to the Young-Helmholtz theory of the perception of light through three optic nerves.

It is because of this relation to the Young-Helmholtz theory of colour that the long description of the High King is presented in terms of a scale of greens and why, as day comes, the movement of the passage is from the violet tones of St. Kevin to the greens associated with the High King to the full colour scale of seven hues involved in the debate about light between Patrick and the archdruid. Out of the three basic colours comes the seven-hued rainbow, which runs through the *Wake*, as a sign. When Patrick invokes the presence of white light in nature against the archdruid's description of many-coloured lights of nature, the actual composition of white lite as a mixture of other lights counterposes the problem of the complexity of perception against Patrick's simple-minded idealism while still justifying Patrick's glorying in the day whose many-coloured lights create the differentiations necessary to make visual communication possible.

Light, as a physical phenomenon closely associated by modern physics with atomic structure, is an important contemporary symbol as well as a symbol from the "ancient legacy of the past," the sundance. The CHAPEL will be illuminated because light acts like a result of wave-like phenomena (A.L.P.) and pulse-like phenomena (H.C.E.) just as the intellect, too, is illuminated because of wave-like phenomena and pulse-like phenomena. Poetically, Joyce is doing what poets have always done, making the world human and inhabitable, for of H.C.E., Anna says: "But there's a great poet in you too" (*Wake*, p. 619).

The engine that Joyce claimed he was making when he described himself as one of the greatest engineers was the vision achieved through his "tetradomotional gazebocroticon." In making this engine (which includes a vision of H.C.E. as transmitter and receiver, transmitted and received), Joyce employs a series of "icons" for his "book" which unites modern physics, modern psychology and modern biology to the "heroticisms, catastrophes and eccentricities transmitted by the ancient legacy of the past" as a means of bringing the world of H.C.E. within creative grasp and at the same time dealing with the actual modes of the creative process. When H.C.E. as Yawn-Whitman says of himself: "I should tell you that honestly, on my honour of a Near-wicked, I always think in a wordworth's of that primed favourite continental poet, Daunty, Gouty and Shopkeeper, A.G., whom the generality admoyers in this that is and that this is to come" (*Wake*, p. 539), one wonders if Joyce remembered the words of Wordsworth's *Preface* when he suggests:

> If the labours of men of science should ever create any material revolution, direct or indirect in our condition, and in the impression that we habitually receive, the Poet will sleep then no more than at present; he will be ready to follow the steps of the Man of Science, not only in those general indirect effects, but he will be at his side, carrying sensation into the midst of the objects of science itself. The remotest discoveries of the Chemist, the Botanist, or Mineralogist will be as proper objects of the Poet's art as any upon which it can be employed. . . .

So the statement that Ivan makes to Izzy—a statement he does not really understand—"sifted science will do your arts good" (*Wake*, p. 440), has an application to the way art can transform the discoveries of science into the materials of human vision. In his works Joyce performs the task that Wordsworth sets down. The modern age has seen the "abnihilisation of the etym" because the same scientific vision that results in a knowledge of atomic structure extensive enough to smash the atom has also provided new descriptions of the structure of language and of symbolic systems, which have broken down the sacred units of the past, but which ultimately reassembles or "reamalgamerges" them into the "sameold, gamebold adomic structure" as long as we realize that the end of the "exprogressive process" is to reconstruct the "seim anew" (*Wake*, p. 215).

This "exprogressive process" which is a "clapper coupling," can describe the act of human generation, the creation of art, or the establishment of civilization. As "dialytically separated elements" combined again and again, the hero of H.C.E.'s dream is at one level Tim Finnegan, a whiskey-loving bricklayer, and at another level, the mythical Finn, the giant who will rise again. In this coalition is joined the notion of the mason as builder and the notion of the builder as civilizer. For this reason, *Finnegans Wake* abounds with the kinds of references to technology that Marshall McLuhan is so fond of borrowing from Joyce. H.C.E., for example, is described as "their tolvtubular high fidelity daildialler, as modern as tomorrow afternoon and in appearance up to the minute . . . equipped with supershielded umbrella antennas for distance getting and connected by the magnetic links of a Bellini-Tosti coupling system with a vitaltone speaker, capable of capturing skybuddies, harbour craft emittences, key clickings, vaticum cleaners, due to woman formed mobile or man made static . . . eclectrically filtered for allirish earths and ohmes" (*Wake*, p. 309). H.C.E. is seen as a human body projecting itself through civilization into a humanist technology so that he becomes the mythical Finn as civilizer of a world. Again and again in the *Wake*, there are references to contemporary communicative technology ranging from references to its cinematic nature, such as "roll away the reel world" to the first bar room television fight scene in literature, written before commercial television had become a reality, a scene where the patrons of H.C.E.'s pub watch a fight between Buckley and the Russian General. The coupling of H.C.E. and A.L.P., as mentioned earlier, is framed by the light coming through a window:

> A time.
> Act: dumbshow.
> Closeup. Leads.
> Man with nightcap, in bed, fore. Woman, with curlpins, hind. Discovered. Side point of view. First position of harmony. Say! Eh? Ha! Check action. Matt. Male partly masking female. Man looking round, beastly expression, fishy eyes, paralleliped homoplatts, ghazometron pondus, exhibits rage. Business. Ruddy blond, Armenian bole, black patch, beer wig, gross build, episcopalian, any age. Woman, sitting, looks at ceiling, haggish expression, peaky nose, trekant mouth, fithery wight, exhibits

fear. Welshrabbit teint, Nubian shine, nasal fossette, turfy tuft, under-
sized, free kirk, no age. Closeup. Play!
    Callboy. Cry off. Tabler. Her move.
    Footage.
    By the sinewy forequarters of the mare Pocahontas and by the white
shoulders of Finnuala you should have seen how that smart sallowlass
just hopped a nanny's gambit out of bunk like old mother Mesopotomac
and in eight sixtyfour she was off, door, knightlamp with her, billy's
largelimbs prodgering after to queen's lead. Promiscuous Omebound to
Fiammelle la Diva. Huff! His move. Blackout.
    Circus. Corridor.
    Shifting scene. Wall flats: sink and fly. Spotlight working wall cloths.
Spill playing rake and bridges. Room to sink: stairs to sink behind room.
Two pieces. Haying after queue. Replay (*Wake*, p. 559).

So that in this one sense, Joyce anticipates the development of the
contemporary erotic cinema of the bedroom.

But how does all of this weave together into a closing vision?
Joyce's own introduction to the closing Easter morning section of
Finnegans Wake goes:

> Sandhyas! Sandhyas! Sandhyas!
>   Calling all downs. Calling all downs to dayne. Array! Surrection.
> Eireweeker to the wohld bludyn world. O rally, O rally, O rally! Phlenxty,
> O rally! (*Wake*, p. 593).

In this phrase, we blend the conceptions of peace and holiness in
"Sandhyas" with the overlayering of erection, both as sex and as building, insurrection as revolution, and resurrection as human renewal.
The phrase intriguingly enough cannot help but echo in Irish ears the
futile radio messages that the rebels tried to send to the world upon the
seizure of the post office, Easter Monday, 1916, but it blends with the
accompanying themes of a liberated human sexuality freed from the
guilt of Freudianism, a liberated humanity freed from the oppressions
of colonial states, and a transformed sense of spiritual salvation which
is found in the sensuous base of resurrection in the material of light, of
life-givingness, and of the marriage of man and wife as analogous to
marriage of Christ and the Church. In such a vision, the objects of
everyday life once again become the possession of man who should be
their maker and controller.

The vision of the *Wake* that I have argued for is one that sees Joyce
as a socialist-humanist, using the place and scenes of Ireland as a way of
dealing with the problems of the international European world to
which he exiled himself. It is interesting, therefore, that his sense of
comedy, as a humanistic and humanizing device, closely parallels the
thought of such Eastern socialist-humanists as Leszek Kolakowski:

> Priests and jesters cannot be reconciled unless one of them is trans-
> formed into the other, as sometimes happens. In every era the jester's
> philosophy exposes as doubtful what seems most unshakable, reveals the

contradictions in what appears obvious and incontrovertible, derides common sense and reads sense into the absurd. In short, it undertakes the daily chores of the jester's profession together with the inevitable risk of appearing ridiculous. Depending on time and place, the jester's thinking can range through all the extremes of thought, for what is sacred today was paradoxical yesterday, and absolutes on the equator are often blasphemies at the poles. The jester's constant effort is to consider all the possible reasons for contradictory ideas. It is thus dialectical by nature —simply the attempt to change what is because it is. He is motivated not by a desire to be perverse but by distrust of a stabilized system. In a world where apparently everything has already happened, he represents an active imagination defined by the opposition it must overcome.[9]

In the light of such a view, Joyce, as a jester, opposing the priests becomes himself a figure of a new material-spiritual order, for just as Erasmus and Rabelais used the modality of the jester in the Renaissance to create the new world of Renaissance humanism, so Joyce, using paradox and dialectics in the comic mode, creates the "seim anew" in the vision of a contemporary socialist-humanist.

---

[9] *Toward a Marxist Humanism*, tr. Jane Peel (New York, 1968), pp. 36-37.

IMAGINATION'S ABODE:
THE SYMBOLISM OF HOUSE SETTINGS IN
MODERN IRISH STAGE PLAYS

Andrew Parkin

J. M. Synge made a crucial point for drama criticism when he stated the reason why a farce or a comedy, as well as a tragedy, can be worth the time and attention of the serious playgoer:

> The drama is made serious—in the French sense of the word—not by the degree in which it is taken up with problems that are serious in themselves, but by the degree in which it gives the nourishment, not very easy to define, on which our imaginations live.[1]

Clearly, "nourishment" for the imagination is not the provision of any one genre. It is my belief that the imagination of the playgoer feeds not so much on particular themes or opinions in themselves, but on characters, situations and settings which are potent enough to embody our national, social, political or personal concerns in such a way as to reveal that they are international, indeed profoundly human. These characters, situations and settings may be particular and specific, but they are also symbolic, in a broad sense, of human experience itself. The human imagination is a cannibal; it takes its nourishment from its own tribe. Plays by Synge, certain plays by Ibsen, or Brecht for that matter, "can no more go out of fashion" for their opinions "than the blackberries on the hedges"[2] because they have presented stage symbols of abiding potency on which our imaginations may dine: we savor the bitter taste

---

[1] J. M. Synge, Preface to *The Tinker's Wedding*, in T. R. Henn, ed., *The Plays and Poems of J. M. Synge* (London, 1968), p. 108.

[2] Ibid.

of Hedda, the great heart of Mother Courage, the warm sagacity of
Galileo.

In the space I have here, I shall content myself with exploring
briefly an abiding example of symbolic setting, in the sense I have
defined, as it is found in a few Irish plays. The imagined abode is a
good setting to discuss in these terms, since it is so basic an image of
human environment, and of course has an ancient and distinguished
stage history. The palace front of classical Greek theatre could evoke
the city state itself, the history of a particular lineage, as with the house
of Atreus, and the tragic fate of a particular (say Agamemnon's) family
group. The palace front, although an external view because of the
circumstances of Greek theatre, is a setting which, besides focusing
social, historical and family forces, is the abode of myth, echoing the
cries if not the whispers of the psyche. The imagination of Greek
civilization seems enormously energetic and healthy, feeding on comedy and tragedy alike. It does not become prurient, though it feeds also
on what lurks within the palace: blasphemy, murder and incest. In
modern drama, of course, the setting is scaled down to the needs of a
more introspective culture, and of an indoor theatre with its interiors
suggested by the small auditorium and proscenium arch.
Compressionism[3] abounds from Ibsen's *A Doll's House* to Ionesco's *The
New Tenant*.

Critics of Irish literature have long noted the importance of the
image of abode or house in Yeats's poetry, from the rude cabin of "The
Lake Isle of Inisfree" to Thoor Ballylee and Coole Park. But the
importance of the house in Irish plays is also difficult to underestimate.
And the house as a stage set has all the immediacy of impact of a
tangible object. It also provides the environment for the actors and
their roles, an environment enriched by voices, sounds and music, and
given atmosphere and mood by its forms, colours, furnishings and
lighting. It can be more than a specific *locus*, for it can represent or
suggest extensions of meaning beyond itself. Since it is an external
object, I would call it a primary dramatic symbol, whereas the verbal
symbols which can occur in the dialogue would be secondary. This by
no means implies that they are less powerful or less haunting than
primary symbols, only that they are different.

The stage set as symbolic dwelling appears in many modern Irish
plays, and an explanation of these settings reveals just how potent the
symbolism is in its rendering of Irish politics and society. It can evoke
not merely the rural and urban life, but also the worlds of myth and of

---

[3] I use Lawrence Kitchin's term *compressionism* to mean the theatrical expression, by
means of stage settings, of that spiritual claustrophobia which marks the anxiety-ridden
condition of modern man.

politics, of specific social issues and universal human needs. A brief glance at Yeats's plays can illustrate this range of symbolic meaning, before we pass on to consider individual plays by other writers which all testify to the unflagging richness of the house as a dramatic symbol.

In Yeats's *The King's Threshold*, the palace front, represented by the great gates before which Seanchan the poet dies, symbolizes the power of an Irish state grown Philistine. The setting is legendary, but the application is modern. In *The Green Helmet*, the mythical world of Cuchulain is presented through vivid, grotesque farce. The set, containing its squabbling heroes, is an Ireland which might achieve unity and joy through heroic and magnanimous leadership. With a boldness to match that of the myth itself, Yeats shows us holes being hacked in the set so that all three heroes' wives may enter simultaneously, none gaining precedence over another. By contrast, the forest hut of *Deirdre* is a compressionist symbol of Ireland as a prison in which double-crossing treachery rules in the person of Conchubar. Tragic love, jealousy, gloating sensual anticipation—these human passions are crammed with the myth into the claustrophobic setting and intensified by the other unities of action and time. Turning to the modern realistic setting of *The Words Upon the Window-Pane*, we notice that Mrs. Henderson's Dublin house is more than her dwelling; the poem on its window-pane makes it a national monument evoking the greatness of Swift's genius and century, but also his personal anguish, his apprehension about the future generations, and the bitter disparity between Swift's Ireland and Mrs. Henderson's, between Swift's passionate ghost and his dying body. But Yeats's most austere and overtly symbolic use of the house to reveal the fall of a civilization, the decay of a culture and the ruin of a class is, of course, the gutted house of *Purgatory*.

A dramatic fragment extant from the early days of the Irish National Theatre Society is Fred Ryan's *The Laying of the Foundations* (Act II).[4] The setting is Michael O'Loskins' office where he works for Dublin Corporation. The office becomes the center of conflict between Michael's duty to the corporation and the poor tenement dwellers and the dubious property deals of Michael's father and his friend Alderman Farrelly. As Michael uncovers cheating and corruption in "The New Building Syndicate," Ryan builds a scathing satire aimed at Dublin's housing conditions. The shaky, half-filled foundations discovered in the play become a symbol of exploitation and corruption in civic life, and, indeed, the undermining of Ireland's hope for a new society.

---

[4] This fragment is contained in Robert Hogan and James Kilroy, eds., *Lost Plays of the Irish Renaissance* (Newark, Delaware, 1970).

The growth of the new patriotic consciousness finds dramatic embodiment too in another early effort, this time by Padraic Colum. *The Saxon Shillin'* is set in the Kearney's house in the village of Convroney on Lord Clanwilliam's estate. The girls Brighid and Maggie are hungry, lonesome, and afraid. Soldiers and police, we learn, have been ordered to enforce evictions. Hugh Kearney enters in his soldier's uniform. The rented house, the environment of a divided family, full of arguments about patriotism and the need to refuse the Saxon shilling, or the £500 a year those more elevated than private soldiers might earn, becomes a microcosm of Ireland itself. Hugh's entry into the set begins a process by which he is changed from a British soldier into a rebel determined to resist eviction and who is shot as a result. The problem of making a living from the land and the constant money troubles of small farmers in rural Ireland are readily expressed by the simple, frugal interiors of farm houses. Lady Gregory's early play *Twenty Five* is just one example. The house stands for a way of life which, despite its hardships, is still enviable to an emigre like Christie Henderson—though he is unsentimental enough to realize that the little Irish kitchen in a cottage on a little bit of land stands for a narrow and hazardous existence.

Synge's shebeen in *The Playboy of the Western World* is not only the most well-known, but also the most complex use of this particular symbolic setting. It houses the joy and laughter as well as the crushing loneliness and sexual frustration, the fighting spirit of a hero and the clumsy sadism of a few villagers. Boring reality breeds the need for mythic inflation and deflation. A lad's growing to manhood needs some ritual of the tribe, or in lieu of that at least some boisterous and dangerous exploits, before he can settle for that vision of the easy, convivial life Christy has at the beginning of Act II, when the set is flooded with the brilliant morning light. The shadow of brutality which darkens Act III becomes, only a few years later, the shadow of revolutionary violence. The turmoil, bloodshed and bitter conflicts, social, political and racial, which demolished one society and started to build another are, of course, powerfully embodied in O'Casey's settings, not only in the Dublin tenement of *The Shadow of the Gunman* and *The Plough and the Stars* but in the emptied, desolate set which ends *Juno and the Paycock*, and in practically any of O'Casey's houses. His sensitivity to place was such that the swelling seemed to him a thing alive; he could not help but make it not merely a scene, but a symbol of the rich life he dramatized, even if he is demolishing it, as in *Purple Dust*.

The Irish playwright who most overtly stated the symbolic use of the house set was, however, George Bernard Shaw in *Heartbreak House*. This play, because it dramatizes forces in England and Europe rather than Ireland, belongs to another discussion, but nevertheless serves to remind us of just how widespread the symbolism is. Denis Johnston's

The Moon in the Yellow River though, clearly owes much to Shaw's play, and provides us with a very brilliant Irish variation. The genial eccentricities and shrewdnesses of the characterization and dialogue, the family relationships within the house, and the incongruous presence, in the end uncomprehending, of Tausch, the German engineer, serve to make the house and its family seem an extremely satisfying symbol of Ireland and the new Free State. The tower and its armory point to the embattled Ireland of old and recent history, while the hum of the turbines and the hooting of ships' sirens suggest the efforts to create a new economic and industrial "modern" society, which is to be resisted. This Irish house is also an educational battleground when Blanaid must learn to prepare for the battle of life with an Aunt who, complaining of too many strangers in the house, churns out political pamphlets, and with a father who spurns her until it is almost too late, for he blames her birth for the death of her mother.

The painful arrival of the new Free State is dramatized in another "house" play, Joseph O'Conor's *The Iron Harp*. Here, the state of Ireland during the "troubles" of the 1920s is symbolized by the mansion which is owned by an Englishman, Tolly, and is an I.R.A. headquarters. Tolly is baffled to find his house "infested by natives with guns, and one strange captain of the British Army who spends his time shooting rabbits."[5] His blind steward O'Riordan is also an I.R.A. officer who has Captain John Tregarthen in his charge as a prisoner. Tregarthen, O'Riordon and his cousin Molly Kinsella have grown to be firm friends while living on the estate in the war-torn circumstances of 1920. Tregarthen and Molly fall in love, but the British officer has to be shot as part of I.R.A. reprisals against the Black and Tans. For Tregarthen the house is both a prison and "an unexpected Paradise," before he knows he has to die. The blind O'Riordan has a more sombre view which makes the setting symbolize not only Ireland, but also the tragic view of human experience itself:

> We're all in prison together, Johnny, one way or the other. I'm a prisoner of the dark, and we're all prisoners of the body, are we not? And if we escape into the mind we find ourselves inside some thick-walled philosophy. And if we escape from life itself, there we are behind the tall bars of eternity. It's a terrible incarcerated existence! Still, so long as we can sing in our cages we shall be happy enough, I daresay, so why worry.[6]

Molly and Johnny Tregarthen pitch their love against the thunder outside, but Sean Kelly arrives like Nemesis with his reprisal orders. The thundery light outside, and the shining silver spoons like stars within the house, seem to promise hope and escape to that vision of a

---

[5] Joseph O'Conor, *The Iron Harp* in E. Martin Browne, ed., *Three Irish Plays* (Harmondsworth, 1959), p. 102.

[6] Ibid., p. 111.

peaceful English village which Johnny describes at one point; but as the
hour for escape approaches, the set itself adds to the suspense and the
feeling of dashed hopes, for we know that though a door can conceal
Johnny briefly from Phelim, soon Kelly will return prematurely, and a
door will open to let him and the cold death into the house.

The great Anglo-Irish houses and their estates were, of course,
often targets of political and class warfare in the early days of the Irish
Free State. The activities of the Irish Land Commission made sure that
many estates were subdivided and parcels of land allotted to local
people and to "migrants" moved in from surrounding districts.
Rutherford Mayne's *The Bridge Head* dramatizes the conflicts which
arise when such redistribution takes place. To some extent it is a
propaganda play, revealing the devotion to duty and government
interests of the officials Stephen Moore and Hugh O'Neill, the latter
sacrificing his love for Cecily Barrington, daughter of the big house, to
the demands of his demanding and often distasteful occupation. But
our sympathies for the Barringtons are given their head, so that doctrine does not cripple the characterization or blind Mayne's vision of
humanity. The set is appropriately Moore's sitting room in Mooney's
Hotel, somewhere in Western Ireland. It is office-cum-living quarters,
suggesting that fanatical living for government work which is the
central theme of the play. The redistribution of land by a government
means that we are all but guests who come and go. The hotel image
seems therefore entirely appropriate. At the end of the play, the only
land remaining for the Barringtons, as for everyman, is the burial plot.
The Japanese, Gosuki, an observer sent by his government, is a convenient character for further emphasizing the basic, universal human
need for land use laws. As we know from our own stance in history, the
concern is not merely that of Ireland in the 1930s. Gosuki, moreover,
gives a satiric and humorous edge to several scenes, since he is a citizen
of the world who observes the society with disarming directness. Such
aspects extend the play beyond its immediate setting in time, and the
shabby little hotel room becomes symbolic of the changing face of
Ireland under the direction of the land "strategists" of the revolution;
Stephen Moore's far-sighted action in getting Dolan to be the "mig-
rant" is vindicated at the end of the play. Moore is like a fanatical
revolutionary commander working from the hotel room as if it were a
field headquarters. As he explains to his assistants:

> . . . Dolan's holding is the one point on the Shivna where we can fling a
> bridge across. No one ever thought, not even the countrymen, of this. No
> ashplant on a cattle drive ever struck a beast on the three thousand acres
> of Fitzgormanstown. Why? Because the Shivna saved it. The greatest
> ranch fortress in the heart of Connaught! Some day we'll capture it, and
> we'll get the money for that bridge![7]

---

[7] Rutherford Mayne, *Bridge Head*, in Curtis Canfield, ed., *Plays of Changing Ireland*
(New York, 1936), pp. 418-19.

The dogged and lonely devotion of the land men in their hotel headquarters is shown to be, though, the austerity of veterans of the revolution, for at the end of the play, the new junior man, Watersley, is a rather feckless young lounger whose main concern is his golf. Fanaticism is beginning to give way to farce. By the time we arrive at Hugh Leonard's brilliant *The Patrick Pearse Motel*, this process seems to have completed itself, and the new society of turbines and tourists can safely ignore the veteran of 1916, who, though bearing the proud name Houlihan, is only a farcically confused geriatric night watchman saluting the pictures of his political heroes who give their names to the motel's tawdry rooms.

If the symbolic abode charts the forces of revolution and social change in modern Ireland, there are two fascinating examples of it which do that and more: they also provide subtle and extremely satisfying images of the dramatic imagination at work. Lennox Robinson's *Church Street* and Michael Molloy's *The Visiting House* are both finished products which explore the processes of dramatic art.

The main setting in *Church Street*, Mrs. Riordan's drawing-room in the National Bank of the small country town of Knock, perfectly symbolizes the boring provincialism of Irish country life as it appears to Hugh Riordan, a playwright who has come home for a few days' rest from the dispiriting and unsuccessful struggle to achieve fame in London. But the ability of this main setting to change its back wall, darken down and become settings for the imagined lives of the characters of his home town in their own houses, bedrooms, lodgings or an abortionist's waiting room, shows that the surface of life is not impenetrably drab, dull and dead. Aunt Moll is a country aunt who is also a variant of the old woman who is Ireland. She rules the house, which is the Jamesian house of Life, the house of the imagination. It is she who insists that Church Street in Knock contains plays which the playwright has to uncover. The scenes which follow Aunt Moll's little chat with Hugh show how an Irish drama can be made out of Irish lives. When friends and neighbors crowd into the little drawingroom for the first time, Robinson directs that:

> The scene which follows must be so well produced that it gives the impression of not having been produced at all. People must move when they should not, mask each other, speak through each other's speeches—and yet every speech must be heard—the audience should say to each other, "what bad acting, what rotten production."[8]

The sudden change of style has the effect of making the guests seem what they are, thematically, the rich raw material of the playwright's imagination, of the selecting and ordering processes of dramatic art.

---

[8] Ibid., pp. 113-14.

The ordering and shaping in this engrossing one-acter is the well-tried play-within-the-play device, here sketched on the scale of scenes-glimpsed-within-the-act. Of course, the effect of modifying very fluently the frame setting, is to make the intervening settings seem very much stage sets, while enforcing the solidity and "reality" of the frame setting itself: the little drawingroom is the microcosm of the reality out of which modern Irish plays are made.

But where did all this modern Irish play-making spring from? A population of vigorous talkers and monologuists[9] seems to have had no strong native tradition of drama before 1900. A large part of the answer, in my view, is revealed in Michael Molloy's masterly play, *The Visiting House*. As he tells us in his opening directions, "Visiting Houses were those institutions that kept Irish folklore alive for a thousand years and left it with one of the greatest folklore libraries on paper and tape of any country in the world; this is one of the last of the Visiting Houses."[10] This setting projects the Ireland which carries the vestiges of the vigorous legends and mythopoetic imagination of a great oral tradition not only handed on by the narrative story-teller, but by improvised plots and japes of the merryman and master of the Visiting House, here embodied in the person of Broc Heavey. The play shows Tim Corry why he must not leave Ireland to work in England. He would be trading the rich poetic and histrionic high-jinks of the Visiting House, and his love for its daughter, against the beer-swilling and cards of the urban pubs. His beloved Mary is the rich folk imagination itself. This basic situation is enriched further by the comic contest in the play between Verb to Be, the Stiff Man of Education, and Mickle Conlon, the Man of Learning, who, like Yeats's Old Man out of mythology in *The Death of Cuchulain*, is the oral tradition of myth learned by heart and in the passionate being. Mickle is a full-blooded Shakespearean (Yeats's Old Man was of the school of Talma) whereas Broc, representative of the Visiting House's last phase "might be described as an actor of the naturalistic school."[11] We watch this extraordinary actor-dramatist-storyteller-farceur with his "mobile face changing from frowns, as he grapples with difficulties, to smiles and triumphant finger-crackings as he solves them. In short, the artist in the throes of composition, an impressive sight when the artist is wholly unaffected and unselfconscious as in this case."[12] Broc has to keep his

---

[9] For further discussion of monologue in drama see the present writer's essay, "Singular Voices: Monologue and Monodrama in the Plays of W. B. Yeats," in *Modern Drama*, 18, No. 2 (June 1975), 141-52.

[10] Michael Molloy, *The Visiting House*, in Robert Hogan, ed., *Seven Irish Plays 1946-1964* (Minneapolis, 1967), p. 32.

[11] Ibid., p. 41.

[12] Ibid.

audience amused and imaginatively enriched night after night by his stories and "plots." The play thus proceeds in the best tradition of the ever-inventive rascally servant of farce by means of one improvised situation after another in which the other characters become victims, audience and actors for the "plots" or japes. Brilliant, fantastic dialogue, monologue and deceptions move abundantly and vividly towards the comedic target of the two marriages which will conclude the play. And all the while, under the comic skirling is the melancholy note of the passing away of a folk imagination in which life was myth, and myth reality:

> **Mickle**:   All right, Verb to Be. Answer this question. What is the most difference between these times and the olden times?
>
> **Verb to Be**:   In these times, Ireland has no ice and is populated with Irish; in olden times, the Icy Age, Ireland was covered with ice and populated with Eskimoes.
>
> **Mickle**:   Verb to Be, that is not the most difference.
>
> **Verb to Be**:   And what's the most difference?
>
> **Mickle**:   In these times, there's nothing talking only mankind; in olden times, everything was talking—animals and birds, and serpents, the dead, and all sorts from the next world, skulls and graves and everything.[13]

Michael Molloy ends his play by giving Mickle, thank God, the last word by means of a magnificent monologue.

In the house of the dramatic imagination there are many mansions, houses which may be derelicts in reality, but which, for audiences and critics who have not lost their hold on personality, are alight with the dramatic and histrionic imagination itself.

---

[13] Ibid., p. 50.

RECURRENT PATTERNS IN O'CASEY'S DRAMA

Ronald Ayling

I

Certain ideas and themes preoccupied Sean O'Casey's mind throughout his life. As we might expect, they recur again and again in his work, in autobiographical narratives and occasional prose writings as well as in the drama.[1] Most important of these recurrent interests, perhaps, is O'Casey's desire to find order and harmony in a world rent by physical and spiritual chaos. A reflection of this concern is shown in his recognition of the same interest in Strindberg's drama:

> Harmony there was none [in the world that the Swedish playwright knew], and Strindberg used all his energy, all his imaginative thought to bring harmony out of disorder and selfishness.[2]

I cannot imagine a better description of O'Casey's own life's work. In his drama emphasis is often placed on disorder and selfishness, shown

---

[1] Unless otherwise stated the texts of O'Casey's plays used in this essay are those printed in the four volumes of his *Collected Plays* (London, 1949-1951), hereafter referred to as *C.P.* For the sake of convenience, where the titles of certain writings are often reiterated, the following abbreviations are used: *The Shadow* represents *The Shadow of a Gunman; Juno* stands for *Juno and the Paycock; The Plough* for *The Plough and the Stars;* and *Red Roses* stands for *Red Roses for Me*.

[2] Draft of a letter on Strindberg's importance to the modern drama copied from one of O'Casey's holograph notebooks among his private papers. The copyright for these writings remains in Eileen O'Casey's possession; I am grateful to her for permission to quote from her husband's notebooks, manuscripts and hitherto unpublished letters. Since the present essay was written a few letters have been printed in *The Letters of Sean O'Casey: Volume I, 1910-1941*, ed. David Krause (New York, 1975).

particularly in social and economic exploitation, and in man's inhumanity to man. This subject is shown, notably, in the degrading effects of war and poverty. At the same time, O'Casey subtly realizes the moral ambiguities inherent in the problems of law and order in a country dominated by a superimposed alien system of morality and justice and therefore particularly vulnerable to revolution and anarchy. These problems are naturally most apparent—and often in the forefront of the action—in the early plays set in Ireland during the period from 1915 to 1922, *The Plough and the Stars, The Shadow of a Gunman,* and *Juno and the Paycock* (to place them in chronological order of subject-matter rather than order of writing). Yet from the evidence of later works like *Purple Dust* and *Red Roses for Me*, where the discussion is continued though in a less prominent manner, it is clear that O'Casey did not consider the matter resolved by the ending of "colonial" rule in Ireland.

It is surprising how writers on O'Casey have ignored the significant number of references to "law and order" which may be found in his writings, particularly the term's multiple occurance in the six-volume autobiographical narrative. Here, in general, the playwright's attitude seems to have been brilliantly anticipated by Oscar Wilde as early as 1889, when he gave the following defintion in his review of a novel about Ireland written by J. A. Froude:

> Mr. Froude admits the martyrdom of Ireland, but regrets that the martyrdom was not completely carried out. . . . Resolute government, that shallow shibboleth of those who do not understand how complex a thing the art of government is, is his posthumous panacea for past evils. His hero, Colonel Goring, has the words Law and Order ever on his lips, meaning by the one the enforcement of unjust legislation, and implying by the other the suppression of every fine natural aspiration.[3]

Similarly, whenever there is an appeal to such a notion, or the phrase itself is introduced in disputation in O'Casey's plays or *Autobiographies* it is invariably in an ironic context. Those who invoke the idea are often the least law-abiding themselves. In *Red Roses for Me*, for instance, it is the fanatical Orangemen, Foster and Dowzard. In a scene in Act IV the two men rejoice that "the King's horses and the King's men" are brutally suppressing a protest march by underprivileged workers. Foster justifies their attitude as follows:

> Law an'ordher in th' State an' law an' ordher in the Church we must have. An' we're fightin' here as they're fightin' there—for the' Crown an' ceevil an' releegious liberty![4]

---

[3] *The Artist as Critic: Critical Writings of Oscar Wilde*, ed. Richard Ellmann (New York, 1970), p. 137.

[4] *Red Roses*, Act IV, in *C.P.*, III, p. 219.

The selfrighteousness of the belief that justice and morality are the exclusive possession of those in power is strikingly epitomized in the words of the French-Algerian colonialist in Genet's *The Screens* who says belligerantly: "My mind won't be at rest till *our* peace and order are restored in this land."[5]

In Act III of *The Plough and the Stars* Jennie Gogan and Bessie Burgess engage in an hilarious argument: their invocation of law and order—both use the expression—as a pretext for "borrowing" someone else's pram in order to carry away goods looted from the shopping center in Dublin affords a brilliant satiric parallel to the political situation of the time. In the latter an alien power (Britain) uses its subject peoples (Ireland among them) to wage a war supposedly on behalf of the freedom of small independent nations—"poor little Catholic Belgium" is instanced in the course of the play—while employing violence and intimidation to preserve law and order at "home," that is, in Dublin and elsewhere.

In *The Shadow of a Gunman*, set in Dublin in the year 1920, the theme of appearance and reality is pursued on various levels, one of which is largely concerned with law and order in the state. By 1920 the large majority of the Irish people no longer respected the political and judicial government of the country and many refused to recognize either (that is, either the Parliament at Westminster, passing laws for Ireland, or the British-oriented law courts throughout Ireland) while they were controlled by England. In 1918 general elections in Ireland had returned a large nationalist majority in the full knowledge that the nationalists were committed to the policy of withdrawal from the House of Commons in London. The elected representatives then established an Irish Parliament (Dail Eireann) in Dublin and a government responsible to it; meanwhile, republican law courts were set up to handle civil cases throughout the country.[6] All three law-making organizations were declared illegal by the established authorities but each continued to operate underground. There was thus a situation in which there were two "governments" in Ireland, both guaranteeing law and order for the people and both resorting to violence to "keep the peace." Against this background, we have, in *The Shadow*, a comic episode where the landlord of a tenement house takes out a summons—presumably in the British-recognized courts—against a tenant who won't pay what the landlord calls his "just and lawful debts." In reply, the tenant warns (in what must be one of the most strongly ironic remarks even in O'Casey's drama): "Just you be careful what

---

[5] Jean Genet, *The Screens (Les Paravents)*, sc. 13, tr. B. Frechtman (New York, 1962), p. 110 (my italics).

[6] In 1918 the Irish people, north and south, elected 73 nationalist representatives in a parliament of 106; Dail Eireann, the Assembly of Ireland, was set up in January 1919.

you're sayin', Mr. Mulligan. *There's law in the land still.*" To which
Mulligan answers, "Be me sowl there is, an' you're goin' to get a little of
it now," while at the same time he hands Shields a notice to quit.[7]

A further satiric variation on the theme of legality occurs a little
later in *The Shadow* when the tenants of another flat in the same house
appeal for legal assistance to the Irish Republican Army, engaged at
the time in undermining the existing forces of order in the country.
Their petition, with its semi-literate use of legalistic jargon, is not only
funny in itself but ironic, too, because it is presented to one who is
himself the shadow and not the substance of an I.R.A. gunman. There
is further irony in that, while the letter is a plea for protection against
violence, it closes with the postscript: "If you send up any of your men,
please tell them to bring their guns."[8] The parallel with the national
political and constitutional position in 1920-21 is obvious.

The will in *Juno and the Paycock*—set in Dublin during the Civil War
of 1922—similarly reflects a significant national issue. Here, the Boyle
family (like Ireland itself in 1921) comes into a modest inheritance only
to find that the document which promised this independence is drawn
up in a dubious way. In the first case the Boyle family loses the legacy
altogether and then disintegrates as a family unit; in the other, there is
civil war over the terms of the Anglo-Irish Treaty by which the Irish
Free State was disinherited of six northern counties.

Whenever O'Casey touches upon the theme of legality in a social
or political context it is invariably in a contradictory and ambiguous
manner. This serves to demonstrate the conviction that consistently
underlies his social morality: that no state in which disorder bred of
poverty is found may be regarded as possessing law and order in any
meaningful sense. From the evidence of his writings there is little doubt
that the Irish dramatist would, by and large, have agreed with the
scornful judgment of Mrs. Alving in Ibsen's *Ghosts* when she says to
Pastor Manders (who, characteristically, had introduced the selfsame
term to defend a morally indefensible attitude): "All this talk about law
and order. I often think that is what causes all the unhappiness in the
world."[9]

In an inseparable counterbalance to O'Casey's concern for order
and harmony there is his abundant use of stage chaos for satirical and
symbolical purposes. Stylistically, this affords one of the playwright's

---

[7] *The Shadow*, Act I, in *C.P.*, I, pp. 101-02. The notice to quit in the play was based
on an autobiographical incident. There is a similar document addressed to O'Casey
among his papers, showing that he was evicted from a tenement in Mountjoy Square
during the "Troubles."

[8] Ibid., Act I, p. 119.

[9] *Ghosts*, Act I, in *Ghosts and Three Other Plays by Henrik Ibsen,* tr. M. Meyer (New
York, 1966), p. 161.

most original contributions to modern drama. Samuel Beckett was one of the first of O'Casey's commentators to appreciate properly this particular feature in his technique. Reviewing *Windfalls* when it appeared in 1934, Beckett singled out the two one-act sketches it contained (*The End of the Beginning* and *A Pound on Demand*) for special praise:

> Mr. O'Casey is a master of knockabout in this very serious and honourable sense—that he discerns the principle of disintegration in even the most complacent solidities, and activates it to their explosion. This is the energy of his theatre, the triumph of the principle of knockabout in situation, in all its elements and on all its planes, from the furniture to the higher centres. If *Juno and the Paycock*, as seems likely, is his best work so far, it is because it communicates most fully this dramatic dehiscence, mind and world come asunder in irreparable dissociation—"chassis" (the credit of having readapted Aguecheek and Belch in Joxer and the Captain being incidental to the larger credit of having dramatised the slump in the human solid). This impulse of material to escape and be consummate in its own knockabout is admirably espressed in the two "sketches" that conclude this volume, and especially in *The End of the Beginning* where the entire set comes to pieces and the chief character, in a final spasm of dislocation, leaves the scene by the chimney.[10]

He ends the article by praising a scene that clearly comes over to him as quintessential O'Casey: "the passage in *The End of the Beginning* presenting Messrs. Darry Berrill and Barry Derrill supine on the stage, 'expediting matters' in an agony of calisthenics, surrounded by the doomed furniture."[11]

Beckett's words command particular attention—retrospectively, that is—because of his own brilliant use of farce and music-hall knockabout and the preoccupation with disintegration in all his work. Indeed, he could well be writing about himself, particularly where he speaks of O'Casey's "disruptive intelligence, exacting the tumult from unity." While it is tempting to look at these ideas, then, as primarily self-revelatory—especially as Beckett has consistently refused to discuss his own writings—it is even more profitable to follow them with regard to the critic's professed subject. And indeed they are not at all far-fetched in relation to O'Casey's intentions, though one cannot imagine him describing his theme and technique in such Beckettian terms. Beckett would appear to be interested in dehiscence and dissolution in their own right as processes, purely and simply, whereas to O'Casey they are means to a greater end, elements subservient (even if, as Beckett suggests, they are often the most successful ingredients) to a

---

[10] Samuel Beckett, "The Essential and the Incidental," *The Bookman*, 86 (Christmas Supplement, 1934), p. 111.

[11] Ibid., p. 111.

more inclusive theme.[12] Deeply concerned that order and harmony be achieved in human society and the individual life, O'Casey is painfully aware of disruptive tensions and disorder in both, and follows the theme through to its *reductio ad absurdum* of destruction. Yet, at the back of the experience, he plainly hints—sometimes not even implicitly but directly—that this anarchy, the product of poverty, bad social organization and individual ignorance, is avoidable. That the theme is treated with great seriousness does not detract from its enormous entertainment value: in full flow, there is no one in modern drama in the English language who can come anywhere near him as a comic writer. (By full flow I am thinking of such scenes as the "sea fantasy" episode in Act I of *Juno*, the squabble over the pram in Act III of *The Plough*, the telephone fracas in Act IV of *The Silver Tassie*, the theological disputation under the table in Act II of *Red Roses*, Mahan and Marthraun discussing the "hierarchilogical crew" on the world's quarterdeck in Scene II of *Cock-a-Doodle Dandy*, and the "Jeeps" sequence early in the second act of *The Bishop's Bonfire*: nor are these merely isolated incidents of comic genius in O'Casey's drama). That he can hugely *enjoy*—in his art, if not in his life—some of the complications and the consequences of dislocation should not obscure his perennial concern with bringing order out of disorder or of using chaos as a warning.

In any case the technique of stage chaos is one O'Casey was to use, with significant variations, throughout his career. Of plays written after 1934, perhaps *Purple Dust* and *Cock-a-Doodle Dandy* provide the most spectacular and hilarious knockabout. In the former, the Tudor manor house at the center of the action takes a prolonged battering at the hands of the workmen supposedly renovating it and by the onslaught of wind, rain and tempest. In *Cock* natural (and possibly supernatural) forces similarly bombard and harass the home and the friends of another money-grubbing businessman. Yet, if later works like, say, *Cock* and *Time to Go* use seemingly supernatural effects and extravagant fantasy in ways that at first appear quite foreign to the basically

---

[12] Like Beckett, O'Casey introduces human derelicts into several of his dramas: men and women maimed by war (Johnny Boyle, Harry Heegan), or slum life (Mollser), or economic hardship generally (the deckchair attendants and the Down-and-Out in *Within the Gates*). The complete or partial destruction of the stage set is a technique used on an even greater—and symbolic—scale in later plays like *Purple Dust, Cock-a-Doodle Dandy* and *The Bishop's Bonfire*. Reviewing a revival of *The Shadow of a Gunman* in 1957, Harold Hobson noted similarities between O'Casey and Beckett in their creation of grotesque tragicomic tramp-figures, and this element could be traced further back, of course, to a Gaelic ancestry that includes Synge and Yeats. In the case of O'Casey and Beckett, however, one wonders whether the tree that miraculously if comically bears fruit in the course of the action of *Time to Go* (published 1951) was known to Beckett before he wrote *Waiting for Godot*.

realistic *Juno and the Paycock*, these differences are more apparent than they are real. In theatrical and symbolic terms we see a particular kind of social order splitting apart at the seams, in the one case in post-Independence Ireland and in the other during the Civil War preceding independence. One does not have to delve too deeply to perceive the logical growth of the later form of drama from the earlier one.

II

In Shakespearian manner, O'Casey is never afraid to put important ideas in the mouths of minor characters, like the anonymous disputants in crowd scenes in *Within the Gates*, or even fools (like the Old Woman in *The Star Turns Red*) who sometimes say things without themselves fully understanding their true significance. A bigoted character such as the Covey in *The Plough* is ludicrously ineffectual as a human being, let alone a revolutionary, yet in his speech he often presents many of O'Casey's political and social convictions. In this respect the Covey is, in some ways, like Trofimov in *The Cherry Orchard*: both look forward, optimistically, to a better future for mankind, and both embody some of their authors' visions, yet we cannot really believe that either character will himself ever achieve his dreams. Both are impractical, immersed in abstract ideas to the detriment of everyday human affairs, curiously afraid of sex, and are often laughed at by the audience as well as by other characters in the plays. We are, in fact, alienated further from the Covey as an individual, though not necessarily from his ideas, because he is a far less pleasant man than is Trofimov, being self-righteous, quarrelsome, and priggish. In such an example, we can see that O'Casey in the early plays written for the Abbey Theatre was like Chekhov in that he treated a number of his own beliefs and ideas in a seemingly ambiguous manner.

In later plays, when O'Casey uses individual figures as mouthpieces for his convictions, they are generally presented in a less ambiguous and in a more attractive way, even though characters like the Dreamer and Ayamonn Breyden are in no way depicted as supermen but as erring and imperfect human beings. In his final plays the dramatist goes further, inventing symbolic figures like Father Ned and the Figuro, who—because they never appear on stage, but work through their influence on the minds and deeds of other people in the dramatic action—can successfully embody the author's ideals without appearing in any way priggish or self-righteous. Arnold Wesker uses the same method in *Roots*, where his mouthpiece Ronnie Kahn is felt as a distinct presence throughout the play without ever appearing on stage. It is not an unusual device, of course, but O'Casey's particular practice in this respect allows him great imaginative freedom in using fantasy and comedy to help realize his didactic purposes.

It is worth noting that his particular device in his final plays had been projected in theory very much earlier. On October 9, 1922, before any of his work had been accepted by the Abbey Theatre, he wrote to tell Lennox Robinson that he was "terribly disappointed" that *The Crimson in the Tricolour* had been rejected. His letter contained a spirited defence of the work against the criticisms of W. B. Yeats, which Robinson had quoted as length as the opinions of one of the theatre's "readers." O'Casey's self-defence concluded:

> One other point: the reader adversely criticises the fact that an action is performed for a man that never appears on the stage. I am glad this is mentioned, for I was thinking of writing a play around Jim Larkin —The Red Star—in which he would never appear though responsible for all the action.[13]

This comment is doubly interesting, in that the description admirably summarizes the central plot motivation in *The Drums of Father Ned* (1960) and *Figuro in the Night* (1961)—both written more than thirty-five years after the letter—but is far from describing the actual drama, *The Star Turns Red* (1940), that he was to write around the figure of Larkin. It is further confirmation of the long-lived continuity of O'Casey's ideas, to be observed at all stages of his development as a writer. His awareness of such longevity in this particular case is apparent from a letter dated December 2, 1947, in which he praises George Jean Nathan for the tribute to Eugene O'Neill in his *Book of the Theatre 1946-47*:

> I think you're right about him going deeper than Shaw or I. And his drawing of a character who never appears is amazing. When I first began play writing—"Crimson in the Tricolour"—I had a clash with Yeats about this. He said it was impossible to put a character in a play who never appeared. I contradicted, and now, many years after, O'Neill proves I was right. (I read "The Iceman Cometh" a week or so ago.)

That O'Casey was here persisting in a traditionally disapproved of theatrical practice is illustrated by the claim made by John Osborne (in an interview in the *Observer Magazine* for December 1, 1974) that one of the most "daring risks" he took in writing *Look Back in Anger* in 1957 was this very "innovation." He added:

> It was almost a rule when I first started working in the theatre . . . that you never discussed anyone on the stage who never appeared because it worried the audience. . . . I knew it was going to be difficult and everybody pointed it out to me at the time.

Judging from the evidence of the extant manuscript of *The Harvest Festival* (completed 1919) and from contemporary comments on the

---

[13] Letter to Lennox Robinson, dated October 9, 1922, now in Southern Illinois University Library.

lost *The Crimson in the Tricolour* (1921), O'Casey's pre-Abbey dramas presented particular viewpoints in an overt and didactic manner. So did a number of his post-Abbey works, written in self-imposed exile. It might therefore appear that, as some critics have claimed, the Abbey plays in between these two phases of development were somehow fundamentally different in kind from either. I do not believe this to be true. Though his "message" in the plays first presented at the Abbey Theatre between 1923 and 1926 is not projected so explicitly through any committed individual or group of figures as it is in either the earlier or later periods, it is not difficult nonetheless to perceive in them where he author stands in moral and human terms. The abundant satire directed against the wastrels and braggarts realizes a large part of the author's social criticism. His understanding and admiration of the imaginative vigour of Dublin working-class life is shown in both the rich comedy and the vivid colloquial language of his drama, while his deep sympathy for the courageous struggles of many slum women clearly emerges from the characterization of his heroines.

III

Throughout his career O'Casey consistently drew attention to the many obstacles in the way of proletarian self-advancement and acquisition of culture. The working people have not only to contend with a social order which gives the poorer children little or no schooling—and what teaching they have often of a mediocre standard—but, frequently, the vehement opposition of parents, neighbours, and friends. The reactions of Mary Boyle's father are typical:

> Her an' her readin'! That's more of th' blasted nonsense that has th' house fallin' down on top of us! What did th' likes of her, born in a tenement house, want with readin'?[14]

One is reminded of "Sailor" Mahan's exclamation, "What do people want with books? I don't remember readin' a book in me life,"[15] which occurs in a play written twenty-five years after *Juno*. As in Mahan's case, Boyle's attitude springs from the common hostility of incorrigible ignorance towards anything not comprehended by it and it is obvious that the author has no sympathy whatsoever with this viewpoint. Boyle's words dimly echo, however, a speech from an earlier play in which a somewhat similar point of view is presented by a character worthy of some respect. Here, five years before *Juno* was written, a tenement mother-figure laments her son's change from being a worshipper within the Anglican community to his becoming not only an

---

[14] *Juno*, III, p. 75.

[15] *Cock-a-Doodle Dandy*, Scene III, in *C.P.,* IV, p. 201.

agnostic but also a militant socialist agitator—this evolution being an exact parallel with O'Casey's own life, of course. In *The Harvest Festival* Mrs. Rocliffe tells the Protestant parish clergyman who is an early model for the Rev. Clinton in *Red Roses for Me*:

> It's the readin' that has ruined him, the readin' the readin'; after awhile when he began readin' I noticed a change in him; how quiet he would sit be the fire, thinkin', thinkin', thinkin', and I liltin' a song to meself, an' pretendin' not to watch him. Whenever I spoke to him he wouldn't hear me, or say yes when he should say no, an' say no when he should say yes. Whatever he saw in the books I don't know, but they were never out o' his hands. An', from bein' gay an' always laughin' he got quiet an' thoughtful, an' for hours an' hours you'd hardly know he was in the house at all, he was that still an' silent. It was the readin' that ruined him—the readin', the readin'.[16]

Though we respect Mrs. Rocliffe, her inherited and initially unquestioned religious and social attitudes are criticized in the course of the action; moreover, like Mrs. Breydon in *Red Roses* (with which character Mrs. Rocliffe has a great deal in common), she herself comes to reverse her earlier defence of established authorities by the end of the play. The mother-son relationship in *The Harvest Festival*—like that in *Red Roses*, written twenty-three years later—has distinct autobiographical overtones and it is probable that Mrs. Rocliffe's outlook parallels that of the playwright's own mother. Whether it does or not, it remains indicative of inherent tenement hostility toward efforts at self-improvement made by members of the slum community: the difference between Boyle and Mrs. Rocliffe in this instance, however, is that the former is wholly antagonistic whereas her complaint is (elsewhere in *The Harvest Festival*) tempered by pride in her son's learning.

IV

With little or no hope of improvement in their standard of living, a complete lack of privacy, and few opportunities for any creative expression of the enormous reserves of imaginative energy latent in them, it is hardly surprising that many of the Dublin slum dwellers seek various forms of escape from reality. The contrasting of illusion and reality, indeed, is a theme that recurs throughout O'Casey's writings. Many of his characters find a refuge in private fantasies—in drink and gambling, for instance—and others in public fantasy as expressed in nationalist rhetoric and slogan cries or in hero-worship of one kind or another.

In *The Bishop's Bonfire* Father Boheroe speaks tolerantly of alcohol, describing drink as a way of "trying to get a glimpse of heaven through

----

[16] "The Harvest Festival" (unpublished handwritten manuscript among the playwright's papers), Act II.

the wrong door."[17] Yet O'Casey himself (like his friend, Jim Larkin, the trade union leader) saw alcohol as one of the chief obstacles in the way of working-class progress in Ireland, and this belief informs his critical portrayal of tenement drinking habits. The desire for an escape from the fearful realities of tenement life is understandable, but excessive drinking is degrading, physically and mentally, and leads to further deprivation for the women. Towards the end of *Juno*, in an obviously escapist gesture, the Paycock leaves the house to spend in a pub the few remaining pence of all his borrowed money; he returns dead-drunk, insensible to the tragedy that has befallen his family, and incapable of standing on his feet, let alone bearing any other responsibility. Similarly, we are meant to be disgusted by Bessie Burgess's first entrance at the beginning of *The Plough*, where she makes a screaming, drunken assault on Nora Clitheroe. Compulsive drinking may be a means by which the horrors of the existing social system are momentarily forgotten; the continuance of the one, however, helps the maintenance of the other, and thus the appalling cycle continues.

In a society of inequality and want, money naturally assumes a major role. Its possession or absence can entail life or death, hope or despair. As one might expect, therefore, money is a predominant theme in O'Casey's drama: money as a talisman, as a panacea for all ills, and as a further kind of escapism in the form of legacies or in gambling on cards, horses, dice, and football pools. The pursuit of money and the morality of money are recurring subjects in O'Casey's work, and in this respect we may place his plays firmly in that long and distinguished dramatic line from Ben Jonson to Bernard Shaw that includes Tourneur, Middleton, Congreve, and Wycherley. This significant thematic element, like the sound of chinking coins and the theme song of "Jingle coins, jingle coins, jingle all the day" (the author's satiric adaptation of the popular Christmas song, "Jingle Bells") in *Time to Go*, runs through the Irishman's work from first to last. In the latter one-act play, subtitled "a morality comedy," the immediate response of the heroine to the first sound of coins clinking together is symptomatic; she says to the small town businessmen in the play:

> A dangerous sound; a sound not to be mingled with the gentle jingle of the Mass bell. Take warnin' from me . . . who lost her virtue for a few lousy coins. Yous may go smilin' through the world, gentlemen, but yous won't go smilin' through heaven. Let yous put more value into what yous give an' less into what yous get, before it's too late.[18]

The play's theme song picks up this idea of judgment:

---

[17] *The Bishop's Bonfire* (London and New York, 1955), Act I, p. 24.

[18] *Time to Go*, in *C.P.*, IV, p. 272.

Jingle coins, jingle on till life has pass'd away,
Then change to foolish cries of woe upon th' judgment day.[19]

The juxtaposition of money and the Mass in the Widow Machree's speech is not fortuitous, of course, for what one might call the two "religions" are often counterposed in O'Casey's writings. In this respect, the very first speech of the young heroine in *Cock-a-Doodle Dandy* is representative. Hearing two miserly but pious employers arguing heatedly over money matters she declares: "Lay not up for yourselves treasures upon earth, where moth and rust doth corrupt, and where thieves break through and steal!" to which Biblical injunction the God-fearing Marthraun replies: "Don't turn your head; take no notice. Don't pretend to hear her lyin' hallucinations!"[20]

In *Juno* the legacy plot, based on an actual case known to the author,[21] enabled O'Casey to write a further variation on the theme of the power of money in an acquisitive society. It also allowed him to portray the impact of money on the lives of his slum characters, and to satirize the ignorance and presumption shown in the ostentatious display of showy furniture and effects in the Boyle household. This exhibition of Paycock finery emphasizes the need for education and for the acquirement of taste and culture—as well as showing the pathetic aspirations toward them—a theme that is also realized on more than one level in the role of Mary Boyle in the sub-plot. The legacy thus operates on several planes of seriousness in the play.

Tommy Owens, in O'Casey's earliest produced play, hasn't got so much as a penny to buy a newspaper, and Mrs. Henderson comments, "I never saw you any other way, an' you'll be always the same if you keep follying your Spearmints, an' your Bumble Bees an' your Night Patrols."[22] In *Within the Gates* and *Red Roses for Me* we find other incidents with characters in rags heatedly arguing the merits of horse-racing form and pedigree in a manner that is vastly entertaining and yet pitiful at the same time. Indeed, within the total pattern of O'Casey's drama the theme contains within itself perceptibly tragic

---

[19] Ibid., p. 273.

[20] *Cock-a-Doodle Dandy*, Scene I, in *C.P.*, IV, p. 129.

[21] It is not generally known that the story of the legacy in *Juno* was based on an actual case known to the dramatist. He himself told me that the poor tenement family to whom a modest fortune had been bequeathed asked him, as one of the few "educated" men in the neighbourhood, to give them legal assistance. As in the play, the family failed to receive a single penny from the legacy because the will (drawn up by an ignorant schoolteacher) had been too vaguely worded. A letter from James O'Connor, of James O'Connor & Co. (solicitors), addressed to O'Casey and dated June 27, 1921, gives further details of the case; the parallels with the will in *Juno* are obvious. The letter is among the playwright's papers in his widow's possession.

[22] *The Shadow*, I, in *C.P.*, I, p. 121.

implications. In *Red Roses*, for instance, a group of unemployed men without hope or vision loses the prevailing mood of apathy only when talking about horseracing. In a drama concerned with the stirring of a dormant people to social and political awareness and activity, one in which the hero sounds a Shelley-like trumpet of prophecy, the following dialogue is full of mordant irony (the very name of the Championship reinforces the point, of course, for "the West's Awake" was the refrain of an optimistic nationalist ballad of an earlier period in Irish history):

> **1st Man**:   Golden Gander'll do it, if I'm e'er a thrue prophet. (*Raising his voice a little*): He'll flash past th' winnin' post like an arra' from th' bow, in the five hundred guinea West's Awake Steeplechase Championship.
>
> **2nd Man**:   In me neck he will! He'd have a chance if it was a ramble. Cooper Goose'll leave him standin', if I'm e'er a thrue prophet.
>
> **Eeada**   (*waking up slightly*):   Prophets? Do me ears deceive me, or am I afther hearin' somebody say prophets?[23]

The theme of money is prominent on various levels of significance in this drama. The workers' strike which is central to the action of the play is an attempt by the men to gain an extra shilling a week in wages, a sum which was of considerable value at the time—the early years of this century—when the action of the play was supposed to have taken place. Here O'Casey writes of that period of his life as a manual labourer, about which the poet Padraic Colum has written:

> Dubliners who come to the re-published *Autobiographies* of Sean O'Casey will feel astonishment, even incredulity as they read the parts dealing with their native city. What will strike him or her as they read chapter after chapter is the penury of the scene. Sixpence represents the difference between gratification and deprivation; men and women sicken and die without the least of the nutriment available today. Then, against prevailing deprivation is the struggle for things that are not of this world: men and women plan, speak and act out of devotion to causes.[24]

This comment regarding the autobiographical writings is equally true of *Red Roses*, where the shilling a week is not only the difference between "gratification and deprivation" but also represents a struggle for things that are not of this world because the finer things of life cannot be obtained without money to purchase (in Ayamonn's case) books and paints and writing paper. Of the ideals of Ayamonn, the play's protagonist, it is said that he died not just for a shilling a week but because he saw the shilling in the shape of a new world.[25] This, for the

---

[23] *Red Roses*, III, in C.P., III, p. 187.

[24] "The Narratives of Sean O'Casey" in *Sean O'Casey*, ed. Ronald Ayling (London, 1969), p. 220.

[25] *Red Roses*, IV, in *C.P.*, III, p. 225.

dramatist, is the true inheritance of the workers (whereas the feverish pursuit of gambling hopes and Boyle's "inheritance" are false talismans): a world in which there is freedom from financial anxiety, and increased leisure in which the finer things of life may be experienced and enjoyed.

At the same time, in the play's sub-plot, there is a parody of the money theme in the over-anxious possessiveness of Brennan o' the Moor regarding his store of money in the vaults of the Bank of Ireland. His persistent enquiries as to the safety of the Bank realize in a comic way a subject which is treated seriously in other plays, where we clearly see how the single-minded pursuit of wealth obscures all other considerations and values for many people. The universality of the theme in O'Casey's drama, whether it be in the form of realism or fantasy, is brought out in his comment on *Cock-a-Doodle Dandy*:

> In spite of the fanciful nature of the play, almost all the incidents are factual—the priest that struck the blow, the rough fellows man-handling the young, gay girl, the bitter opposition to any sign of the strange ways of a man with a maid, the old, menacing fool, full of false piety, going round inflicting fear of evil things on all who listen to him; *and, above all, through the piety, through the fear, the never-ending quest for money.*[26]

However, it is not only acquisitive greed, as in the case of Brennan in *Red Roses* or Michael Marthraun in *Cock'a'Doodle Dandy* or Councillor Reiligan in *The Bishop's Bonfire*, which causes men to put their selfish desires before the needs of others. O'Casey also stresses how harsh economic pressures force people into unnatural and inhuman attitudes. In *The Shadow* this leads to Mrs. Grigson's plaintive enquiries as to her husband's safety during the Black and Tan terrorist campaign. Although the incident occurs at a serious moment in the play, her lament is richly comic:

Mrs. Grigson: Mr. Shields.
Shields: Yes?
Mrs. Grigson: Do the insurance companies pay if a man is shot after curfew?
Shields: Well, now, that's a thing I couldn't say, Mrs. Grigson.
Mrs. Grigson: Isn't he a terrible man to be takin' such risks, an' not knowin' what'll happen to him. He knows them Societies only want an excuse to do people out of their money.[27]

In this case the result of the anxiety over money is, as with Brennan's worries, pure comedy, for no harm befalls Grigson or his wife in the course of the action. But a similar situation in *The Silver Tassie* is presented as a terrible debasement of human and family values. In that

---

[26] *Blasts and Benedictions*, ed. Ronald Ayling (London, 1967), p. 145 (my italics).

[27] *The Shadow*, II, in *C.P.*, I, pp. 136-137.

play, the action of which takes place during the First World War, Mrs. Heegan shows a concern for the safety and welfare of her soldier-son similar in kind to Mrs. Grigson's for her husband. Because she draws maintenance from army authorities while he is on active service, Mrs. Heegan is anxious to pack him off to the trenches for fear that he might over-stay his leave and she lose her allowance. Later, after he has been severely crippled in action, she seems more anxious about the continuance of his disability pension than about his mental and physical sufferings. Here the dramatist depicts in an extreme form the corrupting and dehumanizing power of poverty and of economic pressures arising from it. It is not that Mrs. Heegan has no love for her son —clearly, she has—but that she has had to fight and scheme to eke out an existence for her family for so long that feelings of pity and human sympathy have, finally, been subordinated to economic necessity: as a stage direction puts it, "her inner ear cannot hear even a faint echo of a younger day."[28] Similar experiences are realized in other O'Casey plays without the mother-figure losing so much of her natural compassion. In *The Harvest Festival*, for instance, Mrs. Rocliffe says:

> I wish to God this strike was over; I'm never easy in me mind, the way Jack [her son] does be talkin' about things. He has such a terrible temper, though he was always very gentle with me, an' if he got into any trouble, I suppose they'd take the old-age pension off me; not that it ud be much loss, though we'd miss it now, with nothin' else comin' into the house.[29]

In concrete details, then, as in the broad sweep of theme (or, rather, variations on a theme) we see the pursuit of money and the morality of money as intense preoccupations in O'Casey's mind and art. Development and innovation mark each stage of the playwright's career from first to last, yet the continuity in certain significant themes and ideas is equally remarkable and as well sustained.

---

[28] *The Silver Tassie*, I, in *C.P.*, II, p. 7.

[29] *The Harvest Festival* (manuscript among O'Casey's papers), Act II. Mrs. Rocliffe's attitude here reminds one of Juno Boyle talking about the strike in which her daughter is engaged (*Juno*, Act I).

THE REALISM OF DENIS JOHNSTON

Veronica O'Reilly

The unpublished diaries of Denis Johnston contain an account of an interview with the captured Nazi, Hermann Goering, which ends in the rather surprising gesture of the interviewer's military salute to the condemned German. In this gesture, and in Johnston's explanation of it, is embodied the kernel of a philosophy which he has been developing throughout a half century spent variously as lawyer, playwright, actor, director, war correspondent and university professor:

> If he were the Devil himself, I would salute my Enemy—dead. It is the best tangible expression that I can think of to illustrate the principle embodied in the dictum—I have cast forth the knowledge of Good & Evil. This very peculiar statement does not mean that one does not fight Evil and destroy it whenever it can be destroyed. It does mean that when it is down and out, we can salute it as having been part of life—and something that one has not surrendered to oneself. . . . Life itself is Evil as well as Good. We are all Evil in various ways. I am glad that I did not end that war as a neutral and would like to think that in a small way I helped to contribute something to the end of Goering. Nevertheless, I am also glad to have been, probably, the last person to salute Goering, and that he paid me the compliment of returning my tiny gesture on his way to his fate.[1]

A peculiarly Blakean realm "where Contrarieties are equally true" has been attained by Johnston as a result of a lengthy search for answers to the apparent contradictions in existence. Conventionally reared as a Presbyterian, he was for many years puzzled by religion's failure to give him "an answer to the paradox of Good and Evil—the existence of pain and misery in a world which I want to believe is fundamentally good,

---

[1] One of the diaries entitled "Brit," p. 167.

the inevitability of violence and struggle as part of the fabric of life itself, while religion preached peace."[2] The quandary is hardly unique, but Johnston's "answer," a rejection of the basic Christian myth of Sin and Redemption which necessitates a "demonic" Deity, is founded on an original view of the universe's dimensional character and of God as the deliberate but benignly reasonable creator of Evil. The most accessible locus of his quest and discoveries is Johnston's autobiographical writing, *Nine Rivers from Jordan*,[3] and *The Brazen Horn*,[4] but much of the catechetic also informs his dramatic work.

This cerebral aspect of his plays has limited their popularity in what Robert Hogan calls "a public and, therefore, preeminently naive"[5] medium, and Johnston is the first to state that he has never been a successful dramatist in the sense of the Long Run.[6] But the constant struggle to find a form which will express his vision reflects the serious hope that theatre audiences will one day understand what he is trying to say and acknowledge its importance. Ironically, Johnston's brilliant reputation as the "white hope of Irish theatre" was based on two plays which he now considers "adolescent question marks,"[7] and the works of his maturity are taken as the evidence of unfulfilled promise. A brief survey of an early and a late play, both situate in the ambience of Irish history and both deflating that history's myths, reveals Johnston's continuing efforts to portray dramatically what he feels are matters "of considerable importance."[8] His second play, *The Moon in the Yellow River*[9] (1931), explores the problem "of the friends we have to kill, and the enemies we are forced to admire"[10] against a backdrop of the civil strife which haunted Ireland's newly won independence. Twenty-seven years later *The Scythe and the Sunset*[11] (1958) treats with ironic realism the Easter Rising of 1916, neither endorsing O'Casey's anti-war comment nor debunking what was "a

---

[2] From an unpublished "sermon" delivered at Mount Holyoke and now in Denis Johnston's files, quoted here with the author's permission.

[3] (London, 1953).

[4] (Dublin, 1976).

[5] *After the Irish Renaissance* (Minneapolis, 1967), p. 134.

[6] "Introduction" to *The Golden Cuckoo and Other Plays* by Denis Johnston (London, 1940), p. 6.

[7] "Brit," p. 33.

[8] "Introduction," p. 9.

[9] *Collected Plays* (London, 1960), II.

[10] "Introduction" to *The Cuckoo*, p. 9.

[11] *Collected Plays* (London, 1960), I.

humane and well-intentioned piece of gallantry,"[12] but showing the effect of violence on ordinary people and the confusion of their motives.

The earlier play has discernible Shavian and Chekovian brush strokes in its portrait of a people and a country at a particular historical moment. Ireland in the late twenties could not accurately be described as *fin de siècle*, but the lingering ambiguities of Civil War had created a national malaise which was difficult to face "without a certain feeling of depression."[13] Apparently trivial conversation and hilarious comedy resonate throughout *The Moon in the Yellow River* in an atmosphere tinged with tragedy, and incidents and settings are invested with a symbolic significance. The protracted labour heralding the arrival of the Irish Free State is reflected in the offstage travail of a Mrs. Mulpeter, and is both helped and hindered by the nation's ignorant, superstitious and well-intentioned midwifery. The shape of *The Moon* is the shape of Irish experience as Johnston saw it, and one of the play's greatest strengths lies in the manner in which it derives from the zany peculiarities of a particular situation a texture of common humanity and its concerns. Many themes of Johnston's writing are contained, at least embryonically, in this play and he focusses them around a central trio of characters and a purported act of violence. A well-meaning and cultivated German engineer has come to Ireland with his gospel of progress incarnated in a Power House that is part of the Free State's economic program. Darrell Blake, a well-educated, charming and reactionary idealist, plans to blow up this Power House which threatens his idea of a pastoral Ireland. The encounter between the two takes place in the home of Dobelle, a retired engineer whose cynical disillusionment with life has led him into a nihilistic isolation and cold disdain for his young daughter, Blanaid. When, in the second act, Blake is killed by his former comrade, Lanigan, whose gun is now at the service of the Free State and progress, Herr Tausch refuses to believe that Lanigan's cause and his own are one. In the Preface to this play Johnston had commented on similar happenings in the Free State and remarked that "it is hard to see what other answer could have been made to a continuance of underground warfare, provided of course that we were to have any government at all."[14] *The Moon*, to its credit, does not attempt to answer this problem, but in the person of Dobelle Johnston begins to develop a vision of life which allows an individual to

---

[12] "Up the Rebels!" Preface to *The Scythe and the Sunset* in *Collected Plays*, I, p. 10.

[13] "Let There be Light," Preface to *The Moon in the Yellow River* in *Collected Plays*, II, p. 4.

[14] Ibid.

cope in the face of seemingly inescapable evil. A man who, at the price
of love and hope, has attained insights into the absurdities of life in
general and Irish life in particular, Dobelle is a sort of *raisonneur* who
recognizes the absurdity of his own cynicism in the end. The recognition, barely glimpsed in this play, suggests a vision of life in which Good
and Evil may be accommodated without the loss of compassion and
hope. That vision, expressed only darkly by Dobelle in this play, will be
made more explicit and its ethical implications suggested by 1958 when
The Scythe and the Sunset was first produced.

This late play, although it deals with an event prior to the Civil War,
emerged during the period of Johnston's autobiographical writing[15]
and can be easily glossed by both *Nine Rivers* and *The Brazen Horn*.
Neither a pacifist nor a romantic nationalist, Johnston has, by mid-
century, concluded that "as War appears to be inevitable in this life, it is
more important to keep it the good thing that it is, than to win or lose
it."[16] Within the context of the Rising *The Scythe and the Sunset*
demonstrates his belief that "outside the theatre men do not act from
logical motives as often as they act under the promptings of . . . this
thing that the Orientals call 'face.'"[17] In illustration of his point Johnston gathers in a sleazy cafe on O'Connell Street, Easter Monday, 1916,
exponents of the rebel forces, the "oppressors" and an essentially
disinterested Dublin public. Three rebel leaders, Tetley, Williams and
O'Callaghan, bear more than a casual resemblance to Pearse, Connolly
and Plunkett, and their forces are bolstered by a fanatic Emer Nic
Gabhann of Markievicz stature and a tram conductor/Volunteer,
Michael Maginnis, who may owe something to O'Casey by way of
parody. The imperial view is represented in two officers: Palliser, an
Anglo-Irishman wounded in the first assault on the Post Office, and
Clattering, a rather ridiculous and exasperating Englishman. Three
persons are unconnected with the fighting: Roisin, a waitress in the
cafe and Maginnis's girlfriend, Myles MacCarthy, a Dublin doctor and
psychiatrist, and Endymion, a verse-speaking lunatic with the pre-
science of a Shakespearean Fool. Not a great deal happens in the Pillar
Cafe during the course of the week, but its position as a dressing station
opposite the General Post Office makes it a logical resort for all the
characters. The time span of the play, from Monday forenoon until
Friday evening, allows an audience to become party to the doubts,
disagreements and organizational confusion behind the offstage progress of the Rising. The stance is anti-heroic, a stance central to his belief

---

[15] An interview with *The Irish Times*, 4 July 1951, reveals that the play is being written
at this time.

[16] *Nine Rivers from Jordan*, p. 119.

[17] "Up the Rebels!" p. 11.

that facts are usually very different from official reports, a situation which Johnston finds comic rather than distressing.[18] Through his portrayal, under stress, of brave men who are "always exciting to write about, particularly when they are afflicted with doubts, and deficient in technical training,"[19] Johnston suggests alternative views of violence, death, sex and individual behaviour in the face of seeming inevitability. The effect on an individual of cheerfully accepting Evil in life, without succumbing to it and thereby contributing to its spread, is presented variously through MacCarthy and Palliser, while Tetley's choice, although sympathetically treated, suggests a less desirable alternative. The playwright's decision in March, 1976, to alter the ending of the printed version was made as an attempt to underline further the disparity of outlook between Tetley and Palliser.[20]

A close examination of these three-act "realistic" plays reveals that they are meticulously carpentered to evoke a constantly deepening and altering response from an audience. Johnston's sets become more obviously symbols of the reality he is trying to portray; his characters, described in Shavian detail, flesh out the portrayal, their complexity adduced by dense and ambiguous image patterning and allusions to mythology, history and literature which constantly suggest further levels of meaning. An ironic and often funny juxtaposition of events consistently deflates persons and speeches which might otherwise assume a certain grandeur. The inclusion of short stories or anecdotes which at first seem totally irrelevant except for their fine theatrical impact eventually prove to have subtly reinforced a thematic or emotional point which Johnston is making.

I

The sets for *The Moon in the Yellow River* are carefully detailed to become part of the fabric of Irish life in the late twenties. One set serves the first and third acts and in its untidiness and ill-assorted fittings suggests an uncomfortable accommodation of the present to an all-pervading past. Once the officers' quarters of the fort covering the river mouth, this house has been transformed by Dobelle into a "fairly comfortable, if out-of-the-way residence." That this "heartbreak house" is Ireland becomes increasingly apparent throughout the play as seemingly casual remarks accrete: "Everybody welcome . . . in this house," one character remarks, only to be contradicted later by a hostile remark with a Yeatsian echo: "Sometimes there are too many

---

[18] *Nine Rivers*, p. 111.

[19] "Up the Rebels!" p. 11.

[20] Johnston made the revision while directing *The Scythe* for the Graduate Centre for Study of Drama at Hart House, Toronto, in March, 1976.

strangers in this house." Dobelle refers to it as a "[d]euced unmannerly house," and near the end of the play it is remarked that "Nothing is safe in this house." An extensive library of classical and modern literature is indiscriminately mixed with technical works, suggestive of the complexity as well as the clash of values in the play. The impression is reinforced by direct or indirect allusions in the dialogue to Keats, Browning, Pound, Yeats, Shaw, Schiller, Nietzsche, Shelley, Goethe, Dante, Shakespeare and Aquinas in company with references to Hannibal, Cato, Nero, Horace, the four Evangelists and figures from classical mythology. A toy railway stands in the Dobelle livingroom among the untidy cupboards and sea-stained furniture. Its construction by Dobelle, or at least his preoccupation with it, indicates his remove from what others may consider the "real" world. Redolent of both past and present strife are accoutrements of military life in the set itself, including a cannon port visible across a courtyard. This evidence of violence is more marked in the second set which is the interior of an old armory next door to Dobelle's living room. Presently a store for the Coast Life Saving Service, it is decorated with the Royal Arms, nautical data and gear and a picture of a full-rigged ship. Furnishings are limited to an old piano, a cluttered workbench on which stand four polished four-inch projectiles, a large kitchen clock and what appears to be the muzzle of a gun. The effect is one of violence cheek-by-jowl with lifesaving apparatus. In this room, where preparations are made to save lives, a man is to be killed and a father will reject his daughter. Both sets embody, in their material contradictions, the central paradox of Irish existence as Johnston sees it and the ironical form he uses to convey that vision. The large gun, which finally does not work, is a paradigm of Irish ineptitude and illogicality; George, its creator, has spent eight years constructing it and its four shells so that the "people" can be "free and happy and at peace." Three of the four shells intended for use in destroying the Power House prove useless, but further ironies exist in the fact that the fourth accidentally explodes on a slag heap and demolishes the works.

The set for *The Scythe and the Sunset* remains the same throughout, except for the depredations wrought upon it by proximity to battle and its unwonted role as hospital and internment center. The general impression, which is "unappetizing, and should convey the ever-present smell of cabbage-water," is achieved by the dingy detail of cluttered counter, rickety chairs and soiled table cloths. As in *The Moon in the Yellow River*, a piano stands to one side, and a central pillar decorated with the flags of the "Allies" becomes increasingly significant. The cafe is most probably named from its position near Nelson's Pillar on O'Connell Street, the Pillar which epitomized British dominance in Ireland. The pillar inside, to which Palliser is handcuffed at one point, is stripped of its flags as the play progresses, and, in the final

moments, crashes in ruins. (History has made this symbolism even
more explicit in the removal of Nelson's Pillar and in the placing of
Oliver Sheppard's pillar-statue of Cuchulain in the Post Office.) An air
of "sordid Latin gaiety" is introduced by scenes from the Bay of Naples,
pictures of Bongo dogs, Bairnsfather cartoons, religious emblems and
a portrait of Victor Emmanuel. These somewhat exotic reminders of
the larger world outside Dublin are reinforced throughout the play by
verbal hints—the Nevsky Prospect, Germany, France, Singapore, Belgium, the Geneva and Hague conventions—which tend to alter the
perspective of the on-stage events.

II

"While we continue to live," maintains Johnston, "we each hope to
make ourselves into something we are not, and our lives are a continual
performance, intended to convince ourselves that we have succeeded."
Consequently, he creates characters whose "speech is as often used to
conceal thought as to express it," and this fact, as well as his tendency to
paint the world in technicolor rather than black and white, leads to
plays which "tend to rely upon an audience that does not object to being
left in some doubt as to what side it is on."[21] In *The Moon in the Yellow
River* and *The Scythe and the Sunset* none of the main characters elicits a
simple response, and in the earlier play, in particular, they move in an
ambience of ambivalence heightened by conflicting imagery: fire,
water, heaven, hell, darkness, light, birth and death. The cast, in its
entirety, provides a cross-section of those idiosyncrasies, convictions
and impulses which create the farcical and tragic Ireland of the late
Civil War period.

A servant class is represented by Agnes Reilly and her son, Willie,
who is one of "the boys" in Dobelle's IRA unit. The Ireland which
Johnston portrays in these two seems a far cry from the world of
Dobelle and Blake, and has earned, with some justice, the charge that
he harbors "a superior ascendency smile at the expense of the noble
native."[22] The mutual dependency of the two worlds becomes apparent when Dobelle complains of Agnes's monstrous ways but admits:
"You can't get rid of Agnes. She'd only come back under a different
name. Once you surrender to servants you have no right to live." Apart
from being the servant to whom the family must accommodate its
meals and conversation—a bitter comment upon prevailing tastes
—Mrs. Reilly is another portrait by Johnston of Mother Ireland, whose
"ample breasts and figure bear witness to an all-enveloping matriar-

---

[21] "Introduction" to *The Cuckoo*, p. 7.

[22] "Let There be Light," p. 3.

chy." Less scurrilous than the Flower Woman of *The Old Lady Says 'No!'* [23] (1929), this Cathleen ni Houlihan is terrifying in her fierce, bullying ignorance and outrageous superstition. Willie, a diffident warrior at best, is bullied and disgraced by his mother and his well-meaning stupidity is a constant handicap to and deflation of Blake's romantic idealism. Nonetheless Willie is necessary to Blake; without him there would be no troops to command and no audience to inflame with the blood-soaked rhetoric of the patriot game. At the end of the play Willie will be changed utterly into a serious and deadly gunman by Blake's peremptory murder. The other members of the Dobelle household are female; the engineer's sister, Columba, is an "angular, elderly lady," whose neuroticism, xenophobia and fanatic nationalism are suggestive of an aging adherent of the Cumann ne mBan. The daughter of the house, Blanaid, is a much neglected "incredibly thin, solemn, untidy little girl with short fair hair and bright intelligent eyes." In nearly everyone except her father Blanaid evokes warmth and generosity, the Dobelle family relationships being peculiarly sterile and tenuous at best.

Lanigan, the haunted Free State policeman with "pale saturnine face and sunken cheeks," and an oddly assorted pair of well-seasoned and weatherbeaten salts complete this Irish portrait. The former is a gunman who knows only that he is the court of last appeal in all movements and predictably effective. George and Potts, part of the Live Saving crew, have divided their spare time between the construction of the gun and alcoholic conviviality. The former, "an incurable romanticist" of good family, has returned penniless from a half-century of travel on land and sea without having shed an Irish peculiarity for mocking and misunderstanding "foreigners." Inept, feckless and, withal, generous and affectionate, George and his fat "old Cockney" friend contribute to the sense of illogicality and hilarity that pervades the play.

Dobelle, and Blake, who calls him "coz," share the same nervous sensitivity, witty intelligence and volatile charm. In an "inborn restlessness" of the older man, manifest in the apparent war between a fastidiously cruel mouth and "imaginative and sympathetic eyes," is a suggestion of Shaw's tortured Irishman. Dobelle's patriotism consists in a belief that his country, where people "believe in fairies but trade in pigs," can die for him if it so desires. Blake's romanticism insists that Ireland, in its resistance to industrial progress, remains "one small corner of the globe safe for the unfortunate human race," and he has devoted his considerable leisure, education and imagination to prevent its being turned "into a race of pimps and beggars." Johnston deftly catches the quicksilver wit and warmth of this man for whom it is

---

[23] *Collected Plays*, I.

progress just "to live more consciously and more receptively," and whose sacerdotal blessing of the liquor and graceful familiarity with the classics and Holy Writ are worthy of a politicized Buck Mulligan. In the dialectic with Tausch, Blake recognizes the refutes the German's patronizing notion of progress with rhetoric that is both stirring and convincing. However, his best lines are consistently punctuated and undercut by the inanities of the moronic Willie Reilly, Blake's "left-hand" man. And, despite his humor and generosity, the rebel leader is obviously a man fascinated by danger and intrigue and more than a little possessed by death. Insisting that there is "nothing cruel about her," Blake drunkenly toasts death "that makes the whole world kin." His words sound a bitter echo from *The Old Lady Says 'No!'*:

> Ah, the love of death, creeping like a mist at the heels of my countrymen! Death is the only art in which we own no masters.... Out into every quarter of the globe we go, seeking for a service in which to die: saving the world by dying for a good cause just as readily as we will damn it utterly by dying for a bad one.[24]

Thwarted by Irish ineptitude and the arrival of Lanigan in his attempts to blow up the Power House, a defiant and unrepentant Blake dies with a musical and literary swan song that is not without its qualifying ironies. Seconds before he is shot Blake sings at the piano of the Chinese poet, Li-Po, who died drunk trying "to embrace a Moon / In the Yellow River." The image, from Pound's "Epitaphs," captures Johnston's idea of the illusory patriot dream which has destroyed so many Irishmen. Blake dies as he is wryly reciting the final words of the notoriously dillettantish Nero: "What an artist perishes in me!" His death, the eclipse of "brains and inspiration," solves nothing, although for a time, at least, it appears that the Power House is safe.

The character of Tausch provides an excellent example of Johnston's "technicolor" portrait. A highly civilized and cultured engineer, passionately fond of his family and the music they share, Tausch is devoted to a theory of progress based on freedom achieved through power. Answering the "call of the west wind ... the call of romance," he has come to Ireland to transform that backward land "from the sordid trivialities of peasant life to something newer and better." Not content with providing the Irish with cheap electrical power, Tausch has also studied their language and culture in the praiseworthy belief that "when one goes to live in a strange land, one should try to acquaint oneself with the customs of the people." A series of episodes, calculated to enlighten him to the fact that there are certain customs in Ireland which "would be difficult to understand in München," fail of their purpose, although they provide satirical touch-

---

[24] Ibid., p. 35.

stones for many facets of Irish life. Politely impervious to the rude
truculence of Agnes, the hostility of Columba and the drunken mockery of George, Tausch is merely amused by Dobelle's imaginative
warning:

> ... here we have bogy men, fierce and terrible bogy men, who breathe
> fire from their nostrils and vanish in the smoke.... And we have vam-
> pires in shimmering black that feed on blood and bear bombs instead of
> brats. And enormous fat crows that will never rest until they have pecked
> out your eyes and left you blind and dumb with terror. ... And in the
> mists that creep down from the mountains you will meet monsters that
> glare back at you with your own face.

Unconvinced, Tausch continues to the end of the play convinced of the
worth of his work as greater "even than the life of a man." The thorny
question of progress at the cost of human life is not resolved in the play
and Johnston's use of ambiguous image patterns to delineate Tausch
emphasizes the complexity of the situation. Early on in the play there is
a linking of fire and infernal imagery with Tausch and his Power
House. The "wicked shall be burned with fire," a flippant Blake assures
him and describes the intended event: "Bang goes the gun, up go the
works to hell." Tausch is referred to as a "demon pantechnicon driver,"
one trying "to catch life in a blast furnace." Dobelle reads Dante's
Inferno minutes before the works are accidentally "blown to hell," and a
dismayed Tausch searches the "scorched sod" for the night shift who
are, in fact, "running like hell." At the same time Tausch's many
expletives are invariably addressed to the Almighty; Dobelle resigns
the stubborn German to "higher hands" and Tausch himself remarks
that they "are in the hands of One above." Dobelle tells him that it is
"not the destiny of a man like you to be buried in this accursed hole,"
and Blake, albeit ironically, says: "Tausch said 'Let there be light,' and
the evening and the morning were the first day."

Neither Tausch nor Blake wins finally in this play, a state of affairs
which leaves unanswered questions. The final comment belongs to
Dobelle, whose disillusionment and "satiric neurosis" is more than a
necessary astringent to Tausch's romantic optimism. His wife's death
in childbirth, as a result of some nursing nuns' decision not to abort the
child, soured Dobelle on life so that he has, like Job, retired to "his own
dunghill" in the belief that the world is well lost. He ignores Blanaid
except for elementary provision and an adamant refusal to have her
exposed to a religion in which

> Aquinas tells us that in order that the blisses of Paradise may be more
> delightful to them the blessed in Heaven will be expected to view the
> tortures of the damned and to rejoice.

Evil, Dobelle has decided, is his only Good and the two are irreconcilable: "It is always evil that has made life worthwhile, and always righteousness that has blasted it. And now I solemnly say that I believe in

wrong." To Tausch he says, "I will tell you . . . why we can never be friends. Because you are a servant of righteousness, whilst I have sworn allegiance to the other side." After the destruction of the Power House Dobelle becomes hysterical with laughter which turns quite suddenly to the tears of impotent desperation and an anguished cry of pleading to his dead wife: "*Ah, Bice—la dolce guida* . . . take away this cursed gift of laughter and give us tears instead." In the appearance of Blanaid, very like his wife in the near darkness, a recognition of his own inferno and his own role in remaining in it as accorded Dobelle. This moment of "grace," when it occurs to him that both evil and good have a role to play in life and may be the creation of the same God, is a second chance for Dobelle who, until now, has surrendered to anger and despair. Johnston writes elsewhere[25] of his belief that Evil will always be part of every person's life as the price of moving into the world of experience; but he also believes that we must not succumb to that Evil and blame God for its happening. Instead, when we get involved with Evil, we are to take our punishment, which from a just God will not be eternal, and then brush ourselves off and get on with the business of living. In Johnston's philosophy the moment of accepting God as the author of Evil as well as Good, and of absolving Him from the charge of unfairness and cruelty in His creation, is a moment of grace. Dobelle's groping toward this moment is caught in his closing words: "I suppose the Devil can do nothing for us until God gives him a chance. Or maybe it's because they are both the same person. . . . Darkness . . . death and darkness. Ah, can anything cure them? . . . I wonder." On this interrogative note the play closes as Agnes's entry signifies the safe delivery of Mrs. Mulpeter's baby and the sun rises on a silent morning. None of the questions raised in this play has been answered, but in Dobelle's glimpse of a world that need not deny compassion and hope there is a suggestion of individual redemption.

History is created out of character in Johnston's plays and in the first act of *The Scythe and the Sunset* several facts about the Easter Rising are seen to derive from attitudes and personalities of those gathered in the Pillar Cafe. Characterization is somewhat sparer than in *The Moon in the Yellow River*, the use of imagery and allusion to create effect is less obvious. Yeats and Moore are parodied outright and most of the heroic references, Cuchulain, Maeve, Ferdia, Granuaile, Tristram, Galahad, Don Quixote, are used with deliberate irony. Echoes of *King Lear* sound in the presence of Endymion but it is mainly in the discussion of William Blake that allusions are directly related to the attitudes present in the play. For the most part characters are created with an austere precision in order to establish constant and developing attitudes to-

---

[25] *The Brazen Horn*, p. 170.

wards the Rising, and it is only in the dialectic between Palliser and
Tetley that an audience has "some doubt as to what side it is on."

Roisin, an intrepid working class woman, expresses with deadly
Dublin mockery the "widespread contempt in which the 'Sinn Fein
Volunteers' were generally held prior to the Rising," but in the final act
this woman alters her opinion as she watches O'Callaghan die and
Mickser return triumphant from a battle against great odds. This shift
in her attitude adumbrates Irish sentiment generally, and will provide
Tetley with the encouragement he needs to surrender and be hanged.
"You saw," he explains, "how that shopgirl behaved over poor
O'Callaghan. What will she feel—what will the nation feel—when
fifteen or twenty of us have been treated to what will be called our 'just
deserts?' . . . This week can be turned from a disgrace to a triumph."
Motives for acting are a constant source of interest to Johnston and this
play reveals the unexpected. Roisin's sharp-tongued ridicule and
Emer's bitter taunting drive the confused Maginnis to join the fighting
as Emer's taunting will later drive Palliser to rig an enemy machine gun
and thereby alter the course of the Rising and of History. Williams has
brought the Citizen Army into the Rising in order to make a protest
against British capitalist imperialism, but he is not prepared to continue the fighting indefinitely at the cost of lives and property.
O'Callaghan, obviously ill with tuberculosis, fights excitedly and dies
happily in the knowledge that death is imminent anyway. The British
soldier, Clattering, is anxious to provide some justification for his
existence which will forestall demotion to a "Q Job" in Liverpool, and
proposes turning the Rising into a major military event. Maginnis's
triumph over fear and his apotheosis as a warrior in the last act
illustrates an aspect of Johnston's belief about Good and Evil: "One of
the things we can learn from War . . . brings home the meaning of the
creed of the fighting men—that War is not really such an evil thing at
all. How can it be evil if, in it, one lives more abundantly, and experiences a deeper sense of the meaning of life?"[26] In the character of Dr.
Myles MacCarthy, who is based on the real life doctor, Oliver Gogarty,
Johnston creates a *raisonneur* who most closely approximates an heroic
figure in the plays. MacCarthy is something of an intellectual clown,
much given to ironic witticisms and foolery at moments which others
consider most serious. In fact, he is a competent and compassionate
physician whose insights into and acceptance of life's vagaries allow
him to transcend the partisan aspects of the Rising and celebrate the
facts of life as they are. To Roisin he insists that she accept "the fact that
no primula can live that isn't planted in a reasonable amount of dirt."
Love, he tells her, "is a vegetable that must be planted in a bed pan, and
watered with a nice supply of disappointments." His desire to prevent

---

[26] *Nine Rivers*, p. 119.

unnecessary suffering is manifest in his agreement to act as "dove" between the warring forces and in his vigorous protests against violence in the hospital station. But it is he who turns the occasion of Maginnis's elated return from battle into a celebration with drink, dancing and poetry, and who laments the puritanical and inhibited nature of Ireland as a "land of saints and cemeteries." The Blakean proverbs of Hell might well be taken as an index to MacCarthy's philosophy of life, and in the play he wryly mourns the loss of "the goat's problems." The state of maturity in which one is no longer unduly concerned about justice and gratitude for oneself is wittily exemplified in MacCarthy's refusal to take himself or his safety seriously—despite much play-acting to the contrary.

The creation of Endymion, whose uncanny foreknowledge of the demise of the Empire parallels that of Palliser, is ingenious. Based on a real life character in Dublin,[27] this madman wears his cuffs upon his ankles so that "in a world that's upside down he walks upon his hands." His insight into the illogicalities of life, his knowledge that there are "more ways from Sackville Street than one," are part of the wise innocence that lies beyond the knowledge of Good and Evil.

Tetley, Johnston's gentlemanly Pearse, has urged the uprising, impelled by the fact that many of his compatriots are dying in Europe on the side of the Allies while he remains at home watching the daily attrition of Volunteers. "Face," if nothing else, demands that he act lest his generation "go down in history as being as craven as the last." During the long and disjointed second act, the shape of which mirrors the desultory and confused nature of the Rising throughout the week, Tetley is beset with doubts as failure seems inevitable and the desired effect on the Dublin public has not materialized. Confused, he is yet unwilling to surrender if he can make himself believe that Ireland and its people want him to fight for them. "There we were—in our hands, the first declaration of our independence for the past seven hundred years," he says, in obvious distress. "But there was no sign of understanding in those eyes. . . . Do I have to pretend to myself that I'm another Jesus Christ—that everyone's wrong except me?" in the face of changing public opinion, however, he eagerly grasps the opportunity for martyrdom, convinced that to do otherwise would be to repudiate the purpose of his life. History, of course, has vindicated Tetley's choice, canonizing Pearse and his companions as the saviors of Ireland and Johnston's portrayal is not without a considerable residue of sympathy for this scholarly rebel. In the course of the play Tetley grows rapidly in the Johnston brand of realism, and some of his statements are direct echoes of his creator: ". . . since I've always hated evil and

---

[27] Oliver St. John Gogarty, *As I Was Going Down Sackville Street* (New York, 1937), pp. 1-3.

wanted to fight it . . . I can't be a man of goodwill," he muses. On his way to death Tetley tells Palliser that "whether we win or lose is a matter that only God can decide. How we behave is something that depends on ourselves," a sentiment reflected in Johnston's own writing about war.[28]

Nonetheless, Johnston's play seriously questions Tetley's choice of martyrdom. In the first place, evidence exists within *The Scythe* that the death of Tettley and his companions will serve to initiate further bloodshed, as Blake's death in *The Moon in the Yellow River* foreshadowed that of Lanigan and Willie. At the end of the Rising Tetley tells a delighted Maginnis to report to a Staff Captain Collins, to stay out of internment and avoid being identified. He is laying the foundation here of the Flying Columns which will be a feature of the bloody troubles and Civil War. Through Palliser, Johnston calls Tetley's choice "suicide" which is a "second-rate ambition," and insists, "You don't give a damn about liberty. All you care about is a cause." Palliser's own choice, that of refusing to be a Crown witness at Tetley's court martial and a party to the ongoing violence, is a deliberate foil to Tetley's surrender to the role he feels is forced upon him. In the printed version of the play Palliser stays in the burning building to demonstrate his ability to refuse a vindictive role forced on him by "heaven," and to refuse it without promise of eschatological reward. Johnston has recently changed this ending so that Palliser leaves at the last moment "to go to ground in Greystones until it blows over," because the playwright now feels that Palliser's deliberate death weakens the case against Tetley's suicide and is not in keeping with the character.[29] The Anglo-Irish officer, a type for whom Johnston has expressed great admiration,[30] indicates by his predilection for the poetry of William Blake and his mature, professional attitude toward the Rising, that he, like MacCarthy, accepts the facts of life without rancor. Not without personal vanity, a cheerful cynicism, and a certain irascibility, Palliser is the person to whom Johnston would entrust his world, rather than those of the Company of Tetley.

The latter group belongs to a species whom Johnston feels is characterized by "an active dislike of self, and of self-preservation," which dislike takes "some very curious forms both socially and politically."[31] The earmarks of this particular "distemper" appear to Johnston as "an acute neurosis over Sex that is given voice by SS. Paul

---

[28] *Nine Rivers*, p. 140.

[29] Interview, March, 1976.

[30] *Nine Rivers*, pp. 130, 132.

[31] *The Brazen Horn*, p. 101.

and Augustine," and a "distinct aversion not merely to Evil (which would be understandable), but to certain of the ordinary facts of life." These persons cherish "in the secret places of the heart a deeply rooted, but usually unspoken resentment for what appears to be the unfairness and cruelty of life," and consequently, they become the real Enemy, "out of concert with man as a creature."[32] Throughout *The Scythe and the Sunset* MacCarthy and Palliser have condemned the sexual inhibitions of other characters, Palliser calling Tetley a "fool" for not reciprocating the love which Emer feels for him. The emphasis on the Christian framework of the rebel cause, while not as explicit as in O'Casey's play, nonetheless places it squarely in the context of the "distemper" which Johnston associates with that myth:

> Life itself is an irritating thing these days, if one's mind still works along the lines laid down by St. Paul. But there are other premises on which a more cheerful outlook can be based, and about which I, personally, am not the slightest confused.[33]

III

In suggesting these premises in *The Scythe and the Sunset* Johnston has incorporated many of the early dramatic techniques of *The Moon in the Yellow River*. Apparently trivial conversations resonate, often ironically, in the broader context of the play; a careful orchestration of dialogue, action and sound effects demands split-second timing and professional speaking voices; central symbols, a gun in both plays, are used to focus themes. The dialogue is often witty and sophisticated, although, except in the case of MacCarthy, less self-consciously so than in *The Moon*. Working class speech is pungent and poetic but carefully avoids the floridly sentimental. Music plays a large part in underlining moods and themes in *The Scythe*, and Ravel's "Le Jardin Fecrique" suggests the context for Pallider's exist line and Johnston's definitive comment: "Winter gives back the roses to the frost-filled earth." As a witty and judicious overview of an event often obscured by melodramatic bias, *The Scythe* deserves a better fate than "turning out to be . . . a play without a public."[34] As a work of Johnston's harvest time it embodies, in distilled irony and experienced stagecraft, his mature and moral vision.

---

[32] Ibid., pp. 169, 168.

[33] "Introduction" to *The Cuckoo*, p. 10.

[34] "Up the Rebels!" p. 4.

MYLES NA GOPALEEN

Denis Johnston

At our first meeting we heard a considerable amount of talk about
something that was never very clearly defined—namely, myth. So it
seems appropriate now, at our conference's after-dinner obituary, that
the focus of our thoughts should be a character who died at a lamenta-
bly early age, and more closely approximates to a myth than any other
Irish writer that I can think of, at the moment. Perhaps I should make
an exception of Isaac Bickerstaff who actually *was* a myth, in spite of a
quarter column in the *Dictionary of National Biography* and the im-
primatur of the *Yale Review*. Myles, on the other hand, was a member of
a younger generation many of whose members are still with us. Consequently he has not as yet been canonized, or given the reverential
treatment offered to the distinguished Old Buffs (forgive my Dub-
linism) discussed in the earlier part of our proceedings. Nor, as far as I
am aware, have any doctoral dissertations been written as yet upon his
works. Yet he is a man who shares with the Deity the distinction of
functioning in three Persons: firstly Myles na Gopaleen, the Little
Horse, guardian and friend of the Colleen Bawn; secondly, as Flann
O'Brien, not to be confused with our present popular Postmaster
General; and thirdly, under his own legitimate name of Brian
O'Nolan—no connection with Messrs. Brown and Nolan of Dawson
Street, but a native of Strabane in the Black North, the town that has
given us not only Myles but also that controversial ballad, "The Old
Orange Flute."
　　I have always been impressed, and indeed somewhat intimidated
by the output of University College, Dublin—the English Department
in particular—which, as we all know, is a hotbed of scarifying anecdote
and malicious intelligence carrying on the tradition of our city in a
manner worthy of the scintillating days of Gogarty, Seamus O'Sullivan,

George Moore, and Jimmy Montgomery. The only difference that I can see in the quality of the conversation lies in the fact that in the old days it usually took place at home. There was a time when every evening of the week had its special patron—Gogarty on Fridays, AE on Sundays, and so on. Nowadays they tend to meet in one or two pubs and usually on Fridays, when they are most likely to have any money. This movement away from domesticity I attribute to an increase in the number of impatient wives, and the total absence of skivvies.

Amongst the most notable successors of the Old Gang was a small group from Earlsfort Terrace and the "L and H," sometimes referred to as the Four Cyclists of the Apocrypha—Donagh MacDonagh, the two Nialls, Sheridan and Montgomery, and Brian O'Nolan. A close corporation! They tended to pool their resources and sometimes even each other's gags, and were all the more entertaining on that account. Soon after my first play was produced at the Gate, and a brother barrister—Lord Oxford and Blasket—was trying to get me prosecuted for some lines that he objected to—we took our Theatre seriously in those days—I was visited one evening in my Fitzwilliam Square attic by the two Nialls, then undergraduates and eager to ask me questions about my work to which I might be expected to give some fatuous, quotable answers. Fortunately I was inexperienced in the art of being interviewed at this stage, and was largely unintelligible, from which they wrongly assumed that I was being as smart as they were, and they went away. I was not so lucky in more recent years.

Donagh MacDonagh had quite a different technique, although just as characteristic of that Seventh City of Christendom:

> ... the Dublin of old Statues [he afterwards wrote]
> This arrogant City which stirs proudly and secretly
> In my blood.
>
> And the brewery tugs and the swans
> On the balustrated stream
> And the bare bones of a fanlight
> Over a hungry door.

As a poet, he was the best of the bunch in my opinion. But he had another trick that was all his own, until I started to imitate it myself. This was a practice of telling the truth in an insidious manner that made one assume that it was a lie—a double hazard, as an example of which I remember him assuring me one evening in the Pearl Bar that the Rising of 1916 had to take place at that particular time because Pearse was in trouble over his Income Tax—obviously a joke that nobody would be expected to take seriously. But go now on any Sunday afternoon to that shrine, "Dark Kilmainham Jail," now a Republican museum, and you will find displayed in one of the showcases the actual "Final Demand" addressed to Patrick Pearse in the week before the uprising. Here we have myth in reverse and the cartoon that turns out to be factual.

On the other hand, Myles—to give him his most recognizable name—amused himself in a different way. He was a very accomplished linguist, not only in Irish, but also in Latin, French and God-knows-what-else. He started early in his literary career with an extraordinary booklet in the native tongue entitled *An Beal Boc*, from which I wish I could quote. Here it is, with a cover by Sean O'Sullivan, showing on the cover a half-naked curragh man with a single fish, and two black seagulls hovering overhead. Within the outer boards is a phony map, apparently of Cork Harbour and environs—"Corca Dorca" is what he calls it—with all four arms of the compass pointing west. Dublin City, labelled "Bla Cliath," is somewhere out on Haulbowline Island together with "Sligo Jail" and "The Rape of Baltimore." Two sea markers, labelled "The Buoys of Wexford," are showing the way to a number of Atlantic liners filled with tourists, while the whole of the local population is on the move to Dublin. Other features of this map indicate: "The Sea-divided Gael," the "Pratie Hokers' Route," "G.B.S.," a surplus of "Money Order Offices," and several "deposits" of poteen and cows. The whole work is introduced by two unlikely looking Céildhe dancers in kilts, cloaks, medals and spectacles, while the edition is affectionately dedicated to the Editor of the *Irish Times*. What it is all about I do not know, but I almost started to learn the native tongue in order to find out. Indeed, when its publication was followed by *The Cruiskeen Lawn*, a bi-weekly column in the *Irish Times* entirely in Irish, there ensued before long a popular demand to have it daily and in English, in which form it flourished for years. Even today, long after the author's death, extracts are reappearing in the same newspaper under the title, "The Best of Myles." It may well be that this extraordinary fecundity was aided from time to time by other members of the quadrille, but the proprietor throughout was Myles. Selections have since been published in book form.

Amongst the recurring features of this antidote to bad news we find the Keats and Chapman pun. Cast in the form of a series of supposed anecdotes about these two literary figures, it started off with the lying assumption that Keats and Chapman were close personal friends—unseparated as they actually were by two hundred years. The first of these yarns concerned a painful sore throat from which one of Chapman's non-existent flock of pigeons was suffering. Keats was called in to cure this complaint if possible, and after poking around in the bird's gullet for some time, he took time off to write his celebrated poem, "On First Looking into Chapman's Homer." Needless to say, this paragraph inspired some reader of the newspaper to write a letter indignantly pointing out—as everybody ought to know—that Keats and Chapman were not contemporaries, and that the word "Homer" had been grossly misinterpreted. This of course was precisely what Myles was angling for. Indeed, it is not improbable that he wrote it himself. Anyhow, the opening gambit was followed over the years by a long series of Keats and Chapman stories covering the origin of many other well-known phrases such as "silent upon a pique in Darien" (a quarrel between the two friends while touring Central America), and "magic Casements opening on the foam" (a picture of Tom and his brother Roger opening bottles of Guinness in the Scotch House).

Another sequence centered around something called the WAAMA League—an amalgam of the Dublin Drama League and the newly-formed Writers, Artists and Musicians Association. Out of this melange, Myles constructed an agency that hired out suitably attired escorts to accompany the clients to theatres and concerts where they would raise the social and intellectual status of the employers by talking loudly in stalls and foyers about Beaudelaire, Jimmy Joyce, Osbert, W.B., and that inevitable Mallarmé—the higher the pitch the higher the fee. A devilish development of this industry included a corps of ventriloquists who, by throwing the voice, could make any selected enemy seem to say atrocious things in the public forum of a coffee bar. ("Personally I have always loved the Bus Árus.")

But most original of all was the synthetic personality with which Brian O'Nolan used to envelope himself as the writer of the column. It was the work of "the DA"—Sir Myles na Gopaleen of Santry Hall, the great gates of which, at one time surmounted by coats of arms, are still to be seen on the way to Dublin's airport. From these impressive surroundings reports would emerge giving accounts of the entertainment of distinguished visitors who, as a rule, were actually passing through Dublin, some to receive honorary degrees—from the list of which the name of Myles himself had again been omitted through rank carelessness in the office of Trinity College. Others were said to have come under some official pretext to discuss matters of world concern with Sir Myles, and this sometimes led to denials from the bemused visitor himself. He was sorry, but he had no knowledge of this person, and had not said anything of the sort. Others included Marshal Tito, who of course was never near Dublin in his life, but was hinted to have come to still the objections of the Hierarchy to a soccer match against a Jugoslav team. After the correspondence which followed, the attendance at the game turned out to be much greater than had been expected. When the perennial subject of Dr. Jonathan Swift was in the news I would sometimes find myself referred to in *The Cruiskeen Lawn* as Stella's brother, presumably as an explanation of my interest in the matter. In this case nobody even bothered to phone in a correction, so Myles soon dropped the subject.

In parallel with all of this, there appeared from time to time a number of other characters such as "the Brother." This person had a way of discoursing at some length on the problems of Life, Liberty and Sex in the colorful verbiage of bus queues and bars for which Myles had a deep affection and a wide knowledge. Expressions such as "A lot of Bowsies," "Omadauns," "Wait-till-I-tell-ya" and "Them Gurriers" abounded in these monologues, and in this connection I seem to remember an unsightly object that had been erected in the middle of O'Connell Bridge by the Corporation in honor of some special occasion. Thanks to Myles it soon became known as "The Tomb of the Unknown Gurrier," and finished up in the river—not, of course, by Myles's hand. After all, he was for many years an Unknown Gurrier himself, on account of his multiple pseudonyms. Nobody knew who was writing these things except the boys in the Pearl.

He had a couple of plays produced during the war which did not greatly enhance his reputation, although I always felt that his adaptation of Capek's *Insect Play* was among the best of its kind. But he never really liked writing for the stage, which was too unflexible a medium for one of his mercurial mind. It is on his novels that his real claim to fame must be based outside his native land. But even these experienced a long wait, until *At Swim-Two-Birds* caught the eye of the critics after about twenty-one years and a World War. This, his first novel, was originally published in 1939 under the second of his pseudonyms —Flann O'Brien. It received very little attention until reissued by Longmans, Green, in 1960, after which it sprang in very short time into a fourth edition, and was described by Graham Greene as "the literary debut of the century." As is the usual practice with any new piece of fiction that is at all out of the ordinary in its structure, it was immediately classified by second-line critics as coming from the school of Joyce and Beckett. This is nonsense in my opinion. In the first place Myles belongs on the opposite side of the very significant generation gap that separates him from the "transition" crowd, and he is not writing *about* his homeland, but *in* it. He is neither an *Emigré* nor a nostalgic Yearner for other days. It is true that in his devotion to parody he is at one with most of his Irish predecessors, but his technique and structure are his own inventions.

This first book is about the writing of a book, and consequently it has multiple levels. What is more, it has three beginnings—like the *Book of Genesis*—and it incorporates in the text a number of explanatory comments on itself that would usually be found in footnotes. For example:

> He put the point of his fork into the interior of his mouth and withdrew it again, chewing in a coarse manner.
> *Quality of rasher in use in household:* Inferior, one and two the pound.

It also incorporates passages of parody that include various supposed translations from the Irish:

> Three fifties of fosterlings could engage with handball against the wideness of his backside, which was wide enough to halt the march of warriors through a mountain-pass.

> I am a bark for buffeting, said Finn,
> I am a hound for thornypaws . . .
> I am a windmill.
> I am a hole in a wall.

Shades of Cuchulain, of Frank O'Connor and Alfred Nutt! Elsewhere we find echoes of the Law Reports, and even a superb use of a definition taken from the *Oxford Dictionary*:

> Kiss, n. Caress given with lips; (Billiards) impact between moving balls; kind of sugar plum.

Then we have a couple of original ballads that have since passed into the repertoires:

> When money's tight and is hard to get
> And your horse has also ran,
> When all you have is a heap of debt—
> A PINT OF PLAIN IS YOUR ONLY MAN.

And with it, its Marxist twin:

> THE GIFT OF GOD IS A WORKIN' MAN.

On page 85 the narrative stops for a couple of pages and we are treated to:

> *Synopsis, being a summary of what has gone before,*
> FOR THE BENEFIT OF NEW READERS . . .

and very useful too, for our poor tired minds satiated beyond recovery with the *Tain*, with "Bee Loud Glades," with Finn MacCool and Lugaid MacNoisy, with Maud Gonnorhea and the Pooka Fergus MacPhellimey, and need I add further that there are two conclusions —Penultimate and Ultimate—the Purgatorial and the Just Plain Hellish.

Most of Myles's work is highly critical of the current Irish scene, including the Dail, the Department of Local Government (in which O'Nolan was himself employed), and even of the newspaper that provided the crust of his daily bread. Indeed, in his feature there would appear from time to time a picture of a sinister hand pointing accusingly at the neighboring column in which was appearing his Editor's leading article. Significantly enough, these practices went down better with his Editor than with his superiors in the Government service. However, we may now pass on from this fabulous book, with Dylan Thomas's celebrated comment ringing in our ears: ". . . just the book to give your sister if she's a loud, dirty, boozy girl."

His second novel, *The Hard Life: An Exegesis of Squalor* (1961), was dedicated to Graham Greene, and after a preliminary warning that none of the characters is fictitious even in part, it opens with a text from Pascal to the effect that all the troubles in the world can be traced to the fact that nobody knows how to stay quietly alone in his bedroom. It is

more restrained in its impact than *At Swim-Two-Birds*, and is, on the whole, the least off-beat of Flann O'Brien's works. Much more striking is his third novel published in 1964 and entitled *The Dalkey Archive*, and dedicated this time to his Guardian Angel with a solemn appeal "to see to it that there is no misunderstanding when I go home." Dalkey, a seaside suburb of Dublin—this "vestibule of heavenly conspection" as he terms it—seems to inspire O'Brien to some of the rare moments of coloratura in his prose:

> The road itself curves gently upward and over a low wall to the left by the footpath enchantment is spread—rocky grassland falling fast away to reach a toy-like railway far below, with beyond it the immeasurable immanent sea, quietly moving slowly in the immense expanse of Killiney Bay. High in the sky which joins it at a seam far from precise, a caravan of light cloud labours silently to the east.

It might also be added that this one-time Borough that gives its name to the book had, until recently, one of those rare things—a restaurant that closes for lunch.

The recurrent theme in the novel is concerned with the elusive nature of time, while the plot propounds a theory that James Joyce did not die, as is supposed, in Switzerland, but is living today under an assumed name in this suburb, where he is writing pamphlets for the Catholic Truth Society in expiation for the sins of *Ulysses*, and has totally forgotten all about *Finnegans Wake*.

But to my mind the most illuminating of all his works of fiction is the last—*The Third Policeman*—which oddly enough was not the last to be written, and which I distinctly remember being passed around in manuscript in the Pearl Bar while the war was far from over. Yet it was never snapped up and published until 1967, when the elusive author was dead. Why this should be so I cannot imagine, unless it is because in earlier days some publisher's delinquent reader could not bring himself to study the typescript, owing to the number of pages that consist of enormous footnotes. This, of course, is one of the best spoofs embodied in the book. It looks like a ponderous and unreadable thesis by an aspiring Ph.D., but it reads like a crazy Chinese Box, where each receptacle contains a smaller one. In the course of this hopeless quest for finality the multiple structure of Time and the Universe is illuminated by comments from the characters, such as:

> It's a quare contraption—very dangerous—a certain death-trap—Life.

What an Epitaph! Upon the truth of which only Myles na Gopaleen himself can pronounce, for he died before his book appeared in print, a loss to Irish Letters that occurred at almost the same time as the destruction of another familiar feature of Dublin life—Nelson's Pillar. We would have been better advised to spare our Pillar, and put Myles up there in place of the Onehandled Adulterer. And how his spirit would be laughting! Since he left us, Ireland has become less and less inclined to laugh at anything, which may well be something that our Myles anticipated. He wrote to Saroyan about this same unpublished work:

> It is supposed to be very funny but I don't know about that either . . . I think the idea of a man being dead all the time is pretty new. When you are writing about the world of the dead—and the damned—there is any amount of scope for back-chat and funny cracks.

So how can we be sure that he is any more dead than he alleges Joyce to be? I began by suggesting that this writer was—and is—a myth, and there's many a true word spoken by mistake. Maybe his departure is only one of his greatest hoaxes. After all, it is reported as having taken place on the first of April. Let us not forget that.

*   *   *   *   *

I must not conclude this brief trailer for Myles without mentioning a better summing-up of his background and intentions than I could ever aspire to from my occasional encounters with him. It is written by six of his personal friends, one of whom is his brother, Kevin. Another is one of the four Apocryphers, Niall Sheridan. A third was his Literary Editor on the *Irish Times*, and a fourth was his immediate superior in his Civil Service days—John Garvin, one of Dublin's most perceptive literary critics. The remaining two are J. C. C. Mays, a contemporary scholar, and John Montague, a poet.

This book was published almost contemporaneously with the conference at which these papers were delivered, but I did not see a copy until I had returned to Ireland. It is entitled *Myles: Portraits of Brian O'Nolan*, edited by Timothy O'Keeffe, and is published in London by Martin Brian and O'Keeffe.

IMAGINATIVE PROSE BY THE IRISH, 1820-1970

Kate O'Brien

I fear that what I have to offer in this essay is more in the character of a catalogue than any form of literary comment or criticism. And that is for a reason I could not escape from once I had accepted my need to reply, as fully as possible, to one casual remark made to me a few months ago, and which did truly astonish me.

It was at some luncheon or other in London that a sufficiently distinguished don of Oxbridge—a don of English literature at that —said to me, very politely: "Considering how expert, and indeed famous, you Irish are in words, in manifold use of the word, it is odd to observe how *little* literature you have produced up to now!" "Odd indeed, so to observe!" I thought. But that old knockout feather wasn't needed. I confess I was for a second or two flatly silenced. But then I took a breath, and I think, so far as I remember, that I hit any quiet vis-à-vis with all I could in a flash lay my wits to. I've no reason to believe that my amazed impromptu was at all effective, but at any rate he said no more about Irish writing, and we went our ways. But the exchange gave me to think. And here are some of my not very remarkable reflections.

To begin, in the declining 17th century we gave the English Restoration Theatre its brightest stars—Congreve, Farquhar—and to open the 18th we contributed—to all the world and forever—the terrifying Jonathan Swift, Bishop Berkeley, and later, Oliver Goldsmith. And as if they were not enough contribution to world literature from a very small and unhappy nation, as the century closed we threw in Sheridan and Edmund Burke.

I am concerned here only with the prose, the imaginative prose, that we Irish have written in English. There was, of course, Swift in the 18th century—and it is not necessary to point out that he was an

Irishman of the most troublesome kind, or that he wrote an English prose of perfection in his wild, satiric fictions—*The Battle of the Books, A Tale of a Tub, Gulliver's Travels.* And after him out of our poverty-stricken country came that gentle, curious individual, Oliver Goldsmith. I sometimes think that his exquisite *Vicar of Wakefield* may have had some kind of remote influence on Jane Austen. But that is neither here nor there. Neither of these two writers have anything to give to my present argument. Both, however hard-up or bitter they may have been—and indeed, they had much to suffer as writers —belonged to the ruling caste. They were Protestants; they were members of the class that gave them place in Grammar Schools, and admitted them to Trinity College, Dublin. They were men who were allowed education. So they could write, as educated men, in English, and were admissible to publication in English, and in England.

At the beginning of the 19th century it was impossible for any Irishman who belonged to the Catholic Church to receive education anywhere in his own country. The Penal Laws, which first came in as rule in Ireland under Henry the Eighth I think, were off and on, but always unpleasant, and became finally brutal under Cromwell. When the Confederation of Kilkenny failed, in the middle of the 17th century, then Ireland collapsed into being a kind of serf state. It is terrible what Cromwell did to Ireland. He burnt the country down into a condition of misery and fear. The last courageous attempts to hold on for culture and learning—where in beautiful abbeys and monasteries a few brave priests and monks had tried to hold on and stay with their people—all this was swept away by swords and by physical brutality. This is recorded history. And Cromwell and his men left Ireland empty of all its old and holy culture—and bound by his Penal Laws to a future of illiteracy.

Here I come at last to my theme.

We are an articulate race—and our gift is with words. We are unmanageably literate sometimes; and indeed it is one of the most remarkable ironies of recorded history that it should have been our race, of all in Europe, that was chained down so savagely, for over three hundred years, by those merciless Penal Laws that in fact destroyed for us the life of the word, words being what we are good at—as most students of literature, or ethnology, will concede. Said Cromwell smugly, after he had razed Drogheda and Wexford—Bible in hand, so to speak: "I meddle not with any man's conscience, but as for liberty to celebrate the Mass, I must tell you that where the Parliament of England has power, that will not be allowed." How can anyone talk aloud in such blazing contradictions? Well, when he spoke, it was wretchedly true that the Parliament of England did own Ireland, and was to do so for many bitter generations. And, as I have said, that was an end of education for the Irish race. So, we must jump to the 19th century; and to the arrival on its dark screen of a native son of Ireland, Daniel

O'Connell. No gentleman of the Protestant Ascendancy, no sprig of Trinity College or Dublin Castle, but ordinary Irish Roman Catholic gentleman of modest means and lands in Kerry, O'Connell was educated abroad, in his own church; and he became a distinguished lawyer. After the awful blows and disappointments of the Act of Union in 1800, after the disastrous rebellions of 1798 and of 1803, O'Connell, a constitutionalist and a born Parliamentarian, fought in the English House of Commons for the Emancipation of the Catholic Church in Ireland, for the end of the senseless Penal Laws, in fact. He fought that battle almost single-handed, you could say, and in winning it, oddly, he lost the support of many so-called liberal members of the upper classes in Ireland. But he carried the race itself with him—and gave it back its long-lost self-respect. From 1829 we were indeed, as Thomas Davis was to say later on, a nation once again. We could speak and write again, and hear and sing the Mass in Latin, and bring back the learned priests, and build convents. And we could print our own newspapers, and make a stab for founding our own university. Not that that was going to prove easy—but never mind—we were free to have a go for that great idea. It was a slow, long tidal wave of freedom that O'Connell allowed to curve back to a restlessly intelligent people. It seems to me that we have never been grateful enough to him. But then I am not what one understands by the word "patriotic." When I consider my dear country and its long and tragic history I prefer to praise what our poets and writers have done to honor us, and to work for us—such men of liberal and humane thought as Daniel O'Connell or Henry Grattan. I have been very much moved by what one must call "National" passion—I mean that the idea of being Irish rather than any other breed is important. Because to me it is not. But to be free, to be able to say what you mean—that is vital. And that is what O'Connell wrenched for us from our obstinate old conquerors. Well, no more historic snatches —let us talk now of what matters much more. Of literature, as it evolved, rushing out from this hitherto bound-up and illiterate Ireland of the early 19th century. I have just used the word "rush," but that is a mistake. Literature did not immediately in the 1830s flow out from the hitherto dammed-up Catholic people. No, indeed! Our first important writer from that period was a land-owning Protestant of the Ascendancy—and a woman—Maria Edgeworth.

But this woman, Maria Edgeworth, who is not now every literary person's cup of tea, was really very important to Ireland. She was not witty or sharp-edged like Jane Austen, nor was she passionate in the Bronte mode—and she was not so great a writer as any of these women. But, turning back now after many years of forgetfulness to *Castle Rackrent* and *The Absentee*, one feels at home at once with her certainty and her calm. She heard how we spoke, and she knew what we were talking about; us, the ordinary people of Ireland. She broke through, most amazingly at that time, from all the artificiality of novelists. She

came straight out with what she heard and what she knew of all the
shades and classes of people who were her daily acquaintance around
the County Longford. She set down what she observed, from the point
of view indeed of the lady and sub-grandee that she was, but not at all
with the condescension of later, and lesser, writers. Simply, she found
the life she knew worth steady record, and that is what she brought to
it—with, it must be remembered, her father's great help. He was a
really important "gray eminence" behind her—and she was wise
enough to know that.

We forget how widely Maria Edgeworth was admired, and even
pursued, by the celebrities of her day. One may think that she was
possibly a trifle too commonsensical for her own really great gifts.
More gaiety, a dash of recklessness, would have developed some of
those talents that lie too controlled in her work. She met all manner of
lively people, scientists and people of letters, disturbed and scattered
by the tag end of the French Revolution. She had, I think, some
proposals of marriage from diplomatists and European politicians. But
marriage was not her quarry. She was profoundly attached to her
father—and we do not have to get Freudian about that—because she
also loved very much her many brothers and sisters, and she felt always
that her thought and her duty lay with her own people, of all classes, in
Co. Longford. She was, as Norman Jeffares has said, "so near being a
very great writer that the discriminating will always read her." No
novelist could ask for a better tribute. But, myself, I also take account
for her of some lines of verse which she wrote in the last year of her
life—1849:

> Ireland, with all thy faults, thy follies too,
> I love thee still; still with a candid eye must view
> Thy wit too quick, still blundering into sense,
> Thy reckless humour, sad improvidence. . . .

We have not changed much from that impression, so gentle and so
shrewd.

We were lucky in her. Maria Edgeworth can be said to have
launched Irish writing in English after the breaking down of the Penal
Laws. And could we have had a more sane and honourable pilot? Sir
Walter Scott was a great friend and admirer of this, our first and
important women writer—and that admiration was significant and
would be worth pausing upon. More interesting was what Ivan
Turgenev said: "I do not think that I'd have written *The Sportsman's
Sketches* if I had not read *Castle Rackrent.*" Well, as *The Sportsman's
Sketches* was deeply influential on the Czar Alexander in his decision for
the freedom of the Russian serfs, that is a significant and proud link for
Irish letters with 19th-century Europe.

After Maria Edgeworth we were slow enough in getting really to
work. But the chief thing was that an enormously important point had
been gained—we were literate again, and open to education and self-

expression. And one can imagine that there was a reaction of puzzled relief, and a sense of "there's no hurry now—let's take a long breath," as indeed we were to do, and with great significance for world literature, at the turn of the century.

The middle of the last century did, however, throw up an immense amount of writing, for better for worse, in Ireland. We were free, if you like, to write and to go to school—but of course the long fight for nationhood, and even for the simple idea of Home Rule, was on, and only beginning. Also, although we were free now to go to Mass and to confess our sins, we had a Hierarchy to reckon with, a great body of bishops rightly more sure of its authority over us than England or Westminster could ever be. There were these two Establishments intending to own Ireland, let the Dan O'Connells, the Thomas Davises, and the various kinds of Young Irelanders, Fenians, Ribbonmen, etc., protest as they might. And, of course, protest they did—in successions of rebellions, pamphleteerings, and balladry and propaganda of every quick and fiery kind. The long struggle was on, for legal rights, for education, for self-government—and to get anywhere it was to take a difficult, uncertain century. And naturally, it yields fountains of literature. Most of this was hardly literature at all—though some of it was good fun, and in all it had a tumbling freshness, a kind of courage of release and sudden exclamation. After Maria Edgeworth the first name of any seriousness to emerge into Ireland's imaginative prose was William Carleton. He was a peasant of Tyrone, and it is difficult to know how he got his remarkable stories of Irish country life published in the eighteen-thirties; but he had had some "hedge-school" education, and even learnt Latin well, and something of mathematics. He did a curious thing in middle life, in that he left the Catholic Church of his birth and became, quite formally, a member of the Protestant Church of Ireland. He is much admired by some 20th-century critics—but for my part, I have never found him particularly readable.

The list of middling novelists working the Irish ground in the middle-19th century is long—and some of them perfectly readable. Gerald Griffin, a quiet man out of County Kerry, wrote a long, dramatic novel called *The Collegians*, which was to become famous as a play, *The Colleen Bawn*, and afterwards as an opera, *The Lily of Killarney*. A gentle, very long novel called *Knocknagow*, or *The Homes of Tipperary*, stays much more closely in memory, from one's reading of so long ago. Charles Kickham, who wrote it, died young of tuberculosis, and of general ill-health, from having suffered jail with Mitchel and the Young Irelanders in the uprising of '48. It is a book full of understanding and tenderness and, for all its longueurs it is nearly a masterpiece. I can remember scenes and impressions from it now, without having to search for the book—though it must be fifty years since I as a young girl first read it. Bessie Morris in her white jacket and the English Redcoat following her about the lanes—she really was, I think, a sort of Garbo of a character. And poor Matt Donovan, the great hurler, so sick with love for her; and good Norah Lahy, ready to die for love of Matt. Here we had the sort of novel that was yet to be written; but the young man, Kickham, not long out of jail, did not live to shape what he clearly could have done. He might have been a sort of Irish Turgenev, had he been spared, as they say!

There were Lever and Lover, of course, and Dion Boucicault, and all those rowdies, creators of Charles O'Malley and Handy Andy and the The Shaughraun—all these did much to establish the notorious "stage Irishman." Very successful these writers were, I gather, in their time, but I wonder who reads them now, or when they ceased to be read. I never could read them—not even the idiotic Handy Andy, although when I was a kid one liked a good laugh. But somehow these jokers did seem impossible.

However, as the century lengthened after the awful potato famine, and with the perpetual exodus on the Coffin Ships as sorrow and impatience spread and the Land War revealed the true desperateness of Ireland, as Parnell mounted his noble battle and Michael Davitt went to jail, as the Fenians were shipped to Botany Bay, our race began at last to express itself out of its own voice and its own varied passions, in English.

And what it was going to say—this rising Irish voice—was not, curiously enough, the jingle-jangle of nationalism, or of propaganda. Oh, that was needed, and it was there. We were not unmindful of the simple, clear shouting of Thomas Davis or of Speranza, and we know what Mangan meant when he sang of Dark Rosaleen. All of that was relevant, we knew—I imagine. And we can only hope that our own people, in those dark last decades of the 19th century, after the Famine, after the lonely Fenian risings of the '60s—during the terrible beginnings of the Land War—we must only hope that our people knew what our wildly impassioned young men were set upon, and that they were able to feel with the outpouring propaganda, the songs, the balladry. But, what was happening side-by-side with this desperate, patriotic outcry was something quite other, which on the long view was to be of more significance to Ireland—I say this even now somewhat timidly!—we were beginning to work out a literature which was to be our own, and which would come to be known, oddly and not very satisfactorily, as "Anglo-Irish Literature." This is not a good clue, a good title, for what the Irish have done in English writing in these hundred years, but I cannot think of any descriptive phrase which seems to me to be better.

We have made a literature, slowly and in some pain and confusion, which really is entirely ours, although we have used, and mastered a foreign language in which to make it. But you know, we got a great send-off. While we at home were in the woes of the Land War and, then, the disaster of Parnell, we had by chance sent off to England, to

seek their cheeky fortunes, two quite extraordinarily brilliant men
—Bernard Shaw and Oscar Wilde. Surely it is unique for any small,
poor country to produce at the drop of a hat, as it were, two such
representatives of what she can turn out in the line of wit and entertainment! I grant you, with some exasperation, that they were out of
the Protestant, ascendancy class—and Oscar Wilde had had a Trinity
education before going on to Oxford—but Bernard Shaw had had a
fairly mean upbringing, and neither of them, I think they'd agree with
me, was really out of the top drawer. So that really they can be taken as
fairly ordinary specimens of the Dublin society of their time. And one
certainly doesn't have to carry on about what is only too well known
—how these two men, both with strong Irish accents and idioms, simply
ravished not only London and London society with their brilliance.
The civilized world quickly rang with their fresh gaiety—for poor
Wilde while he lasted, and for Shaw to the end of his long life. I
remember when I was a young woman that I sat on a sofa at a grand
party and assented politely to the grave counsels that Mrs. Shaw was
handing out to me, while her still marvellous-looking husband—God
knows what age he was then, but he was certainly an old man—stood in
the middle of the room, surrounded by ladies of all ages who were in
convulsions of enjoyment while he vigorously lectured them all. I
remember how desperately I was bored by Mrs. Shaw, and how I
longed to be just on the outside ring of that crowd of happy ladies!

However, while Shaw and Wilde—and a little ahead of them
really, but we will return to him, George Moore—were blazing the Irish
trail around London, at home a serious, lonely kind of literature was
being excavated out of our lost traditions. We know what Standish
O'Grady did in digging up and re-presenting the epics of Finn Mac-
Cool and Cuchulain. I read many of those O'Grady reconstructions
when I was a schoolgirl, and I remember how I loved them, without
understanding at all what this erratic man was doing for our poetic
territory—what he was digging up for Yeats, for instance, and after
Yeats for Austin Clarke, and Mervyn Wall and, oh, so many others of
our poets.

Yeats—there he was, growing into a great poet, round Coole; and
there was Lady Gregory herself, whose work in this Anglo-Irish idiom
has never been as much appreciated as I always feel it should be. I think
she was a wittier and more odd interpreter of that society she found
around her house than were some of those whom she promoted with
such generosity. I have always had much respect for her neat and
lonely style.

So, there at the turn of the century the great Irish writing movement was established. The poets. Yeats, and his followers and his
school. AE, also, and Seamus O'Sullivan, and the *Dublin Magazine*
—and on from there. Excellent, and beautiful.

But meantime, a more difficult thing was happening in Irish writing. A boy of six had been brought by his father and handed over to the Jesuits at Clongowes Wood College. That seems improbable to me. I have known many men who have gone through the ordeal of Clongowes, but I have never known any of them being accepted there at the age of six. I have listened with amusement sometimes to this old Jesuit claim: "Give us your child before he is six, and then he is ours, and you can do what you like." But this has always amused me, because no child that I have ever known has gone into a Jesuit school before the age of eight or nine. But this little boy was in fact handed into Clongowes at the age of six—extraordinary!—and his name was James Joyce. He is the one who changed the whole direction of Irish writing. There is no need anywhere now in Europe to open the argument about James Joyce. With Proust he has dominated imaginative writing of the last fifty years. One does not have to claim to understand every word of Joyce, let alone to know exactly what he is saying all the time in *Finnegans Wake*. But one can claim to have entered rich moments of illumination all over all his writings. And he is a genius—only a fool would dispute that. Read *Ulysses*. Read the Hamlet conversation in the National Library. If we seek a proclamation of our literary eminence—and who would bother?—but surely forever we have it here. I must quote Stephen Dedalus, in his superb talk of Shakespeare: "What's in a name? That is what we ask ourselves in childhood when we write the name that we are told is ours. A star, a daystar, a firedrake rose at his birth. It shone by day in the heavens alone, brighter than Venus in the night, and by night is shone over delta in Cassiopeia, the recumbent constellation which is the signature of his initial among the stars. His eyes watched it, lowlying on the horizon, eastward of the bear, as he walked by the slumberous summer fields at midnight, returning from Shottery and from her arms."

I have said that Joyce changed the direction of Irish writing—and of course he did show all anxious young writers a way out, into saying what they desired to say. But now, considering the Irish follow-through, it seems to me that Joyce's influence has been strong and formative in Europe, but not markedly so in Irish letters. And that is curious—if I am right? We have had all kinds of schools of writers come up in the last fifty years or so—some excellent writers—but I would say now, speaking perhaps in a kind of random throw, that the Joyce influence, which is or has been everywhere in Europe, is not now very evident in Irish writing. It is as if there is a kind of revolt against this greatness. One can understand that—and it is part of the destiny of fame. But the paradox of his life—his flight into exile, silence and cunning, out of the deep shadows of which he re-created Dublin, and only Dublin, is paralleled, strangely enough, by the work of his great French contemporary, Marcel Proust. These two geniuses of the novel, inhabiting the same town and leading more-or-less similar kinds of expensive and exclusive lives, met, I believe only about once, and appear to have been no more than politely acceptant of each other's reputations—but their purposes in work, their ruthless industry, their passionate secretiveness and the narrow, deep scheme of each in his total design—in all of these originalities they parallel each other, and offer simultaneously to the world a new and special kind of morality of imagination. Perhaps not exactly new. Flaubert, for one, had had a like frantic and obsessional sense of duty to his own vision and purpose; but that these two together in the opening of the 20th century and side-by-side in the one town should be working almost maniacally on their guarded themes—the Irishman carrying his own small Dublin with him everywhere, night and day, and the Frenchman his equally small and minutely apprehended bits of France—it is interesting to consider how totally and arrogantly they were dissociated from all other men of letters in their time—how alike they were in that, in their profound self-confidence and their indifference to immediacy. They were, each from his own secret workshop—sanctuary—to dominate imaginative prose throughout the self-conscious world, without caring if they did or not—and by their wonderful indifference to contemporary opinion—an indifference more insolent and evident in Joyce than in Proust, but not any more real—they were to establish themselves, infuriatingly to some, as masters of their century. They can be decried now, as they are—and their eminence assaulted. But they never asked for adulation—certainly Joyce did not. And as their century draws towards darkness we must acknowledge that no one has arisen to challenge their stature.

Let me not be thought to belittle the great schools of Irish writing that may seem to have been overshadowed by the extraordinary phenomenon of Joyce. In say a hundred years we have produced a vast and really valuable body of imaginative literature in English—we, the Irish. Leaving our contribution to poetry right out of this address —and that is to say, brushing aside Yeats and his school, dismissing, that is, the very likely greatest poet, in any language, of the past hundred years—and that is something to brush aside, is it not, my friends?—leaving all poetry out of reckoning—we began very seriously to write great and influential prose about the turn of the century. Standish O'Grady, Augusta Gregory, George Moore—those are three names, for a start, that the history of literature has to reckon with. And minor people crowd in around them, gleaning with contributory talent. Such amusing witnesses to Irish life as, say, Somerville and Ross, shone about and made us laugh, perhaps unwillingly, when we were young. They wrote one truly good novel—alarming, in a way—*The Real Charlotte*. But though in certain moods one felt their short stories to be irresistible fun, I have never read them with complete peace of conscience. Because, gifted as those two ladies were, they remained amateurs—in that they wrote from too far outside their subjects. It is essential for a writer to be detached; but the well-tempered ear knows

the difference between the professional detachment of a Flaubert or a
Mary Lavin and the from-above amusement of the jokey, look-how-
clever-I-am writer of the Somerville and Ross mark. So, though those
two ladies cannot be ignored in our Irish canon, they do not ever from
me receive top marks—great fun though they are. And let it not be said
that we touchy Irish cannot take a joke against ourselves. We can—but
we like it to be a professional, well-made joke. We can take, my good-
ness, the savagery of Swift, the contempt of Joyce, the desolate queries
of Samuel Beckett—but our assailers have to be in that top class. I do
not think that we have ever found the Somerville and Ross laugh all
that fair, or true. But God knows those ladies had an ear for our rural
idioms.

At the turn of the century, when Lady Gregory was active, and
before what one may loosely define as the Easter Week school of
writers rose in Ireland, there were some very gifted prose writers.
Apart from Joyce, with his then startling *Dubliners*, there were such
nervously turned artists as Padraic Colum, and James Stephens, and
Gogarty. There was of course at that time, in his flower, George
Moore—a novelist of permanent importance—who has been under
some sort of cloud of critical disapprobation in recent years, I think
—but who could write like an angel in his day, and who will stay in our
canon, and our contribution to Europe.

We, a little provincial clutter, as might be thought by an outsider,
have always had the knack—in our religious history as well as in our
literary—of catching on to Europe—of by-passing our British conquerors in our thought, and reaching out to Spain and France. Italy,
too, but not so much. Italy has always been more the hunting ground of
the English rather than of us. We have sought more for our spirit in
France and Spain. Spain has helped us in our mad wars, and the
Armada fell to pieces off our coast. But before that, Cristobal Colon, on
his way to what he believed to be the empire of the East, called in to
Galway, and prayed for the success of his voyage in the old church of St.
Nicholas. Contemplating America now we can only concede that in
some sense that prayer was heard. We all remember Mangan's cry, in
his great song—"Spanish ale shall give us hope—my dark Rosaleen."

And now, before I leave you in peace, I have to speak of one great
Irishman, now living, now writing. I shall speak with diffidence, as who
would not, of Samuel Beckett. I have not listed out here, as I would like
to, the great number of really accomplished writers which Ireland has
thrown up in my lifetime—but, poets and novelists, they make a fine
array—better, I'd say, better in quality, than most other countries could
muster over the same period. To try to make a list is invidious—one is
sure to omit some excellent writer. Still, they march past—Frank
O'Connor, Sean O'Faolain, Peadar O'Donnell, Liam O'Flaherty, Mary
Lavin, Elizabeth Bowen, Benedict Kiely, John Broderick, John
McGahern, Tom McIntyre, Tom Kilroy, etc., etc. A great list of shining
and promising names.

But I conclude this plea for Ireland's place in the literature of the world by some observations about Samuel Beckett. Beckett has come out of bourgeois Ireland, out of the respectable Dublin suburb of Foxrock, to overwhelm the intellectual world with his meditative sorrow. He is indeed a man of sorrow, acquainted with grief. But he is not the total pessimist that some students of him, wearying perhaps of the question he leaves so sadly open to them, decide that he must be. He is not as easy as that at all. We all know the story of how when he was asked who Godot was he replied that did he know he would have said so in the play. I know that play, *Waiting For Godot*, like the back of my hand —and in fact the last time I saw it was a couple of years ago in Madrid, when I thought it was very well acted, but overplayed for farce. You can, of course, whip any of Beckett's themes of wretchedness right over into the intolerableness of farce—which is to escape from his terrible, unanswerable argument. Beckett is no simple cynic, nor is he what the man in the street means by an atheist, or an agnostic. He is, rather, a mystic, in despair. He stares in consternation at the unfathomable *"Moi."* *Qu'est-que Moi*, of Pascal, who is in a measure his twin, his other self. These two men are alike in being unable to endure the unanswerableness of that question of life, of its fore and aft, its elaborate blankness. All of Beckett's thought and work tramps and tramples round this desolate question—whence and whither—and who am I? Joyce was calmer and more indifferent before all that darkness—and his concern was with man in his flesh and his mortal foolishness. Death? Well, he could only leave it to Glasnevin and the rats. Life was his quarry —specific life in Dublin! And Beckett's question, his anguish, is not at all derived from the master—for whom he did indeed work, with Jolas and Stuart Gilbert and others, in his first days in Paris, but whose pupil, whose neophyte he never was. Beckett has always been his own lonely man—and that isolation, that dark perplexity we reach from every line of his work. Never, I suppose, has there been so lonely a writer—and indeed, hardly ever a nobler.

I come back to the remark that set me out on this discourse—that, for a literary race, we have given so little to literature. Heavens—I have not had time or breath to look at our poets, or our theatre—but when you think of them in merest haste, from Sheridan and Shaw and Wilde, through Synge and Lady Gregory and Yeats to O'Casey and to Brendan Behan—my Heavens, is that not a theatre? Is that not a great slice of the literature of our world?

I think that in letters we Irish do more than hold our own—I think we often grab over, in fact, and snatch a bit from other races. We are an only too lively lot—and for better and for worse I think we were born to write and to talk. No Penal Laws could in the end prevail.

THE LITERARY MYTHS OF THE REVIVAL: A CASE FOR THEIR ABANDONMENT

Seamus Deane

Perhaps the most seductive of all Yeats's historical fictions is that in which he gave dignity and coherence to the Irish Protestant Ascendancy tradition. This was, in itself, a considerable achievement on behalf of a group which Standish O'Grady described, in 1901, as " . . . rotting from the land in the most dismal farce-tragedy of all time, without one brave deed, without one brave word."[1] We tend, perhaps, to forget just how much retrospective glamor the Ascendancy has gained from the Yeatsian version of its achievement in literature. The literary tradition (if one may so hypostatize an elusive concept) in this century has absorbed this fiction as a vital and even unquestionable form of imaginative truth. As a consequence, we fail to see that the heroic impulse which produces the rather ambiguous transformations of the physical force tradition in politics (as in "Easter 1916" or in "The Statues") is the same as that which produces the intellectual chauvinism of that Yeatsian recitation of the great 18th-century names—Berkeley, Burke, Swift, Goldsmith and Sheridan.

Briefly, Yeats claims that the 18th-century Irish writers have in common a specifically anti-modernist outlook. Berkeley's refutation of Locke, Swift's attacks on the Royal Society and on the mercantile system, Goldsmith's lament for the old way of life destroyed by the agrarian revolution and, above all, Burke's great tirade against the French Revolution, were all, in his view, attempts to stem the "filthy

---

[1] Standish O'Grady, *Selected Essays and Passages* (Dublin, Cork and Belfast, n.d.), p. 180.

modern tide"[2] which empiricism, science and the growth of parliamentary mass democracy had swollen to an unprecedented height. It had been, of course, standard, at least since Blake and Coleridge, to blame Locke and/or Newton for the afflictions of modernism. This was as much a stock response on the part of literary men as was the attribution of Europe's problems to Voltaire and Rousseau on the part of political commentators. *"C'est la faute à Voltaire,/C'est la faute à Rousseau"* was a refrain adaptable to almost any persuasion. It is perhaps telling, in this connection, that Yeats did not include the vindictive and well-informed John Wilson Croker, a member of the Ascendancy, in his Anglo-Irish pantheon, even though Croker was perhaps the outstanding Government spokesman against the Revolution and indeed, against France in general.[3] His hostility to the new literature (especially towards Shelley) probably excluded him from consideration. But this merely reveals what an oddly construed Anglo-Irish tradition we have to deal with here. It is essentially a part of the Romantic polemic against the 18th century.

No one but Yeats, however, developed this polemic by choosing a group of writers profoundly steeped in the Augustan tradition, to defend and define this anti-Augustan stance. Indeed, he went further than this when he indicated that the shared anti-modernism of his 18th-century heroes was to be attributed to their Irishness. The Irishness is something which is partly genetic, partly environmental, but, to him, wholly obvious:

> Born in such a community, Berkeley with his belief in perception, that abstract ideas are mere words, Swift with his love of perfect nature, of the Houyhnhnms, his disbelief in Newton's system and every sort of machine, Goldsmith and his delight in the particulars of common life that shocked his contemporaries, Burke with his conviction that all States not grown slowly like a forest tree are tyrannies, found in England the opposite that stung their own thought into expression and made it lucid.[4]

The more one inspects this particular version of 18th-century intellectual and literary history, the more manifestly absurd it appears. But Yeats provides himself with the exit much favored by poets since the Romantic revival, especially those for whom the mythologizing of history exercised an irresistible attraction. Very simply, we are told not to take such myths *as* history; they are myths *of* history. In *A Vision* when speaking of his "circuits of sun and moon," Yeats asks that we

---

[2] The phrase is taken from Yeats's poem "The Statues."

[3] The standard biography on Croker is by Myron F. Brightfield, *John Wilson Croker* (London, 1940). See also Croker's *Essays on the Early Period of the French Revolution* (London, 1857); and L. J. Jennings (ed.), *The Correspondence and Diaries of the late Right Honourable John Wilson Croker*, 3 vols. (London, 1884). His many essays in the *Quarterly Review* have not been collected.

[4] *Essays and Introductions* (London, 1961), p. 402.

learn to regard them as "stylistic arrangements of experience."[5] On that level, it would clearly be foolish to deny the hermeneutic value which his circuits and his version of the Protestant Ascendancy must have had for him. But it should be very clearly recognized that these things have the same status in relation to history. They are metaphors which avail of widely dispersed materials in such a way as to give them a provisional coherence and thereby to make them ductile to their creator's demands. The technique involved is that of the metaphysical conceit; the ambition involved is Hegelian in its range and ambition.

What we meet with in this part of Yeats's writings does not, then, in any serious way constitute a reading of history, even though the first to be fooled into believing so was Yeats himself. When he told the Irish Senate that the Anglo-Irish were "no petty people" he was evidently not thinking of the John Wilson Croker type. He was translating into a proud assertion an almost comically absurd historical fiction. The trouble is that he has been believed. But the absurdity of the historical fiction does not necessarily render it futile. While we may have no very persuasive reading of history in this case, we do have a fascinating theory of history of the kind which we readily encounter in Romantic aesthetics. Whether it be in Coleridge or in Blake, in Carlyle or in William Morris, history is essentially engaged with the fortunes of the Imagination. It is scarcely remarkable, then, that it should therefore be almost indistinguishable from aesthetics. The various histories we have inherited from the *Prophetic Books* or the *Philosophical Lectures* or, indeed, from the essays of T. S. Eliot as well as Yeats, are at root theories of the imagination expressed in historical terms. Or, more simply, they are aesthetic theories rendered as stories. Yeats's Ascendancy is one of the more notable plot systems among these various narratives.

It would not be necessary to labor these distinctions were it not apparent that they are only partially understood or accepted. Insofar as Yeats speaks of the Gaelic and of the Republican traditions, we regard his commentary as very much enhanced by the softening glow of myth. In fact, it is now a common practice to think of such enhancement as dangerous and to exercise upon it that retrospective censorship which Conor Cruise O'Brien so monotonously advocates. But when Yeats speaks of the greasy philistinism of the Catholic bourgeoisie and of the intellectual fragrance of the aristocratic Protestant tradition, it is still common to find him taken literally as though he had in these instances abandoned myth for sociological analysis. This, of course, is very far from the case. The "abstruse research" upon which Yeats's mythological systems are founded is pervasive; we can only assume, as we see the various parts cohere one to the other, that

---

[5] *A Vision* (New York, 1961), p. 25.

"that which suits a part infects the whole."[6] His aristocratic pretensions
are literary, more Mallarméan than anything else. (This is just as well,
as there was little else to go on.) But his association of the two words
"aristocracy" and "Ascendancy" blurs an important distinction which
no worthwhile reading of the Anglo-Irish historical tradition can ignore.

The Protestant Ascendancy in Ireland is now and has for long
been a predominantly bourgeois social formation, a fact of which Yeats
would have been more aware had he known a little more about the
18th-century Ireland in which he discovered his Anglo-Irish tradition.
The Anglo-Irish were held in contempt by the Irish-speaking masses as
people of no blood, without lineage, and with nothing to recommend
them other than the success of their Hanoverian cause over that of the
Jacobites. One can gain a sense of this from the Gaelic poets of that
time. One of the most memorable poems in which the Gaelic pride in
ancestry is revealed is Aodagain O'Rahilly's *Cabhair ní ghoirfead*. The
last line runs:

> Na flaithe fá raibh mo shean roimh éag do Chríost
> (The princes my ancestors served before the death of Christ)[7]

The Protestant Ascendancy, in the eyes of the audience which would
have admired this poem and that sentiment, could never have been
confused with an aristocracy. By the 20th century, this was no longer
true. Since Yeats (but also perhaps since Parnell's death too), a literary
image has emerged which pre-empts most others. It is the image of the
hero surrounded by the mob, of Culture environed by Philistinism, of
civility swamped in barbarity, of a shell-thin civilization tossed upon the
sea of an unruly tenantry which seemed to have become more vulgarly
inclined towards Fianna Fail than towards Unity of Being and the
Abbey Theatre. It is a nice irony that Yeats's view of the rising Catholic
bourgeoisie should have been so similar to Aodagain O'Rahilly's view
of the Anglo-Irish.

Since the success story of the Catholic middle classes is not over
even yet in Ireland, it is not entirely surprising to find that the anti-
Bourgeois literary images and myths bequeathed by Yeats has had a
more extended life than, on the grounds of accuracy or perception,
they may be said to have deserved. The main point, though, is that they
can only be understood as myths, as versions of history converted into a
metaphor which has a bearing that is largely aesthetic and stylistic. The
rather unexpected consequence of all this has been the considerable
resurgence in fiction, rather than in poetry, of the kind of imagery and
of social and historical analysis which we associate with the Yeatsian

---

[6] Coleridge, "Dejection: An Ode."
[7] I am indebted to Dr. Liam de Paor of University College, Dublin, for drawing my
attention to this poem.

attitudes. Since Elizabeth Bowen's fine novel *The Last September* (1929) there have been numerous variations, some of them of virtuoso quality, on the image of the Big House of the Ascendancy surrounded by the Mean Spirit of the gombeen Irish. That image in itself gives a more than notional assent to the Yeatsian version of Irish literary history, an assent which the destruction of Anglo-Irish mansions in the Civil War and of Georgian buildings in general in the last twenty years by the speculative surges of our most recent form of capitalist development have combined to justify. Thus, in works as otherwise different as Aidan Higgins' *Langrishe Go Down* (1966), Thomas Kilroy's *The Big Chapel* (1971), John Banville's *Birchwood* (1973) and Jennifer Johnston's *How Many Miles to Babylon?* (1976), we find this basic image manifesting itself almost as an assumed basis upon which we can interpret either the novel itself or the novel's general attitude towards the culture to which it belongs. Besides, one also finds reflections of this tradition in English writers who "set" their fictions in Ireland. Two remarkable examples here would be Henry Green's *Loving* (1933) and J. G. Farrell's *Troubles* (1972).

This seems odd. The Big House novel, one would think, died in the 19th century or thereabouts, when the Big House, as an important political feature of the Irish landscape, also died. Clearly the repercussions of the Yeatsian myth can survive long after the conditions which initially helped to produce it have vanished. Yet a tradition which continues to interpret its culture in such exclusive terms is in serious danger of petrifaction. The more we look at what Yeats bequeathed to us in this regard in some of his greatest poems and in even more of his highly eccentric essays, the more we realize that his myth of history was an extremely adaptable and subtle figure of thought. This would surely be clear after a careful reading of "Nineteen Hundred and Nineteen" or of "Meditations in Time of Civil War." Nevertheless, the influence of Yeats has been a narrowing one even though his range is greater than that of any Irish writer. His poetry constitutes the real link between the Irish 19th-century novel and its 20th-century descendant. (This is not to ignore the Joyce, Flann O'Brien, Beckett experimental tradition; but that belongs to the cosmopolitan ambiance of modern fiction. Only in John Banville do we sense any effort to conjoin the imagery of the Irish novel as such with the wider questions about fiction, its nature and status, its methods and its philosophy which we associate with Borges, Nabokov, Barth and others.) The re-emergence of the Big House novel, with all its implicit assumptions, demonstrates the comparative poverty of the Irish novelistic tradition and the power of Yeats's presence even now. But the anachronism which bedevils so much Irish fiction of this kind surely relates to the fact that the Big House is more concerned with tourism and tax concessions, the preservation of the artifacts of "Culture," rather than with power or value. It has about as much pressure on contemporary Irish life as the Norman ruins of the

South-East. The extension of a myth into this kind of social literalism has finally led both to its vulgarization and to a failure in the fictional tradition itself. It is surely time to abandon such a myth and find intellectual allegiances elsewhere.

Yeats is not by any means the only example we have of how an author makes history palatable by imaging it forth as a version of the personality. Synge and Austin Clarke come to mind quite readily in this connection. Synge's West and Clarke's medieval, monastic Ireland are not so much historically accurate as they are imaginatively useful in yielding to us in each case a sense of the artist's enterprise in a world which, without these metaphorical suasions, would remain implacably hostile. The sweet-tongued vagrants of Synge's world are memorable Irish versions of the Baudelairian *poète maudit*—healthier and folksier no doubt, but estranged in a similar way. Equally, we can see that the randy clerics of Clarke's beehive-hut civilization are a symptom of that reconciliation between religion and sexuality (Clarke's most obsessive concerns) which 20th-century Ireland had, in his view, rendered impossible. These images do not operate as ideals, nor is there here any insinuation that they are to be deplored because they give social and historical fact such cavalier treatment. But it is surely remarkable that the treatment of history as metaphor by these writers enables each of them in his own particular way to mount an attack upon the small and squalid soul of the modern bourgeois by glamorizing either the Ascendancy, the peasantry or the medieval clergy. In other words, the desire to see Ireland as "a country of the imagination" led to a conclusion that was identical with its premise. That was, as we stated before, the old Romantic premise that the world could be seen falsely in a bleak Newtonian light or truly in a pre-Newtonian aura. The destruction of aura, the stifling of the quick of imaginative life, had led from modern science to the development of philosophies like dialectical materialism, which Yeats, in an astonishing and garbled paragraph, claims "works all the mischief Berkeley foretold."[8] The aesthetic heritage with which we still struggle clearly harbors the desire to obliterate or render nugatory the problems of class, economics, bureaucratic systems and the like, concentrating instead upon the essences of self, nationhood, community and Zeitgeist. If there is any politics to be associated with such an aesthetic, it is the politics of Fascism. It is again surprising that this clear implication should pass almost unnoticed in the body of contemporary Irish writing and in the scattered convictions which many writers still retain about the so-called autonomy of the imagination. The example of Austin Clarke, in his turn from a deliquescent aesthetic to the higher pungencies of satire and of self-discovery, is one that has been too long ignored, possibly because it was not for long

---

[8] *Essays and Introductions*, p. 401.

enough sustained. Clarke is, though, a startling example of the salutary effects which flow from the abandonment of unexamined and therefore misunderstood myths and systems. But of course the great demythologizer, the man who has most deeply influenced contemporary Irish poetry, was Patrick Kavanagh, who repudiated the very idea of the Irish Revival and with that, all its rhetoric of power, suasion and possession. Instead he sought to know the ordinary; and having done so, discovered that it was also the miraculous.

The simplicity of Kavanagh's poetry should not blind us to the fact that it has overcome the rather dreary problem of the relationship between the squalid world and its imaginative version. He frees himself from the shackles of this restrictive and unnecessary dualism by embedding one in the other, by refusing to make the distinction while remaining aware of the difference. Perhaps, though, it should also be noticed that Kavanagh, more than any other Irish poet of any note in this century, simply refuses to play games with history. "The year of the Munich bother" suffices for the Second World War. No images crane for world-historical heights; no traditions are invented to liberate the mind. Among such examples of intellectual promiscuity, Kavanagh was a chaste poet. He still is, because those who have come after him have not retained his purity of commitment to what he knew. Almost inevitably, since the 1950s or early '60s, poets have attempted to blend the fidelity to the ordinary which Kavanagh had taught with the eclectic mythologizing we find in Yeats. History keeps intruding. We historicize in order to poeticize, and Ireland, in consequence, begins to cease to be an actuality and begins increasingly to become a metaphor of the self. It is a strange and vicious circle.

Perhaps, though, it is Joyce's Stephen Dedalus who most clearly displays the dangers of that 19th-century aestheticism when it was inflated into a mythological system. Through Stephen, Joyce details for us the process and the drastic fulfillment of this self-enhancing treatment of history. We must be alert to the operation of the Joycean irony against Stephen if we are to understand the satiric edge which redeems much of the soft sympathy of A Portrait of the Artist from the excesses of sentimentality and which of course pervades Ulysses in so many structural and rhetorical guises. For the present purpose, it is sufficient to say that the kind of aesthetic tradition to which Yeats (and Synge and the young Austin Clarke) belong is parodied in Ulysses.

Stephen's almost endless capacity to mythologize experience is based upon a belief in the validity of that strict dualism between the world of fact and the world of myth which has already been mentioned. The radiant arena of art is created by the stress of the imagination operating in the dusty area of life. The conversion of one into the other defines the transubstantiating power of the imagination. The daily bread, which Stephen has to monotonously earn, is transmuted into the eternal host of art. The very strictness of this dualism (later to be repeated in Flann O'Brien and in Samuel Beckett with even greater exploitation of the comic potential implicit in such a schismatic vision) and the inevitable sense of total isolation which is either its prerequisite or its consequence are two features of Stephen's universe which we are persuaded, through the mediation of Bloom in particular, to repudiate.

If we take just one small segment of Stephen's system we should be able to see in it Joyce's marvellously precocious analysis of the kind of thinking which the heroic conception of literature necessarily involves. We learn almost immediately in *Ulysses* that Stephen wishes to disengage himself as much as possible from the Irish version of Catholicism into which he had been indoctrinated. He chooses to do so by associating himself at an early stage with heresiarchs and Gnostics like Arius, Valentine, Photius and Sabellius, all of whom had been guilty in one way or another of heresy against the doctrine of the Holy Trinity as that was expounded in the Nicene Creed. This doctrine deeply attracts Stephen, partly because of its applications to his own trinity of the artistic process (Author-Work-Inspiration), partly because through it he was able to release and give justification for his anti-maternal obsessions. Thus when he speaks of the Mariolatry of Irish Catholicism, of that image of the Madonna "which the cunning Italian intellect flung to the mob of Europe" we begin to see a very peculiar version of Church history being invented for the sake of liberating its creator from the difficulties of a personal crisis. For, by virtue of this reading of the development of Catholicism, Stephen brings in the image of the Holy Family as the plebeian vulgarization of the doctrine of the Trinity (which he understands in a semi-heretical manner anyway). Through that manoeuvre, he attempts to release himself from "the agenbite of inwit" which he suffers at the thought of his own dead mother, of Mother Ireland and of Mother Church, all of whom (along with "our great sweet mother" the sea) occur in the first few pages of the novel. Escape from the sentimental squalors of the culture into the impersonal heaven of art is Stephen's aim, although his trinitarian passion is comically enmeshed in the mock Holy Family situation in which he plays his Christ the Son role between Leopold-Joseph and Molly-Mary. There are many other complications attendant upon this particular aspect of Stephen's thought, but this brief excursion into some of them should serve the present purpose.[9]

That purpose is to demonstrate the fact that Joyce shows us in Stephen the figure of the Wildean artist; and that it is this figure, armed with a more ponderous aesthetic than Wilde would ever have deemed it necessary to imagine, which is incarnated in Yeats and

---

[9] The quotations in this paragraph are from *Ulysses* (London, 1960), pp. 266 and 3 respectively. I have discussed this issue at greater length in "The Joycean Triumph: *Ulysses*, Fifty Years After," *Encounter*, 39, No. 5 (November 1972), 42-52.

through him becomes the type of the artist in the literature of the Irish revival and much Irish literature since. It has for long been customary to read this literature as expressive of regionalism and of nationalism, but this can lead us into serious error if we do not at the same time recognize that these things exist as integral parts of a total aesthetic in which the primary figure and the primary interest is that of the heroic artist. The importance of being earnest about art is senior in such writings to the importance of being accurate or even perceptive about other things. I think that an investigation of, for example, Parnellism in literature as against the Parnell of the biographers and historians would reveal the kind of discrepancy of which I speak. Barry O'Brien's early biography of Parnell gives us a view of the man which is sadly out of line with the myth. Parnell was not simply an important man. He was the nucleus of the impulse to make the defeat of heroism a kind of basic pattern of Irish life. But Parnell is simply the artist in an Irish historical disguise, particularly powerful because he seems to represent simultaneously the Yeatsian Ascendancy ideal and the Joycean artistic ideal. But insofar as he has an historical reality in, say, *Ulysses* it is of the same kind as that which we attribute to Arius or Sabellius; and in Yeats's poetry, it is of the same kind as that which we attribute to Berkeley or Burke.

Having said this, the plain fact of the continued loyalty of contemporary Irish literature to what I have suggested are outmoded or anachronistic modes of thought clearly needs to be explained. In the first place, we can very simply refer to Yeats and to Joyce and ask what else there is which could in any way be taken as sufficiently representative of a tradition. The answer, alas, is nothing. The more we look at the 18th and 19th century, the more we despair of perceiving therein a principle of continuity that could be said to have more substance than the Yeatsian Ascendancy ideal. This doesn't even help with the 19th century anyway, unless we wish to make some elaborate issue of the effects of the Union upon the Ascendancy spirit which had produced Grattan's Parliament as well as Burke's political writings. It is perhaps more honest and sensible to admit the discontinuity which marks the various achievements of those Irish authors who wrote in the English language during these centuries. Continuity is the invention of the Revival, but it is not one which has worn particularly well, even though it cannot be gainsaid that any possibility of speaking in terms of a specifically Irish tradition in the English language belongs to the period between 1880 and 1940. But this was a period which made a fetish of continuity, partly because that concept was for the writers involved an enabling instrument, a kind of legal fiction which proposed the idea of an Irish Social Contract as the basis for the belief in the existence of a specifically Irish civilization. But our present dilapidated situation has borne in upon us more fiercely than ever the fact that discontinuity, the discontinuity which is ineluctably an inheritance of a colonial history, is more truly the signal feature of our condition. One could, finally, add to this the remark that the dream of an evolutionary continuity in a civilization which fetches its origins from some misty past is also a characteristic of the conservative politics which the main line of European Romanticism has always held in considerable affection.

So, the Revival's myths survive because they have no serious competitors. In the second place they survive because they contain perceptions about our situation which are true. It can hardly be denied that the view of the middle classes which we discover in Yeats and in Joyce has a good deal to be said for it. The facility of the distinction is, however, its most fatal element. Not only does it glamorize the artist, but it also frees him from the responsibility of actually *seeing* the middle classes. Their cultural immiserization is itself a phenomenon which to some degree explains the esoteric forms of Irish literary culture; but these esoteric forms do not explain that immiserization. They merely use it as the warranty for their own love of the arcane and the complex. The truth about the middle classes (and about the proletariat as well) which we find in our literature is so partial that it has become a distortion. The rupture between men and their culture has itself become part of the *raison d'être* of culture itself.

Although these are explanations for the survival of the old myths they are clearly not offered as justifications for it. By virtue of this survival we are faced with an assumed separation between "High Culture" and the general populace. Of course the ambition we discover in Yeats especially (but in later writers too) is the overcoming of this separation. But the ambition is bogus precisely because the method of overcoming (an appeal to peasant or to aristocratic values) is grotesquely impractical. One might find in Joyce a deeper sense of the solidarity of men, although this is perhaps reduced in *Ulysses* to a kind of spiritualized vitalism, a late version of the unconquerable will of the little man. But this Charlie Chaplin view of Bloom is hardly sufficient, not even when it is expanded into the dreaming Everyman of *Finnegans Wake*. Nevertheless, the Joycean analysis of the relationship between the high Stephenesque culture (brought to a point of exhaustion, to be sure) and the mass Bloomian culture is the most fruitful we have. For in it we learn to regard art as the activity which clarifies this relationship, rather than as an activity which, in order to be authentic, must disdain it. Besides, it is clear that for all the commentary which surrounds Joyce, his effect on Irish modes of thought has (sadly perhaps) been negligible compared with that of Yeats and even of Synge.

However, when we turn to contemporary poetry we can see that the example of Joyce and of Kavanagh has begun to take effect. This effect I would describe very simply as a diminution of the heroic impulse, a certain modesty in relation to history and its malleability, a scepticism or at least an anxiety about the status of the autonomous art-object. This is not a personal discovery on the part of any particular individual, nor is it a crusade against all that Yeats and the Revival stand to represent. More probably, the maturity of contemporary poetry can be explained as the result of contemporary conditions in Ireland. For it is the intractability of our situation, the impossibility of converting it (except at profound cost and maybe in profound dishonesty) into myth which has at last begun to free poets from the semantic straitjacket, from the aesthetic and heroic vocabularies of the Revival. Poetry, more than the novel, has begun to read its past intelligently; it therefore creates its present more authentically, facing its difficulties in a more plainly steadfast manner than seems to be available to our novelists. (The role of the drama is less clear, partly because drama inherited little in the way of myth, but much in the way of various styles and forms, none of which seem pertinent to the situation today. This is perhaps because the kinds of public commitment which the drama more severely than either fiction or poetry entails are not happily served by the rather limited naturalistic-expressionistic and symbolist modes which have come and gone in random fashion on the modern Irish stage.)

Examples of the maturity I claim for Irish poetry are too numerous for any detailed account to be given here. But we might call attention to the achievement of Thomas Kinsella whose work already seems to have achieved two phases. One, from 1956-68, is marked by a succession of lyric steps in each of which we see the consciousness becoming aware of the difference between its growth and the growth of other things in the world:

>   He must progress
> Who fabricates a path, though all about
> Death, Woman, Spring, repeat their first success ("Interlude").

Here we have again the disjunction between the artist and his world. But it is not in this case a matter of hostility; it is more clearly a matter of difference. Up until 1968, Thomas Kinsella explored the nature of that difference. Since then, especially since "Nightwalker" and "Phoenix Park" he has begun to explore the various ways in which this difference is mediated (although never lost) through the otherness both of art and of other people. His poetry produces for us none of the almost canonical pathos about alienation. Instead it recognizes that the various, unavoidable forms of alienation with which consciousness deals are in themselves the impulses which make the consciousness grow. Since 1968, we observe in him a reconstitution of the idea of what poetry is in its relation to personal experience, history and natural process. This enterprise has reached a new intensity in *Notes from the Land of the Dead, One* and *A Technical Supplement*. The important point for the moment, though, is that this poetry has evidently been educated in the Irish tradition and yet is in no pejorative sense derivative. The highly serviceable myths of the Revival have been abandoned and the intellect and imagination have created for themselves a careful freedom.

John Montague is also a poet who has broken new ground, partly after the example of Kavanagh (since the ground is that of the local parish), partly on his own. His verse is, above all things, elegant, spare in its diction, tender in its tone, oblique in its consideration of the problems we have been speaking of here. In a prose-poem, "Coming Events" (from *Tides* [1970]), the poet contemplates a painting in which a man is being flayed; and the piece ends thus:

> The whole scene may be intended as an allegory of human suffering but what the line of perspective leads us to admire is the brown calfskin of the principal executioner's boots.

Here again we have a disjunction between the aesthetic and the human response, a view of how history manifests itself not only in art but also as art. This is something which John Montague wishes to repudiate. His act of repudiation is to be found in *The Rough Field* (1972) and again, in the subsequent volume *A Slow Dance*. In the former we have two vocabularies, those of the poet and of history, the private and the public, each posed against the other in such strict counterpoint that we initially feel their mutual intractability and finally feel the vigor that such a recognition can produce. For history here is not given over to myth or to the heroic artistic impulse. Instead, the imagination has now learned the art of coexistence, favouring neither its own perceptions nor the brute facts of the public world. Such poetry achieves a poise between the two worlds which relieves it of that hectoring oratorical possessiveness which Yeats so brilliantly developed. We learn to admire the nervous and yet pure lines of the lyrics in this sequence and to contrast them with the statuary rhetoric of the public prose. In such austerely modelled verse we find ourselves at a great remove from the denser ambiance and excitements of the poetry of the Revival.

One could perhaps extend this discussion to the poetry of Derek Mahon or of Seamus Heaney or to almost any other poet of the new Northern Revival. It would be unjust to attempt to deal with any one of these writers in such short space as this. Perhaps it is sufficient to say that Mahon, more sensitive than any other to the unavailability of myth, alert to the lostness of the imagination in the world of Northern Ireland, writes a poetry which craves silence, which is based upon the art of reduction carried to the point almost of abolition. In Heaney's case, we find the mythological impulse erupting again, although in his case there is no heroicizing impulse involved. In him too the imagination is less imperial, the myth less likely to be taken as an omnicompetent mode of meeting experience. If history exists for him it is almost as a form of the occult. Domineering it is the Kavanagh landscape of the parish, of the personal encounter with experience.[10]

In all of these contemporary poets, experience is not made ductile by the stress of rhetoric. Instead, it is rhetoric itself which comes under interrogation, and in our best poems its capacity to take the stress of experience is tested and retested. If any proof were needed of the necessity to abandon the mythological mode of thought which characterized some of the best work of the Revival, it is surely there in the poetry of the last decade. We still, though, need to feel the full weight and not just acknowledge the sentiment of Anthony Cronin's lines:

> How can we praise in our poems the simplified heroes,
> Or urge to the truth we can never be true to ourselves?

---

[10] See also more detailed discussions of these poets in my essays in *Two Decades of Irish Writing,* ed. by D. Dunn (Carcanet Press, 1975), pp. 4-22; and *The Sewanee Review* 84 (Winter 1976), 199-208.